WITHOUT EXCUSE

THE COMPELLING EVIDENCE FOR CREATION

T0166254

JULIE VON VETT

BRUCE MALONE

INTRODUCTION

This is our fourth book showing how the marvels of nature confirm the accuracy of God's Word – making a total of almost 1,500 nuggets of truth revealing the creativity, beauty, and genius of our Creator. Because these books are being read to, and by, tens of thousands of children, you will notice that many articles end by acknowledging that God is the "designer, programmer, organizer, systems maker, instinct giver, provider, artist, genius, engineer, or creator" behind the wonders of nature. It is this acknowledgement which has resulted in the harshest criticism of these books. Why?'

Our public education system and media systematically train generation after generation to view the marvels of nature through a lens which leaves out any possibility that God supernaturally and recently created its wonders. Those trained to think in this way all too often become blinded to any possibility of God being involved in nature and claim that Christians just "throw God at the problem" and pretend this explains it all. Yet, evolution believers do exactly the same thing. The only difference is that chance occurrences (mutations) and vast time periods are *their* "god." Yet bacteria-to-man evolution and "deep time" have enormous scientific problems that are simply faulty interpretations based on bad assumptions, not absolute scientific realities.

Throughout history, mankind has worked to escape accountability to God or make God into an image that we can control by following some set of rules in order to pay for our own shortcomings. It never works. God will not be molded by our desires. The cosmic battle of the ages is whether we will believe God or believe a lie. Evolution is the ultimate lie of our age – that everything can be explained without a Creator. Test the truth claims of God (found in the Bible) and you will find that they are true, just, and accurate.

Soli Deo Gloria – "Solely to the Glory of God"

According to Romans 1:18-24 God holds us accountable for **knowing He exists** (vs. 19-20). God is angered when this evidence is denied and suppressed (vs. 18). Furthermore, the denial of the obvious blinds people to the truth (vs. 21) - resulting in their thinking becoming utterly foolish (vs. 21-22) and following sinful desires rather than truth (vs. 24).

What is the solution to curing the increasing blind foolishness we can observe all around us? **Making the truth about history, reality, and science known.** Jesus said the same thing when He told us to place our light on the hill and not hide it under a basket (Matthew 5:14-15). The Great Commission commands Christians to, "teach all nations... teaching them to observe all things, whatsoever I have commanded you..." (Matthew 28:19-20). The implication of the text is to share with the world all that Jesus has done – this includes Creation, the Fall, and the Flood.

That is the power of this book. Molecules-to-man evolution is the ultimate in false revisionist history that blinds people to reality. Putting the truth of creation in front of people has the power to open their eyes and set them free from deception, ultimately leading them to accept that God loves them enough to have become a human and died in their place as payment for their sins. Enjoy and share these daily nuggets of truth about the wonder and beauty of creation. This is the evidence which leaves all of us without excuse for believing (and obeying) our Creator and our Savior.

Video Links Throughout This Book

Throughout this fourth creation devotional we have placed QR codes that open 2-3 minute Youtube video teachings on the subject addressed on those pages. These videos are called *"Without a Doubt"* and make wonderful visual reinforcements for parents and teachers sharing the creation science concepts of these books with students. Here is a link to the playlist of all the *"Without a Doubt"* devotional series.

DEDICATION

There are numerous brilliant and dedicated scientists who have endured censorship and ridicule by the academic world. Yet they persevere in acknowledging God's interaction and the Bible's accuracy with observations of scientific evidence pointing to the reality that we have a Creator (and a Savior.) We dedicate this book to those heroes of the faith – Dr. John Sanford (genetics), Dr. John Baumgardner (geophysics), Dr. Steve Austin (geology), Dr. Jerry Bergman (human physiology), and many others.

We also dedicate this book to those Christian missionaries who have given their lives to presenting truth to those who would never otherwise have any opportunity to hear it. Kory Mears and Fred Brashear (and their families) have worked tirelessly to bring the evidence for creation and our *Pearls in Paradise* devotional to every high school student in Fiji. Jim and Ari Hirtzel, Gary and Lori Ellison, and Jeremy Pinero all helped to open the schools in Vanuatu to our presentations and books. Marilyn and Bob Stefan and Matthew Wolff have hosted multiple mission trips to the Philippines and distributed over 30,000 of our books. Thank you all for your partnership in sharing the Gospel.

ACKNOWLEDGEMENTS

We would like to thank and acknowledge the work of hundreds of creation researchers and scientists who have written and published articles on the evidence for creation which were used as source material and summarized in *Without Excuse*. Without their work, this book would not be possible.

Illustrations bring books to life. It is impossible to overstate our appreciation for the creativity of Jamie Walton who has spent countless hours finding the perfect illustrations and layout for each page of our book. Thank you for taking on this project while working full-time for the national Assembly of God chilren's mission department.

To some degree, all authors are blind to their own errors. Not only have both authors meticulously reworded and corrected each other's work, but our spouses, Vince Von Vett and Robin Malone provided significant input on changes and suggested improvements. We could not have produced this book without their help and support.

The final step before publication was to have others familiar with creation evidence check the text for any errors or needed clarifications. We would like to thank Don and Jeri Slinger, Marilyn Stout, and Bryce Gaudian for providing this service.

ABOUT THE AUTHORS

Julie Von Vett has been teaching creation science since 2003 to homeschoolers, churches, and community events, providing science training to approximately 500 home-schooled studented all over the state of Minnesota. Prior to this, Julie home educated their children, Annette and Caleb, through high school. She realized that the foundation of a Biblical worldview begins with creation, Genesis 1-11. Julie received her B.A. from St. Olaf College. She lives with her husband Vince in Minnesota. *"I accepted Jesus as LORD and Savior but once I realized He was also the Creator, I felt I was 'twice born.' I then saw Him as the Creator of the heavens and the earth and all that is in them.... that is one Powerful God!!! Our prayer for you is that you too can see His power displayed through what He has made. May He richly bless you as you see His fingerprints in His creation. The entire universe truly declares His Majesty!"*

Bruce Malone has spent the last 30 years bringing the scientific evidence for creation to churches and schools at seminars throughout the United States and 16 foreign countries. He has also authored or co-authored ten books on the evidence for creation with over 500,000 copies in print and produced an 18 part video series, *The Rocks Cry Out*, used in small groups and churches to train others on the evidence for creation and accuracy of God's Word. Bruce has 27 years' experience as Research Leader with the Dow Chemical Corporation, but left in 2008 to act as full-time Executive Director of Search for the Truth Ministries with the vision of *"Awakening Hearts and Minds to Biblical Truth."* This organization widely distributes Bible-affirming creation materials to students and prisoners – giving away over 300,000 books in the last 10 years. Bruce has a B.S. degree in Chemical Engineering from the University of Cincinnati and holds 17 patents for new products. Bruce and his wife Robin have been married for 36 years and have four grown children and five grandchildren. They reside in Midland, Michigan.

JANUARY

JANUARY

"HE THAT HONOURS ME, I WILL HONOUR."

– Anonymous note given to martyred missionary and national Scottish Hero, Eric Liddell (1902-1945), before he competed in the 400 meter race at the 1924 Olympics. Liddell refused to run the race he had trained for (the 100 metres) because it was held on Sunday and felt this would dishonor the Lord. With little time to train for the 400 metres race (which was held on a weekday), he miraculously won the gold medal.

"…For I will honor those who honor Me. And those who hate Me will not be honored."

– 1 Samuel 2:30b (NIV)

JANUARY 1

Did you know that there is a sea slug (*Elysia chlorotica*) which behaves and looks like a leaf? This animal lives in the salt marshes along the coast of North America and steals chloroplasts from algae. You may be wondering, "*Why would an animal want to steal chloroplasts?*" Chloroplasts are organelles (like tiny machines) in which photosynthesis takes place. Plants use sunlight to convert carbon dioxide and water into the plant's food, and it is within the chloroplasts that photosynthesis takes place. Chloroplasts contain chlorophyll which is what makes plants green.

This slug feeds on filamentous algae by cutting it open and sucking up the algae's chloroplasts, almost like slurping down a milkshake through a straw. Specially designed cells line the wall of this slug's digestive tract which allows it to store the algae's chloroplasts without digesting them. The sea slug eats lots of these chloroplasts during its transition from larva to adult. Once it reaches its 2-inch-long adult shape, the slug has all the chloroplasts it needs to survive for the rest of its life (about one year). **Here is an animal that survives by feeding itself using the food generating machinery stolen from a plant!** When the sun shines, the animal eats. Even more curious is the shape of the sea slug - it looks like a leaf!

Think of the hundreds of chemical and biological changes needed for this animal to start using a plant's food-making mechanisms. They all had to happen at once or nothing would have worked. How was it able to not digest a certain part of the plant? How did it know to store the chloroplasts? And how did the sea slug know what a leaf looked like? Slugs don't know these things, but an intelligent Creator does. God shows His creativity through the creatures He has made!

The earth is the LORD'S, and the fulness thereof; the world, and they that dwell therein.
– Psalm 24:1 (KJV)

JANUARY 2

In the Minnesota Museum of Mining in Chisholm, MN, visitors are surprised to see a sign next to stone candlesticks which reads, *"petrified candles."*

PETRIFIED UNDERGROUND CANDLES USED FOR LIGHT

These rock candlesticks were found in an underground mine. **How could wax candles become petrified in such a short period of time?** Up until World War II, most mines were dug via underground tunnels. Miners were given a weekly ration of 5-6 candlesticks. They would attach one to their helmet and stash others in openings in the mine walls. Many of these underground mines were wet and had to be constantly pumped out.

After World War II, the underground mines were closed; pumps were turned off and many of the mines flooded with water. With the need for iron increasing, open pit mining became popular. As the miners were digging these open pits, they would come across the old drifts and shafts which contained forgotten mining items. Candlesticks were one such item. Some of the candlesticks were found to be petrified. How did they become petrified? Mineralized waters saturated the soft wax candles turning them into rocks. Does it take millions of years to petrify as commonly believed? No - just the right conditions.

Iron is taken from the earth...they search out the farthest recesses for ore in the blackest darkness. Far from human dwellings they cut a shaft... - Job 28:2,4 (NIV)

JANUARY 3

The large number of comets still circling our sun is direct observational evidence that the solar system is quite young. This observation is inconvenient baggage to the philosophical belief that the solar system evolved long ago rather than being recently created. In order to explain the presence of abundant comets still present within our solar system, Dutch astronomer Jan Hendrik Oort proposed that there is a depository containing billions of comets outside of our solar system which has occasionally kicked new comets into orbit around our sun. A comet is made up mostly of ice and dust with smaller amounts of carbon dioxide, ammonia, and methane.

This "solution" to the dilemma of how these comets could still exist if the solar system were billions of years old has become a dogmatic belief taught within astronomy. However, this cloud of ice balls has never been observed, nor have any new comets purportedly originating from it been identified. Furthermore, it has been shown to be statistically improbable to account for even a fraction of existing comets in this way. In essence, what Oort did was add an unobserved "fudge factor" to explain the existence of comets within the dogma of a billion-year-old solar system. A fudge factor is a made-up addition to a problem to produce the answer you desire. It is a story. **This fudge factor of modern astronomy (The Oort Cloud) is no different than using your imagination to add extra numbers to a math problem in order to get the answer you believe to be correct.** Fudge factors, whether in math problems or astronomy, will never lead to the truth – our solar system was recently created by God.

Your word, LORD, is eternal; it stands firm in the heavens. – Psalm 119:89 (NIV)

JANUARY 4

Your body has 11 different systems that work seamlessly together. This unified 'system of systems' had to work perfectly the first time, or humans could not exist. Consider these 11 systems:

1. **Respiratory system:** brings oxygen into our body through our lungs and expels carbon dioxide.
2. **Digestive system:** processes which bring nutrients into our body while eliminating waste.
3. **Circulatory system:** pumps blood with nutrients and oxygen to every cell in our body.
4. **Immune system:** sends white blood cells to battle pathogens and clears the body of toxins.
5. **Urinary system:** cleans our blood through the kidneys and removes waste.
6. **Endocrine system:** glands which produce hormones to regulate growth, sleep, reproduction, mood, and metabolism.
7. **Nervous system:** our bodies' electrical wiring; allows the brain to send and receive signals that zip through the body.
8. **Muscular system:** allows us to run, write, sit, talk, and express emotions.
9. **Integumentary system:** our skin, hair, nails.
10. **Skeletal system:** sturdy bones to support our body.
11. **Reproductive system:** enables us to produce new human beings.

Each one of these systems is very complex and well designed in itself! Yet, all 11 systems are also interdependent. If you remove one system, it affects the other systems. For example, the respiratory system provides oxygen, the digestive system supplies nutrients, and the circulatory system sends the oxygen and nutrients around the body to the cells. All three must be working simultaneously or the body will die. Evolution cannot explain even one system's gradual step-by-step development - let alone having 11 of these complex systems working simultaneously and interdependently! The only possible explanation for the existence of the human body is that there is a great designer that put it all together at once. That Designer is Jesus, our Creator and our Savior!

I will praise Thee, for I am fearfully and wonderfully made; Marvelous are Thy works; and that my soul knoweth right well. - Psalm 139:14 (KJV)

JANUARY 5

Was he a monkey or a man? That was the question before visitors to the Bronx New York Zoo in the early 1900s. "Where is the pygmy?" was a common question from an estimated 40,000 visitors. "In the monkey house," came the reply. Sure enough, housed with an orangutan was Ota Benga, on display to promote the belief in human evolution to a gullible public.

Darwin believed that humans descended from apes and that some races were less evolved. **Evolution is firmly rooted in blatant racism.** Darwin was so convinced that blacks were an "inferior race" of less evolved humans that he wrote, *"The civilized races of man will almost certainly exterminate and replace throughout the world the savage races...the break will then be rendered wider...than the Caucasian and some ape as low as a baboon, instead of as at present between the negro or Australian and the gorilla."* This idea permeated the thinking of the intellectual community for the next 100 years. As late as the 1960s, Afro-Americans were still being sterilized and prejudice was being justified throughout the South on the basis of science and evolution. The abuse of Ota Benga, 23-year-old, 4'11" tall, 103-pound man brought over from the Congo is representative of the evils evolution has spawned. The unsuspecting public was taught that pygmies were *"small apelike, elfish creatures"* that *"exhibit many ape-like features in their bodies."*

In reality, pygmies are intelligent, talented, nimble, quick, and superior hunters. Ota Benga was culturally different, not inferior. Other pygmies were also brought to America for evil purposes. Falsely assuming brain size to be an index of intelligence, scientists murdered a pygmy, severed his head from his body, and boiled it down to measure his brain size. They were amazed to find the pygmy had a larger brain than American statesman Daniel Webster. We should look back in horror at the evil fruits of the belief in human evolution.

The Bible documents a different view - that all humans are brothers and sisters. **We are all closely related as descendants of Adam and Eve.** We did not evolve from apes! There are no races. In fact, the Bible does not even use the word race when speaking of people, but it does say we are *"one blood."*

And hath made of one blood all nations of men for to dwell on all the face of the earth...
- Acts 17:26 (KJV)

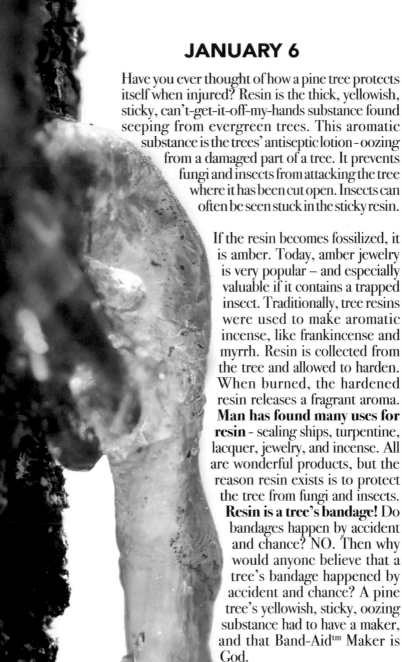

JANUARY 6

Have you ever thought of how a pine tree protects itself when injured? Resin is the thick, yellowish, sticky, can't-get-it-off-my-hands substance found seeping from evergreen trees. This aromatic substance is the trees' antiseptic lotion - oozing from a damaged part of a tree. It prevents fungi and insects from attacking the tree where it has been cut open. Insects can often be seen stuck in the sticky resin.

If the resin becomes fossilized, it is amber. Today, amber jewelry is very popular – and especially valuable if it contains a trapped insect. Traditionally, tree resins were used to make aromatic incense, like frankincense and myrrh. Resin is collected from the tree and allowed to harden. When burned, the hardened resin releases a fragrant aroma. **Man has found many uses for resin** - sealing ships, turpentine, lacquer, jewelry, and incense. All are wonderful products, but the reason resin exists is to protect the tree from fungi and insects. **Resin is a tree's bandage!** Do bandages happen by accident and chance? NO. Then why would anyone believe that a tree's bandage happened by accident and chance? A pine tree's yellowish, sticky, oozing substance had to have a maker, and that Band-Aid™ Maker is God.

But I will restore you to health and heal your wounds, declares the LORD.
– Jeremiah 30:17 (NIV)

JANUARY 7

Scientists get bogged down with trying to define intelligence and how to measure it. The bigger the head, the smarter the person...right? Did you realize that men's brains are on average about 10% larger than women's? Did you also know that our brains shrink as we get older? That would then mean that men are more intelligent than women and teenagers are smarter than adults. **Something is obviously wrong with the brain size versus intelligence theory.**

Since the 1800s, evolutionary paleontologists have lined up skulls of monkeys, apes, and various humans in order of brain size. They assume that smaller cranial capacity means a person is less evolved, therefore less intelligent. What scientists are discovering is that **brain size does not determine intelligence.** If so, elephants with their huge brains would be way smarter than humans! Ravens are smarter than monkeys. Yet, ravens have a smaller brain size (14 g or the size of a walnut) than a monkey (53 g or the size of a pear). It was found that ravens have more densely packed neurons than monkeys. So, is it the packing of neurons in the brain that make you smarter? What about synapses?

It has been determined that the number of synapses (bridges between neurons) determines overall intelligence. This is called synaptic density. Intelligence is more closely related to the total number of brain cells and connections rather than the old evolutionary assumption of skull size. *Homo floresisnsi* is a recently found fully human fossil from the Indonesian island of Flores. It had an extremely small body and skull. Nicknamed "the Hobbit," he had a cranial capacity of just 400 cc - yet made stone tools and built boats. Neanderthal brain size is about 1350cc (larger than modern humans). They buried their dead, painted on cave walls, hunted in groups, made musical instruments, did leatherwork, and developed inventive adhesives. Both were fully functioning humans. Brain size does not determine the human kind. More importantly, no matter how science determines intelligence, we all have the ability to know God.

The fear of the LORD is the beginning of wisdom: and the knowledge of the holy is understanding. – Proverbs 9:10 (KJV)

JANUARY 8

What is the fastest creature on earth? The peregrine falcon. During its steep dive, it can exceed more than 200 miles/ hour (322 km/hr.). From its streamlined body to swept-back wings, **this raptor is designed to dive**. But what about its eyes? How do the eyes stay focused on prey a mile away and adjust its missile-like trajectory as needed?

1. The falcon has 4-5 times more visual cells in its retina than we do.
2. The falcon has a third clear eyelid, a nictitating membrane. It's like having flying goggles so the wind doesn't dry out the eyes.
3. Just below the peregrine's eyes are dark patches, which works like a football players' dark patches for minimizing glare.

Breathing is the next critical design issue at such accelerated speeds. If it were not for the falcon's specialized cone-shaped bone protruding from its nostrils, the bird could not breathe while diving at these speeds. This bone acts as a baffle to deflect shockwaves of air away from the nasal passage, allowing the falcon to breathe while diving. **Engineers have, in essence, copied this design with the cone at the opening of jet engines.** When flying at supersonic speeds, engines can "choke." The air flow seems to *"hit a wall"* and flows around the engine resulting in the jet stalling. With the cone in place, air flows through the engine opening instead of around it. All large jet engines have these cones at their center. Human engineers had to solve this problem for jets flying at supersonic speeds, just as the Engineer of the peregrine falcon had to solve this same problem for the fastest creature on Earth. If I see design, why isn't there a designer? Jets have people, peregrine falcons have God.

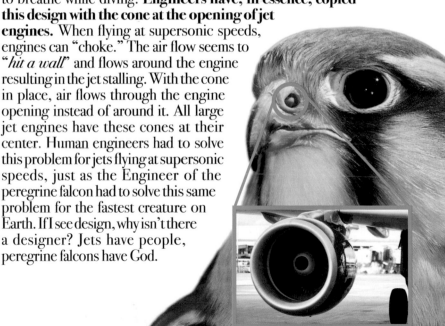

Lord, our Lord, how majestic is your name in all the Earth! – Psalm 8:1 (NIV)

JANUARY 9

How do I get nutrients from an apple into my big toe? Your part is merely to chew and swallow the apple - your body does the rest through the digestive process. After thoroughly chewing, it enters a 10-inch long tube called the esophagus, flows past the opening to the lungs (without a speck of apple pouring into them), and arrives in the stomach. The top of the stomach has a valve (the esophageal sphincter) which opens to let food in and closes once it arrives; while the bottom of the stomach has another valve (the pyloric sphincter) which opens at just the right moment in the digestive process to let the food out.

Muscles in your stomach mix the apple with acids and enzymes. Powerful hydrochloric acid dissolves the apple. Question: If the stomach is able to dissolve an apple, then why isn't your stomach digested? No one has been able to answer this question fully, but we do know that the cells in a stomach's lining are constantly and rapidly replaced. When your apple is thoroughly mixed and dissolved, a signal is sent to the lower sphincter to open and the mixture is released into the small intestine.

If there is oil in the food, it triggers the gall bladder to release chemicals which help dissolve the oil. Other complex digestive chemicals are released from the pancreas. These juices are critical for breaking down fats, proteins, sugars, and starches into smaller particles. The apple mush continues to move through the 20 feet of the small intestine. Through its entire length, tiny fingers called villi are protruding from the walls. These villi absorb any valuable nutrients from the apple and send them into the blood vessels. Now an entire new system, the circulatory system, has to take over to carry the food to every cell in your body. So that is how an apple gets to your big toe! Meanwhile, any food not absorbed is sent to the large intestine and out of your body.

Did this incredible system "evolve" over millions of years? Notice how many parts are needed to make the digestive system work: mouth, esophagus, stomach, small intestine with villi, gall bladder, pancreas, and large intestine. If the villi were not there from the beginning, we would not be able to absorb food. What if the stomach hadn't evolved? What if there were no valves to allow the food in and out? All the parts had to be there from the beginning, or we would be long dead. When we see a system with lots of parts working together, we know there must be a system maker. What a system Maker is our God!

Your hands made me and formed me; give me understanding to learn your commands.
– Psalm 119:73 (NIV)

JANUARY 10

Do you lay awake at night thinking about slug slime? Apparently, some researchers do! There is one slug species found in North America and Western Europe, *Arion subfuscus*, which glues itself to wet surfaces when scared. The slug's glue remains soft and stretchy as birds try to pry them off the sidewalk. **Slugs glued to wet sidewalks are much more difficult for birds to remove!** Glue that works on wet surfaces is needed for surgeries, a glue that can repair organs without stitches or staples. Slime from scared slugs to the rescue!

However, scientists were not able to start slapping slug slime onto patient wounds immediately because how would they get enough slime to supply the market need? Imagine lining up slugs in front of a screen to watch movies of scary birds...and then collecting their slime as they glued themselves to their seats! **Slug farms just didn't seem practical.** Instead, they studied the slime to discover how it worked. The result was a nontoxic, super-stretchy, works-on-wet-surfaces, super-wound glue.

So, what is the lesson? If you want to be a great inventor, look at what God has created and just copy Him (He doesn't mind at all!) Who would have thought that slug slime would inspire a wonderful new flexible medical glue? What a "slugger" of an idea!

But now ask the beasts, and they will teach you;
And the birds of the air, and they will tell you.
– Job 12:7 (NKJV)

JANUARY 11

Why would land animals be buried with ocean animals in the same fossil bed? Recently a duck billed dinosaur (hadrosaur) was found in a layer of ocean stratum. In 1999, south of Lima, Peru, a fossil graveyard of both marine and land creatures was uncovered in the same "aged" layer. There, marine creatures - sharks, whales, fish, turtles, seals, and porpoises were buried with land creatures - ground sloth and penguins. In Egypt, a fossil crab was found alongside a dinosaur. In Mongolia, Belgium, Tanzania, and at other sites, including Agate Springs, Nebraska are found a variety of animals mixed with sea and fish life.

If you believe in evolution, these land animals evolved millions of years after marine life and would not be buried together. If you believe in a global flood, then these fossils are not out of place. The Flood waters poured onto land along with the contents of the oceans - marine animals. These marine animals were buried with the land animals because they had been swept up in the tsunamis covering the land. Marine animals buried with land animals are not a problem for the catastrophic worldwide Flood that is mentioned in the historical book called the Bible.

And, behold, I, even I, do bring a flood of waters upon the earth, to destroy all flesh, wherein is the breath of life, from under heaven; everything that is in the earth shall die. - Genesis 6:17 (KJV)

JANUARY 12

When looking at the fossil record as a whole, what do we find?

- 95% are marine invertebrate, those without a backbone or vertebra. This would include clams, coral, and trilobites.
- 5% are plants such as algae, ferns, or buried trees.
- < 1% of all fossils are vertebra - primarily fish.

After 150 years of searching, the total number of nearly complete dinosaur skeletons is estimated to be only about 2,000 "good skeletons."

Why are most fossils marine invertebrates? During a worldwide flood, the creatures buried first would have been ocean invertebrates. As the tsunamis swept over the land, they carried with them marine creatures, burying them in massive numbers. Meanwhile, land creatures moved to higher ground but finally succumbed to the flood waters. Most animals would bloat, float, and would rarely have been preserved as fossils. Occasionally, flood waters could have swirled some into areas where they were covered by sediments creating dinosaur graveyards. **The fossil record is best understood as a result of the Genesis Flood.**

[The waters] rose greatly on the earth, and all the high mountains under the entire heavens were covered. – Genesis 7:19 (NIV)

JANUARY 13

Have you considered the cardinal fish that lives in the reefs of tropical oceans? Once a female cardinal fish's eggs are fertilized, the male scoops them into his large mouth. But even if dad is hungry, he does not eat eggs, but rather, protects them. For the next 10 days, he incubates them in his closed mouth until they hatch. Imagine holding something in your mouth for 10 days without swallowing it! To make sure they receive enough oxygen, he will open his mouth every minute so that the eggs receive a fresh supply of oxygen-containing water. When hatched, the fingerlings (baby fish) swim in and out of his mouth until they are ready to be on their own. **From fertilization until the young fish are on their own, the father eats absolutely nothing!**

Cardinal fish survive by eating small fish and other sea creatures around a reef. Why does the male n___ his own babies? How does he know to protect them in his mouth? If animals evolve by "survival-of-the-fittest," why wouldn't the first male cardinal fish have eaten his young? If he had, there would have been no more cardinal fish. For the male to care for his young in such a manner shows love and creativity, which points to a Creator. God loves to amaze us with His creation!

The Lord will keep you from all harm – he will watch over your life. – Psalm 121:7 (NIV)

JANUARY 14

Survival-of-the-fittest has always been a central teaching of the theory of evolution. It is the idea that if any organism is more fit, it will have an advantage and ultimately take over an animal group and become dominant in an environment. If this happens over and over again, evolutionists believe one animal can change into a completely different type of animal. But what makes an organism more fit? It has some characteristic allowing more of its offspring to survive than another similar animal in its vicinity.

Let's examine this idea in more detail. Suppose an animal in one generation decides to eat its young. During its lifetime, that animal would have a huge advantage. It would have a readily available food source and become far more "fit for survival" than other animals that did not eat their offspring. Yet this logical advantage would end the existence of his genetic line. Animals do not have foresight. They cannot see into the future to understand the consequences of their current actions. Evolution cannot explain how any animal could have learned to protect the next generation at great cost to its own existence (not eating a readily available food source nor eating anything for weeks).

A central mechanism of evolution, survival-of-the-fittest, does not work when we take time to think about it more closely.

They exchanged the truth about God for a lie, and worshipped and served created things rather than the Creator – who is to be praised.
– Romans 1:25 (NIV)

JANUARY 15

Penguins are birds, which mean they have feathers. Penguins hop in and out of the freezing Antarctic Ocean in an environment where winds can reach 90 m.p.h. (144 km/hr.) One would think ice would cake up all over their feathers. Yet penguins are able to handle extremely cold temperatures AND remain ice-free!

Using a scanning electron microscope, researchers were able to study the fine details of the penguin's feathers. The feathers contained the typical network of barbs, barbules, and miniature interlocking hooks, but also had *"many elaborate wrinkles."* Not only were there *"elaborate wrinkles,"* but the feather structure had microscopic grooves causing air entrapment on a microscale. *The Journal of Physical Chemistry* reported that this miniature structure, along with the penguin's special preening oil, kept super-cooled water from sticking. Researchers then built a replica of the Humboldt penguin's feathers and no ice formed even when the model was sprayed for hours with super-cooled water. Scientists have copied the feather's **unique structural design in an effort to develop an ice-free fiber membrane.** Penguin feathers have a wonderful architectural design which means there had to be an architect. There is and He is God.

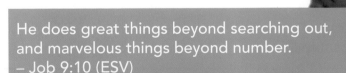

He does great things beyond searching out, and marvelous things beyond number.
– Job 9:10 (ESV)

JANUARY 16

When you step outside on a starry night, thousands of visible stars shine down upon you (unless light pollution is hiding them). Which stars do you connect to make a picture? It is not that easy. Yet in essentially every early culture around the world, you find the same pictures recognized - constellation names and patterns.

Orion the hunter is found in Greek mythology AND with Indigenous Australian people. Another example is the star cluster called Seven Sisters (or Pleiades) which is also found in both Greek mythology and Australian Aboriginal dream stories as well as mentioned three times in the Bible. Surprisingly, the stories are the same. How did Greek mythology transfer to an isolated aboriginal "stone age" culture? Evolutionary anthropologists are fairly certain that no such contact took place. Then how can they have the same constellations and stories? References to the Seven Sisters also appear in early Guatemalan cultures, Ukrainian folklore, and about 15 other people groups. In fact, the early Andean farmers of South America used the Pleiades to decide when to plant. At a certain time of year, if they saw the Seven Sisters dimming day after day, they knew the rains would be late and, therefore, delayed planting. The Seven Sisters are not spectacular and nothing about these seven brighter stars in a group of about 800 stars shows sisters or even a woman. Yet, this concept shows up in various early cultures across the world. **This suggests a common origin.**

When we read the history of people in the Bible, we find that ALL peoples/cultures of the world today are descendants of those that dispersed from the tower of Babel about 4,000 years ago. As the people groups moved out to fill the earth, they brought with them the same knowledge of the same constellations.

ASTRONOMY

These three were the sons of Noah, and from these the people of the whole earth were dispersed. - Genesis 9:19 (ESV)

FLOOD GEOLOGY

JANUARY 17

Millions of fossilized clams have been found in sedimentary layers around the world. Billions probably exist. So what, you may ask; fossils are common everywhere. But **these clams are found with their two halves firmly shut.** Who cares about closed clams? Those looking for the truth about the past!

Clams have two shells that are hinged together. When a clam dies, its muscles relax and the shell naturally opens. Yet, around the world, we find fossilized clams in a closed position. **Clams are "digging machines" that can easily burrow out, even if they are suddenly buried in more than ten feet of sediment.** The fact that billions are buried with their shells closed means they were buried alive, buried fast, and buried very, very deep! Rapid, deep, catastrophic burial is exactly what we would expect from the Genesis Flood. So the next time you see a fossil clam, check to see if it is closed; if it is, it was buried alive and died in the Flood of Noah. **Fossilized** closed clams witness to the worldwide Genesis Flood and the accuracy of God's Word!

The voice of the LORD is upon the waters: the God of glory thundereth: the LORD is upon many waters. The voice of the LORD is powerful; the voice of the LORD is full of majesty.
– Psalm 29:3-4 (KJV)

JANUARY 18

Does your skin have the same sensitivity all over your body? No, some parts are more sensitive than other parts. Why? Because the number of nerve endings vary with location. There are actually about 20 different types of nerve sensors: touch, temperature, and pain are examples. Each sensation is produced by a different type of nerve receptor. The more nerve endings in a patch of skin, the more sensitive that spot is to its specific sensation. **Certain patches of skin are far more sensitive to touch than others** - the most sensitive being our fingertips, hands, face, and lips. Your fingertips have more touch sensing nerve endings than the palm of your hands or your legs. Have you noticed how your legs are not as sensitive to touch as your fingertips? If we had the same concentration of "fingertip" touch nerve endings distributed all over the body, our brain would be overwhelmed with information.

Yet when it comes to heat and cold, our hands and face have fewer temperature sensing nerve endings than the rest of the body. That is why you can leave your face exposed when you go outside in the winter and not feel the cold. Your hands may feel comfortable touching bath water, so in you go... then you discover the water is too hot. That is why mothers test a baby's bath water with their elbows (which are far more sensitive to temperature changes than the hands). Also, they test the temperature of baby's formula on their wrist.

If evolution were true, then how did we get certain patches of skin that are more sensitive than others? And how were certain areas chosen? If our fingertips were not touch sensitive, then how would we pick up a thin dime? What if our feet were as touch sensitive as our fingertips, could we even walk? **Our skin, with its varied distribution of nerve endings, did not haphazardly come together**, but was wonderfully designed. If there is a design, there must be a Designer and He is God!

ANATOMY

Thou hast clothed me with skin and flesh... - Job 10:11 (KJV)

The Portuguese man o' war is one crazy looking animal (well, really it is a colony of four types of polyps which can't survive by themselves). Its gas-filled, blue bladder floats on the ocean surface (acting like a sail, because it can't swim) and it has long tentacles which can stretch as much as 150 feet below the surface (acting like fishing lines). Each tentacle is armed with thousands of poisonous stinging cells (called nematocysts) which it uses to stun and capture its prey. The stings from the Portuguese man o'war are excruciatingly painful for humans, but don't cause death. Fish make up 70-90 % of the Portuguese man o' war's diet. Yet a little fish, called the Man of War fish or bluebottle fish (*Nomeus grenovii*), makes the Portuguese man o' war's tentacles its home (There are several others, including the yellow jack and clown fish). How can it survive when most other fish are paralyzed and eaten?

This type of fish can tolerate much stronger venom than other fish and skillfully avoids touching most of the nematocysts on the stinging tentacles. The bluebottle fish benefits the Portuguese man o' war by being a fishing lure to attract prey that cannot withstand the stinging tentacles. The Man of War fish eats leftovers - keeping the tentacles clean and even nibbling on the tentacles (which grow back.) It also receives protection from larger fish wishing to eat them. So, the **little Man of War fish gets food and housing while the Portuguese man o' war gets a fishing lure and a housekeeper!**

Evolution believes this relationship came about by accident and chance mutations. How did this relationship begin? And how did the Portuguese man o' war know it needed a housekeeper and fishing lure? This relationship was designed with a purpose. A win-win purpose. Such a design points to a designer and that Designer is God. If a little fish can trust in God's protection, how much more can we!

O taste and see that the Lord is good; blessed is the man that trusts in him. – Psalm 34:8 (KJV)

JANUARY 20

Have you ever heard of stinging ocean waters? Swimmers often feel the stinging effects of the upside-down jellyfish, even if they do not touch the jellyfish. These upside-down swimming jellies are found in the warm coastal waters from the Florida Keys to Australia to the Red Sea. Upside-down jellies feed by releasing a cloud of mucus. The mucus is then sucked back in, containing stunned shrimp and plankton. What is in the mucus that stings and immobilizes the jellyfish prey? Scientists found microscopic stinging cells, called nematocysts.

Most jellyfish have nematocysts attached to their tentacles. Upside-down jellyfish have a different technique for stunning their prey - they launch stinging cells by mixing them with mucus and "spitting" them upward into the water. These tiny masses of stinging cells are able to move independently because of tiny attached filaments. **These jellyfish literally produce "moving torpedoes."** Each torpedo is covered with thousands of stinging cells. What an ingenious way to stun and eat prey. Do we believe torpedoes happen by accident and chance? Then how could the upside-down jellyfish's torpedoes happen by mutational accident and chance. If you are ever swimming in the ocean and the water starts to sting you, you are probably being "torpedoed" by a jellyfish.

For the Lord is a great God, and a great King above all gods…The sea is His and He made it…
- Psalm 95:3,5 (KJV)

JANUARY 21

What's the oldest toothpaste formula? Prior to the time of Colgate in 1873, people used soapy water with salt to brush their teeth. Yum! So was Colgate the first to invent good tasting toothpaste? Not even close!

The oldest toothpaste formula was found written on the back of a Egyptian papyrus document dating from the 4th century A.D. The recipe written down for *"white and perfect teeth"* called for soot, gum Arabic, mint, salt, grains of pepper, and dried iris flowers. **The dried iris flowers were the main ingredient in the formula.** What is surprising is that dental researchers have only recently discovered the beneficial properties of the iris flowers. It has been found to be an **effective deterrent against gum disease.** Egyptian toothpaste was presented at a dental convention, where it was described as being *"ahead of its time."* WAY AHEAD OF ITS TIME! It was even noted by the papyrus researchers that the toothpaste formula was written by someone who knew medicine, for he used abbreviations for medical terms. One dentist at the convention brushed his teeth with it and said, *"I found that it was not unpleasant...afterwards my mouth felt fresh and clean."*

The belief in evolution carries with it the baggage of assuming that the farther back in time we go the less intelligent people were. Yet the Bible tells us that Adam and Eve's children were raising crops and livestock. And that their grandchildren and great-grandchildren developed musical instruments and forged tools out of bronze and iron. People have always been smart and creative. If only people had passed down the ancient toothpaste formula, we wouldn't have needed to use soapy water with salt and needed to re-invent toothpaste!

Moses was educated in <u>all the wisdom of the Egyptians</u> and was powerful in speech and action. - Acts 7:22 (NIV)

JANUARY 22

Have you considered how the Closed Bottle Gentian (*Gentiana andrewsii*) is pollinated? This late summer-fall flower found in the woodlands of Northeastern America remains closed. **The flower petals do not open when in bloom!** But big burly bumblebees force open the closed petals and crawl inside. There they find a rich source of nectar made by the nectarines (glands in the flower). The bumblebee's long tube-shaped tongue sucks up the nectar. During this time, the bumblebee gets covered with pollen. After leaving the flower, it finds another Closed Bottle Gentian, forces open the closed petals, and crawls inside. While eating more nectar, some of the pollen it has been carrying falls off - thus pollinating the next flower.

Only bumblebees pollinate this flower. **They are the only insect burly enough to get inside the flower**. The bumblebee pollinates the Closed Bottle Gentian and the Closed Bottle Gentian gives the bumblebee a rich supply of nectar. Both benefit (mutualism) and, furthermore, cross-pollination produces stronger seeds. What advantage is it to a flower to be difficult to pollinate? How did this flower know a big burly bumblebee could open it up and get inside? Flowers with tightly closed petals and hard to get nectar would be at a continuous disadvantage over long periods of time and go extinct – not thrive. From the beginning, a bumblebee and the Bottle Gentian had to work together. As you take a walk in the early Fall, look for this violet colored flower and take a close look at how God designed this flower to be pollinated.

...Great and marvelous are thy works, Lord God Almighty... - Rev. 15:3 (KJV)

JANUARY 23

Built for speed - that is the design of a cheetah. Cheetahs are the fastest land animals. They can go from 0 to 60 m.p.h. in 3 seconds! To be able to run that fast requires special design features. A heavy lion's body (550 pounds on a four-foot frame) would not work well on the cheetah's three-foot frame, so cheetahs weigh in at a lighter weight 80-140 pounds. Check out these other design features:

- The main design change needed to support its speed is its spine - it is highly flexible, curving in and out with each stride. In fact, the vertebrae can even spread apart!
- The hind legs have a high percentage of fast-twitch muscle fibers allowing for explosive energy.
- The cheetah has an extra-large heart and lungs; and oxygen comes in through the extra-wide nostrils, allowing the muscles to be well oxygenated.
- It's one thing to be speeding along, it's another to be able to see without blurriness. Cheetahs have extra neurons in the eyes to help their focus remain sharp. To reduce glare, cheetahs have those black tear lines under the eyes, now copied by football player's black face paint lines.
- But what about not crashing at these speeds? It's in the tail! The long tail swings back and forth working like a boat rudder stabilizing and counterbalancing. The tail allows for sudden sharp turns at high speeds.
- The cheetah's semi-retractable claws act like cleats - gripping the ground.

Cheetahs are uniquely built for speed; this did not come about by accident and chance over eons of time. Just as when we see a Ferrari, we know there must be a race car designer; the fast-moving cheetah had a Designer and He is God.

Let us run with perseverance the race marked out for us. – Romans 12:1b (NIV)

JANUARY 24

Have you heard of fossilized dinosaur eggs? How do they fit into the flood of Noah's day? First though, are dinosaur fossilized eggs rare? No. Since 1996, paleontologists have discovered almost 200 locations with dinosaur eggs. At one location in Spain there are as many as 300,000 eggs. In the U.S.A., Egg Mountain in Montana has dozens of egg clutches. In Argentina, thousands of eggs are found in six different rock layers within several square miles. Worldwide, millions of eggs and hundreds of egg clutches have been found.

Interestingly, the egg clutches are in close proximity. **Eggs are rarely found inside the dinosaur mom; finding a developing embryo inside the egg is also very rare.** Paleontologists find very few egg nests. Most of the eggs are laid on flat, bare sediments. (Alligators and crocodiles lay eggs in "nests" they have dug and then covered their eggs in sediment or vegetation). Many of the fossilized dino eggs show unusual traits such as double shells or thin, easily broken shells.

These eggs were rapidly laid in the midst of an enormous worldwide catastrophe – Noah's Flood. The stress of the rising flood would have caused many pregnant females to rapidly drop their eggs on flat, bare sediments without taking time to prepare nests or allow the eggs to properly develop. The poor diet of fleeing dinosaurs might also have caused the eggs to lack calcium, having a thin shell. Other females, attempting to delay laying, could have produced eggs with a double shell. These eggs would have been subsequently buried by rapidly rising, sediment-filled water and later became fossilized.

Do we see eggs becoming fossils today? No, it takes special conditions and the flood of Noah's day would have provided those conditions. When you see a fossilized dino egg in a textbook, museum, or on the internet - *you are looking at an egg laid by a stressed-out dinosaur trying to escape the judgment of the Genesis Flood.*

For the Lord giveth wisdom, out of his mouth cometh knowledge and undrstanding.
- Proverbs 2:6 (KJV)

BOTANY

JANUARY 25

Have you considered that the plant called the skunk cabbage (*Symplocarpus foetidus*) has its own hand warmers? This Eastern North American woodland plant emerges from the ground in late winter when snow is still on the ground. When you are walking through the snow, you may notice a few slushy spots. Take a closer look and see if there are thick leaves in the center, the size of a softball with flowers. Now smell them. Does it have a "skunky" smell? Then it is skunk cabbage.

Other spring flowers are still in winter dormancy. This remarkable plant can generate its own heat! **It melts the snow in its vicinity by maintaining a temperature of 72°F.** How can a plant make its own heat? Scientists have found that skunk cabbages' cells contain mitochondria. Within these mitochondria is an enzyme called alternative oxidase (AOX). AOX is used in an exothermic chemical reaction, producing heat which melts the snow. In a similar way, commercial hand warmers contain chemicals that combine with oxygen to produce heat.

We know that someone made the hand warmers, that they did not come about by mutational accident and chance. Then why would we say the skunk cabbage, with its ability to produce heat for several weeks, happened by accident and chance. When we see hand warmers we know that there must by a hand warmer maker. When we see skunk cabbage with their own hand warmers, we know that someone made it, and that Someone was God.

Then God said, "Let the land produce vegetation: seed-bearing plants and trees on the land that bear fruit with seed in it, according to their various kinds." - Genesis 1:11 (NIV)

JANUARY 26

How does a skunk cabbage help a bear? It is early spring, and the black bears have been in winter hibernation for months. **They can go 100 days without eating, drinking, urinating, defecating, or exercising.** When they emerge from their dens, they seek out skunk cabbages. This flower grows in late winter or early spring and emits a slight skunky odor. Skunk cabbage is sometime called bearweed because bears love to eat the buds and leaves. The bears have not defecated for a long time. There is a fecal plug up to a foot long in their lower intestines. That plug has to be unplugged before feasting on grubs and grasses.

Enter in the skunk cabbage - it's literally the bear's laxative. When the bear eats this plant, things get moving and the bear becomes unplugged. Skunk cabbage restores their normal bowel movements. Remember, skunk cabbage are among one of the very first spring plants to emerge and snow is often still present. The skunk cabbage is there for the bear at the exact time the bear needs it. Happen by chance? We would have a lot of plugged-up bears if the skunk cabbage was not present! **God's ready-made pharmacy!** Evolution can't explain this, but our Creator can!

...if you accept my words and store up my commands within you...then you will understand the fear of the Lord and find the knowledge of God. - Proverbs 2:1,5 (NIV)

DESIGN

JANUARY 27

Where does beauty come from? Did beauty evolve by accident and chance over eons of time as evolutionists believe? No. Look at a beautiful, intricately designed flower. Furthermore, there is no evidence that pollenating insects are attracted to beautiful flowers, such as orchids, dahlias, or roses, to a higher degree than to the drab flowers of weeds. Did flowers get together and decide to become beautiful? No. Flowers do not have brains. **Randomness does not create beauty.**

How about a butterfly's beauty? Where did that come from? Butterflies are like winged flowers – absolutely stunning in their colorful designs! Yet, butterflies come from worm-like caterpillars. Did these worm-like caterpillars get together and decide to become "jeweled" flying flowers? Did they program their DNA with beauty genes? No, caterpillars have no ability to create beauty.

Even the setting sun can paint the entire sky with a vast array of beautiful colors. **Everywhere we look in creation there is beauty that serves no direct functional purpose except to reflect the nature of its Creator.** When we see beauty in a flower, butterfly, or colorful sunset we should be reminded of the one who is the beauty-Maker - Jesus Christ.

For since the creation of the world God's invisible qualities—his eternal power and <u>divine nature</u>— have been clearly seen, being understood from what has been made, so that men are without excuse. – Romans 1:20 (NIV)

JANUARY 28

Do radiometric dates provide conclusive evidence for purportedly billion-year-old Earth rocks? One common type of radiometric dating uses potassium argon (K-Ar). Ten years after Mt. St. Helens erupted, Dr. Stephen Austin collected cooled rock from the newly formed lava dome at Mt. St. Helens. The potassium-argon (K-Ar) date for a 10-year-old rock was 350,000 to 2,000,000 years old. Confused? Yes, the dates don't match. Other tests over the years have been just as wrong.

Here are a few examples

Location	Years since eruption	Measured Result
Mt. Etna-basalt	29	35 million years old
Sunset Crater-basalt	950	27 million years old
Kilauea, Hawaii - basalt	<200	21 million years old
Mt. Stromboli	38	2.4 million years old

The Grand Canyon also yields some bizarre results. A lava flow from a volcano at the top of the canyon was dated at 1.34 billion years old, while the Cardenas basalt layer, among the lowest strata of the Grand Canyon (Precambrian), yielded a date of 1.07 billion years old. Notice the two dates: 1.34 billion on top and 1.07 billion on the bottom. The date on top should be younger but it is not! How can the top of the canyon be older than the bottom of the canyon? Confused? You should be!

So what do evolutionary geologists say about these dates? They simply call them "*discordant,*" claiming they are from "*old material mixed into new flows,*" and ignore them. Yet many dates for rocks of known age are clearly wrong (as the chart above shows). If radiometric dates give an incorrect age of known rocks, how can they be "trusted" to date rocks of unknown age? The whole of deep time is collapsing, yet evolutionary geologists continue to use it!

...you may command certain men not to teach false doctrines any longer nor to devote themselves to <u>myths and endless genealogies</u>. These promote controversies rather than God's work... - 1 Timothy 1:3-4 (NIV)

AGE OF CREATION

JANUARY 29

Have you considered how a frog gets its meal? Frogs will eat insects, spiders, and even small birds, mice, and fish. But how does a frog capture its food? It's all in the tongue and the spit!

The frog has a super-soft tongue (think of a marshmallow). As the tongue is launched, its super-soft tongue hits its target and curls around the prey. The tongue alone isn't enough to hold the prey, but the frog's super-sticky spit will. The frog's saliva is very thick when it is in the mouth (think of room temperature honey). When the tongue hits the target, the saliva instantly thins and oozes over the prey. As the tongue retracts, the saliva thickens again. But there is yet another problem. Now the prey is in the frog's mouth, how is the frog going to release it? At the exact moment the food reaches the frog's mouth, its eyeballs sink into its head, causing the food to be pushed down the throat, which again causes the spit to thin, resulting in freeing the prey so it can be swallowed. **Ahhh, lunch is served!**

Did this incredible system just make itself? What if the tongue was not soft like a marshmallow? Experiments have shown that if a frog had a human-like stiffer tongue, it would have an 80% decrease in contact area. What if the tongue had no super-sticky saliva? What if it had super-sticky saliva but could not change from thick to thin to thick and finally thin again at exactly the right moments? And what if the eyeballs did not sink into the head, so the saliva could change, and the prey released? **All these factors have to work together perfectly or no lunch for the frog.** God's fingerprints are all over a frog's marshmallow tongue, thickening/thinning spit, and sinking eyeballs!

Sing unto the LORD with thanksgiving…He giveth to the beast his food…
- Psalm 147:7a,9a (KJV)

JANUARY 30

Were Neanderthals dumb? Scientists studying the teeth of Neanderthals from Belgium and Spain have decided that these guys were pretty smart! Paleoanthropologists were studying the stuff that clings to teeth, called plaque (*calculus*). Dental plaque hardens into tartar if not brushed. As tartar accumulates, it stores information about our diets.

It was determined that Neanderthals from the Spy Cave in Belgium mainly subsisted on wooly rhinoceros, wild sheep, and wild mushrooms. A Neanderthal from the El Sidron cave in Spain showed the individual suffered from a dental abscess on its jawbone and had an intestinal parasite (microsporidian) which causes severe diarrhea. So what did the tartar show that this individual ate? He had a steady diet of mushrooms and plants, including poplar (Populus sp.). Poplar bark contains salicylic acid, the active ingredient found in aspirin. He was also eating plants covered in penicillium mold, which is an antibiotic. Noted the researchers, *"We've got a guy self-medicating…He is eating aspirin (poplar bark) and we're finding penicillin mold in him."* Dumb Neanderthals? Hardly! Neanderthals were fully human descendants of Noah and his family and not some half man-half ape transitional creature.

Then God said, "Let us make man in our image, in our likeness…"– Genesis 1:26 (NIV)

JANUARY 31

There are vast differences between ape and human footprints:

- Apes leave a flatfooted print, while humans have an arch which leaves a distinct right/left footprint trail.
- Humans have a distinctive ball on the heel of their foot.
- Apes have an elongated thumb-like big toe, while humans have all five toes which line up at the front of the foot.

Thus, it is exceedingly easy to know whether fossilized prints have been made by a human. Human feet are made for up-right walking and ape feet are made for living in trees. Whenever footprints of australopithecines like Lucy are found, they have ape-like footprints.

Multiple examples of footprints showing a right/left arch, heel, and aligned toes have been found:

- The Taylor trail at the Paluxy River in Texas, was documented to have every characteristic of human prints and extended for 14 steps along the riverbed.

This trail was found in Cretaceous limestone (placed at over 60 million years by evolutionists).[1]

- The Laetoli trail of 70 human prints were uncovered by paleontologist Mary Leakey's team in Tanzania in 1978. These prints were *"indistinguishable from prints made by habitually barefoot modern humans."* They were found in volcanic ash and placed at 3.6 million years by evolutionists.[2]

- An accredited archeology website admits that, *"Recent discoveries suggest that human footprints are more common than previously supposed...,"* showing pictures of what are clearly human prints, and listing technical articles describing these finds in Kenya, Tanzania, England, Italy, Columbia, South Africa, Australia, Namibia, Korea, Tennessee in the United Sates, and other places.

All of these findings show that humans have always been humans, leaving distinctively human footprints in rock layers *"where they shouldn't be found."* Whenever these human prints are found where they are not supposed to have existed, paleontologists make these kinds of assumptions:

a. The human prints were made by ape-like creatures with human-like feet (when actual fossil evidence contradicts this belief).
b. The prints are dinosaur tracks, erosional features, or worm trails.
c. The rock layers containing human prints are not as old as identical "millions of years old layers" that did not contain human prints.

In reality, these prints were made by the descendants of Adam and Eve. They were either descendants who missed the boat and perished in Noah's Flood, or they were people living after the Flood and subsequent geological activity captured these human footprints.

How beautiful on the mountains are the feet of those who bring good news, who proclaim peace, who bring good tidings, who proclaim salvation, who say to Zion, "Your God reigns!"
– Isaiah 52:7 (NIV)

FEBRUARY

"HE IS NO FOOL WHO GIVES WHAT HE CANNOT KEEP TO GAIN WHAT HE CANNOT LOSE."

– Jim Elliot (1927-1956), martyred missionary

The next day John saw Jesus coming toward him and said, "Look, the Lamb of God, who takes away the sin of the world!"

– John 1:29 (NIV)

FEBRUARY 1

Johannes Kepler, one of the greatest astronomers of all time, proposed that planets moved in regular predictable patterns. Kepler used years of observation to discover three very specific laws of planetary motion:

1. All planetary orbits are elliptical, not circular.
2. Planets slow down when farther from the sun and speed up when closer.
3. $T^2=R^3$; A planet's orbit time (T) varies with its average distance from the sun (R).

Let's examine the first two planetary motion laws. Does the earth actually speed up and slow down while orbiting the sun? Because the elliptical orbit of Earth is not perfectly centered on the sun, at times our earth is 91 million miles away from the sun and at other times it is 94 million miles away. When the earth is closer to the sun, it is winter in the northern hemisphere (because of the tilt of the earth.) Since Earth is moving faster, fall and winter last only 179 days. When the earth is farther away from the sun, it should be moving slower and these seasons should last longer. And that is exactly what we find. Spring and summer in the northern hemisphere last a full seven days longer or 186 days. Precisely as Kepler predicted.

Why did Kepler see these patterns when no one else was even looking? **This great founder of modern science believed in God.** He reasoned that a Creator would create the universe based on logical, observable, and understandable laws. The laws of logic, uniformity of nature, science, and underlying orderliness all require the mind of an intelligent Creator - which is outside of the limits we are familiar with; time, space, matter, etc. One of Kepler's beliefs was that examining nature was merely, "*Thinking God's thoughts after Him.*" He also warned against "*Glorifying our own minds instead of giving God the glory.*"[1]

The fear of the LORD is the beginning of wisdom: and the knowledge of the holy is understanding. – Proverbs 9:10 (KJV)

FEBRUARY 2

Have you heard of a whale with a tusk? It's called a narwhal. These whales live in the remote waters of the Arctic Ocean where for half of every year these waters are in twilight or dark all day long. A 17-foot-long narwhal can have an ivory "tusk" over nine feet long protruding from its mouth. This odd tooth is spiral shaped and its purpose is not clearly known. Males will often stick their tusks straight up out of the water and wave them around. At other times, the males will spar with them. **Narwhal's tusks have a hypersensitive outer layer - with 10 million nerve endings!**

In one interesting experiment, a researcher poured fresh water and salty water on the tusk and noted a heart rate difference. Because of the tusk's sensitivity, it can detect slight changes in water salinity, temperature, and pressure. In the Arctic Ocean, salt concentrations fluctuate as the seawater freezes and thaws. Narwhal's tusks may be used as a sensory device to determine if they are near freezing or closing ice. This can be very helpful as narwhals dive up to a mile deep to feed on Greenland halibut and other fish in total darkness. This leaves little time for them to resurface and get air between their dives which can last as long as 25 minutes. A nine-foot-long ice-sensing tusk in jet black water sounds like a pretty useful feature! However, it is only the males who have a tusk.

What is the purpose of the narwhal's tusk? Science hasn't proven it yet, but has uncovered some interesting clues. If a scientist approaches this mystery from a Biblical viewpoint, he would see purpose and design in all things. **As Johannes Kepler noted, it is a scientist's job to, "*think God's thoughts after him*" in order to understand purpose and design.** The narwhal's tusk is a mystery just waiting for us to discover and give glory to God, acknowledging His awe-inspiring creativity.

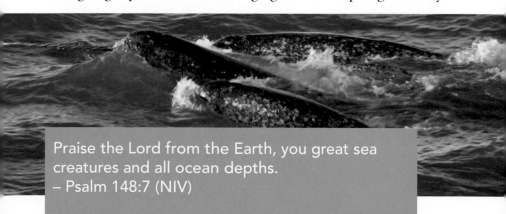

Praise the Lord from the Earth, you great sea creatures and all ocean depths.
– Psalm 148:7 (NIV)

FEBRUARY 3

Antarctica has a rainforest?! Well not anymore...but below the ice is the fossil record of a lush rainforest that once grew in Antarctica. **This discovery has completely baffled evolutionary scientists.** How could tropical plants survive in total darkness for four months? Yet the evidence is undeniable - pristine samples of forest soil with pollen from tropical flowers, spores and root systems - even the cell structure could be seen. A lush rainforest once grew here.

If we take the Bible's teaching about ancient history seriously, the rainforest was buried during the Flood. At this time, Antarctica was a part of a Pangaea-like supercontinent. As the Flood continued, Earth's tectonic plates moved rapidly apart, resulting in Antarctica moving into today's position. Before the Flood, this supercontinent would have had Antarctica near the 45-degree south latitude, about the equivalent of southern New Zealand. Surprise! The types of trees and flowering plants that we find in New Zealand's South Island are the same types that are found in Antarctica's fossilized rainforest. **The lush rainforest did not grow in the present-day Antarctica, but far from the South Pole, where they were buried, fossilized, and rapidly moved to their current location.** When we put on our Biblical glasses, fossilized rainforests in Antarctica are not at all baffling.

In the six hundredth year of Noah's life, in the second month, the seventeenth day of the month, the same day were all the fountains of the great deep broken up, and the windows of heaven were opened. - Genesis 7:11 (KJV)

FEBRUARY 4

Your kidneys are a fantastic filtering system for cleaning your blood. Within the kidney are nephrons. Each is a capillary cluster with a coiled tube attached to it. There are more than 1 million nephrons in your kidneys. As blood passes through the nephron's capillary clusters, waste products are filtered out. Blood is about 55% water, and the filtered blood is returned to your body, leaving a concentrated wastewater solution to be discarded.

This waste trickles down tubing to the bladder. When the bladder contains about a pint of waste fluid, it sends a message to the brain, "time to go to the bathroom." How does a bladder, which is just a holding bag, know to send a message to the brain? What if the bladder could not communicate with your brain? **You would be spending your day in the bathroom!** How do a million nephrons know what to filter out and what not to? What if they did not filter the correct things?

Medical engineers have spent millions of dollars and decades designing kidney dialysis machines for people whose kidneys have failed. These artificial kidneys are huge and nowhere near as efficient as the ones God designed. Here in our body is the real kidney machine, yet evolutionists say it happened by mutational chance accidents. Was not the artificial kidney – the kidney dialysis machine, designed by looking at the real kidney? If I told the engineers who made the artificial kidney that they did not really make it, they would be insulted. Telling the Creator that He did not make our real kidneys is also an affront. When we see an artificial kidney, we know there must be an artificial kidney maker. Likewise, when we see a real kidney, we know there must be a real kidney maker and that Maker is God.

ANATOMY

Your hands shaped me and made me...
– Job 10:8a (NIV)

FEBRUARY 5

Piltdown man, the purported ape-man fossil, convinced much of the world that man evolved from an ape. For more than 40 years, this specimen played a pivotal role in the theory of human evolution. More than 500 scholarly articles were written and references to Piltdown man in textbooks and popular media numbered in the thousands. **Piltdown was no minor fossil find; it was central to popularizing the concept of human evolution.**

Here is the back story: Charles Dawson, a young geologist, noticed the type of rock that workers were digging in order to repair a road near Piltdown, England and thought the site might contain humanoid fossils (½ man - ½ ape). What he found was introduced to the world in 1912 as "Piltdown Man." The "evidence" consisted of skull fragments, a jawbone and a single tooth. The *New York Times* headline proclaimed, "Darwin Theory is Proven True." Replicas of the skull were made and spread throughout the world. The American Museum of Natural History prominently promoted Piltdown man. High school students and their teachers visited in ever increasing numbers to see for themselves the "proof" that human evolution was true. Back in England, the Piltdown site was declared a national monument.

Then in 1949, a scientist who wanted to prove beyond a doubt that Piltdown man was the "missing link" used a new dating method based on fossil fluorine content. Instead of revealing a primitive humanoid, the test revealed that Piltdown man was less than 10,000 years old. Curious and puzzled, the bones were removed from the safe and critically examined. The result:
a.   The skull was determined to come from a modern human.
b.   The jawbone was actually from an orangutan.
c.   The teeth had been filed down, stained to appear old, and impregnated with sand grains - so as to 'imitate" fossilization and fit into the skull.

Years passed before the truth came out. Finally, the **embarrassing hoax was revealed in 1953**...but not before doing 40 years of irreparable harm to two generations of students. It influenced millions of people to accept evolution as a fact. It was even used at the Scopes Trial as proof of evolution, which caused evolution to be taught in the public schools of the U.S.A. All based on a lie! Forty years of deception and lies. How many people walked away from their faith in God because of this lie?

Lying lips are abomination to the LORD:
but they that deal truly are his delight.
– Proverbs 12:22 (KJV)

FEBRUARY 6

In 1917, Harold Cook found a tooth in the northwestern part of Nebraska. Some five years later, the tooth was given to Henry Fairfield Osborn, a noted paleontologist, and the President of the American Museum of Natural History in New York. Without investigating, Osborn declared the tooth America's first half man/half ape *Hesperopithecus haroldcookii!* Osborn was a leading member of the ACLU and believed in evolution. Being aware of the ACLU's desire to challenge a ban on teaching evolution in schools, the tooth from Nebraska appeared to provide a useful tool for the support of evolution. It was widely publicized for years prior to the famous 1925 Scopes Trial. **This trial was a key turning point for promoting evolution throughout America's educational system.**

Was Nebraska man an "apeman"? A few years after the Scopes Trial, the real evidence surrounding the Nebraska tooth came out – it was the **tooth from an extinct pig!** Here is a case where a pig made a monkey out of a man. Osborn should have admitted his mistake before the Scopes Trial began and not continue to promote this tooth. So whatever happened to Nebraska Man? On one of my journeys out west, I wanted to discover the place that Nebraska man was first discovered in 1917. Yet when I arrived at the Agate Fossil Beds National Monument, not a word was on display and the rangers seemed completely perplexed when I mentioned this infamous fossil. Nebraska man, an extinct pig's tooth, helped usher evolution into our public schools, yet this horrible mistake has simply been forgotten in the dusty halls of history.

Whoever speaks the truth gives honest evidence, but a false witness utters deceit.
– Proverbs 12:17 (ESV)

FEBRUARY 7

Gorillas were unknown to Europeans until the late 1800s. The first scientific description of a gorilla came in 1847 from a missionary, Thomas Savage. A decade later, the first European zoologist confirmed that gorillas existed. Gorillas live in family groups, often led by a single mature male called a silverback (because of the patch of gray hair on its back). He often is the father of all the baby gorillas in the group. Gorillas are both social and smart. One famous gorilla, named Koko, learned 1,000 signs of American Sign Language. She knew the words but lacked the grammar rules (syntax). The discovery of gorillas at almost the same time as Darwin's publication of *Origin of the Species* (1859) caused many people to wonder if they had evolved from gorillas.

Gorillas have a slightly similar appearance (about 83% similar DNA), behave in some ways like us, and eat similar foods. But this does not prove common decent. Any good designer would use the same design when designing structures for similar purposes. Although gorillas have some similarity of design, they have an enormous missing piece - they are spiritually dead. They simply cannot understand the majesty of God or the atoning work of Jesus Christ. The book of Genesis tells us that man was made in the image of God. This is a spiritual likeness, not a physical likeness. We understand spiritual things, whereas a gorilla does not. God could have made us as the gorilla, without spiritual understanding, but He did not. God gave us a spiritual side. With this spiritual side comes the ability to wonder, worship, and communicate with the Creator of the universe. Neither a gorilla, nor any other animal, has this privilege.

For not all flesh is the same, but there is one kind for humans, another for animals, another for birds, and another for fish.
- 1 Corinthians 15:39 (ESV)

FEBRUARY 8

Have you considered that the sun's solar winds protect us from deadly cosmic rays of interstellar space? In 1977, two space probes were launched by NASA, Voyager 1 and 2. These probes have finally reached interstellar space, about 11 billion miles from the sun.

Far outside of our solar system, interstellar space is filled with high levels of cosmic radiation. Startling discoveries from these space probes have found our sun emits solar winds so powerful that it creates a protective bubble which deflects this harmful radiation. The sun's solar winds are themselves full of charged particles that could easily destroy us on Earth, **but the earth's magnetic field acts as a protective bubble inside the sun's protective bubble to protect us!** We see the result of the earth's protective magnetic field in the northern or southern lights. The Voyager probes found these solar winds were still blowing way beyond the planets - creating a special bubble around us. This heliosphere (or solar wind bubble) protects everything, even our fragile DNA, from the high energy radiation of interstellar space. Is there anything God has not thought of!

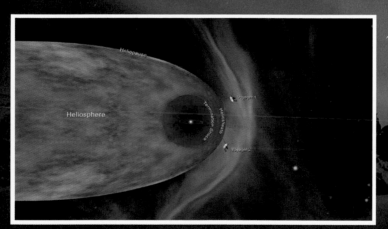

Praise him, sun and moon, praise him, all you shining stars. - Psalm 148:3 (NIV)

FEBRUARY 9

Koalas are marsupials, which are mammals that give birth to live young, but these babies are premature and not fully developed. Therefore, to survive, the offspring finish their development by nursing in their mother's pouch. Kangaroos are also marsupials, but their pouches are forward-opening and when the mother is ready for a new joey, it licks the pouch clean. However, the koala's pouch is rear facing; it would be impossible for the koala mother to lick it clean. But how do koalas keep their backwards-facing pouches clean?

During the non-breeding season, the koala pouch is filled with crusty brown crud. During the breeding season, droplets of clear material are secreted. The pouch becomes squeaky-clean, glistening, and pristine. The tiny baby koala (the size of a small baked bean) has no immune system so it cannot combat disease. It has been found that the droplets that are secreted to clean the pouch also contain powerful proteins that kill dangerous microbes. Do germ killers happen by accident and chance? No, there has to be a germ-killer maker and the **koala's super-duper, antibiotic ointment Maker and pouch cleaner...is God.** Now the baby koala has a germ-free, squeaky-clean nursery.

The LORD is gracious, and full of compassion... The LORD is good to all: and his tender mercies are over all his works. – Psalm 145:8a,9 (KJV)

FEBRUARY 10

Have you considered the baby kangaroo when it is born? It is about the size of a bean and it is blind, deaf, hairless - like a tiny worm. When it emerges from the birth canal, it should just drop onto the ground and die, but it doesn't. Somehow it knows to hold on tight to the mother's fur and climb into the mom's pouch. This takes about three minutes. Once in the pouch, it finds the mother's nipple and latches on. The mother's nipple swells in the joey's mouth and it cannot be easily removed. By the time the joey is 7 to 10 months old, it leaves the pouch but stays with the mother for up to two years. As soon as that joey leaves the mother's pouch, a new joey is born. The new joey and the older joey have different nutritional needs. Surprisingly, the mother makes two different kinds of milk, one for the new baby on board and another for the young joey outside of the pouch who reaches in for a drink. **Two different types of milk – tailor-made for different sized joeys.**

The mother also needs to keep the pouch clean for the developing baby, so **the baby joey on board is potty trained!** When the mother cleans the pouch by licking it clean, she gives the joey a thorough washing at the same time. The joey on board doesn't urinate or defecate until it feels its mother's tongue. As she cleans the smaller joey, a tiny wee-poo goes straight onto the mom's tongue. It's not a lot - just a droplet of waste (remember the joey is the size of a bean.) Even the pouch is designed to protect the tiny joey. When relaxed, the pouch is open and airy, but it all changes when the mom hops. Suddenly the pouch becomes like a pressure bandage with powerful muscles that quickly tighten. Thus, as mom hops away, the joey is tucked safe inside and not jostled around or falling out.

How does evolution explain this birthing, two types of milk, potty training, and muscle tightening upon hopping? All these features are wonderfully designed for the kangaroo by our creative Creator!

Let everything that hath breath praise the Lord. Praise ye the Lord. – Psalm 150:6 (KJV)

FEBRUARY 11

Was Jonah swallowed by a whale? It says in Jonah 1:7, *"God had prepared a **great fish** to swallow Jonah."* Henry Clay Trumbull made a valid point when he wrote,

*"What better heralding, as a divinely sent messenger to Nineveh, could Jonah have had, than to be thrown up out of the mouth of a great fish, in the presence of witnesses, say on the coast of Phoenicia, where the fish-god was a favorite object of worship?...a multitude would be ready to follow the seemingly new avatar of the **fish-god**, ... where the **fish-god** had its very centre of worship."* [1]

After three days in the fish's digestive acid, Jonah's skin would have been bleached white. A bleached man vomited out of a great fish would have caused quite an uproar! But what fish could swallow a man? **The sperm whale is one possibility** AND was known to have lived in the Mediterranean Sea. A sperm whale's favorite food is giant squid, so it could easily swallow a man-sized object. *The Princeton Theological Review* (Oct 1927) reported on two incidents, taking place in 1758 and 1771, in which a man was swallowed by a whale and vomited up shortly thereafter. Sperm whales are also known to eject the content of its stomach when dying.

Another possibility is a shark. A Madras (India) newspaper, *The Mail*, reported on November 28, 1946 that, *"A twelve-foot tiger shark, weighing 700 lbs., was dragged ashore last evening at the Sasson Docks. When the shark was cut open a skeleton and a man's clothes were found. It is thought that the victim may have been one of those lost at sea during the recent cyclone. The shark was caught by fishermen thirty miles from Bombay."* Also, Great White sharks can be over thirty feet long, weighing thousands of pounds, and could swallow a man alive.

Is the account of Jonah and the whale a myth? **Jesus didn't think so!** He compared the events of Jonah's life to His own future death and resurrection.

> "For just as Jonah was three days and three nights in the belly of the great fish, so will the Son of Man be three days and three nights in the heart of the earth. The men of Nineveh ... repented at the preaching of Jonah, and behold, something greater than Jonah is here."
> - Matthew 12:40-41 (ESV).

FEBRUARY 12

What's the oldest living thing on earth? High in the remote, cold, dry air of California's White Mountains lives a bristlecone pine tree called Methuselah - named after the longest living human. This tree was placed at 4,789 years old based on tree ring studies done in 1975. Normally, when trees are dated by counting their growth rings, only one summer/winter ring is assumed for each year. This is generally true; however, it has been demonstrated that in years of good growth (warm, moist conditions), more than one growth ring can occur. In one experiment with Bristlecone pine seedlings a heat lamp was added to their "normal" winter daylight. **The result: extra rings grew.** After the Flood of Noah's time, there would have been centuries of warm, moist weather with abundant rainfall. Thus, Methuselah likely rooted immediately after the Flood of Noah and is only about 4,500 years old, not 4,789 years old.

How can the bristlecone pine trees live so long? Their highly resinous wood enables them to resist attacks from fungus, bacteria, and insects. They grow extremely slow. With the harsh conditions at 10,000 feet, the annual growing season is only 45 days long, so in 100 years they may add a mere one inch of girth. The second oldest living tree (measured by tree-ring counting), has an estimated age of 3,631 years. It's an Alerce Tree (or Patagonia Cypress) and grows in Chile, South America. So why are there not older trees? If trees can last 3,660 - 4,500 years, why not longer? When

doing a straightforward tree-ring counting, why do we not find a 9,000-year-old tree? What happened about 4,500 years ago? The Flood of Noah. The Bible records a yearlong worldwide Flood which obliterated everything. As the Flood waters drained off the land, a little bristlecone seed landed in a remote part of the White Mountains and has been growing ever since.

And all the days of Methuselah were nine hundred sixty and nine years: and he died.
– Genesis 5:27 (KJV)

FEBRUARY 13

The other day, my friend pulled out of his pocket some beautiful agates and an arrowhead.
He asked me, "Which one was made by someone?"
I pointed to the arrowhead.
"How do you know that," he asked.
"The design." I replied, "No rock could weather that way."
"Then what about my hand" came his reply. "Is my hand, that is holding the arrowhead, designed?"

Evolution teaches that people evolved over time from a single cell. So **to an evolutionist, the hand is not designed but is the result of chance mutations.** Yet my hand has a unique arrangement of parts. The hand is controlled by muscles in the forearm. Long tendons in the fingers pass through to the forearm. The forearm muscles control the movement of the bones in each finger like a puppet. Imagine, instead, our fingers being controlled by fat muscles and no tendons, how would we pick up anything? Instead, we have an ingenious boney puppet. To cushion the nerve endings, the skin has special fat cells. Within each fingertip are four different kinds of nerve receptors: touch, pain, temperature, and pressure (light and deep). This helps us judge how firmly to hold something. Did our hands happen by accident and chance? The more we study our hands the more we see design.

Just as the arrowhead shows design, so too the hand that is holding it. If there is a design, there must be a designer, and the Designer is God.

But now, O Lord, you are our Father; we are the clay, and you are our potter; we are all the work of your hand. - Isaiah 64:8 (ESV)

FEBRUARY 14

Over the course of the last two hundred years, science has been slowly changed from its original understanding as, "a systematic method of studying creation in order to understand the principles by which it operates," to "the naturalistic understanding of the universe." In other words, science, by today's definition, cannot even consider the possibility of God's existence or God's interaction with creation anytime in the present, past, or future.

I vividly remember a conversation I had with a Ph.D. archaeologist over twenty years ago who had repeatedly insulted me in public letters to the editor in our local newspaper. At the time, I was writing a weekly column explaining the scientific evidence supporting creation, and this scientist accused me of undermining the Constitution of the United States and trying to drag our country back into the Dark Ages. I challenged him to a public debate on the issue and asked to meet him in his office to talk about the details. As we met, I explained that someone finding an arrowhead could choose to believe that random blows from other falling stones had created the arrowhead, but the symmetry and purpose of the object would make the truth obvious – it had to have been designed by intelligence. The complexity and interdependence of the parts of even the simplest living cell makes this truth even more obvious. I further explained that I simply wanted students to hear all the facts so that they could determine the truth for themselves. This scientist got increasingly agitated as I talked, and by the time I finished, he stood up and literally shouted that, "Science is not searching for the truth (here he traced a capital "T" in the air), just the best natural explanation for things. If you want to search for truth - go home and do it, that search does not belong in a science classroom."

How sad that a religious belief (evolutionism) has taken over the very methodology of scientific exploration. This is not how the founders of modern science (almost all of them believed in a literal, recent creation) viewed science.

...Jesus answered, "You say that I am a king. In fact, the reason I was born and came into the world is to testify to the truth. Everyone on the side of truth listens to me." – John 18:37 (NIV)

FEBRUARY 15

Australia has some interesting animals, and one such animal is the snake called a floodplain death adder snake. The adder snake dines on frogs. He quickly strikes these frogs, using his fangs to inject the venom. Most frogs die quickly and are immediately eaten after being bitten by the snake, but the adder uses a different plan with two special Australian frogs. When the floodplain death adder snake strikes a marbled frog, **the irritated frog secretes an amazingly sticky, glue-like mucus onto its skin.** If the snake gets this glue on its skin, then dirt, sticks, and leaves will stick to him. Who wants a mouth full of glue? No thank you! **So the snake waits about ten minutes** before eating the dead frog. By this time the frog's sticky glue has degraded to one-third its original stickiness.

The other frog is the Dahl's frog. It is so poisonous that it can kill a snake immediately. After the snake's first strike, the Dahl's frog's poison causes the snake to thrash around and lie on its back with its mouth hanging open. So the adder snake waits about forty minutes before eating the frog, and by this time, the poisons have degenerated to nontoxic levels. Two different substances, two different break-down rates, yet the floodplain death adder knows the difference; **he just sits back and waits.**

How does the floodplain death adder know to wait exactly the right amount of time, either ten minutes or forty minutes? Was this learned or programmed within? If he ate either frog sooner, his mouth would have been glued shut or he'd be dead. It had to be programmed within the snake's instincts; which means there is a programmer, and that Programmer is God.

[An unjust ruler's] venom is like the venom of a snake, like that of a cobra that has stopped its ears. – Psalm 58:4 (NIV)

FEBRUARY 16

"What type of crazy plant is that?" wondered botanist Friedrich Welwitsch. He was exploring southern Angola's Namib Desert in 1859 when he came across a weird plant. The plant was a gymnosperm, (think evergreen) yet it had leaves instead of needles. This unique plant has roots and two leathery, broad and strap-shaped leaves. These leaves lie on the ground, and as the plant ages, the leaves become shredded. Carbon dating places many of these plants living from 500 - 2,000 years!

Being a gymnosperm, it reproduces using cones. Gymnosperms are mostly wind pollinated, but not this one; it is pollinated by insects. But how does the plant attract insects to pollinate the cones? This gymnosperm makes sweet nectar!

This plant, the *Welwitschia* (named after the explorer), is able to survive in a harsh dry desert because of the morning fog. During the night, cool air from the cold Benguela current in the South Atlantic meets the hot air from the Namib Desert and a thick fog blankets the region. The fog droplets condense on the bending ribbon-like leaf and the water rolls down to the base of the plant and into the soil which the roots quickly absorb. **This is not a weird plant, but one that is wonderfully designed to thrive in the desert.** When we see design, we know there must be a designer and that Designer is God.

O give thanks to the Lord of lords...To him who alone doeth great wonders, for his mercy endureth for ever. – Psalm 136:3a,4 (KJV)

FEBRUARY 17

The next time your Mom or Dad asks, *"Do you have rocks in your head?"* answer them, *"Of course, and so do you!"* These tiny rocks are called *"ear rocks."*

Located in the inner ear between the cochlea and semicircular canals are two tiny sacs. These sacs are filled with a jelly-like substance in which there are sensory hairs. Also inside each sac are the tiny rolling rocks (also called otoliths).

The ear rocks help you maintain your balance. If you are moving forward and stop suddenly, or if your head nods forward, these ear rocks move forward and bump into sensory hairs - which send a signal to your brain. If you tilt your head to the right, gravity causes the ear rocks to bump into tiny hairs on the right and a signal is sent to your brain which is interpreted as leaning or moving to the right. If you were going up in an elevator (a vertical linear movement) and stop, the ear rocks bump into the vertical sensory hairs in this sac and send yet a different signal to the brain. This is a very elegant and precise balance system. Doctors know very well the consequences of any part of this elegant system not working correctly. There are toxins that affect ear rocks, like streptomycin. Also, aging can cause the deterioration of these ear rocks - causing an elderly person to have balance problems. Any change or deterioration means the entire system will not work correctly. And the brain has to know what to do with the signals or they are worthless noise. We needed this complex system to work correctly from the beginning.

Evolutionary scientists say it took millions of years for things like the ear's balance system to develop. Imagine a life with no ear rocks or those rocks in the wrong position. **Your life would be one of dizziness and constantly falling down.** Those rocks in your head needed to work correctly from the beginning! Our complex balance system is useless and detrimental until it is in its finished form. That simple fact rules out evolution. A system requires a systems maker, and our System Maker is Jesus Christ.

But blessed are your eyes, for they see: and your ears, for they hear. – Matthew 13:16 (NIV)

FEBRUARY 18

Have you considered your earwax? Your ear canal has approximately 4,000 glands that produce wax. Why do we need earwax?

- First, **it moisturizes the skin** and keeps it from becoming dry and itchy in the canal.
- Second, earwax contains special chemicals which **fight off infections,** particularly when you go swimming in dirty water.
- Third, earwax is noxious to most bugs. The hairs in the canals also aim outward. **God wanted to make sure bugs did not constantly crawl into your ears!**
- Finally, earwax coats the ear canal **acting like flypaper to trap dust and dirt.**
- It is interesting that the cells in the canal grow differently than cells on your body. Skin cells grow up and are sloughed away as they die. The cells in our ear canal are like people-movers at an airport; they move laterally and are sloughed off outside the ear. As the cells grow, they automatically carry the old wax, which has the debris on it, out of your ear.

Sometimes ears become impacted with earwax because the "conveyor belt" was not working properly. However, this does not happen often because our ears are designed to clean themselves. Isn't it incredible how God is concerned with the smallest of details, even earwax removal!

And your ears shall hear a word behind you, saying, "This is the way, walk in it," when you turn to the right or when you turn to the left. - Isaiah 30:21 (ESV)

FEBRUARY 19

Have you ever thought about how mudrock (shale), or other rocks made of mud formed? Try this experiment:

- Fill a jar with water.
- Add dirt made of mud, silt, and sand and then shake the jar vigorously.
- Sit it in a still location to allow the sand and silt particles to fall rapidly to the bottom.
- Observe how long the mud stays suspended in the water.
- It will take much longer for the mud particles to sink to the bottom.

Mud particles are thin and flat, like snowflakes, taking a long time to settle to the bottom. This type of experiment led scientists to believe that shale layers, like the 500-foot-thick Bright Angel Shale in the Grand Canyon or the 900-foot-thick Marcellus Shale in the Pennsylvania area, took millions of years to be deposited. Because mud particles settle so slowly, geologists teach that these thick layers took millions of years to form. HOWEVER, we now know that mud particles settle quickly in <u>rapidly moving water.</u>

Scientists used a racetrack flume in which water and mud flowed around and around in an oval, like a racetrack. The fast-moving mud particles clumped together becoming the size of sand grains. Mud particles have a weak residual electrical charge. In fast moving water, these tiny mud plates were forced so close together that the oppositely charged particles attracted each other, causing them to clump. This caused the clumped mud to settle quickly, resulting in mud layers forming instantly.

Shale makes up the majority of the sedimentary geological rock layers, more than limestone and sandstone. Scientific evidence shows that shale layers can form in minutes; it does not take millions of years! The worldwide Flood resulted in limestone, sandstone, and shale all forming rapidly.

The earth, O LORD, is full of thy mercy: teach me thy statutes. – Psalm 119:64 (KJV)

FEBRUARY 20

Within this book you will find hundreds of examples of the evidence for design in nature:

- Beauty
- Mutually dependent organisms that rely on each other for survival
- Specifically designed parts all working together to achieve a common function
- Intricately designed chemicals within every cell
- Systems where all components are needed or nothing works correctly

There are only two possible explanations for all of this design – either it was created or it made itself (evolution). We often end articles by contrasting these two diametrically opposite viewpoints. The only mechanism evolution has for creating new information is random mutational change (i.e. chance occurrences). Thus, **we are really comparing chance and mistakes with design and purpose** as we look for a source of the beauty and intricacy of life.

Believing that random mutations could create complex design is analogous to throwing scrabble letters onto the floor and expecting to eventually find meaningful sentences spelled out. This will never happen. **Random mutations improving life is impossible.** Evolution pretends that there is a force in nature called natural selection that can select "good" changes and eliminate "bad" changes, but 99.9999% of all changes are negligible in their effect, good or bad, yet these small changes slowly destroy the information contained in the DNA.

Chance mutations are mistakes and will never increase the complexity of life. **Nothing can stop the slow downward deterioration of life because we live in a fallen, sin-ridden universe.** The mechanisms of evolution simply do not work to explain life's development, beauty, interdependency, and existence.

...thorns and thistles for you...All your life you will sweat to master it, until your dying day.
– Genesis 3:17-19 (ASB)

FEBRUARY 21

A unique fossil bed in Clarkia, Idaho contains millions of leaves that have not been mineralized. **They are so fresh looking** that many still contain red, yellow, orange and green colorations. Once exposed to the air, these colors rapidly fade. Some samples even retain the smell of rotting leaves.

Geologists teach that this deposit formed around 16 million years ago. Textbooks presume to explain the intricate preservation of over 120 different species of tree leaves in a single location as having slowly formed at the bottom of an 800-foot-deep lake where the anaerobic (low oxygen) conditions preserved the vegetation. For 16 million years? This explanation does not make sense because other such lakes do not preserve leaves in such a manner AND the wide variety of leaves are from vastly different ecological zones! A MUCH better and more logical explanation is that these leaves were washed together during Noah's Flood and preserved by fine volcanic ash that settled in this unique location about 4,500 years ago.

These non-mineralized leaves are very unique because much of the carbon in their cells has not been replaced by minerals. Many leaves have their original structure and have not completely decayed. **Finding these leaves is equivalent to finding "soft tissue" within dinosaur fossils!** There is even DNA present within the leaf cells. University researchers verbally admitted to amateur paleontologist Stan Lutz that Clarkia leaves have 1/400 - 1/500 of modern DNA levels. Since the half-life of DNA is about 500 years, it would take about 8 half-lives, or approximately 4,500 years since their burial to reach this level of residual DNA. What happened about 4,500 years ago which would have buried massive numbers of leaves? The Flood of Noah!

This privately owned fossil bed is open to anyone wishing to collect samples for a modest fee. These non-mineralized "fresh" leaves containing significant quantities of DNA, confirm the Biblical accuracy of the Flood. If these leaves are not millions of years old, neither are the rock layers, and the entire evolutionary house of cards collapses. Hopefully, careful documentation and publication by scientists will make this significant find more widely known in the near future.

[In 7 days] I will cause it to rain upon the earth forty days and forty nights; and every living substance that I have made will I destroy from off the face of the earth. – Genesis 7:4 (KJV)

Have you ever looked at fossilized leaves? They are wonderfully preserved! Plant leaves curl and shrivel up within hours or days when separated from their source of nutrition. But this is not what we find when we look at fossilized plant leaves. How did they become so exquisitely preserved? During the Flood of Noah's time, leaves were ripped off plants. These fresh leaves would have floated on the ocean and absorbed water causing them to straighten and become flatter than what we normally see in life. Then the leaves were buried with sediment before having a chance to decay. All around the world we find these amazingly preserved, flattened leaf fossils, which give testimony the global Flood of Noah's time.

FLOOD GEOLOGY

I am the vine; you are the branches. If a man remains in me and I in him, he will bear much fruit; apart from me you can do nothing.
– John 15:5 (NIV)

FEBRUARY 23

Sunflowers are heliotropic, meaning they follow the sun from east to west. But how do the young sunflowers move their blooms to face the sun all day? And why do mature sunflowers stop turning? In the morning, the sunflower head faces east. By design, the stem grows faster on the east side. The uneven stem growth forces the head to turn west following the sun. At night, the west stem side has a higher growth rate and the sunflower returns to face the eastern rising sun in the morning.

Researchers do strange things. They decided to anchor the plant's head so it could not move. The result - the flowers had smaller seeds and leaves compared to flowers that could move with the sun. As a sunflower reaches maturity, the plant's growth decreases and the flower faces the morning sun continually. "Torturing" more of the poor flowers, researchers forced half the mature flowers to grow only facing west and half to grow facing only east. The east-facing sunflowers had five times more pollinating insects visiting them than the west-facing flowers. Why? Bees prefer the east-facing warmer flowers.

How did sunflowers "**know**" that to have larger seeds, they needed one side of the stem to grow more cells so it would elongate and the head follow the sun? How did the sunflower "**know**" that at blossoming, warm flowers attract more pollinators and thus settle on an eastward-facing direction? A sunflower doesn't have a brain; **it was programmed to do this from the beginning.** If there is a program, there must be a programmer and that Programmer is Jesus.

Let the name of the LORD be praised, both now and forevermore. From the rising of the sun to the place where it sets, the name of the Lord is to be praised. – Psalm 113:2-3 (NIV)

Would you believe flowers "hear" a bee's buzzing and respond by increasing nectar sweetness? Bees need nectar to produce honey, so the sweeter the nectar the better. Bees have been designed with the ability to detect nectar sugar level differences as small as 1-3%. Because they visit sweeter flowers more often, and stay longer, the sweeter the flower the more effectively they are pollinated.

What area of the flower picks up the bee's buzzing sound? The flower's petals. When a buzzing bee comes near, the flower's petals vibrate. Researchers tested this with a laser vibrometer (a machine that picks up the tiniest movements). When the petals were removed, the flower did not vibrate as much, and the nectar was not as sweet. The bowl shape of a primrose flower is shaped like a satellite dish and is particularly effective at picking up vibrations. **Researchers found that when they played a recording of a bee buzzing, this flower's nectar sweetness increased by 20% within 3 minutes!!!** Researchers even went on to say that the flower's petals functioned like an "ear."

For a flower to have the ability to make nectar sweeter only when a buzzing bee is nearby would save its resources to use only when needed AND reward the bee with the best nectar - thus resulting in pollination. What a complicated but efficient system that benefits both organisms! The wonders of nature reveal God's genius.

BOTANY

He covers the sky with clouds; he supplies the earth with rain and makes the grass grow on the hills. – Psalm 147:8 (NIV)

FEBRUARY 25

Before creation there was no time, space, or matter. God had infinity to plan the creation of every human being who would ever live. With an eternity of time to work with, He could change anything at any time to affect any future set of circumstances. God knows in advance the impact that every choice will have on the future of each person it affects. And because God is outside of creation, and therefore "outside of time," He had to know all this even before each of us were created.

In addition to making the physical universe, God made the angels to witness the creation of the universe, life, and mankind. Only mankind and the angels were created with the freedom to choose right over wrong and obedience over rebellion. But why would God allow such a choice when he knew 1/3 of the angels and all of mankind would choose rebellion?

- Without choice, there is no freedom.
- If we have no freedom to choose disobedience - trust and faith in another person is not possible.
- Without trust and faith, we are really just biological machines or robots – running by pure programming.
- There can be no true relationship with a robot.

Our Creator desires and values our faith and obedience, but He does not "need" it, like an egotistical ruler needs approval. In spite of all the heartbreak and pain our free-will has brought into creation, God will never force us to trust and obey Him. Through observing creation, there is abundant and undeniable evidence that He exists, but God does not force anyone to have faith in Him. Jesus desires a relationship but loves us too much to force us to love Him back.

This is how God showed his love among us: He sent his one and only Son into the world that we might live through him. - 1 John 4:9 (NIV)

FEBRUARY 26

What is this - a bird, a reptile, or a mammal? It's a platypus. A platypus has a tail like a beaver, fur like an otter, a bill and feet like a duck, and lays eggs like a lizard. The first early white settlers to Sydney, Australia in 1797 couldn't believe what they saw. When a stuffed platypus was sent to England, one zoologist thought it was a fake - sold to a gullible seaman by Chinese taxidermists. Another zoologist used scissors to try and cut the bill off (you can still see the scissor marks on the platypus in the British Museum of Natural History in London). It was not a hoax, but a real mammal with unique characteristics.

The bill of the platypus is especially unique. When a platypus submerges, it firmly closes its eyes and ears. So how can it find food? **Its duck-like bill has approximately 40,000 sensitive electro-receptors that pick up the weak muscle contractions** in shrimp, insect larvae, tadpoles, and other aquatic animals. Even in murky water or under a rock, the prey cannot hide because of the platypus' electro-receptors. It is almost like the platypus has a very advanced metal detector. Do metal detectors happen by accident and chance? No, an engineer had to design one. Then why would we say that the platypus' "metal detector," which is more advanced than humans, happened by accident and chance mutations? This very unusual animal, with its otter-like fur, reptile-like eggs, beaver-like tail, and electro-receptor duck-like bill is a mammal that gives glory to God's creativity.

Great is our Lord, and of great power; his understanding is infinite. — Psalm 147:5 (KJV)

Did you know that no scientist can really explain what gravity is? We can feel it, measure it, mathematically show how it functions, and use it in a myriad of ways, but what is this that we call gravity? Gravity is the weakest of all elemental forces (10^{38} times weaker than the force that holds atoms together), yet it holds planets in their orbits, us here on earth, and can bend the path of light as it passes by stars. It must be precisely correct. If it were even a trillion, trillion, trillion (10^{36}) times weaker, the universe would have long ago flown apart, and stars would not be able to burn. If it were a one trillionth, trillionth, trillionth times stronger ($1/10^{36}$), the universe would long ago have collapsed back into itself.

Gravity cannot be blocked or stopped and continues to work no matter how far the distance. It can pass through the vacuum of space, solid lead plates, entire planets or stars, breeze right through magnetic and electrical fields, and even prevent light from escaping enormous stars called black holes. Nothing seems to stop it. Yet we really have no idea what gravity really "is."

God is kind of like gravity. We can feel Him, see what He has made, read about His characteristics in the Bible, and know that He exists... but as finite humans, we cannot even begin to truly understand the infinite nature of God. He is everywhere at once, has always existed and will always exist, is perfectly just and will leave no sin unjudged, is outside of time, knows every thought and every action of every human before time started, created the entire universe from nothing, and is perfect love. He loved us so much that this infinite God became Jesus, a finite human being, to die in our place because of the sin that separates us from Him. **Such love is incomprehensible and is offered to all as a free gift.**

He is before all things, and in him all things hold together. – Colossians 1:17 (NIV)

FEBRUARY 28

Thirsty? Try living in one of the driest deserts on earth, such as the Namid Desert in Africa, where it rarely rains. This desert is home to the unique fog harvesting beetle. **Have you ever tried to catch water from fog?** It's hard, but the Namid beetle knows exactly how to do it. This ingenious critter climbs to the top of the sand dunes in the early morning, faces into the wind, stands on its head, and collects water from the fog that rolls by. How does this work?

As fog-laden winds blow across the dry sand dunes, microscopic fog droplets accumulate on the beetle's bumpy back. When a water droplet grows large enough, it rolls down the grooves and into the beetle's mouth. Ahhhh, wonderful water! Scientists designed different textures (bumps, grooves, and smooth) on several spheres and found the bumpy surface was a fog magnet. The size, arrangement, and location of the bumps were all critical. Also, the waxy surface of the beetle's exoskeleton allowed the water not to stick but kept it moving into its mouth. This method of fog harvesting has caught the attention of scientists concerned for thirsty communities. Of course, evolution would say that nature created this fog harvesting method. Well, who created nature? **Our Creator God Who is concerned with even the tiniest little beetle living in a dry desert.** And by studying what God has made, we may be able to provide more water for thirsty people!

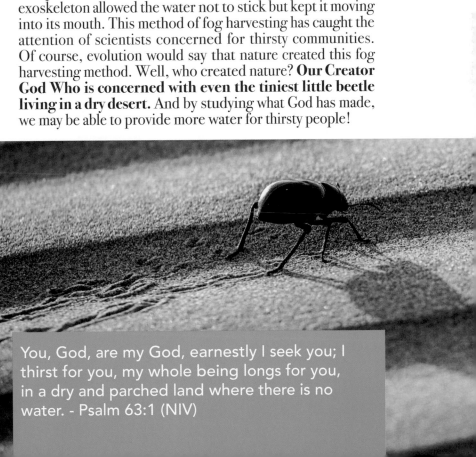

You, God, are my God, earnestly I seek you; I thirst for you, my whole being longs for you, in a dry and parched land where there is no water. - Psalm 63:1 (NIV)

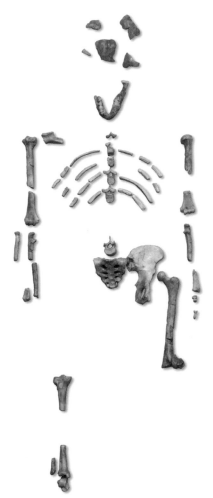

FEBRUARY 29

If asked to name a supposed ape-to-human fossil link, almost any student in America is likely to respond, "Lucy." Donald Johanson, the paleoanthropologist who discovered this set of bones in Ethiopia (consisting of only 20% of the animal's original skeleton), did a masterful job of marketing to both the scientific community and the general public that this is the definitive link between our purported apeish ancestor and modern humans. Numerous facts are left out of essentially all museum displays and textbooks.

1. Johanson's initial research report stated that he had found fully human bone fragments in the same vicinity as Lucy. Only later did he claim these larger bones were from larger animal males of the species. This interpretation was rejected in numerous papers by other evolutionary experts. Johanson promoted the idea (that these human bones were not really human) because if humans lived at the same time and in the same vicinity, Lucy was merely an ape variation, not a human ancestor.

2. No hand or foot bones were found with Lucy, but another researcher (Mary Leakey) found fully human footprints in the same general rock strata, located 1,000 miles away in Tanzania. Because of these prints (found in another country!), Johanson ASSUMED his creature walked upright with human-like hands and feet! **Every textbook and museum display show Lucy with human feet.** Yet other fossils of this chimp-sized creature (*Australopithicus*) show they had the hands and feet of a branch-grabbing monkey, which are completely different than human hands and feet. This is conveniently ignored.

3. Numerous technical papers on Lucy-type fossils have documented that these tiny (less than 4' tall, 65 pound) creatures had arms hanging down to the knees (like an ape); the brain size, skull, face, and jaw of an ape; the shoulders, rib cage, and spine characteristic of apes (not humans); and the hips, knees, hands, and feet of an ape! In other words, Lucy was an ape!

4. An increasing number of researchers place Lucy (and the entire australopithecines family), as simply an extinct variation of some ape-like creature. Yet the media, textbooks, and museums continue to promote her as our ancestor. Lucy is not the missing link; she was at best a degenerated human, but most likely just a variation of an ape. All of this is meticulously documented in the book, ***Contested Bones***, by John Rupe and Dr. John Sanford.

They were banished from human society... forced to live in dry stream beds, among rocks and holes in the ground. They brayed among the bushes...A base and nameless brood, they were driven out of the land. Job 30:5-8 (NIV)

MARCH

"YOU ARE ALL STARDUST...ALL THE THINGS THAT MATTER FOR EVOLUTION [THE ATOMS IN YOUR BODY] WERE CREATED IN THE NUCLEAR FURNACES OF EXPLODING STARS ...SO FORGET JESUS, THE STARS DIED SO YOU COULD BE HERE TODAY.."

– Lawrence Krauss (1954 -), popular atheist astrophysicist, cosmologist, and college lecturer

---

for in [Jesus] were all things created, in heaven and upon the earth...all things have been created through him, and unto him; and he is before all things, and in him all things consist.

— Colossians 1:16a,17 (ASV)

MARCH 1

The bola spider received its name from the Argentinian gauchos (South American cowboys) who flung bolas from horseback to bring down cattle. A bola has two or three cords with rocks or weighted balls attached to the end of each. The cowboys swing the balls in a circle and release them, aiming for the cow's legs. When the bola hits, the cords wind around the legs causing the animal to stop in its tracks.

A female bola spider has its own version of a bola. The bola spider makes a short, strong thread and puts a glob of sticky glue on the end. Next, the bola spider secretes chemicals that smell like a female moth. The male moth smells the supposed female moth and flies close to check it out. The spider skillfully begins to whirl her weapon. When the moth is near enough, **she flings the bola and it wraps around the moth**. She reels it in, bites it, and wraps it in silk until she is ready for supper. The bola spider hunts at night, when the moths are out, so their ability to lasso prey in the dark is even more impressive.

Evolution believes this happened over millions of years. **Did the bola spider just start making random smells** and after a million tries one just happened to smell exactly like a female moth? What about the glue? Glue doesn't happen by accident and chance, someone has to make the glue. And then the skill in using a bola... this also happened by accident and chance??? Try telling a cowboy from South America that his abilities just happened by chance. You may find yourself "bolaed!"

The spider tketh hold with her hands, and is in kings' palaces. – Proverbs 30:28 (KJV)

MARCH 2

Have you heard of a diving bell spider? In the ponds of northern Europe lives a tiny brown spider, *Argyroneta aquatic*, that spends its entire life underwater! It needs oxygen to breathe (just like all spiders), so how does it survive underwater? This spider spins a tiny web to hold air bubbles; it goes to the surface and brings back a bubble of air that is trapped to its hairy abdomen and legs. The water spider then puts the air bubble in the "diving bell." Now it has its own underwater "diving bell" to live in!

Scientists have discovered that the "diving bell" also acts like a gill-taking in oxygen from the surrounding pond water. As the spider breathes, it removes oxygen from the "diving bell," while more oxygen flows in to replace it. This allows the spider to only surface once a day to grab additional air bubbles.

- This spider also lays her eggs inside of the "diving bell." As they hatch, each baby spider lives in its own "diving bell" nursery, as small as the head of a pin.
- As the water spider catches tadpoles and larvae, it puts them inside the "diving bell" to eat as needed.
- When the spider wants to rest, it just goes into its "diving bell" for a nap.

The incredible ability and instincts required for this spider to live its entire life underwater is awe-inspiring and not a result of a few random changes over time. **It would have needed its abilities and instincts to succeed from the beginning.** The diving bell spider gives glory to its Creator.

As for God, his way is perfect: The LORD's word is flawless; he shields all who take refuge in him.
– Psalm 18:30 (NIV)

BIOLOGY

MARCH 3

During the Flood of Noah's time, when the world was totally covered with water, the earth's rotation would have created large-scale circulating oceanic currents, called gyres. Scientists have calculated that these gyres would have flowed at 90-180 m.p.h. (40-80 m/s) for distances of 1,500 miles (2,500 km). In addition, the moon's gravitational pull would have caused enormous twice-daily tides.

This massive water flow would have caused cavitation around the globe. Cavitation results from high-speed water flowing across a surface - creating tiny vacuum bubbles as water is pulled away from the surface. These bubbles burst supersonically, producing temperatures as high as 27,000 °F, enormous local pressures, and pitting of the underlying surface. In 1983, the Glen Canyon Dam, near the Grand Canyon, saw the destructive power of cavitation. Heavy rains threatened to overflow the dam, so water was discharged to the spillway tunnels. This heavy discharge resulted in cavitation which caused chunks of concrete, sections of rebar and pieces of sandstone to be ripped from the tunnel.

The Genesis Flood would have caused gyres (large-scale currents) and tidal forces to produce cavitation on such a wide-scale basis that **huge volumes of rock would have been eroded and transported over widespread areas of the world in a short time.** The Genesis Flood was truly a catastrophic worldwide event.

The floods have lifted up, O LORD, the floods have lifted up their voice; the floods lift up their waves. – Psalm 93:3 (NIV)

MARCH 4

Evolutionists assume that the entire universe, and life, originated by accident and chance because they leave God out of consideration. Let's check their logic.

Take a box of puzzle pieces, shake vigorously, and toss all the pieces high into the air. **Did the pieces come together when they hit the table?** Did even a few pieces start to form any coherent picture? Try it again...and again. Did the pieces, even though they were designed to fit together, fall into place? These few pieces are nothing compared to the millions of complex parts...that make up the trillions of cells...that make up your body! How did the trillions of pieces (cells) come together without someone putting them in the right place! Just like it takes a person to put together a puzzle, it takes Someone far more intelligent and powerful than any human to put together a human. The One who put you together was none other than your Creator and Savior – Jesus Christ.

For you formed my inward parts; you knitted me together in my mother's womb.
– Psalm 139:13 (ESV)

MARCH 5

When scientists first discovered this fish, they had never seen anything like it. This fish has a transparent forehead filled with clear liquid. Inside this clear liquid are two tubular eyes shaped like barrels, so the fish is called a "barreleye fish." This deep-sea fish lives a third-of-a-mile below the surface and looks up to capture its prey - jellyfish. The tube-shaped eyes are perfect for this task, allowing it to see farther away - like looking through binoculars. In the pitch blackness of water, almost 1,600 feet deep, the barreleye fish looks up, scanning for the faint outline or glow of a bioluminescent jellyfish. When it sees its prey, the barreleye fish swims up towards the jellyfish. **Once level with its prey, the fish's tubular eyes rotate in its head so it can see the jellyfish in front of its face.** This is highly unusual, because other animals with tubular eyes cannot move them.

Jellyfish are known for their powerful stinging tentacles. No problem for the barreleye fish because its eyes are protected inside their transparent fluid-filled forehead. What a wonderful design feature, a protective shield for precious binocular eyes! Evolution teaches that this all happened by accident and chance over millions of years. Getting stung in your eyes every time you try to eat lunch doesn't sound very healthy! The barreleyes' uniquely designed eyes are impossible to explain by slow and gradual evolutionary processes. These eyes were perfectly designed for this fish's deep-sea living and jellyfish eating. If there is design, there must be a designer and that Designer is God.

Let the heaven and earth praise him, the seas, and everything that moves in them.
– Psalm 69:34 (ESV)

MARCH 6

Have you ever seen a sunburned fish? If you were at the beach all day, you would need sunscreen. Well, imagine the zebrafish, it lives in shallow reef waters and is exposed all day to the sun's harmful ultraviolet rays. Earth's atmosphere protects us from the deadliest rays, except ultraviolet A and B (UVA, UVB). UVA penetrates deeply into the skin causing wrinkling and aging while UVB reddens the skin and causes sunburn. Both can cause skin cancer. We use sunscreen or sun block to stop the UVA and UVB. How does a zebrafish protect itself from UV rays?

The zebrafish makes its own sunscreen compound, called gadusol, which filters out ultraviolet light. **Sunscreen lotions were not widely available until the 1970s - after extensive development over the previous 30 years.** Did this development happen by accident and chance? Then why would zebrafish sunscreen happen by accident and chance? In both cases, there had to be a sunscreen maker. For the zebrafish, that Maker is God.

BIOLOGY

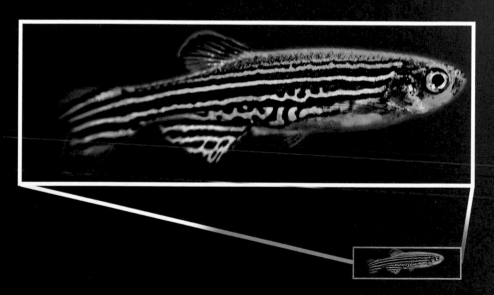

And God said, "Let the waters swarm with swarms of living creatures, and let birds fly above the earth across the expanse of the heavens."
– Genesis 1:20 (ESV)

MARCH 7

Did you know that geckos can launch water off their skin like popcorn popping! Tiny nano- hair-like structures cover their bodies which helps the water droplets coalesce. When the water droplets are large enough, they are hurled off the skin and away from the body. Any dirt that is present is collected by the water droplet and flung away with it. The coalescing of water droplets and the launching off the skin happens so quickly that a gecko is called "super-hydrophobic."

Biomimicry scientists are excited about the gecko's skin design and are thinking of ways to create a self-cleaning, water-repelling fabric as your next piece of clothing! **These scientists recognize a great design when they see it!** If there is a design, there must be a designer and that Designer is God.

For he maketh <u>small the drops of water</u>: they pour down rain according to the vapour thereof: – Job 36:27 (KJV)

MARCH 8

Opossums are rather homely animals that come out at night and are frequently hit by cars. Apparently, they are neither fast moving nor smart. So, what good are they? Perhaps they benefit us more than we realize. Even secular ecologists have noted that when people and animals are allowed to share an ecosystem, they benefit one another in an interdependent win-win interrelationship.

Take the case of Lyme disease. This debilitating, and sometimes deadly disease is spread by certain ticks and likely manifested itself only after mankind's rebellion against God at the Fall. For more than twenty years, the Cary Institute of Ecosystem Studies in New York studied what type of animals carried the specific species of tick infested with Lyme disease. These scientists live-trapped hundreds of woodland mammals and counted the number of ticks they had. They counted these ticks on squirrels, shrews, deer, opossums, etc. During their research, the team discovered that **a single opossum could eat 5,000 ticks each season**. It seems like God has provided opossums to moderate the effect of sin and death for us by having them gobble up deadly ticks. As opossums walk through the forest, they can collect as many as 200 ticks, but an opossum is a fastidious groomer, and most will be gobbled up. Don't get "ticked" off with opossums - welcome them as gifts from God, for they are tick eaters. As one researcher stated, "*They're net destroyers of ticks.*" So, don't run over that opossum in the road, God has sent them to help with your health.

When you besiege a city for a long time, making war against it in order to take it, you shall not destroy its trees by wielding an axe against them. You may eat from them, but you shall not cut them down. - Deuteronomy 20:19 (ESV)

MARCH 9

Mercury, the closest planet to the Sun, is causing big problems for the belief in cosmic evolution.

1. If Mercury is billions of years old, it should not have a magnetic field; **but it does**. Its magnetic field strength is decreasing, with a half-life of 320 years. So, every 320 years the field strength is halved. The magnetic field should be completely gone if Mercury is billions of years old.

2. It should not have blue hollow valleys; **but it does**. These blue colored pits or depressions can be miles in diameter and have every appearance of a quite recent formation. Mercury is supposed to be old and burned out, so how could these geologic features have formed recently?

3. Mercury has a high density core; **when it shouldn't**. It is thought to have an iron core occupying some 75% of its diameter. Evolution's slow and gradual processes cannot explain this high-density core. They postulate that some cosmic collision occurred removing Mercury of its low-density material and leaving the iron core. If this were true, then sulfur would have vaporized during the impact and escaped into space. However, sulfur is present in high concentrations!

Mercury, with its rapidly decaying magnetic field, fresh looking blue hollows, and high sulfur concentration, declare it to be young - just as the Bible says.

When I consider your heavens, the work of your fingers, the moon and the stars, which you have set in place, what are human beings that you are mindful of them... - Psalm 8:3-4 (NIV)

MARCH 10

Uranus, the farthest planet from our sun, is a methane gas giant and the coldest planet in our solar system at -371 degrees F. (-224 degrees C). Uranus is also unique in many other ways.

- Uranus is tipped on its side with an angle of approximately 98 degrees. This means it rolls along, traveling around the sun on its side.
- Uranus rotates backwards of other planets. So now it is rolling on its side but backwards. Evolutionists teach that the planets were formed by the nebular hypotheses - a rotating cloud of gas and dust coalesced to form the planets. This should have resulted in all planets rotating in the same direction. Venus is also an anomaly - rotating backwards.

How did this happen? The story told to astronomy students is that a collision in the distant past reversed the spin of Uranus and flipped it on its side. This is just assumed to be true with no evidence to support it and ignored are the enormous problems with this hypothesis:

1. The mass of Uranus is 14.5 times the mass of Earth and it rotates in 17 hours - faster than Earth. This means Uranus is like a giant gyroscope, resisting any change in rotational direction. For Uranus to spin backwards and on its side, an Earth-sized planet would have to hit it, at exactly the right speed and angle with a glancing blow near one of its poles to produce exactly the right amount of torque without tearing apart the planet. The chances of such an event are essentially zero.
2. Uranus' orbit is almost circular; a collision would not have resulted in a near perfect orbit.
3. If Uranus had been hit, its 27 moons and fine delicate rings would have been scattered. Therefore, a hit could not have taken place.

Uranus defies naturalistic explanations. The only logical explanation is that God created Uranus the way it is.

Ah, Sovereign Lord, you have made the heavens and the earth by your great power and outstretched arm. Nothing is too hard for you.
- Jeremiah 32:17 (NIV)

ASTRONOMY

MARCH 11

When God created the earth, He made massive amounts of rock to form the very foundation of the entire planet. Rock is used dozens of times throughout the Old Testament as representation of the mighty strength, safety, and non-changing nature of God. This theme continues in the New Testament as Jesus taught that we need to act on His words like "*a wise man who built his house <u>on the rock</u>*" (Matthew 7:25-27) and that upon Peter's revelation that Jesus was Son of the living God, "*<u>on this rock</u> I will build My church, and the gates of Hades shall not prevail against it.*" (Matthew 16:18)

Those living in first century Judah knew exactly what Jesus was referring to when saying He would build His church "on a rock." This referred to the massive cornerstone upon which a structure rests and everything else in the building is aligned to that "rock." Then Jesus used the Greek word "ekklesia" for church. This word does not refer to a building but was commonly used for any gathering of people. **"The Church" is not a building or even a denomination** but any group of believers whose doctrine and priorities center on the acknowledgement that Jesus is the Savior and Redeemer of mankind who died in our place for our sins, rose from the dead, and provides the only pathway back into eternal fellowship with God. Jesus is the ROCK which aligns everything in people's lives, sets their priorities correctly, and changes their eternal destiny.

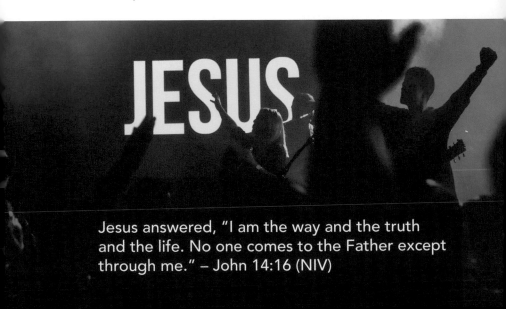

Jesus answered, "I am the way and the truth and the life. No one comes to the Father except through me." – John 14:16 (NIV)

MARCH 12

Is your body the same as when you were a teenager? Are you physically the same person from ten years ago? Not even close!

The bones that make up your skeleton are totally replaced every ten years, cell by cell. Some bone cells (called osteoclasts) break up and remove bone material no longer needed. Other bone cells (called osteoblasts) add bone structure where it needs to be stronger. This constant remodeling needs to be done to meet the needs of a changing skeleton: such as during a pregnancy or when weightlifting.

How about a new stomach? Every two weeks a new stomach lining is produced because the acid in your stomach is constantly eating away at the stomach lining! Your liver, which cleans out toxins, must be totally replaced every 13 months. Interestingly, if only 25% of the liver is present, it can regrow itself. No other organ can do this!

What about those ever-expanding fat cells? Your fat cells are replaced every 10 years. Your top skin layer (the epidermis) is replaced about every 27 days. It simply wears out and requires frequent regeneration. Your taste buds are replaced every 10-14 days, or you would no longer be able to taste foods. Most frequent of all is the cerebrospinal fluid surrounding our brain and filling our spinal cord. This critical fluid is totally replaced every 24 hours; each day we make about a pint's worth of fresh brain fluid.

There are a few parts of your body that are never replaced, such as your tooth enamel, your brain's cerebral cortex neurons, and your eye lenses core cells. But for the most part, you really are a "*new you*" even though you may feel and look the same. Wouldn't it be great if our car could replace its parts continually? Or how about your house adding another room when needed? Our bodies are incredible! Your cells are constantly rebuilding *the new you*, they work like clockwork. Do schedules that work like clockwork happen by accident and chance? Evolution believes that things happen with randomness and no purpose. How does each area of your body know when to replace its cells? It's on a schedule. Such schedules take a schedule maker and that schedule Maker is God.

It is of the LORD'S mercies that we are not consumed, because his compassions fail not. They are new every morning: great is thy faithfulness. – Laminations 3:22-23 (KJV)

MARCH 13

What fish swims in 28°F water without freezing AND has a white heart? The unique Antarctica icefish. It makes its home in the frigid ocean waters off the coast of Antarctica where ocean water is well below freezing because salty water freezes at a lower temperature than freshwater. **The icefish blood contains special proteins which act like an antifreeze** so that its blood does not solidify in subfreezing water. As the blood begins to crystallize, the antifreeze proteins fasten onto the growing ice, forcing the water molecules to scatter and remain fluid.

Most warm-blooded creatures react to cooler temperatures by thickening their blood. Yet the icefish has blood that remains thin at subfreezing temperatures. This happens because icefish have NO red blood cells or hemoglobin in their blood. No other vertebrates (animals with a backbone) are designed in this way. Red blood cells and hemoglobin transport oxygen from the lungs to other parts of the body. Icefish transport oxygen in a completely different manner. Antarctic water is more oxygen-rich than other oceans and icefish absorb oxygen directly through their skin and gills. Oxygen in the water diffuses directly into the fish's blood plasma, which is the liquid portion of blood (mostly water). It is then circulated to every cell in the body. **Without red blood cells the icefish has translucent blood and a white heart!**

No other vertebrates have this way of absorbing oxygen, so this fish has no known ancestor. How could such ability slowly develop and leave no ancestors? **It couldn't.** How  could it just get rid of all its red blood cells? **It was designed to function without them from the beginning.** The abilities of the icefish are a testimony to the creativity of our Creator.

For You are great, and do wondrous things; You alone are God. – Psalm 86:10 (NKJV)

Words matter. When Charles Darwin coined the phrase "natural selection" to supposedly explain how simple organisms evolved to turn into the variety of complex life on Earth it was a stroke of deceptive genius. The idea of natural selection is that there is a "natural" process by which nature itself "selects" **useful positive changes** in each new generation of any creature while **rejecting less fit negative changes.** It is repeated so often and sounds so feasible (on the surface) that it is almost universally accepted and repeated by evolutionists and creationists alike. But is it true?

Without a doubt every form of life reveals enormous variety. Mutations (which destroy information) do cause changes within every generation of organism. However, "nature" has no "mind" and cannot "select" anything. In reality, the genetic mechanisms within every cell and every organism are programmed to continuously adapt to environments, stresses, mutually beneficial relationships, and inherent abilities. Any animal not already programmed with the ability to adapt can do nothing when thrown into a new environment. It is going to die, not be "selected" for survival. Think of a pigeon being relocated to Antarctica or a fish being thrown into a desert!

What God built into the biological world is the programmed ability to adapt and fill an almost infinite variety of new environments. **But programming REQUIRES an intelligent programmer**, not some "natural" process of "selection." Without the program to provide the changes needed to fill new environmental niches (programmed filling) there would be mass extinction, not massive variety of life on Earth. Natural selection is a deceptive misnomer which hides the truth of God's existence.

Let no one deceive you with empty words, for because of these things the wrath of God comes upon the sons of disobedience.
– Ephesians 5:6 (ESV)

ANATOMY

MARCH 15

Take a deep breath. Air rushes into your nose and down your trachea to your two lungs. Your left lung is not as large as your right lung because it has to make room for your heart. Air travels from the trachea (or windpipe) into the bronchi and on into even smaller tubes called bronchioles. Bronchioles are about the same thickness as a strand of hair. At the end of each bronchiole is a special area that leads into clumps of teeny, tiny air sacs called alveoli. There are about 600 million alveoli in your lungs and if you spread them out, **they would cover the area equal to an entire tennis court!** It is here on this tennis court-sized surface that the miraculous happens.

Each alveolus has a mesh-like covering of very small blood vessels called capillaries. These capillaries are so tiny that the cells in your blood need to line up single file just to march through them. **This is where the exchange of oxygen and carbon dioxide take place.** Oxygen passes through the walls of each alveolus into the tiny capillaries that surround it. The oxygen enters the blood and hitches a ride on the red blood cells. The oxygenated blood cells travel to the heart where they are pumped throughout the body - delivering needed oxygen to every cell in our body. Then the cell's waste product (carbon dioxide) hitches a ride on the red blood cells back to our lungs where this waste gas passes through the wall, into the alveolus, and is breathed out of our lungs. Our very life depends on both oxygen and the removal of poisonous carbon dioxide.

Isn't it interesting how the respiratory system works in unison to complete these tasks? Yet we are told to believe that this all somehow happened by mutational accidents and chance! **Evolution is impossible.** Even millions of years would never have developed the respiratory system, with all of it parts. Such an intricate system, with its thousands of individual parts, had to all be together from the beginning.

You hide Your face, they are troubled; You take away their breath, they die and return to their dust. - Psalm 104:29 (NKJV)

MARCH 16

Did you know that within our lungs there are "vacuum cleaners" collecting and removing particles that enter our lungs? These vacuum cleaners are special cells called macrophages. Macrophages (meaning "big eaters") work in the deepest part of the lung, in the alveola. They are flat and mobile, patrolling like flat fish on the ocean bottom, looking for particles or bacterial invaders to consume which have escaped the air cleaners above. They reach out with tubular extensions to engulf any particles. **One macrophage can clean an area forty times its size.** When they are finished with their work, they make their way to the mucus escalator which moves them up through the lungs to the windpipe where they are plunged into the pool of death – i.e., the stomach acids. If macrophages are facing an infectious invasion, they signal white blood cells into the area to help. A widespread lung infection is called pneumonia. If we did not have these macrophages, our lives would be in constant danger. The alveola area of the lung is a warm, wet climate – the perfect place for germs to grow. So, macrophages act like vacuum cleaners to keep us from major infections.

Do we say a vacuum cleaner happened by accident and chance? Then why would anyone say that our macrophages, which act like vacuum cleaners, happened by mutational accidents and chance? And **Who is our lungs' vacuum cleaner maker?** Who else – God!

Who knoweth not in all these that the hand of the LORD hath wrought this? In whose hand is the soul of every living thing, and the breath of all mankind. – Job 12:9,10 (KJV)

MARCH 17

Are jackalope's (rabbits with antelope-like horns) real? As a child traveling to Wall Drug, South Dakota, we often stopped and saw the infamous giant jackalope. We laughed at it! But here is the rest of the story.

During the 1930's, hunters in Iowa reported seeing rabbits with horn-like structures on their heads. When Dr. Richard E. Shope heard of these rabbits, he started to investigate. He first found specimens of these "horned" cottontails in the high plain states of the U.S.A. Upon further investigation, he discovered that these odd-looking horned rabbits were mentioned as far back as 1789, even illustrated in a French encyclopedia. Research revealed the protrusions to be a result of a virus, the cottontail rabbit *papilloma* virus. **Dr. Shope's research revealed for the first time that a virus could cause cancer.** Cancer is a mistake in the programming of a cell that results in out of control reproduction of that cell. The virus which created the horns out of the infected cells was caused by a virus - a mutation.

Are mutations which produced "jackalopes" useful? Not really. In reality, muations always distort or destroy information.

- Over 99% of mutations are harmful.
- The remaining 1% are too insignificant to matter.
- A miniscule percentage serve some useful function.
- **All mutations destroy functioning information within a cell.**

Evolution relies on mutations adding complex and useful information to a cell. Observational science shows us that mutations do not do this.

For the creation was subjected to futility....
- Romans 8:20a (ESV)

MARCH 18

Want to share the Gospel with someone who thinks God is not important? Ask them to consider Pascal's wager. Blaise Pascal was a brilliant 17th century scientist. The unit of pressure, the pascal, is even named after him. Atmospheric pressure in weather is measured in kilopascals. Pascal was also a Bible believing Christian and proposed this wager:

- There are only two possibilities for God's existence: God exists, or God does not exist.
- There are two basic responses to this: live as if God exists or live as if God does not exist.

1. If you combine these two, there are four possible results: If God does not exist and you live as if God does NOT exist, nothing was gained during life and nothing is lost when you die. Everything starts as dust and returns to dust. One thousand years from now nothing you do will be remembered.
2. If God does not exist and you live believing that God does exist, nothing is lost when you die, but you will live a far more meaningful, hope-filled, purposeful life.
3. If God does exist and you live as if God does NOT exist, you lose big time after death as His righteous judgment falls upon your unbelief and sinful life!
4. If God does exist and you live as if Jesus (God) does exist, you gain everything – hope and fulfillment while alive and eternal life and fellowship with your Creator and Savior after death!

Pascal's Table

	GOD DOES NOT EXIST	GOD DOES EXIST
LIVE AS THOUGH GOD **DOESN'T** EXIST	LOSE NOTHING	LOSE EVERYTHING
LIVE AS THOUGH GOD **DOES** EXIST	LOSE NOTHING	LOSE NOTHING GAIN EVERYTHING

How can you lose if you choose to become a Christian? Are you gambling with your eternal life? What if there is a God?

And ye shall seek me, and find me, when ye shall search for me with all your heart.
- Jeremiah 29:13 (KJV)

MARCH 19

Did you know that there is a clock in your body? Not just one clock but trillions of them. Since the 1960s, a whole new field of biological studies has developed - chronobiology. Nearly every living thing - plants, animals, and fungi - have these clocks. Even single-celled bacterium tracks the day-night cycle with amazing accuracy. For humans, at night, the body's growth hormones increase so skin cells regenerate, muscles repair, and kids grow. Why do teenagers sleep so much? They are growing!

Our master clock is located in the part of our brain called the hypothalamus. This timekeeping computer is called the suprachiasmatic nucleus. But there are more clocks in your body that run different organs and tissues. It turns out that almost every cell in the human body has its own clock!

- **Hair cells**: divide at a particular time every evening - which means our hair grows mostly at night.
- **Brain**: has a sleep-wake cycle and the brain is most alert about 10 a.m.
- **Heart**: blood pressure rises sharply around 6:45 a.m. and peaks at 6:30 p.m.
- **Liver**: most active during the day.
- **Lungs**: most prepared to fight disease during our most active hours. Asthma is most pronounced at night.
- **Stomach**: eating at odd times, such as late at night, may cause weight gain because other organs are not ready to use the food.
- **Pancreas regulates insulin**: an out-of-whack clock can lead to diabetes.
- **Body fat**: has a clock and if out-of-whack, it can contribute to obesity.

Research into diabetes and dieting has found the time of day you take your medicine will have a profound affect. It has been found that blue wavelengths are beneficial during normal daylight hours, boosting mood, attention and reaction time. Viewing electronic screens late at night zaps you with blue light, confusing the body into thinking it is 12 noon. Clocks in our body are well interconnected and complex! Did this happen by accident and chance? Clocks require a clockmaker, and this Clockmaker is God. Truly you are fearfully and wonderfully made!

> To every thing there is a season, and a time to every purpose under the heaven
> - Ecclesiastes 3:1 (KJV)

MARCH 20

Where is that horrible, stinky smell coming from? Oh, the corpse flower or *Titan arum*. The corpse flower is native to Sumatra, Indonesia. At the base of the tall spadix (spike) are the tiny male and female flowers. Surrounding the tall spadix is the bright green spathe which looks like a pleated skirt.

For an entire decade this plant stores up energy underground, then the bloom grows rapidly. The stalk can grow up to 15 feet tall and the bloom can be 3 feet wide. Chemical analysis of the flower's smell reveals dimethyl trisulfide (limburger cheese), indole (mothballs), dimethyl disulfide (garlic), trimethylamine (rotting fish), and isovaleric acid (stinky socks). This flower literally smells like the rotting carcass of a dead animal. **Not a good flower to give to your wife on Valentine's Day!**

While in bloom, the plant heats up to more than 98°F. This allows the scent to spread farther, especially at night, and attract flies and beetles looking to feed on what they are tricked into believing is decomposing meat. The flies and beetles crawl deep within the flower structure which has two rings of flowers, one ring of female flowers and one ring of male flowers. **The flies and beetles just love being there**, romping around, laying eggs, playing in what they think is a dead piece of rotting meat. The female flowers are pollinated and soon die. The plant even traps the insects forcing them to spend the night. The next day pollen from the male parts of the flower rains down on the insects before they are released. These insects, covered in pollen, then fly to the next corpse flower to pollinate the female flowers.

Interestingly, in 2016, scientists noticed that corpse flowers all over the world bloomed within weeks of each other. Evolution will tell you this plant and its pollination style came about by mutational accidents and chance. How does a plant, without a brain, know what rotting meat smells like or that flies and beetles love rotting meat? How does the plant know how to trap insects so it can rain down pollen the next day? The corpse flower shows design - which points to a designer - Who is God.

Dead flies cause the ointment of the apothecary to send forth a stinking savour: so doth a little folly him that is in reputation for wisdom and honour - Ecclesiastes 10:1 (KJV)

MARCH 21

In the hills of Tennessee is a tree that is a rock. Actually, it is a petrified tree that extends upward through multiple layers of rock. Geologists call these kind of fossils polystrate fossils because they extend through many (poly) layers (strata). Evolutionists believe that layers were laid down slowly over time, so this tree would need to stand tall over millions of years as it was ever so slowly buried and the rock layers were forming. Wrong! That is clearly impossible because when a tree dies, it decays, falls over, and is recycled into soil. A tree cannot stand for millions of years while sediments slowly cover it, inch by inch.

The Flood of Noah's day would have been the event that would have rapidly laid down layers of strata, buried trees, and had the necessary conditions for fossilization.

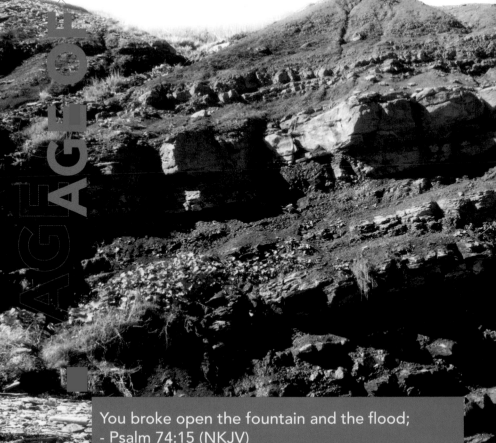

You broke open the fountain and the flood;
- Psalm 74:15 (NKJV)

MARCH 22

In the vicinity of Nova Scotia, Canada is an old coal mining town called Joggins. Joggins is located on the shore of the Bay of Fundy, which is famous for having the highest tides in the world, **48 feet - twice a day**. The incredible tides are caused by the bay's unique shape and orientation. The continual eroding of the surrounding cliffs exposes new fossils. The cliffs are 82 feet high and have multiple strata or layers. Within these layers are the famous polystrate fossils. A polystrate fossil is one that cuts through multiple layers of rock. Within the Joggins cliffs are dozens of polystrate lycopods and calamites (giant, hollow reeds up to 10 feet tall).

As Dr. Derek Ager, former President of the British Geological Association, wrote, "*Obviously sedimentation had to be very rapid to bury a tree in a standing position before it rotted and fell down.*" **To preserve a vertical reed would require rapid burial**, otherwise the exposed part of the plant would quickly decay. Evolutionists believe these polystrate plants grew slowly in place for hundreds of years before being slowly buried and preserved. How could a reed remain partly unburied without rotting? These polystrate fossilized plants show no evidence of rot. Polystrate fossils, like these at Joggins, give us evidence of rapid burial. The hollow reed lycopods and calamites were caught in the Flood of Noah's time, buried quickly, fossilized, and the daily tides of Joggins continue to reveal their catastrophic past.

They did eat, they drank, they married wives, they were given in marriage, until the day that [Noah] entered into the ark, and the flood came, and destroyed them all. - Luke 17:27 (KJV)

AGE OF CREATION

MARCH 23

Charles Darwin's book, *The Origin of Species*, was published in 1859 and promoted the theory of evolution. Only a few accepted it at first, but by the 1920's, the theory of evolution was starting to make inroads toward public acceptance. Many parents worried that their children were being taught to distrust the Bible in the public schools. Teaching molecules-to-man evolution (without pointing out the enormous problems with this belief) does exactly that. By 1925, twenty states had passed laws not allowing schools to promote the idea that man evolved from an ape as a fact of science.

The Butler Act from the state of Tennessee was one of these laws. At this time, the ACLU put ads in newspapers to challenge this law. A friend of John Scopes wanted to bring notoriety to a small Tennessee town, so he convinced Scopes to accept the ACLU offer. John Scopes was a football coach, not a science teacher. He later admitted that he had not even taught evolution during the two weeks he acted as substitute teacher for an ill science teacher. But the case went to court and became known as the "Scope's Monkey trial." **It is considered the "trial of the century" in the 1900s because of the ramifications it had on both public education and Biblical credibility.** There was no particular animosity towards either side and a circus-like atmosphere prevailed throughout Dayton, TN during the eight-day trial.

Although John Scopes was on trial for teaching evolution and ultimately charged $100 for his offense (nothing was ultimately paid), he was not the focus of the trial. **The goal of the ACLU was to crush public trust in the Bible by making believers look like idiots.** They succeeded beyond their wildest dreams. [To Be Continued...]

...trial of the State of Tennessee v. John Thomas Scopes, July 20, 1925.

You broke open the fountain and the flood;
- Psalm 74:15 (NKJV)

MARCH 24

The evidence that was presented at the Scopes Trial to "prove" evolution has essentially been proven wrong. For example:

- Vestigial organs were presented as left-over vestiges from a person's evolutionary past as they slowly changed from green slime into people. 180 vestigial organs were once proposed such as the tailbone, appendix, tonsils, and Thymus gland. The tailbone is now known to be a place where muscles are attached so you can go to the bathroom. The appendix is now known as a place where good bacteria are harbored until needed to reboot into the intestine. Tonsils are now known to provide a first line protection from diseases. The thymus gland is now known to help our immune system.
- Evolutionists presented many supposed ape-man fossils at the Scopes Trial. Piltdown man was later discovered to be a hoax. Heidelberg man (known as Neanderthal man today) is universally recognized as fully human. Java Man was simply a *Homo erectus* fossil; this category of fossils is best interpreted as humans who are degenerated by inbreeding and nutrition deprivation. We are not finding the missing link between ape and man. It is still missing.[1]
- Human baby embryos were presented as "proof" of evolution, because at a certain stage of development, they seem to have gill slits, egg sac, and tails. Experts assured the public that this showed human's evolutionary past as fish (gills), reptiles (egg sacs), and ultimately monkeys (tails). No physiologists today promote this superficial mistake. The "gills" are a development area for our ear and various glands; the "egg sac" is a source of critical blood cells which is often different than the mother's blood type; and the "tail" is the development area for our spinal bones.[2]

Authoritative sounding scientists convinced a listening nation that all these mistakes were actually facts of science. Today we know that these evolutionary mistakes were not true, yet these lies influenced Christians. Christian leaders did not know how to respond to attacks upon the Word of God by "authoritative science." [To be continued...]

...for behold, the wicked bend the bow; they have fitted their arrow to the string to shoot in the dark at the upright in heart;
- Psalm 11:2 (ESV)

Following the "expert" witnesses testifying to the "fact" of monkey-to-man evolution, William Jennings Bryan took the witness stand to defend the accuracy of the Bible. When asked where Cain could have found a wife to propagate the human race after he killed his brother, Bryan responded, "*I'll leave the agnostics to hunt for her.*" He also had few satisfying answers when asked about Jonah being swallowed by a whale, how a woman could be created from the rib of Adam, and other questions aimed at undermining belief in God's Word. The climax of the trial came as atheist Clarence Darrow asked, "*Do you really believe the Earth was created in six days?*"

Answered the man defending Christianity, "*Not in six days of 24 hours.*" Asked the atheist, "*Doesn't the Bible say so?*" Answered the man explaining why we need to trust the Bible, "*I do not see that there is any necessity for construing the words, 'the morning and the evening,' as meaning necessarily a twenty-four hour day...*" Asked the man who called Christianity a '*fool's religion' during the trial, "So creation might have been going on for a very long time.*" Answered the professing Christian, "*It might have continued for millions of years.*"

In essence, to the entire listening nation, the Bible was portrayed as meaning anything anyone wanted it to say, full of errors, and wrong about history, biology, geology, and cosmology. Church leaders in many denominations were so embarrassed by the trial that they backed away from teaching Genesis as true history and just concentrated on matters of faith. The famous Scopes Trial was staged to counterattack the influence of creationist thinking in America and the teaching of creation in schools. Once the Church quit believing the Bible as true history, everything else fell like a row of dominos. The Supreme Court, in 1948, endorsed the 'separation of church and state.' Beginning in the 1960's, the Bible, the 10 commandments, and prayer were outlawed in school. Today, God is not present in public schools, He has been kicked out! The domino to start it all was the Scopes Monkey Trial, and that domino fell with a resounding crash!

We destroy arguments and every lofty opinion raised against the knowledge of God, and take every thought captive to obey Christ,
- 2 Corinthians 10:5 (ESV)

MARCH 26

Albert Einstein made the following statement once he came to understand the nature of time, "*People like us, who believe in physics, know that the distinction between the past, present, and future is only a stubbornly persistent illusion.*"

Space is measured in three dimensions – length, width, and depth. All physical objects are also measured using these three dimensions. Time has been called the "fourth dimension" and has been found to be part of, not independent from, the physical universe. Interestingly, it also is measured in three ways – past, present, and future. Einstein and his experiments have shown that the rate at which time moves is affected by the amount of matter in its immediate vicinity, and by the speed and acceleration with which any object is traveling through space. This modern understanding of time leads to some interesting conclusions about the nature of God.

God is the Creator of the universe, and time is part of that creation. Thus, God is totally and completely outside of time as we know it. This is why God calls Himself the "Eternal One" and the "Alpha and Omega" (beginning and the end). **Our Lord and Maker simultaneously sees everything which has ever happened, is happening, and will ever happen.** The many specific prophecies in the Bible demonstrate this timeless nature of God. Bible prophecies assure us that the Bible is indeed authored by the One who created the universe; therefore, He is outside of time and knows the future.

This should give us rock-solid assurance that nothing is happening which God has not allowed and we can depend upon and trust Jesus to get us through our problems.

And we know that all things work together for good to them that love God, to them who are the called according to his purpose.
– Romans 8:28 (KJV)

BIOLOGY

MARCH 27

Have you considered the Luna moth of North America? This beautiful pistachio-green moth comes out at night. Its 4-7 inch wingspan (almost the length of an I-phone) allows room for a beautiful black eyespot on each wing. Evolutionists teach that artistic designs like this evolved to scare off predators, but moths fly at night not during the day, and predators cannot even see the eyespots at night. So, this is just storytelling, not science.

At night, the Luna moth's predator is a bat and they hunt with sonar, not by sight. That's where the elongated ruffled tail of the Luna moth comes in handy. These twisted tails spin as the moth flies – like a spinning whirligig in the wind. This causes the bat's sonar to become scattered. As a result, the bat often misses the moth completely or just gets part of the tail. Did this type of tail happen by accident and chance as evolution states? How would the Luna moths know they needed a twisted tail? Did they know that bats used sonar to catch them, so they created a way of making the sonar to be deflected? Do moths have the ability to add a spinning tail to their bodies? How many were eaten before they evolved this specialized sonar confusing mechanism? **When we see such engineering, we know there must be an engineer behind it and who is that great Engineer? God Himself!**

Praise be to the LORD God, the God of Israel, who alone does marvelous deeds.
– Psalm 72:18 (NIV)

It was a dark night over England and specially designed radar picked up something never before seen - the night migration of moths. Silver Y moths spend their summers in Greenland, Iceland and Scandinavia, but each fall, they fly over England on their way to North Africa. When they return each spring, they breed before dying (in some years two generations can be born). So, these migrating moths are returning to the wintering place of their parents or grandparents, **having never been there before!**

Researchers found the moths flying as much as 2,600 feet above the ground and achieving speeds as high as 66 mph. Why do they fly so high and how do they fly so fast? The moths take flight when high altitude winds align toward their destination and if not precisely correct, they adjust their trajectory for sideways drift. Their mass migration usually happens on only one night per year and using the jet stream, they travel some 1,200 miles to their destination in just 3-4 nights. They also have some sort of internal compass which tells them if they are travelling in the correct direction; if not, they bail out of the jet stream and wait for the return of winds to take them in the correct direction. It was found that moths knew of the correct higher elevation wind conditions even though there were no obvious clues at ground level.

How a little moth can calculate where to go, when to go, measure wind speeds, and make course corrections is not known. Evolution thinks this skillful navigation happened by accident and chance mutations. We know navigational skills require a navigator. The Navigator Who designed it within their DNA for this type of behavior is God.

Who *are* these that *fly* as a cloud, and as the doves to their windows? – Isaiah 60:8 (KJV)

MARCH 29

Is evolution, where one creature turns into a different creature, found in the fossil record? Let's take a look:

Ants have been found in amber assumed by evolutionists to be 92 million years old, yet they look like today's ants. **Where is the evolution?**
-   Chambered nautilus fossils are assumed by evolutionists to be over 100 million years old, yet they look like today's chambered nautilus. **Where is the evolution?**
-   Ginkgo leaf fossils are assumed by evolutionists to be over 200 million years old, yet they look like today's ginkgo leaves. **Where is the evolution?**
-   Horseshoe crab fossils are assumed by evolutionists to be 200 million years old, yet they look just like today's horseshoe crabs. **Where is the evolution?**
-   Hundreds of other fossil organisms look the same as today's counterpart. Here are a few examples:

    -   Cockroach (supposedly 250 million years old)
    -   Crocodile (supposedly 140 million years old)
    -   Frog (supposedly 275 million years old)
    -   Parrot (supposedly 70 million years old)
    -   Shark (supposedly 400 million years old)
    -   Spider (supposedly 400 million years old)

As scientists continue to dig up organisms, they find that they match their counterpart of today. Fossil organisms, looking like today's organisms, are the norm for the fossil record, **showing us that no evolution has taken place**. If evolution were true, we should not find stasis (a lack of change) in the fossil record, yet that is exactly what we observe. God stated ten times at the beginning of the Bible, He created creatures "after their own kind." There is enormous variety within a kind, but basic body structures stay the same. God made each basic "kind" of creature unique from the beginning.

And God said, Let the earth bring forth the living creature after his kind... - Genesis 1:24a (KJV)

MARCH 30

In 1994, in a remote gorge in the Blue Mountains of Australia, a stand of Wollemi pines was discovered. So what, you ask? This pine tree was thought to be long extinct, known only by fossils. It was believed to have thrived during the time of the dinosaurs, so finding a grove of them was touted as the equivalent of finding a living dinosaur roaming earth. The **Wollemi pine shows no change from its fossil counterpart**. It is called a '*living fossil*.'

'Living fossils' are living creatures or plants which are identical to the fossil form taught to have lived millions of years ago. Here are just a few of the hundreds of examples of living fossils:

- Fossil coelacanth fish, dated using evolutionary assumptions to be 340 million years old, look essentially the same as the living coelacanth fish of today.
- Modern-looking duckbill platypus fossils have been found which are presented as a fact as being 150 million years old.
- Fossil nautilus, placed at 100 million years, look essentially the same as today's nautilus.

There are hundreds of other examples of these types of living fossils. Why have these life forms remained unchanged? **Where is the evolution?** What we observe is that modern plants and animals stay the same as their fossilized ancestors. I ask again, where is the scientific evidence for evolution when we have hundreds of 'living fossils'?

So if you visit Sydney, Australia go to the Botanical Gardens (it is right around the corner from the famous Opera house) and see the Wollemi pine thought to have been extinct for millions of years. The Wollemi pine gives evidence for creation and NO evidence for evolution!

FLOOD GEOLOGY

That which has been is what will be, That which is done is what will be done, And there is nothing new under the sun. – Ecclesiastes 1:9 (NKJV)

BOTANY

MARCH 31

When walking through a forest, you may hear a bird singing or see a beautiful tree, but have you thought of what is under your feet? Sure, there are tree roots, but scientists are discovering that these roots are intertwined and intricately connected to a network of microscopic fungus.

When people think of fungus they think of mushrooms. Mushrooms are the "fruit" of the fungus, like apples are the fruit of an apple tree. Most of the fungus lives underground, in the soil, wrapped around tree roots in a vast network of tiny "threads" called mycelium. If you pulled back the bark of a decaying tree you may see these tiny white threads. These tiny threads form a network called the mycorrhizal network. This network of threads is connecting two very different organisms. Trees and fungus share both water and nutrients in an amazing way. For example, if saplings are growing in a shady area and there is not enough sunlight for photosynthesis, the saplings receive nutrients and sugars from the older, taller trees who send it to them through the mycorrhizal network!

The University of Reading in England studied Douglas-fir and found that the trees actually recognized the root tips of their relatives and sent carbon and nutrients through the fungal network to the less fortunate. In return, the mycorrhizal network retains about 30% of the sugars from the trees.

The sugars received from the trees fuels the fungi ...which collects phosphorus and other nutrients into the network...which is then sent to other trees. The oldest trees typically have the most fungal connections. Thus, they can detect distress signals from neighbors, and can send them needed nutrients!

Trees have a well-developed and complex symbiotic relationship with fungus. The trees need the fungus and the fungus needs the trees. It is a win-win situation. God in His wisdom knew that the trees would need help and the fungus would need help, so He designed a beautifully beneficial network. This is called mutualism and is one of the strongest evidences that evolution could not possibly be true. A one step at a time change cannot explain how two vastly different organisms could learn to depend upon each other. Who would have thought so much was happening under our feet as we walk through the forest!

Show me the wonders of your great love, you who save by your right hand...
- Psalm 17:7a (NIV)

APRIL

"EVOLUTION DESTROYS UTTERLY AND FINALLY THE VERY REASON JESUS' EARTHLY LIFE WAS SUPPOSEDLY MADE NECESSARY. DESTROY ADAM AND EVE AND THE ORIGINAL SIN, AND IN THE RUBBLE YOU WILL FIND THE SORRY REMAINS OF THE SON OF GOD. TAKE AWAY THE MEANING OF HIS DEATH. IF JESUS WAS NOT THE REDEEMER WHO DIED FOR OUR SINS, AND <u>THIS IS WHAT EVOLUTION MEANS</u>, THEN CHRISTIANITY IS NOTHING!"

– Richard Bozarth, (1949 -), 'The Meaning of Evolution', American Atheist, p. 30, February 1978.

And if Christ be not raised, your faith is vain; ye are yet in your sins...But now is Christ risen from the dead... For as in Adam all die, even so in Christ shall all be made alive.

– 1 Corinthians 15:17,20,22 (KJV)

APRIL 1

Sometimes God creates animals with characteristics which seem designed to confound those who deny His existence! The nine-banded armadillo, *Dasypus novemcinctus*, is such a creature. The only species of armadillo living in the U.S. and the state animal of Texas, this creature has a protective shell, or carapace, made of bony plates in the skin. These plates not only cover its body, but also its head, limbs, and tail. Evolutionists explain away its unique plates by assuming they developed over time because they are useful for protection...but an eighth, quarter, or half protected armadillo would easily be eaten by predators as it gradually evolved enough protective plates. But its babies are even more confounding to evolutionary beliefs.

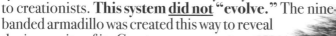

This armadillo is the only vertebrate that gives birth to identical quadruplets every time! Once the single egg of a female is fertilized, the egg splits into four embryos, each identical, that share the same placenta. This results in four identical armadillos at birth. How and why this unique reproductive system could have "evolved" is a mystery to evolutionists but not to creationists. **This system <u>did not</u> "evolve."** The nine-banded armadillo was created this way to reveal the ingenuity of its Creator.

For every beast of the forest is mine, and the cattle upon a thousand hills. - Psalm 50:10 (KJV)

APRIL 2

Suppose you get pregnant but want to still fit into that flattering evening gown. No problem – just delay your baby's growth for four extra months! Or perhaps you'd like your children's birthdate to fall on a certain day of the year. No problem - just put things on hold so the actual birth happens on the day you want. No more hot summer pregnancies! No more pregnancies interfering with vacations, holidays, and hospital schedules. All you need to do is grow an armored coat and become an armadillo!

The nine-banded armadillo can put their pregnancies on hold! Like several other types of mammals, including bears and badgers, armadillos can choose longer gestation periods by putting a baby in a dormant state until conditions are good for growth or birth. Armadillo offspring take about four months from inception to birth, but mom can give birth to her cute little guys up to 8 months later if she chooses. Her body is constantly gathering data from the area she is living in and responds appropriately.

Thousands of programming and chemical changes to the armadillo would be required to allow this creature to achieve such a feat. Programming changes do not occur by random chance. **God gave this amazing creature its super pregnancy powers.** This could not happen by chance and has clearly been designed by God.

O sing unto the LORD a new song; for he hath done marvellous things. - Psalm 98:1a (KJV)

BIOLOGY

APRIL 3

Have you heard of the polka-dotted zebra? This zebra is the result of a rare genetic mutation affecting the zebra's melanin (pigment) production resulting in an abnormality in its stripe pattern. Zebras with this mutation do not survive as long as zebras with the normal stripes. This indicates that this mutation is **NOT** an improvement to the gene pool.

Why do zebras have stripes at all? Ideas have ranged from camouflage to the stripes of a rapidly running animal messing with the mind of pursuing predators. One of the latest proposals is that the black-and-white pattern functions as a fly repellant! It seems that the stripes mesmerize and disorient flies, causing them to have difficulty in landing. This is good! Zebras have very thin coats, which makes it easier for flies to bite and penetrate their skin. African flies carry a number of diseases that are fatal to zebras.

This polka-dotted zebra has a mutation and won't survive long. Are mutations helpful and good? Not in this case. Evolution teaches that mutations have advanced a small single-celled organism all the way to a human. Mutations are overwhelmingly bad and are a symptom of the world held in bondage to decay - just as the Bible tells us.

His delight is not in the strength of the horse, nor his pleasure in the legs of a man, but the Lord takes pleasure in those who fear him, in those who hope in his steadfast love.
- Psalm 147:10-11 (ESV)

APRIL 4

Florence Nightingale is known as the world's most famous nurse. Nursing during the Crimean War was her training ground for changing the health of the common man in England. After the war, she contracted a debilitating inflammation of the vertebrae (spondylitis) and often found herself bedridden. So, she started to collect data from the Crimean War military hospitals where the wounded soldiers had recuperated. These hospitals were poorly ventilated, filthy, and overcrowded. **The death rate at these horrible hospitals was greater than the number of soldiers who died in the field.** Nightingale came up with a new type of graphic illustration known as a coxcomb - a circular design divided into 12 sections, each one representing a month. The coxcomb graphically presented a relationship between improved sanitation, which had been implemented, and a plummeting death rate. Because of her presentations, the military improved their hospitals and Parliament approved the first comprehensive sewage system for London.

Nightingale then sent questionnaires to hospitals, collected data on every aspect of medical care, and correlated the data verses age, gender, disease length and death rates. Nightingale came to believe that, "*using statistics to understand how the world worked was to understand the mind of God.*" She led the way for public health legislation in England. As a result, the average life expectancy in England increased from 40 years to 60 years. Nightingale had given her life to Jesus as a 16-year-old and later in life she wrote in her diary, "*Would I do good for Him, for Him alone...?*" Trust and belief in a Christian God led to Nightingale's passion, and as a result, nursing methods improved, and millions benefited from longer healthier lives.

176   THE ILLUSTRATED LONDON NEWS   [Feb. 24, 1855.

That thy way may be known upon earth, thy saving health among all nations.
- Psalm 67:2 (KJV)

APRIL 5

In the first edition of *The Origin of Species*, Charles Darwin proposed that North American black bears, which were known to catch insects by swimming in the water with their mouths open, had slowly turned into whales by this process: "*I can see no difficulty in a race of bears being rendered, by natural selection, more aquatic in their structure and habits, with larger and larger mouths, till a creature was produced as monstrous as a whale.*"

The idea didn't go over very well with the public. Darwin was so embarrassed by the ridicule he received that the swimming-bear passage was removed from later editions of the book. One-hundred sixty years later the evolution stories still continue. Only now unsubstantiated storytelling is given scientific sounding names. Below are some of the extinct land animals commonly promoted as whale links in today's textbooks:

Pakicetus: This fossil has no blowhole, no flippers (only hooves), and no whale neck (just a neck typical of land mammals). The ear-bone does not look like a whale's which has finger-like projections but looks like a land animal with plate-like bones.

Ambulocetus: The ear bone is not like a whale's ear bone and there is no fossil evidence of a blow hole.

Rodhocetus: There is no fossil evidence for a tail or flippers.

Evolutionists essentially teach that Darwin had the right idea but the wrong animal. Instead of looking at bears, students are now told to believe that some sort of cow or hippopotamus crawled back into the ocean and slowly turned into a whale. Now that is a whale of a fairy tale.

Beware of false prophets, who come to you in sheep's clothing but inwardly are ravenous wolves - Matthew 7:15 (ESV)

APRIL 6

For over 3,000 years, horses have been domesticated and bred to help mankind. For centuries, horses were bred and used for many purposes. We developed war horses to fight battles and Clydesdales or Percherons for pulling heavy loads. Cleveland Bays were bred to pull carriages and Shetland ponies were bred to work in the mines. There are about 200 breeds of horses ranging in size from the tallest horse, a Belgian draft horse at 6 ft. 7 ½ inches (shoulder to hoof) to the miniature brown mare "Thumbelina" at 17 ½ inches. This is not evolution, but pre-programmed variation within a horse kind.

The wide variety of horses is a result of man's breeding expertise. Just as a musician plays the notes on his instrument to create a vast array of harmonies, so play the genes. However, the musician can only play the notes that are already on his instrument. In the same way, the horse kind can only play the genes it has. In Genesis 1:24, it states that creatures *reproduce after their own kind.* "*Kind*" is based on the animal being able to reproduce with another animal. Is a zebra of the horse kind? Yes. So, what happens when you breed a zebra and horse? You get a zorse, of course! Is a donkey of the horse kind? Yes. So, what happens when you breed a donkey and a zebra? You get a zonkey. What about a Shetland pony and a zebra? A zoney. God created the wonderful horse kind, which enabled man to breed variety for his benefit!

"The witless can no more become wise than a wild donkey's colt can be born human."
- Job 11:12 (NIV)

APRIL 7

Did you know that stories about a worldwide flood are found in historical records all over the world? After the Flood, people built the tower of Babel and were dispersed. As these people groups traveled and finally settled, **they brought with them the stories from the past.** There are more than 360 Flood stories from around the world. One such story comes from South America.

When the Spanish settlers encountered the Carib Indians in eastern Venezuela, they found them to be fierce fighters, often eating their prisoners. It is believed the term "cannibal" came from their name. Their name was also given to the Caribbean Sea. According to one Carib story, they were created from the bones of an enormous dragon or snake. The Karina people also have a flood legend. Here are some of the highlights:

The supreme sky god (Kaputano) came down to earth and warned the people about the coming worldwide Flood. Only 4 couples (8 people) believed, the others scoffed. The supreme sky god helped them build a very large canoe. It was so large that they gathered two of each animal to put on board. Then the rains came, and the rain was so great that not even the tops of the tallest trees were visible. The entire world was covered with flood waters. Then the waters began to recede, and the land began to dry out. The four couples left the canoe and looked at their new world, empty and void. Kaputano created a new earth for the Karina. Kaputano took the form of Orion and is now in the night sky.

Notice the similarities with the Genesis account: a warning, scoffers, floating vessel, destruction by water, 8 people saved, animals taken on board, a worldwide flood. Today, there are only 11,000 Carib ancestors alive but they still hold many of their ancient beliefs, including the Flood account. If a group of people survived a global flood, wouldn't that event be passed on from generation to generation? This is what we find all over the world, a common remembrance after thousands of years found in the stories from hundreds of diverse people groups scattering across the world after Babel. The most accurate and comprehensive of these Flood accounts is found in the historical account in Genesis.

So the Lord scattered them abroad from there over the face of all the earth, and they ceased building the city. Therefore its name is called Babel, because there the Lord confused the language of all the earth... Genesis 11:8 (ESV)

APRIL 8

The ancient Miao or Miautso people (known as the Hmong) preserved their history in song and passed it down generation to generation. They have an amazing song about historical events found in Genesis chapters 1-11, recorded before western missionaries arrived. Here is what the song contains:

- It begins with the creation of the world, the first man being **made from dirt.**
- All the **people became wicked** except righteous Nuah (Noah) and his family.
- They were saved from a **worldwide flood** in a boat along with two of each kind of animal.
- It rained for 40 days with the flood eventually covering all the earth, a dove was sent out, and the earth eventually dried.
- After the flood **a tower was built**, and all people spoke one language. Then God caused them not to understand each other and people dispersed.
- The Miao (Hmong) left the tower and traveled to China and eventually to where they live today - in the hills of Thailand, Laos, Vietnam and China.

In the song, it is revealed they are descendants of Jah-phu (Japheth), the oldest son of Nuah (Noah). Can you imagine being able to take your genealogy all the way back to Japheth, Noah and Adam? What a heritage! The Hmong people once knew the one true God of the Bible. The God of the Bible is not just a Western religion. Pray that they might find their way back to trusting the entire Bible and Jesus Christ for their salvation.

Then the Lord God formed the man of dust from the ground and breathed into his nostrils the breath of life, and the man became a living creature. - Genesis 2:7 (ESV)

GENETICS

Communist governments maintain control with oppression and coercion. They are inherently atheistic because the State is the ultimate authority and no allegiance to a supreme God or absolute moral truths can be tolerated. Communism requires that evolution is creator, not God. This is why all communist governments strongly promote evolution as the only possible explanation for our existence.

Evolution presumes that random chance and mutations explain the upward advancement of life. Imagine an experiment to test the concept of mutations producing improved humans. Such an experiment was actually done in the Soviet Union in the 1950's. **The government forced unprotected pregnant mothers to watch nuclear testing, knowing this would cause the babies to be born with severe mutations.** Our hearts grieve for these deformed babies because mutations never produced the hoped-for "super race" of Soviets, just tragic pain and early death to innocent babies.

Every mom inherently knows that mutations (birth defects) are not good. Evolution, taken to its logical conclusion, produces evil results.

But each person is tempted when he is lured and enticed by his own desire. Then desire when it has conceived gives birth to sin, and sin when it is fully grown brings forth death.
- James 1:14-15 (ESV)

APRIL 10

The world is filled with plants and animals designed to adapt and function in a myriad of environments. Even evolutionists frequently use the word "design" as they describe various organism's abilities and features. Yet evolutionists adamantly deny that a Creator designed these creatures, attributing their design to mutations and natural selection. They also adamantly deny evolution is driven by **random chance and mistakes**. They teach that things like a hummingbird's flying ability or a butterfly's metamorphosis are the result of the elegant action of mutations guided by natural selection and do not see this as a random process. Keep this universal truth in mind - **just because a blind person denies that he is blind does not change his blindness.**

The only source of new information for evolution are mutations and mutations are random mistakes. Mutations are exactly like randomly re-arranging the letters in a book in the hope of making a new book with improved information. IT WILL NEVER HAPPEN! **Natural selection can never create anything new and mutations are mistakes which randomly destroy information.** Information is non-material. It is a coded message with an intended purpose and/or an expected action. A mind is required to make new information. There can be no new information without an intelligent, purposeful sender.

No matter how steadfastly evolutionists deny that they are teaching that mistakes and random chance designed the amazing creatures featured in this book...**that is exactly what they are teaching students to accept.** Sadly, their blinded viewpoint is all too often the only explanation shown to students throughout our education and media system.

He also told them a parable: "Can a blind man lead a blind man? Will they not both fall into a pit? - Luke 6:39 (ESV)

GENETICS

APRIL 11

Do you realize that the mineral nickel can be used as a clock? There are many minerals that enter and leave the Earth's oceans and nickel is one of them. The age of the oceans can be estimated by determining how much nickel flows into the ocean every year and then calculating how many years it would take to reach the ocean's current nickel concentration. **This "clock" puts a maximum age of the oceans at 6,500 years!**

Evolutionists say the oceans are billions of years old. But wait, can nickel be removed from the ocean? Nickel can be removed from the water in the form of manganese nodules. On the sea floor are lumps of metal called manganese nodules composed mainly of manganese, iron, and nickel. It is estimated that there are about 500 billion metric tons of these nodules on the sea floor.

If **ALL THE NICKEL** that flowed off the continents went into these nodules how old would the oceans be? The maximum age of the oceans would still only be 133,000 years. Remember, evolutionists need the oceans to be very old. Vast age is evolution's magic wand that supposedly transformed bacteria into people. The low nickel concentration in ocean water points to the recent creation of the Earth's oceans. This is very good, because too much nickel in the oceans would be toxic! According to UK environmental health guidelines, concentrations higher than 30 parts per billion are toxic to marine life, and that would have been reached in only 850,000 years if we used todays current rates of input. Oceans cannot be billions of years old according to the nickel "clock."

For the earth shall be filled with the knowledge of the glory of the LORD, as the waters cover the sea. - Habakkuk 2:14 (NIV)

DESIGN

Homing pigeons have been used throughout history. Caesar used pigeons during his Gallic Wars for communication. Genghis Khan used pigeons to stay in contact with distant parts of his empire. During World War II, "pigeon posts" became so valuable that the British Air Ministry had a registry of carrier pigeons and sought to destroy all peregrine falcons which ate pigeons. But how do pigeons know where to go?

People have used magnetic compasses for hundreds of years to tell direction. How do they work? The floating metal needle always points north because our earth acts like a huge magnet with a magnetic field surrounding the entire globe. During the 1970's, bits of magnetite were found in the beaks of homing pigeons and other birds. **It was even discovered that the microscopic iron particles changed direction, like a compass needle, as the bird turned!**

How does evolution explain this compass in the beak of a pigeon? How does the pigeon know what to do with the changing direction of the iron particles in its beak? Compasses do not happen by accident and chance. When we see a compass, we know there must be a compass maker; and the pigeon's compass Maker is God.

Trust in the Lord with all thine heart; and lean not unto thine own understanding. In all thy ways acknowledge him, and he shall direct thy paths. - Proverbs 3:5,6 (KJV)

APRIL 13

CarbFix, a company in Reykjavik, Iceland, is working with the power station to properly dispose of carbon dioxide (CO_2). The CO_2 from the hydrothermal plant's steam vent is first captured. Next the captured CO_2 is dissolved in water. Think of sparkling water with a fizz. **This carbonated water is pumped into 3,200 feet deep rock layers near the plant.** Iceland is made from volcanic rock (basalt). This type of basalt resembles Swiss cheese with holes made by leftover gas bubbles when the basalt was cooling. The injected carbonated water percolates through the holes in the basalt, reacting with magnesium and calcium.

More than a year later, CarbFix drilled down to check the progress. **Surprise!** The basalt's Swiss cheese-like holes were filled with white carbonate minerals. Prior to checking the injection sites, scientists thought that it could take thousands of years for the CO_2 to turn into rock. This was based on evolutionary assumptions that it took thousands to millions of years to form the carbonate rock layers of the earth. CarbFix researchers discovered that with the right conditions it only took a year.

During the Flood of Noah's day, volcanoes were releasing massive amounts of carbon dioxide and this would have dissolved in ocean waters, subsequently turning into rock. The bulk of the world's extensive carbonate rock deposits could have formed in months. It does not take millions of years for rock to form, just the right conditions.

I lift up my eyes to the mountains - where does my help come from? My help comes from the LORD, the Maker of heaven and earth.
– Psalm 121:1,2 (NIV)

APRIL 14

Thick beds of limestone are found worldwide and make up about 10% of all sedimentary rock. Today we see limestone forming slowly in the still ocean waters by the mechanical weathering of shells which form lime muds and limestone. Because limestone can form very slowly, evolutionists believe the earth is old. However, does today's limestone look like limestone formed in the past? NO! Modern limestone has larger crystals and a different composition than "ancient" limestone. There is an exception though; limestone formed in hurricanes (a catastrophic event) in the Florida-Bahamas area, pick up large quantities of lime mud and redeposit it - resulting in limestone looking like the "ancient" limestone.

Another problem for evolutionists is "ancient" limestone contains many well-preserved fossils. This attests to rapid limestone formation; otherwise the plants and animals would have decayed or have been eaten by scavengers before they could have been captured in the forming rock layer. To find fossils in limestone means the limestone had to form quickly. All this speaks of a catastrophic event in the past, such as the Flood of Noah's day.

Why, mountains, did you leap like rams, you hills, like rams? Tremble, earth, at the presence of the Lord. – Psalm 114:6,7 (NIV)

APRIL 15

A sunken 1622 Spanish treasure ship, the *Atocha*, offered more than gold coins. This sunken ship off the coast of Key West, Florida contained grape, olives, apricot, and beggar ticks (*Bidens alba*) seeds. The beggar tick, a 40 inch tall weed with prickly fruit, that facilitate seed dispersal by sticking to the fur and clothing of any animal or human that brushes against it. **Amazingly, the beggar tick seeds sprouted after 350 years in saltwater muck!** So, why is this important? A year-long Flood covered the entire world with salty water during the time of Noah. One would think that seeds would be destroyed by salty water.

The beggar tick seed's ability to germinate and grow after 350 years demonstrates that seeds can survive in saltwater for long durations. On Noah's 601st birthday the land was dry and ideal growing conditions existed for as far as Noah could see from the Ark. The ocean temperature may have been as high as 90°F (from all the volcanism and land movement during the flood) so the air temperature was warm and humid. The land had also been flooded with rich nutrients from the sea water. The nutritional benefit of sea water covering land was seen after the December 26, 2004 Indonesian tsunami which caused bumper crops in 2005. Trillions of seeds could and did sprout, making the world green with food when Noah, his family, and the creatures departing from the Ark about 87 days after coming to rest upon the mountains of Ararat.

Then the dove came to him in the evening, and behold, a freshly plucked olive leaf was in her mouth; and Noah knew that the waters had receded from the earth. - Genesis 8:11 (NKJV)

APRIL 16

Do you like oysters? Oysters are not only good for eating but are a good fossil find. Evolution teaches that in the past, the flat oyster (*Ostrea sp.* on the left) evolved into the "Devil's toenail" shaped coiled oyster (*Gryphaea sp.* on the right below). Millions of students were taught that this example was "one of the best documented cases of evolution" found in the fossil record.

This has now been shown **not to be evolution in action**, but the oyster having a built-in programing response to its environment. The oyster is free-swimming for the first few days of its life, after which it attaches itself to a site permanently. If the site is firm, the oyster grows into a flat fan-shaped form (on the left). If the site is muddy, the oyster grows into a coiled cup-shaped form (on the right). To coil or not to coil is based on the organism gathering data, making decisions and responding appropriately, based on a muddy or firm foundation. NOT evolution!

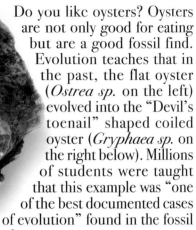

He is the Maker of heaven and earth, the sea, and everything in them – he remains faithful forever. - Psalm 146:6 (NIV)

APRIL 17

Did you know there are several types of tears? Each has its own unique chemical make-up.

Continuous tears are the ones you have all the time. These basal tears keep your eyes moist so you can see clearly. Each time you blink, fluid oozes from two small lumpy glands (lacrimal glands) just above the outer side of each eye. This fluid washes away dust and germs. The fluid is mostly water (with a pinch of salt), but there are also lysozymes which prevent bacterial infections. This prevents your eyes from getting bacterial infections. Special oils in the tears also help reduce evaporation. We have the perfect amount of tear fluid for the optimal vision possible. All this gives our eye a smooth surface for optimum vision.

The second type of tears are reflex tears which protect us from irritants; the onion you are cutting, smoke from your campfire, a gust of wind and so much more. These antibody containing tears are produced in the greatest quantities.

The third type of tears are emotional tears. These tears result from sadness, frustration, or being overwhelmed by joy. Emotional tears contain chemicals (hormones) caused by or related to stress and pain management. Some of these actually leave your body when you cry. So, having a "good cry" really does help. **God sees your tears and saves them by putting them in a bottle.** That's how much He cares for you!

You number my wanderings; Put my tears into Your bottle; Are they not in Your book?
- Psalm 56:8 (NKJV)

APRIL 18

What happens to the tears that continually flow across your eyes? Once a tear flows across your eye, it drains down through tiny holes (lacrimal puncta) in the inside corner of your eye. Gently pull back the inside corner of your eye and you can see a tiny, almost insignificant hole - that's where your tears go. The tears continue through this tubing and into your nose. When the tears reach your nose, they spread out and are evaporated by the air entering your nostrils. This also provides moisture for your airway. If you have been crying, there is too much fluid to evaporate, so you have a "runny" nose. If we did not have this tubing to the nose, we would have eye problems. Consider some of the problems of a blocked tear duct: recurrent eye infection, inflammation (pink eye), crusting of the eyelids, and blurred vision.

Waiting for evolution to evolve a tear duct would be a mess! **Those tiny tubes are not so insignificant after all.** Who was the One who drilled a hole in the bone and laid the water pipe for the removal of this fluid? None other than our Creator.

He is the Maker of heaven and earth, the sea, and everything in them – he remains faithful forever. - Psalm 146:6 (NIV)

APRIL 19

Have you considered how the continental margins (continental shelf and continental slope) were made? There is much evidence that during the first four months of the Flood of Noah, the Earth's continental plates rapidly moved into their current positions to form the Earth's current continents. This movement caused thousands of massive tidal waves and tsunamis which ground up the surface of the planet and deposited massive underwater sediment layers on the surfaces of the continental plates. As Noah's Flood wound down (in months five through twelve), the continents rose, causing flood waters to rush off of the newly deposited continental surfaces. These fast-moving sheets of water eroded vast amounts of recently deposited sediments. Immense amounts of water traveled so fast that sediments, sometimes miles deep, were carried off the rising continents. As the currents slowed down, these sediments dropped to the ocean bottom - forming the continental margins (shelf or slope) that surround all continents.

Continental margins make up some 20% of the ocean floor; the remainder are deep ocean basins. **These margins are made of sedimentary rocks which can be up to 12 miles deep!** Sedimentary rocks formed from sand or other particles which flowed into position, settled, and formed new rock layers. The continental margin is fairly flat and varies in width from a few miles wide to 250 miles wide (one shelf is 600 miles wide)! The continental slope averages 430 feet in depth continuing down to 4,900-11,500 feet.

From an evolutionary viewpoint, there should be NO continental margins! The existence of continental margins is a problem for evolutionists. How could it form with slow and gradual processes? It couldn't! However, the rapid runoff from the Genesis Flood is the perfect explanation for the continental margins.

[Wisdom was there] when [God] gave the sea its boundary so the waters would not overstep his command, and when he marked out the foundations of the earth. - Proverbs 8:29 (NIV)

ANATOMY

APRIL 20

If your brain was the President, the pituitary gland would be the Vice-President. **This pea-sized gland is considered the "master gland"** because it controls most other endocrine glands by secreting hormones (chemical messengers to keep your body running smoothly). Here are just a few things controlled by the pituitary gland:

- Bone growth
- Kidney output of excess water
- Body's metabolism when under stress
- Womb contraction at the birth of a baby

The pituitary gland, along with the hypothalamus, constantly monitors temperature, blood pressure, blood chemistry, and then makes critical adjustments as needed.

For many years, evolutionists considered the pituitary gland a useless or vestigial organ. **They falsely believed the same thing about 170 other parts of the human body!** Imagine life without a pituitary gland! Would you want it removed? It is dangerous to declare an organ useless just because we do not understand its purpose and design. The belief in bacteria-to-human evolution has been a detriment to the advancement of scientific knowledge and truth. We have needed the pituitary gland right from the start - fully formed and fully functional!

Know that the Lord, he is God! It is he who made us, and we are his; we are his people, and the sheep of his pasture. - Psalm 100:3 (ESV)

APRIL 21

Did you know all deciduous trees have flowers? Of course, you say, look at fruit trees - they are covered with beautiful flowers in the spring and are pollinated by insects like bees. But where are the maple tree flowers and how are they pollinated? Observe the maple tree closely in the early spring. High up, the branch tips are reddish-looking; these are teeny, tiny flowers. Are they insect pollinated? No, they are wind pollinated.

Other wind pollinated trees, such as the birch, have flowers that hang down called catkins. Wind tends to blow more often and more steadily in the spring as air temperature increases. Summer often has days with absolutely still air. Notice also, that in the spring, the tree leaves have not unfurled yet. Most wind pollinated tree flowers come out before the leaves. This allows the pollen to move around much easier. What if the pollen was blowing during the summer through a forest of leaves? Much less pollen would get to another tree flower. Wind pollinated trees need:

1. Wind (more frequent and constant winds tend to come in the spring).
2. No leaves (less obstruction for the pollen to reach another tree flower).

When we see such design, we know there must be a designer and that Designer is God. So, take a look up in the deciduous trees in the spring and see if you can locate the tiny flowers ready to be wind pollinated. Enjoy discovering tree flowers!

Consider the lilies, how they grow: they neither toil nor spin, yet I tell you, even Solomon in all his glory was not arrayed like one of these.
- Luke 12:27 (ESV)

APRIL 22

What kind of egg is so small that it can be flung out of its nest by a single raindrop? Surely there is no creature so small that it makes a half-inch nest filled with such miniature eggs. In actuality, it is a fungi. The bird's nest fungi is common in forests throughout the world. Nests generally contain 5-8 eggs (peridioles) in which are spores which must be dispersed to grow new fungi. The nest and eggs are an ingenious bit of engineering.

The "nest" is simply a dispersal aid: each nest is designed so the energy of an entering raindrop violently throws the "eggs" out of the nest, some eggs landing up to 6 feet away. One species of bird nest fungus has an extra engineered detail: attached to each egg is a long-coiled thread with a sticky end. When a raindrop falls into the nest, the eggs are hurled through the air, the cord is unleashed, and if twigs are near, the sticky end winds around the twig, suspending the egg above the ground. Now the spores can be released and dispersed to a further distance.

How does evolution explain this dispersal method? If it took millions of years to evolve, what if the nests weren't designed so the eggs could be ejected? The spores would stay where they were. How does a fungus <u>know</u> to engineer this dispersal method (it doesn't have a brain)? **God must have enjoyed engineering this fun way for fungus to disperse its spores.** So as you take a hike in the forest, looking for the miniature bird's nest fungus, but make sure it's not raining, or you might get hit with flying "eggs"!

Then I will give you rain in due season, and the land shall yield her increase, and the trees of the field shall yield their fruit. - Leviticus 26:4

APRIL 23

If a butterfly is caught in a rainstorm, will it survive? Sure, it heads for protection under trees. But in the process, what if its fragile wings are hit by a few raindrops? Raindrops can fall up to 22 miles per hour, and depending on their size can make quite an impact. A raindrop hitting a butterfly's wing is analogous to a bowling ball falling from the sky and hitting sus. **Getting hit by even one raindrop is a dangerous event for a butterfly.**

Scientists from Cornell wanted to know how a butterfly's thin delicate wings could survive the impact of a raindrop. They discovered that the wings surface has two special design features. Tiny bumps on the wing disperse the force of a raindrop by rupturing the raindrop and shattering it into tiny droplets. At the nano-level, these bumps are also covered with a thin layer of wax. The droplets are then repelled by the nano-wax layer.

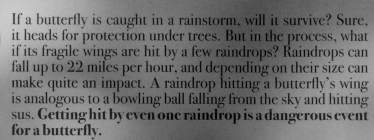

How do evolutionists explain these two design features: micro-bumps and nano-scale wax? As the butterfly was evolving, how would it survive with no micro-bumps when it rained? *"**Rats, I haven't evolved micro-bumps yet and my wings are full of holes, again!**"* Think about the wax: does wax come about by accident and chance? Wax for your car was developed by an engineer. Wax for the butterfly was developed by the Great Engineer, God Himself!

Remember his marvelous works that he hath done; his wonders, and the judgments of his mouth; - Psalm 105:5

APRIL 24

Quick, get a pencil. Now balance the eraser on your index finger with the pencil tip pointed straight up. **Continue to balance the pencil as you move it up toward the ceiling.** If the pencil tilts and falls off your finger, you lose. The pencil is representative of a rocket being sent to the moon. During the Apollo missions this is one problem the engineers had to consider and solve. Below are a few other problems these rocket scientists had to solve to get man to the moon:

• Launch the largest (30 stories high) and heaviest (6 million pounds) rocket in history.
• Go from 0 to 17,000 mph in minutes (the required speed to escape Earth's gravity).
• Drop off pieces of the rocket at right times as fuel is used up.
• Exit earth's orbit and head towards the moon (at EXACTLY the perfect moment).
• Enter lunar orbit (at EXACTLY the perfect angle).
• Separate the lunar landing module from the command service module.
• Keep the command service module in perfect orbit.
• Safely land the lunar module on the moon surface.
• Launch the lunar module off the moon and dock it with the orbiting command module.
• Leave the Moon orbit with the exact needed trajectory to head back to Earth.
• Survive reentry and splashdown.

And these scientists did their work mainly with slide rulers, not computers!

NASA engineers used operational science to get man to the moon. Operational science is solving problems, building stuff. **Molecules-to-man evolution is speculative science - based on proposed beliefs about the past which cannot be tested or proven.** Molecules-to-man evolution is a belief, not rocket science. To get man to the moon was not based on speculative science (like evolution) but on "operational" science.... and that is what should be taught in schools.

DESIGN

The moon and stars to rule over the night, for his steadfast love endures forever;
- Psalm 136:9 (ESV)

APRIL 25

Do you realize that an owl has its own satellite dish? An owl's exceptional hearing is due to its entire head being involved in hearing. You may think that the owl's ears are those two tufts sticking up; those are just feathers. The owl's true ears are on either side of its head, just behind the eyes, hidden by feathers. An owl has a concave round face with a facial ring of stiff feathers. As sound waves approach, the feathers act like a satellite dish, catching, reflecting and directing sound into the ear holes. An owl can actually move its facial feathers to improve its sound reception. It is kind of like forming a cup shape with your hand around your ear. You'll hear faint sounds better because the sound waves are being directed into your ears. Try it.

In many species of owls, the ears are placed asymmetrically, with one ear located higher than the other ear. Owls can tell where the sound is coming from by judging the time delay, i.e. the microsecond longer that it takes a sound to travel to the ear that is slightly farther away. Humans have symmetrical ears; we only hear the direction the noise is coming from. **Owls can pinpoint the direction left to right and the direction up and down!** The owl' hearing is so precise that they can locate their prey within 1.5 degrees both vertically and horizontally. That is why an owl can swoop in on the exact location of a mouse hidden under snow.

We use a satellite dish that allows us to receive information, like our favorite TV show. An owl's hearing system is like a satellite dish. Do we say a satellite dish happened by accident and chance? Then why would we believe an owl's satellite dish happened by accident and chance? There had to be a satellite dish maker, and for the owl, the satellite dish Maker was God.

O Lord, our Lord how majestic is your name in all the earth! - Psalm 8:9 (ESV)

APRIL 26

BIOLOGY

Have you considered the Great Horned owl? It nests in January and February. Why would it nest in the coldest part of winter? Great Horned owls begin their mating in January. To find their mate, the hooting begins. After mating, the female searches for an abandoned crow's nest and adds a few branches and feathers. Soon three white eggs are laid in the coldest part of the frozen northern winter and she incubates her eggs. The female is unable to leave the nest for even an hour, or the eggs would freeze. For weeks she endures the hardships of no food, snowstorms pelting her feathers, and below freezing nights. *"Oh why didn't I just fly south for the winter?"*

Finally, the eggs hatch and cute, hungry little downy owlets emerge. Now begins the job of feeding them, and **they have enormous appetites.** Because the Great Horned owl has her babies in February, forest rodents are very easy to see and catch. Leaves are not on the trees and white snow makes a great backdrop for seeing scurrying rodents. How did the first Great Horned owl come up with this timing? Did it look on its calendar and decide to nest in the middle of a cold winter? An owl does not think about such matters; it is by instinct. This timing had to be preinstalled on the owl's hardware (that's its brain). When we see such preinstalled software, we know there must be a software maker and that software Maker is God. So, when you hear the Great Horned owl hooting in the dead of winter, think of that great software Maker, God.

All creatures look to you to give them their food at the proper time. - Psalm 104:27 (NIV)

TRUTH

APRIL 27

Our five senses are wonderfully crafted (engineered). Our bodies work with our mind to actively gather data via sight, hearing, touch, smell, and taste. Our brain then processes this data and reacts in a multitude of ways, learning from the response in order to modify future responses. Here is a partial list of abilities which depend on our brain's programming to evaluate and respond to the information received from our five senses: balance, body position, chemoreceptors, familiarity, healing of our body, language, hunger, intuition, itch, muscle tension, breathing, pain, pressure, movement, temperature sensing, thirst, and time awareness.

Our bodies are consciously and continuously tracking, responding, and adapting to EVERYTHING going on around us - allowing us to live healthier. Combining God's pre-programmed engineering (subconscious systems) with our individual choices (our conscious mind) we are provided with a sense of understanding of ourselves, our environment, and God. Through our beautifully crafted senses we are capable of learning about and acknowledging the exquisite skill, wisdom, power, and intelligence which was needed to create these abilities. In other words, by observing the craftsmanship and complexity of creation, even if we had never heard of God, we know that He exists. This is why every culture in the world has an inherent understanding of the existence of God, even if their religious belief is a distortion of His true character. We are without excuse. **We should clearly stand in awe of our Creator**, but He does not force us to do so.

O Lord, how manifold are thy works! In wisdom hast thou made them all: the earth is full of thy riches. - Psalm 104:24 (KJV)

APRIL 28

The Vikings put dragon heads on their ships 1,000 years ago. Why would they do that? Well, they knew about the great dragons of the sea. They called one of them the "Kraken." **Kraken, a gigantic sea monster, was the stuff of Scandinavian legends.** Krakens were popular not only in Norse and

Icelandic stories, but also with American whalers and even Peruvians. Peruvian fishermen called it a water demon, but their description closely resembled the Norse stories. It was portrayed as an octopus or squid with tentacles so long they could drag a ship under water. Pliny the Elder wrote at length of Krakens in his Naturalis Historia (1st century A.D.). He described this fierce beast with long tentacles and a sharp parrot-like beak. Yet naturalists for centuries thought Krakens were imaginary creatures.

It was not until 1873, when a full giant squid washed up on the shore of Newfoundland, that giant cephalopods were taken seriously by the scientific community. The first living giant squid was photographed in 2004 when a whale watching association caught sight of it off the coast of Japan. In recent years, complete specimens of the giant squid and *"the much bigger and badder"* colossal squid have been found. The colossal squid can grow to be twice as long as a city bus with eyes the size of dinner plates. It has 8 arms, and in the middle of each arm, there are 25 tooth-like hooks. **These have razor sharp edges and can rotate 360 degrees, like a circular saw!** The colossal squid also has a "beak" shaped like a parrot. Sound like the stuff of drunken sailor yarns? Krakens do exist, they just live very deep in freezing ocean waters. The oceans make up 70% of earth's surface and much of its depth has been barely explored. There is much to be discovered in God's world.

Here is the sea, great and wide, which teems with creatures innumerable, living things both small and great. There go the ships, and Leviathan, which you formed to play in it.
- Psalm 104:25-26 (ESV)

APRIL 29

ASTRONOMY

"**Once upon a time**, billions of years ago, there was a Big Bang and from that Big Bang came all the stars and planets. One of those planets, in that swirling mass, came together and formed a hot ball of rock which we call Earth. This happened about 4 billion years ago. This is our rock. Then it rained. From this primordial soup, all the diversity of life we see today arose." That is the evolutionary story, that you are evolved from a rock and some rain.

The creation account tells us that we were created by God on Day 6 of the creation week - fully formed. God made you in His image, to feel, to think, to create, to love... He created you a little lower than the angels for His pleasure. You are the crown of His creation. He did not want to make you a puppet, so He gave you free will. This was a dangerous move because "the created" could choose to reject "the Creator." The Creator created you to live forever, but sin happened. A Holy and Just God cannot tolerate or allow sin to punished. Death throughout creation was the result. But God made a way so that you would appear holy before Him. He provided a covering for your sin. That covering is the blood of Jesus. You just need to accept this covering in order to appear before the Holy God Who created you. God loves you intensely and desires for you to spend eternity with Him. Put on His free covering by accepting Him as your Savior. To not accept His free covering, well, ...

"It is a fearful thing to fall into the hands of the living God." - Hebrews 10:31 (NKJV)

APRIL 30

Have you considered that the Earth is located in the "Goldilocks' Zone" – not too hot...not too cold...it is "just right." It takes Earth 24 hours to rotate. **That gives us just the right amount of heat and coolness.** Jupiter has a 10-hour day, so it spins very quickly. If the earth spun that fast-violent hurricanes would happen almost continuously. Venus rotates slowly; a day on Venus is 243 Earth days. If Earth rotated that slowly, our day would become too hot and the night side would become too cold. As it is, we have **just the right** amount of spin, 24 hours so Earth does not become too hot or too cold.

Earth's tilt, at 23 degrees, **is also just right**. This is perfect for moderating seasons. Mercury has essentially no tilt and no seasons. If Earth had no tilt, the equator would be hotter and the poles colder. Uranus has a 97.8-degrees tilt which results with it rolling sideways like a ball rolling across the floor; this produces wild weather! Our tilt is also stabilized by the moon. If there were no moon, our tilt would fluctuate over time from 0 to 85 degrees. Living on Earth would be like living on a carnival ride!

Perhaps one reason God made such a variety of planets in our solar system is so that we can compare them to Earth and then give God the glory for our **Goldilocks planet**. The earth is just right for habitation. It is too perfectly deigned to have happened by accident and chance.

ASTRONOMY

Thus says the Lord who made the earth, the Lord who formed it to establish it—the Lord is his name: - Jeremiah 33:2 (ESV)

MAY

"IN MY VIEW, THE CHRISTIAN RELIGION IS THE MOST IMPORTANT AND ONE OF THE FIRST THINGS IN WHICH ALL CHILDREN, UNDER A FREE GOVERNMENT, OUGHT TO BE INSTRUCTED... NO TRUTH IS MORE EVIDENT IN MY MIND THAN THAT THE CHRISTIAN RELIGION MUST BE THE BASIS OF ANY GOVERNMENT INTENDED TO SECURE THE RIGHTS AND PRIVILEGES OF A FREE PEOPLE."

– Noah Webster (1758 – 1843), Father of American scholarship and education.

It would be better for them to be thrown into the sea with a millstone tied around their neck than to cause one of these little ones to stumble.

– Luke 17:2 (NIV)

MAY 1

Most toads lay their eggs in water and leave them to develop. Not the midwife toad (*Alytes obstetrians*). Once the female lays a long string of eggs, about 20 or more, the male pushes her away and puts his hind legs through the mass of eggs. For the next three weeks the male carries the egg mass around on his body. He must be careful that the eggs do not dry out, so he spends his day in shady damp places and only ventures out at night. If the eggs start to dry out, he gives them a bath in the nearest pond. His mid-wifery comes to an end after three weeks when the eggs hatch into tadpoles. While the tadpoles are still inside the jelly-like skin, the male takes them to the pond where he places them in the water, they chew their way out, and swim off.

Evolution believes this happened over millions of years. How did the first midwife toad know **not** to lay her eggs in the water? How did the male know that he had to care for the eggs on his body, making sure they had the right moisture? Furthermore, how did the male know that after three weeks he needed to go to the pond to release them? Each step had to work correctly the first time or no midwife toads. God created these toads to do exactly what they do from the very beginning: precisely pre-programmed. There was no evolution here!

Blessed *be* his glorious name for ever: and let the whole earth be filled *with* his glory;
– Psalm 72:19 (ESV)

MAY 2

What does it take to receive a letter? An address. Most countries use a hierarchical system with house number, street, city, territory and country. Many countries have a wonderful postal system that has been set up by a system maker. On the other hand, there are places such as Nigeria in which only 20% of the homes have an address – making it difficult to receive mail. Do you realize that other living things have a delivery system also?

Within every cell (except red blood cells) are kinesin molecules that haul cargo along roadways (microtubules). **Kinesin are little biological robots, designed for carrying loads from one spot to another.** They are shaped with two "arms" for carrying the cargo and two "legs" for walking on the microtubule roadways within the cell. Every cell that has a nucleus needs to move proteins and other things to specific places at specific times within the cell. Once a specific protein is made, the cell's Golgi apparatus packages the "part" and puts an address on it. Next the kinesin is summoned. It picks up the package and walks along the roadways (microtubules) delivering the package. The motor powering the kinesin is 50% efficient while your car engine is only 20% efficient. It is also able to walk 100 steps per second. If the load is too heavy, another kinesin robot helps. Sometimes the kinesin robots act like a relay race, handing its payload to a "fresh" kinesin robot. Kinesin also know the best route to destinations, like today's GPS. If the delivery system goes wrong, serious health problems arise - such as cystic fibrosis and other hereditary illnesses. **Kinesin is similar to a great mailman.** Do postal delivery services happen by accident and chance? Ask a Nigerian who would like to receive his package. It takes a system maker to make such a system and the system Maker is God.

Your hands made me and formed me; give me understanding to learn your commands.
– Psalm 119:73 (NIV)

MAY 3

Animals produce dung and the Australian native bush flies love to breed in it. That's what Aussies discovered when cattle first came to Australia in 1788. As cattle farming spread throughout the country, so did the bush flies. There were so many bush flies that all sorts of innovative devices were invented to help control the fly plague. Australian folklore even has women wearing hats with corks dangling from the brim to deter the flies. Sure, Aussies had dung beetles that dealt with kangaroo and wombat dung but not cattle manure. To solve this problem, Aussies introduced a type of dung beetle that loved cattle dung.

When cattle deposit a pile of dung, the odor attracts the beetles. The beetles arrive, burrow into the dung, grab little pieces of manure, form it into balls, roll the manure balls away from the manure pile, and bury them in the ground. Some beetles lay their eggs in the dung balls while others just use them as a food source. Either way, once the dung is buried, it is no longer available as a place for flies to breed.

Dung beetles are the janitors of the world, living on all continents except Antarctica. Imagine the tons of waste with flies and parasites spreading diseases if the dung beetle was not created to clean it up. By burying the waste, the beetles fertilize the soil at various depths, thereby improving the health of pastures used by the cattle. These beetles also tunnel into the soil - providing a pathway for water to infiltrate which reduces runoff and prevents soil erosion. **Dung beetles are amazing!** In fact, the "sacred" scarab (*Scarabaeus Sacer*) of ancient Egypt is a dung beetle. Dung beetles could not exist without the animals to make dung. And animals have a much better life with dung beetles around to keep the grasslands well fertilized. These vastly different creatures depend on each other. What a creative way God provided for keeping the environment clean and healthy!

> Let the fields be jubilant, and everything in them...Let all creation rejoice before the LORD, for he comes to judge the earth.
> – Psalm 96:12a, 13 (ESV)

MAY 4

There are many seed dispersal methods. Some seeds are shaped to float or glide through the air and are dispersed by the wind. Other seeds may be transported by water. Still other seeds explode out of a pod shooting them far from their parent. But have you heard of the seed that looks and smells like poop and is dispersed by a dung beetle?

Dung beetles like to eat dung, raise their children in it, roll it, and bury it. **Dung beetles love dung**. Scientists found that large brown seeds from a *Ceratocaryum argenteum* (a grass-like plant) looked like the dung of local antelopes (and smelled like it too). This tricks the dung beetle. Once the fooled dung beetle buries the seed, it sprouts and grows. Large seeds do not get easily buried by themselves. Also, this area of South Africa is known for its shrublands catching fire so being buried prevents the seeds from burning.

How does evolution explain this? How does a plant without eyes know what antelope dung looks like? How does a plant without a nose know what antelope dung smells like? How does a plant without a brain know that a dung beetle is attracted to dung? Did this happen by mutational accidents and chance? Hardly! Created by God to get the seed planted? Yes!

Be thou exalted, O God, above the heavens; let thy glory be above all the earth.
- Psalm 57:5 (KJV)

BOTANY

MAY 5

Does lightning travel up or down? Cloud-to-ground lightning begins when ice crystals and raindrops are violently colliding with each other in a storm cloud. This produces electrical charges. As a result, lighter positive charges end up near the top of the cloud while negatively charged particles are near the bottom of the cloud. Meanwhile, on the ground below the storm cloud, positive electrical charges build up. These charges can make your hair stand on end right before/after a lightning strike. Now the stage is set for a lightning bolt.

Starting in the cloud, small streamers of sparks, called *stepped leaders*, shoot downward. As the downward leader streamer approaches the ground, it meets the upward streamers. When this happens, an invisible channel is formed and a lightning bolt is born. The flash is the heated air from the return upward stroke. Then, a return stroke from the cloud, called a *dart leader*, flashes downward through the channel. The second return stroke flashes upward. Even though lightning seems to shoot down from the cloud we are actually seeing the return stroke from the ground streamer. All your eye sees is one flash of lightning. I bet you didn't realize a "simple" bolt of lightning was so complicated!

So does lightning travel upward or downward? It does both! Notice lightning flows in a channel or way, just as Job 28:26 (KJV) states, "*When He made ...a __way__ for the lightning of the thunder.*" This was written about 4,000 years ago. Whenever the Bible speaks on scientific issues, it is correct and science eventually catches up.

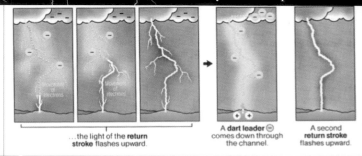

...the light of the **return stroke** flashes upward.

A **dart leader** ⊖ comes down through the channel.

A second **return stroke** flashes upward.

Listen to this, Job; stop and consider God's wonders. Do you know how God controls the clouds and makes his lightning flash?
- Job 37:14,15 (NIV)

MAY 6

Millions of different kinds of tiny organisms reproduce by asexual reproduction, making copies of themselves without the need of male and female counterparts. They have a complex method of "splitting in half," with each half resulting in an exact copy of the original. This works perfectly for producing more of the same kind of organism, and these bacteria, protozoa, and plankton are considered "simple" forms of life. Those who leave God and the Bible out of their thinking (even many Christians are guilty of this), assume that these simple forms of life evolved into more complex forms of life which require male and female counterparts to reproduce the next generation. Let's think about this.

Thousands (maybe millions) of complex programming changes which would be required to transform a creature which reproduced copies of itself into a creature who could no longer reproduce copies of itself but produce only half of the DNA information – "the male seed." Meanwhile, thousands (maybe millions) of complex programming changes would be required to transform another creature of the same kind to produce the other half of the information – "the female egg." And these amazing changes would have to happen in exactly the same generation. The now different creatures would have to find each other, and they would need to know how to reproduce. If all this did not happen simultaneously, both would go extinct in one generation! The odds against this happening even once are impossible.

Furthermore, having two sexes is far more difficult and far less efficient than having a single organism with everything it needs to reproduce – putting such a bi-sexual organism at extreme disadvantage. Evolution would prevent, not allow, two sexes from evolving. If there were no other evidence for the existence of God, the existence of males and females should be enough to convince any open-minded person of His existence!

So God created man in his own image, in the image of God he created him; male and female he created them. – Genesis 1:27 (NIV)

MAY 7

One of the most baffling geological features of the Grand Canyon is the canyon cutting through a great plateau and not around the plateau. This plateau arose before the river was in place. **Water runs around hills, not through them!** The Grand Canyon should not be where it is.

North of the Grand Canyon is the Colorado River. This river runs south and then it abruptly turns 90 degrees and into the heart of the uplifted Kaibab Plateau, which is 3,000 feet higher than the river. Evolutionists believe that the Grand Canyon was carved over millions of years by a little bit of water. What is the Biblical perspective? During the Flood of Noah, sedimentary layers were laid down. At the end of the Flood, Psalm 104:8 speaks of the mountains rising and the valleys sinking. As the continents rose, the Flood waters drained off the continents into the newly formed ocean basins. While the continents were being lifted up, massive sheets of water, deep and wide, were scouring the landscape. Just north of the Grand Canyon, this erosion rapidly carved the Grand Staircase, a sequence of ascending cliffs, leaving behind the colorful cliffs of Zion and Bryce National Parks. **In this area alone, it has been estimated that this sheet-like erosion removed 100,000 cubic miles of sediments!** This material formed part of the continental shelf off the west coast of North America. When standing at the Grand Canyon rim, look up and imagine one mile of dirt above you!

The uplifting of the continent caused flood waters to drain off the earth in vast sheets. As the water became shallower, channels started to form. This channelization would have cut the initial path of the Grand Canyon. To the north and east of the Grand Canyon, Flood waters were trapped and large lakes formed. These lakes contained water estimated to be three times the volume of Lake Michigan! The impounded lakes would have continued to increase in size until they weakened and eventually breached the natural dams. Now the lakes emptied, and the water rushed forward exploiting ar channels already carved. **The Grand Canyon was formed rapidly**. The Grand Canyon was carved by a lot of water in a short time not by a river flowing uphill over millions of years.

Before the mountains were brought forth, or ever thou hadst formed the earth and the world, even from everlasting to everlasting, thou art God. - Psalm 90:2 (KJV)

The Grand Canyon is 277 miles long, about a mile deep, and 4 to 18 miles wide from rim to rim. But did the Colorado River carve this canyon over millions of years? Some geological facts to ponder:

1. <u>Missing dirt</u> - Simple calculations indicate 1,000 cubic miles have been removed. Normally the sediments would be at the delta of a river. Look at the Colorado River's mouth. **There is virtually no delta!** The little sediment found at the delta represents thousands of years of erosion, not millions of years. So where is the dirt?
2. <u>No Talus</u> - Talus or debris is lacking at the bottom of the cliffs. If the canyon was millions of years old, there should be vast amounts of talus or rock debris at the base of the cliffs. Do you see rubble (talus) piled up below every cliff face? Now check the side canyons ending in the U-shaped amphitheaters, do you see talus? NO! They are clean. Some amphitheaters are hundreds of feet deep and extend back a mile from the river. Most have no water source to remove the possible talus. **The lack of talus affirms a recent and catastrophic event.**
3. <u>No Erosion</u> - The below the Colorado River rest enormous boulders which are not slowly disappearing by erosional processes. Despite massive floods flushing through the canyon over the last 100 years **there is no evidence of the supposed slow erosion** over purported millions of years causing the canyon to slowly deepen.

The Grand Canyon was carved rapidly with lots of water in a short amount of time, thus no delta, no talus, and no indication of current erosion. The Grand Canyon is a testimony to recent catastrophic processes, i.e. it was carved out as a result of Noah's Flood.

The valleys of the sea were exposed and the foundations of the earth laid bare at your rebuke, LORD, at the blast of breath from your nostrils. – Psalm 18:15 (ESV)

MAY 9

Marx and Hitler both cited Darwin as scientific evidence in support of their evil actions.

After Marx read Darwin's *The Origin of Species* he wrote, "*This is the book which contains the basis in natural history for our views.*" The century following the publication of Darwin's book proved to be the bloodiest in all human history with Marxism directly responsible for 100 million deaths.

Hitler saw Darwinism as providing the scientific justification for racism. The full title of Darwin's book was, *The Origin of Species by Means of Natural Selection, or the Preservation of Favoured Races in the Struggle for Life.* Did you notice the racist language, "*Favoured Races?*" Hitler believed what Darwin had written and it formed the basis for his passion for extermination of the Jewish people. His goal was, "*to promote the victory of the better, the stronger, and to demand the submission of the worse and weaker.*" He saw the Holocaust as the "Final Solution" to humanity's ills and himself as merely aiding the natural processes of evolution. **In his mind, the Aryan race was superior to the others.** Hitler promoted propaganda throughout Germany that, "*The Jews formed a sub-human counter race, predestined by their biological heritage to evil, just as the Nordic race was designed for nobility.*"

Even when he was losing WWII and his troops desperately needed supplies, Hitler refused to divert trains from delivering Jews to their death to delivering supplies to his troops. He felt his greatest contribution to humanity was to eliminate unfit humans from its gene pool. When you studied WWII, did the writers and teachers ever tell you that Darwin's book on evolution was a key motivation behind the Holocaust? If there had been no Darwin, there would have been no corrupting view of reality influencing Hitler to annihilate millions. The 75 million lives lost during WWII could have been avoided.

The combined deaths caused by WWII and Marxism was 175 million people. The inspiration and justification for all this death was Charles Darwin's belief in animal-to-man evolution.

> The wicked draw the sword...to slay those whose ways are upright. But their swords will pierce their own hearts, and their bows will be broken.
> – Psalm 37:14,15 (ESV)

MAY 10

Dinosaurs evolving into birds is taught as an evolutionary fact in essentially every textbook, natural history museum, and nature program dealing with birds or dinosaurs. Yet this belief has enormous problems which are either glossed over or ignored. Here are a few of those problems:

Solid to hollow bones - Dinosaurs are reptiles and reptiles have solid bones. Birds have hollow bones. How would solid bones evolve into hollow bones with the required struts and crossbars to make sure the newly hollowed bones did not collapse? A bird with solid bones would have great difficulty flying because solid bones would be so much heavier.

Cold-blooded to warm-blooded - Dinosaur metabolism is not fully known but all modern reptiles are cold-blooded and have a predominately lethargic lifestyle. Compare that to a bird, which is warm-blooded and has an exceptionally high metabolism.

Reptilian lungs to avian air sacs – Reptile respiration is like human respiration, working like a bellows with the in-and-out movement of air. Birds have a radically different breathing system. The air flows continually in a one-directional loop going through 7 to 9 air sacs. Birds are never out of breath and enormous internal changes would be required to change one system into the other.

Skin to feathers - Reptilian skin is like a folded drapery; one big piece. Reptilian scales are just thickened folds of skin, while feathers grow out of skin follicles. Each feather is lost one by one.

Size - A t-rex evolving into a hummingbird? That means the t-rex had to shrink some 200 times to get to the size of a hummingbird.

These are just some of the major obstacles that evolution would have to overcome for a t-rex to evolve into a hummingbird. Can a half bird/ dinosaur survive on its way to becoming a bird? Also consider that most of these characteristics must be acquired at the same time or they serve no purpose. A dinosaur evolving into a bird just doesn't fit the facts of science.

So God created ... every winged bird according to its kind. And God saw that it was good.
– Genesis 1:21b (NKJV)

MAY 11

What's egg shaped, bright blue and the size of a human's palm? An Australian fruit called the cassowary plum (*Cerbera floribunda*). This poisonous fruit is only eaten by, you guessed it, the cassowary bird. The cassowary is an almost 6-foot tall, jet-black, flightless bird. Its only coloration is its fabulous blue, red, and purple head and fleshy pouches on its neck. The cassowary is able to eat the poisonous plum with no ill effect because the fruit passes through its short digestive system relatively intact.

The cassowary bird and the cassowary plum benefit each other mutually, i.e., they have a symbiotic relationship. The plum provides food for the cassowary and the cassowary spreads the seeds of the tree. As the bird travels around the rainforest of northeastern Australia, it defecates the seeds, thus the plant is spread throughout the jungle. **Cassowaries are a major seed disperser in Australia**; more than 100 plant species are dependent on cassowaries to disperse their seeds. The seeds of a rare Australian tree, *Ryparosa kurrangii*, actually showed increased germination after passing through a cassowary's digestive system. Only about 4% of the seeds germinated without passing through the bird, but seeds defecated by the cassowary germinated 92% of the time. The cassowary moves around spreading seeds for a non-moving plant. Another example of God's ingenuity!

The LORD reigns, let the earth be glad; let the distant shores rejoice. – Psalm 97:1 (NIV)

MAY 12

The bird called the Clark's nutcracker and the whitebark pine tree (pinus albicaulis) have a perfect symbiotic relationship. The pine needs the nutcracker and the nutcracker needs the pine. The tree is totally dependent on this bird for seed dispersal. When the seeds are ripe, the pinecone does not open and there are no wings on the seeds to let them ride the wind gusts. **The seeds are literally trapped!** But just when all seems lost and these trapped seeds are fat and full of nutrition, the Clark's nutcracker comes to harvest them. The Clark's nutcracker is the only bird which pries open the cone to get at the seeds inside!

A single bird can hold up to 150 seeds in a pouch under its tongue. Then the nutcrackers bury these seeds in storage "caches" to be eaten later. They are buried at a depth of about an inch, which turns out to be the perfect depth for germination. **In one year, a nutcracker "*plants*" up to 100,000 seeds!** Nutcrackers have excellent memory, being about to find their "caches" nine months later, even under three feet of snow. The seeds not eaten by the nutcracker may grow into new whitebark pines. This is the only way this pine tree is propagated, and their seeds are the major source of food for the bird. Both bird and pine were needed from the beginning, so no evolution here.

BIOLOGY

If we were to compress all the living vegetation on the earth today, how much coal could be produced? Only about 3% of the earth's coal reserves. Then, how did we get all this coal? The world prior to Noah's Flood was very different.

1. There was **greater land area**. Instead of 30% land and 70% seas; it was probably 50% land and 50% shallower seas.
2. The vegetation found in coal beds is different from today's vegetation. North America's "carboniferous" coal beds consist largely of giant lycopod trees, giant ferns, conifers, giant rushes and extinct seed ferns. Most had hollow stems and roots. These plants were part of vast mats of floating forest which hugged the coastlines. It has been suggested that ½ **the seas' surfaces had these floating forests.**
3. The land would have been **lush with vegetation** and had no ice sheets or deserts. Including the floating forests, 75% of the world would have been covered with lush foliage. Today it is less than 20%.
4. Experiments have shown that at temperatures of only 257°F. and relatively low pressure (being buried under 6,000 feet of wet sediments) **coal can be produced within 75 days**. Coal formation does not take millions of years.

Imagine the Genesis Flood waters catastrophically sweeping across the land and burying much of the vegetation upon the earth. Water permeating through the deeply buried vegetation worked with clay catalysts to start converting it into coal beds within months. Coal is a memorial to the worldwide Genesis Flood and the conditions upon the earth before the Flood explain why so much coal exists today!

He blotted out every living thing that was on the face of the ground, man and animals and creeping things and birds of the heavens. They were blotted out from the earth. Only Noah was left, and those who were with him in the ark.
- Genesis 7:23 (ESV)

MAY 14

What a nose a bloodhound has! Bloodhounds can pick up a scent that is 12 days old. That would be like **still smelling the perfume from someone who walked past you 12 days earlier**. This dog can detect a scent trail of only a few molecules of a given scent. Let's sniff out how a bloodhound can do this.

Once a molecule of scent is picked up in the large nasal chamber of the dog, which has 300 million scent receptors (compared to a human's 5 million scent receptors), the message is sent to the brain's olfactory bulb. The olfactory bulb's job is to sort out smells. This organ is 40% larger in a bloodhound than in a human. Bloodhounds literally "see" smells. Every smell has a "scent picture." When a bloodhound is on the trail, folds of skin fall around its eyes and act as blinders, helping the dog stay focused. Meanwhile, its large drooping ears can act like scent sweepers, dragging the ground and sweeping the scent toward its nose. The wrinkled skin also picks up stray scents and channels them to the nose. **Bloodhounds have been known to follow a scent trail for more than 130 miles!**

How does evolution explain the nasal chamber with its 300 million scent receptors, huge olfactory bulb, the dog's ability to recognize specific scents, and its capability to follow that one scent while ignoring all others? Even if a dog could evolve the millions of scent cells it would have no way of processing them in the olfactory bulb. Both these and other abilities had to be present from the beginning for the bloodhound to be one of creation's greatest sniffers.

[Isaac] smelled the scent of his clothing, and blessed him, and said, "Look, the scent of my son is as the scent of a field which the LORD has blessed." – Genesis 27:27 (NHEB)

BIOLOGY

ASTRONOMY

MAY 15

There are hundreds of clues which help to determine the age of the earth. **Even asteroids provide one of these indications.** An asteroid hitting a solid surface body generally results in an impact crater. Craters are common on all of the studied solid-surface bodies in the solar system except the Earth and Io, Jupiter's moon. There are three primary areas where asteroids are located in our solar system:

1. The asteroid belt between Mars and Jupiter
2. The Trojan asteroids whose orbits are hidden within Jupiter's orbit
3. Near-earth asteroids

Near-earth asteroids are asteroids whose orbits cross earth's orbit, introducing the potential of collision. We are actively tracking the paths of about 500 near-earth asteroids. There are only about 175 undisputed impact craters identified on Earth's surface. If the earth is 4.5 billion years old, then **we should find far more impact craters.** The lack of impact craters upon the earth reveals that our planet is young.

By wisdom the Lord laid the earth's foundations,
by understanding he set the heavens in place;
- Proverbs 3:19 (NIV)

MAY 16

Between the orbits of Mars and Jupiter is the astcroid belt. of the largest space rocks in this orbiting debris field is a dwarf planet called Ceres. Recently, NASA sent a space probe to inspect Ceres. Surprise! **If Ceres were billions of years old, it should NOT be geologically active**, but Ceres was found to be erupting mud from "cold volcanoes." Cold volcanoes or cryovolcanism is where chemicals such as water, ammonia and methane under the surface are heated by volcanic activity and erupt into space where they quickly freeze because of the intense cold.

Evolutionary astronomers couldn't believe these cold volcanoes were ejecting mud! How can the inside of Ceres still be hot, AND shouldn't all the water and other gasses have been used up long ago? Ceres is too far away from large planets to be affected by their gravitational pull, so what's happening? Ceres' hot interior is a witness that it is not millions of years old but only a few thousand years.

Similarly, over one hundred water jets have been photographed gushing upwards at 800 miles per hour on Saturn's moon Enceladus. Nanograins of silica, formed when 200+°F liquid water and rock interact, were identified in the ejecting plumes. This is possible only if Enceladus is thousands of years old, not millions.

The most widely read historical book of all human history (the Bible) states that the universe was recently created. Ceres and Encedeldus testify to this truth.

The heavens declare his righteousness, and all the people see his glory. – Psalm 97:6 (KJV)

Modern medical practices are not so modern after all. The earliest writing on sound public health practices are found in the first five books of the Bible.

Leviticus chapters 13 – 15 warn us to:
Isolate and in some cases quarantine the sick, destroy contaminated objects, burn used dressings, bury fecal waste outside of the camp, avoid eating animals that have died of natural causes, wash hands, keep clean, and take precautions when touching anything infected or deceased. *We now know that all of these precautions help prevent the spread of bacteria and viruses.*
Leviticus chapter 18 warns:
Not to engage in sexual relationships outside of marriage. We now know 100% of sexually transmitted diseases can be avoided when the family unit is exclusive.
Exodus 15:26 promised:
If the Israelites obeyed the Word, they would enjoy great health; if not, they would have sickness.

During the Middle Ages, the Bible was de-emphasized and superstitious ideas from Plato and Aristotle took over. The Bible was set aside with its practices of hygiene and infection control. As a result, medieval humanity experienced centuries of misery, suffering, and premature death. During the Protestant Reformation, devout men desired to "think God's thoughts after Him." In returning to Scripture, sound public health practices came into vogue. Modern medical science began in 1876, when Robert Koch and Louis Pasteur proved that disease contagion passed from one individual to another by microbial life. Life comes only from life - *just as the Bible states.* Germs DO NOT arise spontaneously - *as evolutionary theory and Greek philosophy teaches.*

The establishment of germ theory has extended millions of human lives over the last century. Yet all life, even bacterial life, comes only from previously existing life, just as the Bible stated. Is modern medicine a modern idea? Hardly! Whenever the Bible speaks on a scientific matter, it speaks the truth.

> If you listen carefully to the LORD your God... if you pay attention to his commands and keep all his decrees, I will not bring on you any of the diseases I brought on the Egyptians, for I am the LORD, who heals you. – Exodus 15:26 (NIV)

MAY 18

The book of Ecclesiastes speaks of the wind moving in great circuits around the globe. King Solomon wrote of this some 3,000 years ago, when it was thought that winds just blew in a straight line. We did not "discover" the jet stream until World War II. During the 1940's, bomber pilots flying westward towards their targets found they were making little forward progress as they navigated against 230 m.p.h. winds. Islands in the sea below appeared to be stationary. **The pilots were "swimming upstream" against the wind**, unable to deliver their bombs to their designated targets. These pilots had inadvertently discovered the jet stream.

The jet stream is a fast flowing river of air moving at 50-300 m.p.h., hundreds of miles wide and located about 7 miles above the surface of the earth. There are several of these rivers of moving air that completely circle the earth. Pilots today avoid these channels of wind when flying west and often go with the wind when flying east.

During late 1944 and into 1945, Japan launched 9,300 hydrogen-filled balloons, each carrying explosives or forest fire starting devices. They had studied the jet stream and knew the balloons would travel eastward to the United States. About 280 are known to have accomplished their mission, with at least two going as far east as Michigan!

These jet streams have an important effect on our weather. When the northern west-to-east flowing jet stream dips southward, it carries colder air with it. If it stays to the north, the weather further south remains warmer. The southern jet stream brings storms and heavy rain, depending on the direction it varies. The Bible spoke of "circuits of wind" some 3,000 years ago before man knew the jet stream existed. When the Bible speaks on a matter, it is always correct.

The wind goes toward the south and turns around to the north; the wind whirls about continually and comes again on its circuit.
- Ecclesiastes 1:6 (NKJV)

MAY 19

What bird would be foolish enough to build its nest above hungry alligators in Florida's Everglades? Apparently, wading birds such as herons and egrets. These birds have a problem with hungry predators (such as raccoons and opossums) climbing into their nests and eating their eggs. But if alligators are present, these predators first have to get past them. In other words, **the herons have their own personal bodyguards**. But what do alligators get? Often in nesting colonies (rookeries), birds lay more eggs than they can raise, and parents will adjust the brood size according to the food available. A chick or two may be pushed out of the nest to the waiting alligators below. Gators also receive other food dropped from the nest as chicks are fed and even feast on a few raccoons in the process of raiding the nests.

Researchers have found that alligators living within 650 feet of a bird colony were significantly healthier than those who did not have a bird colony nearby. A six-foot alligator living close to the rookery typically weighs six pounds more than one living a mile away. This is symbiosis, a win-win situation. The gators get fat while protecting the nesting birds. So the next time you see an alligator in the wild, check to see if it has its own rookery.

Honour and majesty *are* before him: strength and beauty *are* in his sanctuary. – Psalm 96:6 (KJV)

MAY 20

Did you ever wonder why alligators and crocodiles have bumps on their faces? It's not for beauty! The bump's positions are so unique that they can be used to identify individual crocodiles – like a fingerprint. But what are these bumps for? While a crocodile is covered in an armor of hard scales, the bumps on its face are delicate sensors of touch, vibrations, and pressure. These bumps have an array of nerve fibers leading to the brain. Researchers have discovered that **alligator and crocodile bumps are ten times more sensitive than our fingertips!** Further study revealed that alligators can detect the ripples from a single drop of water and orient themselves toward these ripples in complete darkness. Researchers experimented by dropping food pellets into pitch-black croc tanks and filming the results using infrared cameras. The crocodiles would turn towards the ripples, sweep their heads side to side and once their skin touched the food, they snapped it up - all within 50-70 milliseconds.

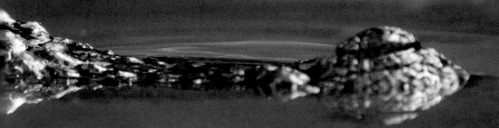

Crocodiles and alligators have a highly developed nerve system not only to find food and know what is going on around them but to protect their young. Most of the bumps are near their teeth. This is a good design, because mother crocs often carry their eggs, and then their babies, in their jaws. A sensitive nerve system is critical to prevent the mother from harming her young as she carries them in her mouth.

The next time you are tempted to put your hand into a southern pond or stream... think about your ripples activating the bumps of an alligator jaw so he can zero in on you! Who would have thought those ugly bumps helped the alligator? But of course, the Designer put such a design into His creation so it can survive and thrive!

Shout for joy to the LORD, all the earth...Let the sea resound, and everything in it, the world, and all who live in it. – Psalm 98:4a,7 (NIV)

HISTORY

MAY 21

The mysterious Nazca lines are massive drawings in the sand/ rock of an arid plateau in Peru. This 37 miles by 15 miles plateau is one of the driest deserts in the world. On the very flat Nazca Desert are etched over 800 straight lines, 300 geometric figures and 70 animal and plant designs. Some of the straight lines run up to 30 miles long. **There is a monkey the size of a football field and a parrot that could fill two football fields.** Other figures are a 315-foot hummingbird, a 213-foot killer whale, and a 446 foot condor. From ground level, the designs are nothing more than furrows from 4-12 inches deep but from the air they are astonishingly massive artistic pictures.

A Peruvian archeologist in 1926 was the first to systematically study the lines, but it was almost impossible to identify what the lines were until planes started to fly over them. It soon became apparent how stunningly straight the lines were. **Only sophisticated instruments could account for their laser straightness**, and the builders even took into account the curvature of the earth! At other times, when a line comes to a hill, it stops and then proceeds on the other side at precisely the same linear path. Many consider it unimaginable that ancient people had the ability to make these laser-straight lines and produce giant drawings of plants and animals. Now consider that they could not even see the results of their own efforts because they can only be seen from the air! Did these ancient people know how to fly, perhaps in gliders or hot air balloons? From an evolutionary viewpoint, ancient people were unintelligent and primitive. Yet here we see the proof, in the Nazca lines, that these ancient people were extremely adept and intelligent. We still do not know the technology these Peruvians possessed to have built such wonders. But, why should we (especially Christians) be surprised? The Bible tells us that mankind was created in the image of God (intelligent and creative). Adam was very intelligent and within the first ten generations, they had already built cities, forged brass, and iron and made musical instruments. The Nazca lines are evidence that mankind has always been intelligent.

The Lord came down to see the city and the tower the people were building. The LORD said, "…nothing they plan to do will be impossible for them." - Genesis 11:5,6 (NIV)

When one hears of birch bark, birch bark canoes come to mind. Birch bark is **extremely water resistant and durable**, so it was a perfect canoe construction material. If you ever take a hike through the northern forests, you will notice that fallen birch trees have completely rotted out from within, while the white layer of birch bark remains on the ground completely intact. Birch bark is also perfect for starting fires and burns with extreme heat because **it is filled with natural oils**. These oils render the bark both rot and water resistant.

Another reason that birch bark is rot resistant is because it has chemicals to slow the growth of bacteria and fungus. This antibacterial and antifungal property was used by Indians to preserve food longer naturally. Native Americans used birch bark to make containers to store foods like blueberries. Do germ killing substances happen by accident and chance? If there is an antibacterial substance, then there has to be an antibacterial maker and that Maker is God. Birch bark is a wonderful bark that is water and rot resistant with germ-killing properties. What a wonderful design God gave us in birch bark.

BOTANY

Great is the Lord and greatly to be praised...
- Psalm 48:1a (KJV)

MAY 23

There are dozens of well-documented finds of soft tissue in fossils from 1966-1997. The first widely reported soft tissue found in dinosaur fossils was reported in 2005. Since that report was published, over 120 peer-reviewed papers have reported soft tissue being found in fossils. Can "soft tissue" really last millions of years? When an animal dies, within a short time, the carcass is normally destroyed by scavengers, water, and microbes. Rapid burial is needed to make a fossil. But there is one natural process that continues even when something is buried: chemical oxidation. Experiments have shown that the chemistry of decay works on bone collagen and DNA. Laboratory studies have revealed that buried bone collagen (soft tissue) could last 900,000 years **at the maximum** and detectable DNA fragments could last 650,000 years **at the maximum**; NOT MILLIONS OF YEARS! Dinosaurs did not die out 65 million years ago. **If the dinosaur bones are not millions of years old, then the rock layers are not millions of years old.**

There are hundreds of documented reports of soft tissue in a wide variety of dinosaurs including a t-rex, triceratops, and hadrosaur. In addition, detectable fragments of DNA have also been identified in a wide variety of fossils believed to be 10 to 200 million years old. Evolution claims that dinosaurs died out 65 million years ago, yet neither dinosaur soft tissue nor DNA could last that long. The Biblical viewpoint accepts the reality of a catastrophic worldwide Flood only about 4,500 years ago. Did dinosaurs die out 65 million years ago? Empirical science says NO.

Where is the wise? where is the scribe? where is the disputer of this world? hath not God made foolish the wisdom of this world?
-1 Corinthians 1:20 (KJV)

MAY 24

Recently in the fossil-rich Messel Pit in Germany, scientists discovered a fossilized bird's oil gland of which part was still soft tissue. A bird's oil gland is used for preening. How can an oil gland be soft after a purported 48 million years? It can't, from an evolutionary viewpoint but; from a catastrophic Flood viewpoint, it can. About 4,500 years ago there was a worldwide Flood that covered the bird, and with the right conditions it became a fossil.

Here is the fossil recipe:
1. Fast coverage.
2. Deep coverage.
3. Limited oxygen slowing decomposition.
4. Lots of water. The water percolated through the layers picking up minerals and depositing them into the animal.

In the case of soft tissue, the minerals did not deeply penetrate; it still remained soft. Soft tissue could never survive for 48 million years. The bird's soft oil gland shouts that it was recently buried. **That means the fossil is not millions of years old.** All of this fits perfectly with a worldwide Genesis Flood about 4,500 years ago.

And behold, I, even I, do bring a flood of waters upon the earth, to destroy all flesh, wherein is the breath of life, from under heaven; and everything that is in the earth shall die.
– Genesis 6:17 (KJV)

MAY 25

Did you know that in the past there existed gigantic monsters? Here is a partial list:

1. Sharks (megalodons) 80 feet long (today's great white shark reaches only 20 feet).
2. Camels reaching 13 feet tall (compared to today's 7 foot tall camels).
3. Beavers standing 8 feet tall - the size of a black bear.
4. Penguins almost 7 feet! Today's tallest penguin, the Emperor, is less than 4 feet.

Fossils of these giant creatures have been discovered all over the world. Obviously, in the past there was an increased variety of mammals, birds, insects, and sea life. These different kinds of creatures were created by God and displayed enormous diversity. This original creation was perfect until sin brought death in the world. After the Fall, the entire universe began to deteriorate. Noah's Flood killed and buried all living animals that "had the breath of life in its nostrils." (Genesis 7:22) and were not brought on the Ark. After the Flood, animals from the Ark repopulated the world.

The Flood set up the right conditions (warmer oceans with more evaporation) for the one and only Ice Age. One third of the earth was covered in ice (the higher latitudes) while other parts of the world experienced lots of rain. It took hundreds of years for the oceans to cool off, at which point the entire Earth's climate dramatically changed. Tropical regions of the world dried out and became deserts. With a smaller food supply, these giant creatures were at a distinct disadvantage and most became extinct. Today we are left with smaller animals and less variety throughout the animal kingdom. In his book, *Untold Secrets of Planet Earth: Monumental Monsters*, Vance Nelson documents the demise of 35 giant animals.

The diversity of life in the animal kingdom is declining. Evolution would have us believe that things are getting better and becoming more diverse - but that is not what we observe. The world is decaying and running down. The extinction of these wondrous giant creatures from the past is a testimony to the truth of God's Word.

"Come out of the ark... Bring out every kind of living creature that is with you--the birds, the animals, and all the creatures that move along the ground--so they can multiply on the earth and be fruitful and increase in number on it." – Genesis 8:16a,17 (NIV)

MAY 26

Our skeleton is amazingly designed. Let's take a look at the arm. The upper part of your arm is made of one bone, the humorous. The lower part of your arm has two bones, the ulna and the radius. The ulna is on your pinky finger side, while the radius is on your thumb side. These two bones are able to twist, with the radius rotating while the ulna stays put. Hold out your arms and twist them. Notice how you can move your hands in almost any direction.

If you only had one bone in your lower arm, life would be very hard. Try this: pour a glass of water and drink from it without twisting your arm. Evolution would have you believe that these two bones in your lower arm made themselves just because they are useful. Really? What would life be like with one bone instead of two? What we see is brilliant design, which means there had to be a brilliant Designer. His Name is Jesus. In the simple movement of our lower arm, we can see the work of His intelligent mind.

Surely the arm of the LORD is not too short to save, nor his ear too dull to hear.
– Isaiah 59:1 (NIV)

ANATOMY

ANATOMY

Have you considered how your teeth fit together like pieces of a puzzle? Find a mirror and take a really close look at your teeth. Do you notice the variety of shapes? **The incisors are in front**, sharp and straight, designed for biting. **The cuspid** (or canine teeth) are pointed and are used for tearing. **The molars and premolars are flat, located in the back**, and used for grinding food. If you had only canine (tearing) teeth, you would have a hard time chewing. Alligators have all tearing teeth and have to swallow their food in large chunks. If you had only molars (grinding teeth), you'd have to chew for hours like a cow and eat your food in only small pieces. **Each tooth has a different shape and purpose.**

Now notice how the teeth fit perfectly together. There are a variety of dips, grooves, bumps and hills, but the teeth fit together like puzzle pieces. Imagine each tooth not fitting together like misplaced puzzle pieces. What havoc would be happening in our mouth! It's a good thing that when we bite down, we have the perfect fit. Did this happen by accident and chance? Does a puzzle happen by mutational accident and random change or is a jigsaw puzzle designed by intelligence? The next time you are at the dentist, look at his model of the teeth and realize our teeth are like a three-dimensional puzzle designed by God for our benefit and His glory.

> For his merciful kindness is great toward us: and the truth of the LORD endureth forever. Praise ye the LORD. – Psalm 117:2 (KJV)

MAY 28

Did you have your wisdom teeth pulled out as a teenager? I did, and I also had my children's wisdom teeth removed. **Where did this idea of pulling out wisdom teeth come from?** Darwin was the first to popularize the idea of wisdom teeth being a left-over vestigial organ from our ape-like ancestors. A vestigial organ is a purported left-over which now serves no good purpose (from our purported evolutionary past.) Let's check this out.

Wisdom teeth are also known as the third molars and usually appear between 15 and 27 years of age in both the upper and lower jaws of humans. When there is adequate room for development, they function for chewing like the first and second molars. **Wisdom teeth are useful, not useless!** Because of this evolutionary idea that wisdom teeth are useless, dentists in the past routinely removed them whether there was a problem or not. It has been estimated that only 20% of people develop problems with the third molars, yet for many years, 90% of American teenagers with dental insurance had their third molars extracted. Why were perfectly good healthy teeth being removed? Ideas have consequences!

ANATOMY

For since in the wisdom of God the world through its wisdom did not know him...For the foolishness of God is wiser than human wisdom, and the weakness of God is stronger than human strength. – 1 Corinthians 1:21,25 (NIV)

MAY 29

So, what do salamander eggs have to do with green algae? Apparently life itself!

In eastern North America, spotted salamanders emerge from the ground and head for the breeding pools each spring. The salamanders lay their large gelatinous egg mass in seasonal ponds, tire tracks filled with water, and roadside ditches. These pools of water are generally low in oxygen and not good for salamander development.

Enter in the green algae called *Oophila amblystomatis* or "love of salamander eggs." The developing salamander eggs need oxygen to survive and the algae thrives on carbon dioxide. The green algae use photosynthesis to produce oxygen, and since they grow on the egg capsules, they surround the egg mass with needed oxygen. Meanwhile, the salamander embryo is giving off carbon dioxide and a waste product, nitrogen. Nitrogen is a nutrient for plants and algae is a green plant. If the nitrogen stayed with the developing embryo, it would become toxic. But no problem, the "salamander egg loving" algae gobble it up!

This mutualism is a win-win relationship! The algae give oxygen to the salamander eggs, while the eggs give carbon dioxide and nitrogen to the algae. How does evolution explain this? If algae were not present, there would be no salamanders. The algae had to have been there from the beginning. Here is a cleverly designed relationship, which means there must be a Designer and He is God.

He gives food to every creature. His love endures forever. Give thanks to the God of heaven. – Psalm 136:25,26 (NIV)

MAY 30

Evolution teaches as a fact that mankind came from some animal which must have had a tail, thick hair all over its face and body, and ran around on all four legs. All of these features have multiple survival advantages. For example, a tail provides balance, an extra grip when climbing, and a fifth "hand" for gripping items. Body hair conserves warmth and provides camouflage. Animals with four limbs almost universally outrun animals restricted to two legs. Belief in evolution requires that each step of the evolutionary change must provide some advantage to the next generation of animal. How could losing a useful feature do this?

Any animal losing a useful feature would be at a disadvantage every step on the way. Why lose a very useful tail? Why would we shed thick body hair and now have to wear clothes? Why would humans jettison four legs if it were faster? **When we take time to critically examine the foundational principles of evolution, that belief system fails.** God created a vast variety of creatures, with different features and functions, to display His creativity and power.

For although they knew God, they neither glorified him as God nor gave thanks to him, but their thinking became futile and their foolish hearts were darkened...and exchanged the glory of the immortal God for images made to look like a mortal human being and birds and animals and reptiles. – Romans 1:21,23 (NIV)

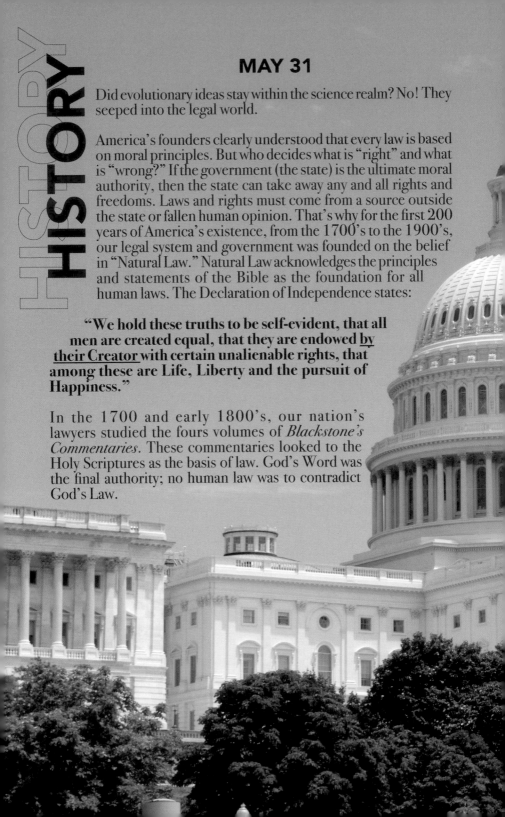

MAY 31

Did evolutionary ideas stay within the science realm? No! They seeped into the legal world.

America's founders clearly understood that every law is based on moral principles. But who decides what is "right" and what is "wrong?" If the government (the state) is the ultimate moral authority, then the state can take away any and all rights and freedoms. Laws and rights must come from a source outside the state or fallen human opinion. That's why for the first 200 years of America's existence, from the 1700's to the 1900's, our legal system and government was founded on the belief in "Natural Law." Natural Law acknowledges the principles and statements of the Bible as the foundation for all human laws. The Declaration of Independence states:

"We hold these truths to be self-evident, that all men are created equal, that they are endowed <u>by their Creator</u> with certain unalienable rights, that among these are Life, Liberty and the pursuit of Happiness."

In the 1700 and early 1800's, our nation's lawyers studied the fours volumes of *Blackstone's Commentaries*. These commentaries looked to the Holy Scriptures as the basis of law. God's Word was the final authority; no human law was to contradict God's Law.

What happened to our legal system to the point where even the words of our Constitution are now considered "fluid" and can mean anything those in control of government want them to mean? In the 1800's, the cutting edge law program was at Harvard University. In 1869, Harvard's President, Charles Elliot, installed Christopher Columbus Langdell as head of the law department, over the protests of the law professors. Why? Langdell was not qualified to head the Law Department, but Elliot and Langdell both strongly believed in evolution and thought the principles of evolution (slow modification over time) should guide all areas of thinking. Over time, Langdell trained generations of law students that:

"Law, considered as a science, consists of certain principles or doctrines...Each of these doctrines has arrived at its present state by slow degrees; in other words, it is a growth, extending in many cases through the centuries."

This led to the current belief, first promoted by one of Landell's colleagues John Chipman Gray:

"The law is a living thing, with a continuous history, sloughing off the old, and taking on the new."

We rejected the absolute basis of law upon which our country was founded (God and the Bible) and accepted the faulty principles of evolution in its place. The result: the current arbitrary nature of law, with government edicts as the ultimate source of authority.

Do not be deceived, God is not mocked; for whatever a man sows, that he will also reap.
– Galatians 6:7 (NKJV)

JUNE

JUNE

"THE ONLY FOUNDATION...FOR A REPUBLIC TO BE LAID IS RELIGION. WITHOUT THIS THERE CAN BE NO VIRTUE, AND WITHOUT VIRTUE THERE CAN BE NO LIBERTY, AND LIBERTY IS THE OBJECT AND LIFE OF ALL REPUBLICAN GOVERNMENTS."

– Benjamin Rush (1775-1813), signer of the Declaration of Independence and Father of American Psychiatry.

Create in me a clean heart, O God; and renew a right spirit within me...Then will I teach transgressors thy ways; and sinners shall be converted unto thee.

– Psalm 51:10,13 (KJV)

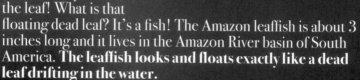

JUNE 1

Along the Amazon River drifts a dead leaf with its stem pointing downward. Thinking nothing of it, a small fish swims by. In an instant, the little fish is swallowed by the leaf! What is that floating dead leaf? It's a fish! The Amazon leaffish is about 3 inches long and it lives in the Amazon River basin of South America. **The leaffish looks and floats exactly like a dead leaf drifting in the water.**

Its flat body has a black line running down the length of its body looking like the midrib of a leaf. A fleshy region in the lower jaw looks like a leaf stem. It hangs with its head down in a completely unfish-like manner. It lies still in the water, just drifting, like a leaf. If it needs to move a bit, its transparent fins push just ever so slightly. Always lurking, the leaffish waits in ambush for an unsuspecting fish or insect; then it strikes and swallows the prey. The leaffish is nature's master of camouflage, hiding in plain sight among the other leaves and vegetation of the river.

Did this fish decide it needed this type of camo for hunting? Did a non-camouflaged fish change its DNA so it would look like a leaf? Would it have that ability? Oh, I want my children to be tall so they can dominate on the basketball court...**can I change my DNA so my children will be twelve feet tall?** Of course not! Neither could the leaffish. The leaffish was created by God from the beginning to look like a leaf. God loves to show His creativity, including through mimicry!

I will ponder all your work, and meditate on your mighty deeds. - Psalm 77:12 (NIV)

JUNE 2

Have you considered the cornea of your eye? It is one of the most uniquely designed parts of our body. This front covering of your eye allows light to pass through it so you can see clearly. The cornea is a glass-makers dream – it is crystal-clear! No blood vessels are in the cornea; in fact **it is the only part of the human body that has no blood supply.** It would be very difficult to see if blood vessels were present in the cornea. So how does the cornea get its nourishment? The oxygen it needs comes from the air. The aqueous humor (the liquid just behind the cornea), and the tear fluid (on the front), both nourish the cornea.

What if you scratch your cornea? Daily the cornea is exposed to dust, grit, pollen, chemicals and other small particles which could cause scratches. To heal, healthy cells quickly slide over and patch the scratch - before infections take place and vision is affected. Normally, if we receive a scratch, the healing is from the bottom up, while the cornea is healed from the top down. This also helps prevent scar tissue from forming. Imagine if every time you scratched your eye, scar tissue resulted; in a short time, you would not be able to see clearly. **The cornea is the fastest healing tissue in the human body**, healing within 24-36 hours.

How did the cornea know that if it was scratched it needed to heal quickly and differently? How did the cornea know that it needed to have no blood vessels to feed it, so it can remain crystal clear? These are just a few ways the cornea maker used purposeful problem solving when designing this lens. It is crystal clear that our cornea was made by God!

I will praise thee; for I am fearfully and wonderfully made: marvellous are thy works; and that my soul knoweth right well.
-Psalm 139:14 (KJV)

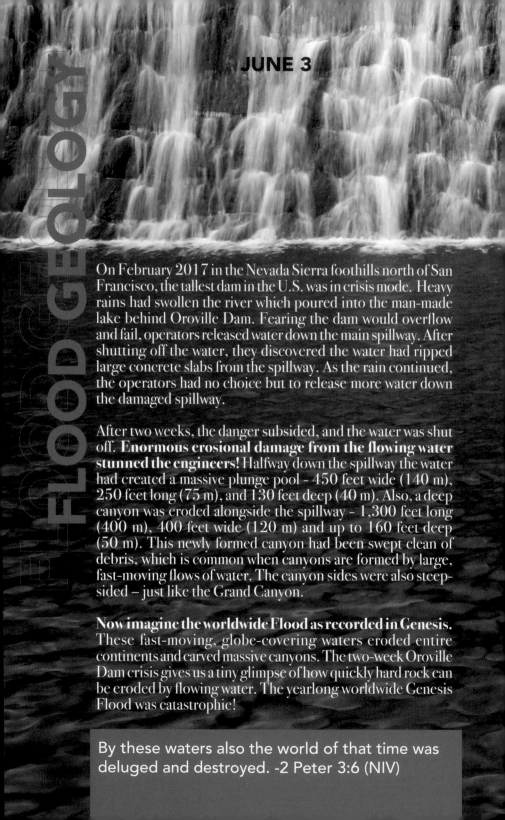

JUNE 3

FLOOD GEOLOGY

On February 2017 in the Nevada Sierra foothills north of San Francisco, the tallest dam in the U.S. was in crisis mode. Heavy rains had swollen the river which poured into the man-made lake behind Oroville Dam. Fearing the dam would overflow and fail, operators released water down the main spillway. After shutting off the water, they discovered the water had ripped large concrete slabs from the spillway. As the rain continued, the operators had no choice but to release more water down the damaged spillway.

After two weeks, the danger subsided, and the water was shut off. **Enormous erosional damage from the flowing water stunned the engineers!** Halfway down the spillway the water had created a massive plunge pool - 450 feet wide (140 m), 250 feet long (75 m), and 130 feet deep (40 m). Also, a deep canyon was eroded alongside the spillway - 1,300 feet long (400 m), 400 feet wide (120 m) and up to 160 feet deep (50 m). This newly formed canyon had been swept clean of debris, which is common when canyons are formed by large, fast-moving flows of water. The canyon sides were also steep-sided – just like the Grand Canyon.

Now imagine the worldwide Flood as recorded in Genesis. These fast-moving, globe-covering waters eroded entire continents and carved massive canyons. The two-week Oroville Dam crisis gives us a tiny glimpse of how quickly hard rock can be eroded by flowing water. The yearlong worldwide Genesis Flood was catastrophic!

By these waters also the world of that time was deluged and destroyed. -2 Peter 3:6 (NIV)

JUNE 4

After the Flood of Noah's day, the Ice Age began. During this Ice Age, there were over 100 lakes in the southwestern U.S.A. One of the largest lakes, Lake Bonneville, was located in Utah with a surface area roughly equal to Lake Michigan. Lake Bonneville covered present day Salt Lake City to a depth of 800 feet and the ancient shoreline can be seen on the surrounding hillsides. Pressure built as the water continued to fill the basin until it spilled over and a "natural dam" broke at Red Rock Pass - catastrophically releasing almost 1,000 cubic miles of water and eroding more than 340 feet of bedrock.

It is estimated that at its peak, the Bonneville flood released water through the spillway at **35 million cubic feet per second.** This huge lake would have taken weeks to empty, cutting a three-fourth mile wide spillway through Red Rock Pass. We can follow the path of the Bonneville flood northward from Red Rock Pass into the Snake River of Idaho, on into the Columbia River in Washington, and finally dumping into the Pacific Ocean. Along the way, we can see evidence of the catastrophic flood - giant gravel bars, ripped up boulders, sharp steep cliffs. The Snake River Canyon was deepened in many places, creating the spectacular Shoshone Falls and Twin Falls. As the Ice Age ended, the climate changed. Imagine the Bonneville Salt Flats under 1,000 feet of water. Now that's climate change!

From whose womb comes the ice? And the frost of heaven, who gives it birth? The waters harden like stone, And the surface of the deep is frozen. - Job 38:29,30 (NKJV)

JUNE 5

Have you considered the relationship between the passion fruit vine and the *Heliconius* butterfly? This tropical butterfly lives from Florida to South America and has a longer life than most butterflies, up to 9 months. Each day the butterfly flies a certain route through tropical forests, visiting the flowers of the passion fruit vine for nectar and pollen. With all the pollen on them the butterflies pollinate other vines. This butterfly is unusual in that it secretes enzymes to break down the pollen into liquid form and then eats it. In other words, **this butterfly makes its own protein shake!**

When it is time to lay its eggs, the butterfly again returns to the passion fruit vine. After the eggs hatch, the voracious caterpillars consume huge amounts of leaves. Generally, most passion fruit vines are protected from insects devouring them because the leaves are poisonous. Passion fruit vines' leaves have cyanogenic glycosides, chemicals that release cyanide when digested. Yet these caterpillars do not die, they keep on munching. **The cyanide collects in their body and protects them from predators.** To prevent too many eggs from being laid, the passion fruit vine has small yellow structures on its leaves that resemble the eggs of the butterfly. The female butterfly looking for a place to lay her eggs sees the "no vacancy" sign and moves on to another vine to lay her eggs…or just lays fewer eggs.

Evolution falsely looks at this arrangement as an *"arms race,"* one organism evolving a strategy which is then countered by the other. **Why not look at this as design?** The butterfly is rewarded with pollen and in turn pollinates other flowers. The fake eggs limit the number of caterpillars, so the vine is not decimated and so survives for future generations of caterpillars. The cyanide remains in the body of the butterfly and protects it from predators. Design strategies are present, which means there is a designer, and that Designer is God.

Sing to the Lord, praise his name; proclaim his salvation day after day. Declare his glory among the nations, his marvelous deeds among all peoples. – Psalm 96:2,3 (NIV)

JUNE 6

Ethiopian forests were almost decimated during the 20th century with a growing population and multiple famines. The forests were being cut down to make way for farms. The Christian church in Ethiopia believed they needed to save the forests, so they preserved 35,000 tiny "islands" of green forests scattered within the farm land. Some of these green islands are as small as 5 acres, while others are up to 1,000 acres. Why did the churches feel the responsibility to preserve the forest when food was so desperately needed? The clergy and church members believe they are the caretakers of God's creation. **Were it not for the belief in God's Word**, there would be no forests left in Ethiopia! They saw forests as symbols of the Garden of Eden.

For the people of Ethiopia, entering these green spaces is a little like going from hell to heaven. They have the brief opportunity to leave the hard labor of dry hot fields to enter the coolness and beauty of the forest. Modern conservationists have partnered with the churches to encourage them to take the stones from the fields and build walls around their forests. These walls have allowed the forests to thrive, even to the extent that the stone walls have to be extended outward. Because the church followed the dominion mandate given in Genesis 1:28, Ethiopian forests, with all their biodiversity, have been preserved.

And God blessed them, and God said unto them, Be fruitful, and multiply, and replenish the earth, and subdue it: and have dominion over the fish of the sea, and over the fowl of the air, and over every living thing that moveth upon the earth.
- Genesis 1:28 (KJV)

TRUTH

JUNE 7

The beautiful tiger swallowtail butterfly has distinct yellow and black stripes on its wings. They are called swallowtails because of the long "tails" attached to the back of their wings. Like many other butterflies, the swallowtail is common to the woodlands and grasslands of the Eastern U.S. and Canada. This is the life cycle of a butterfly:

- The adult butterfly lays eggs on the specific leaves needed as food for caterpillars.
- After a caterpillar emerges from the egg, it eats voraciously.
- Three to four weeks later, it pupates and seals itself inside a hard chrysalis shell.
- Ten to twenty days later, the pupua emerges as an adult butterfly.

How does a caterpillar undergo the miracle of metamorphosis - becoming "caterpillar soup" and rearranging itself to become a butterfly? How could a creature with six pairs of simple eyes that see in black and white, dissolve and create two compound eyes that see in color? How could a creature with a chewing mouth that only eats salad, dissolve itself and then recreate itself with a long tongue that only sucks nectar through a straw? How could a creature with sixteen legs and zero wings become jelly and reemerge with six very differently shaped legs and four wings? The butterfly is the only one to make babies - not the catapillar. How could this life cycle happen by chance? God, the Master Engineer, designed the catapillar to make the chrysalis, dissolve itself into soup and reemerge as a butterfly. As you a take a walk, look for the tiger swallowtail and marvel at our Creator's exquisite and highly engineered work!

... I will astound these people with wonder upon wonder; the wisdom of the wise will perish, the intelligence of the intelligent will vanish.
– Isaiah 29:14 (NIV)

JUNE 8

Can a Christian believe in evolution? Yes, because like all fallen human beings, Christians are capable of believing in all sorts of things that are not true - but believing something that is not true will hinder our Christian growth and effectiveness. Christians who choose to believe in evolution are Biblically inconsistent. Let's examine both worldviews:

BIBLE TEACHES	EVOLUTION TEACHES
In the beginning Earth was covered with water	In the beginning Earth was covered with molten lava
Grasses were an early life form	Grasses evolved millions of years later
Flowers were made days before insects	Insects evolved before flowering plants
Earth was made before stars	Stars evolved before Earth
Mutations are a curse: bringing an ever-increasing levels of brokenness.	Mutations are a blessing, they provide the raw material' for upward progress
Originally created universe was "very good"	Original universe was chaotic
Man is fashioned after God's image	Man's closest relative is a chimp-like creature
Man originally a vegetarian	Man originally a hunter-gatherer
God's work of creation is finished	Process of evolution is not finished
Death, struggle, bloodshed are due to man's rebellion in the garden	Death, struggle, bloodshed predate man and are the very means by which he arose

Did God use evolution to create the world? Not according to Scripture. As Christians, we should believe the Bible and trust in His Word. Do not be conformed to this world! Evolution and the Bible do not mix. God did not use evolution to make the world. The Bible and evolution are two VERY different worldviews. Trust what God's Word actually says!

Be not conformed to this world: but be ye transformed by the renewing of your mind, that ye may prove what is that good, and acceptable, and perfect, will of God. – Romans 12:2 (KJV)

JUNE 9

Wernher von Braun is known as the father of space flight. During WWII the Nazis developed the first viable rocket technology. In 1942, when Germany launched V-2 rockets in attacks on civilians in London, von Braun objected and was briefly jailed but subsequently released because he was so critical to the German war effort. In 1945, his entire team and their families - some 5,000 people- surrendered to the Americans. These transplanted Germans essentially became our American space program.[1,2]

Relocating in Texas, von Braun was invited to an American church and shortly thereafter gave his life to Jesus. Under his influence, the Bible and creation were openly welcomed at NASA. This renowned rocket scientist made the following statement concerning our origin: *"One cannot be exposed to the law and order of the universe without concluding that there must be design and purpose behind it all...To be forced to believe only one conclusion - that everything in the universe happened by chance - would violate the very objectivity of science itself. What random process could produce the brain of a man or the system of a human eye? It is in scientific honesty that I endorse the presentation of alternative theories of the origin of the universe, life, and man in the classroom. It would be an error to overlook the possibility that the universe was planned rather than happened by chance."* [3] This is not the statement of an unintelligent, uninformed, non-scientist, but the **conclusions of a key person involved in sending mankind to the moon.**

From the founders of modern science to modern scientists such as von Braun, there have always been brilliant scientists who see no conflict between belief in God's Word and the observations of science.

In the beginning God created the heaven and the earth... – Genesis 1:1 (KJV)

JUNE 10

Like America, NASA (National Aeronautical Space Agency), was strongly influenced by Christians and Christian beliefs in its foundational years. NASA's first director was the brilliant Wernher von Braun who led the agency's race to the moon from 1960 to 1970. Von Braun underwent an evangelical Christian transformation after his years of working for the Nazis and was not at all shy about acknowledging his faith, making public statements such as, *"The farther we probe into space, the greater my faith."* [1]

This faith was shared by many of the early astronauts involved in America's space program. The first astronauts to travel to the Moon recited Genesis 1:1-10. While on Apollo 8, on December 21, 1968, Bill Anders read verses 1–4, Jim Lovell verses 5–8, and Frank Borman read verses 9 and 10. The entire listening world heard **God's revelation about the origin of the universe at the very pinnacle of mankind's greatest technological achievement!** It was no happenchance accident that the astronauts chose to acknowledge and give credit to God for His creation as they explored His creation.

Another example is James Irwin, the eighth man to walk on the moon during the Apollo 15 mission in 1971. He said that his experience in space made God more real to him and stated that his Christian rebirth happened while he was in space! For the rest of his life, Irwin called himself a **"Goodwill Ambassador for the Prince of Peace."** According to this acclaimed astronaut, "Jesus walking on the earth is more important than man walking on the moon." In his book, *More Than Earthlings*, Irwin expressed his view that the Genesis creation account, including the fact that the Ark landed on "the mountains of Ararat," was real literal history. Because of his belief, Irwin made multiple trips to the permanently snow-covered, 16,000 feet Mt. Ararat in search of the remnants of Noah's Ark. [2]

And God called the dry land Earth; and the gathering together of the waters called he Seas: and God saw that it was good. – Genesis 1:10 (KJV)

JUNE 11

On the morning of July 16, 1969, an estimated one million spectators watched from the highways and beaches in the vicinity of Cape Canaveral, Florida as Apollo 11 lifted off to take men to the surface of the moon for the first time. The launch was televised live in 33 countries, with an estimated 25 million viewers in the United States alone. Apollo 11 was manned by Neil Armstrong (the first man to walk on the moon), Buzz Aldrin (the second man to walk on the moon), and Michael Collins (in charge of piloting the orbiting Command Module).

Buzz Aldrin, a strong Christian believer **took communion while sitting in the lunar lander** and read Jesus' words from John 15:5. He was forced by NASA to keep this ceremony a secret because of a lawsuit over the reading of Genesis on Apollo 8! In 1970, he commented: "*It was interesting to think that the very first liquid ever poured on the Moon, and the first food eaten there, were communion elements.*" In response to his actions on the moon being censored by NASA officials, Aldrin hit upon a more universal reference to his faith on the voyage back to Earth by publicly broadcasting the reading of Psalm 8:3–4, "*When I considered the heavens, the work of Thy fingers, the moon and the stars which Thou hast ordained, what is man that Thou art mindful of him.*"

These great explorers and men of science saw no conflict between their belief in God, their trust in God's Word, and the achievements of science. Their words and actions indicated that they actually depended upon and credited God for mankind's greatest achievements.

"I am the vine. You are the branches. Whoever remains in me, and I in him, will bear much fruit; for you can do nothing without me."
– John 15:5 (NIV)

JUNE 12

Apollo 13 was the 3rd Apollo mission aimed at landing men on the Moon. The craft was launched from Kennedy Space Center on April 11, 1970, but the lunar landing was aborted after an oxygen tank in the service module (SM) failed two days into the mission. The only option for getting the crew home was to have them continue to the moon and use its gravity to slingshot them home. The Command Module's (CM) systems had to be shut down to conserve its remaining resources for reentry, forcing the 3-man crew to transfer into the tiny two-man Lunar Module (LM) as a lifeboat.

Although the LM was designed to support two men on the lunar surface for only two days, Mission Control in Houston improvised new procedures so it could support three men for four days. The crew experienced great hardships including extreme cold, limited oxygen, and limited power. But the worse problem was having only enough fuel for one major course correction as they came around the moon to head home. Elzie Gerrels was an engineer working in the Apollo program at that time and told me personally that the general feeling amongst Mission Control was that, - *"Apollo 13's odds of getting home safely were about the same as throwing a dart across a room and hitting a piece of paper on its edge."* From the moon our atmosphere literally appears as thin as a s paper. If the recovery capsule (RC) hit Earth's atmosphere at too steep an angle it would burn up, or at too shallow an angle it would bounce off. **There was no margin for error** as they burned almost all their fuel adjusting course to escape the moon's gravity!

On April 15, 1970, President Nixon **asked the entire nation to pray for the safe return** of the astronauts. The crew returned safely on April 17, 1970. When our entire nation humbled itself in unified prayer and dependence on God, lives were saved.

If my people, which are called by my name, shall humble themselves, and pray, and seek my face, and turn from their wicked ways; then will I hear from heaven, and will forgive their sin, and will heal their land. – 2 Chronicles 7:14 (KJV)

JUNE 13

In 1959, Russia shocked the world by placing the first manmade orbiting satellite (Sputnik) into orbit around the Earth. Amerca wondered, "*If they could do this with a small satellite, why not with nuclear weapons?*" and "*Who would ultimately control space around the world?*" President Kennedy rallied a nation around the goal of sending man to the moon and returning them safely within ten years. We were years behind the Soviet Union as we entered the "Space Race," yet over the next ten years America achieved the astounding: far surpassing the Communists while making enormous advancements in computer and communications technology, yet never militarizing the space above the earth. Why?

It has far more to do with God's blessing than man's ability. America's space program was run by strong believers in God and the Bible who had broadcast Scripture from space, experienced a born-again salvation in space, and took communion on the moon. America is FAR from perfect but as long as God and God's Word are openly acknowledged and obeyed, He will continue to bless our nation (and the rest of the world through us) in amazing ways. **BUT, if we, as a nation, deny our Christian heritage and withdraw our public support of Biblical truth, God's blessing will diminish.**

Therefore whoever confesses Me before men, him I will also confess before My Father who is in heaven. But whoever denies Me before men, him I will also deny before My Father who is in heaven. – Matthew 10:32,33 (NIV)

JUNE 14

What explains the existence of information and knowledge? Information comprises the non-material foundation for machines (biological or technological), mathematics, music, works of art, and so much more. But where does this information come from?

Understanding why information exists is a partial answer to one of life's ultimate questions. At its most basic level, "information" is a coded message with an intended purpose or expected action. It can be transferred by letters on a page, electromagnetic waves sent through space, numbers stored in the hard drive of a computer, dots/dashes of Morse code, or meaning assigned to smoke symbols. When a man's sperm combines with a female egg all the DNA information we will ever have is already present for our physical bodies to be assembled. DNA is the most compact source of information in the known universe and has all the attributes below of being intelligently designed:

Statistics – non-repeating symbols which could not statistically align by random processes

Syntax – arrangement of symbols via "grammar" – i.e. a code which is agreed upon between sender and receiver

Semantics – assigned ideas with an understood meaning, message, and/or conclusions

Pragmatics – actions which are implemented by the coded information

Apobetics – pre-determined purpose and achieved result

What is required to add information? An intelligent mind and purposeful sender. To explain the vast amount of information in biological systems the information must have been formed prior to the existence of life. Thus, the originator must exist outside of the limits of time (eternal), be all knowing (omniscient), and all powerful (omnipotent). Only the God of the Bible meets these criteria. As Creator, He is outside of the limits we experience - such as time, space, matter, energy, etc. In the beginning there was God, and God spoke - creating information.

And God said, "Let there be..."
- Genesis 1:3,6,9,11,14,20,24,26 (KJV)

One of the most bizarre fish in the world is *Anableps anableps*, commonly called the 'four-eyed fish.' **These fish have eyes that see both above and below the water surface at the same time!** Imagine two large bulging frog-like eyes that are located on top of its head. Each double-lobed eye is divided in half, with the upper half for vision in air and the lower half for vision underwater.

Each upper and lower lobe has its own cornea and retina (the cornea is like a camera lens and the retina is like the film of a camera). **Two eyes each seeing two images, hence the name 'four-eyes.'** When examining the eyes closely, the upper lobe is flattened, while the lower lobe is rounded. The lens of each eye also varies in thickness from top to bottom to compensate for the differences in air and water vision. As 'four-eyes' swims along the surface of the water, the top part of the eye can spot predators or food in the air; meanwhile, the lower eye also looks for predators and food under the water. Four eyes working simultaneously!

Evolution cannot explain this special eye. Remember, the eyes are very complex requiring a brain set-up with the ability for each eye to decode two images received by two retinas. To evolve four times would be impossible. The only real possibility is that God Who created this bizarre 'four-eyed' fish for His glory.

The hearing ear and the seeing eye,
The LORD hath made even both of them.
– Proverbs 20:12 (KJV)

JUNE 16

Have you ever heard of synovial fluid? Probably not, but it is vital for pain-free movements. A joint is a place where two bones meet. Having bone rub against bone produces friction and pain. Thankfully, by design, the ends of bones are covered with cartilage. This rubber-like material allows bones to glide more smoothly over each other. However, if a joint just had cartilage, movement would still produce enough friction to harm the bones.

Rapidly rub your hands together - do you feel the heat made from the friction? Now add some lotion and rub. Notice how much easier it is for your hands to slide? Synovial fluid works in the same way to protect your joints. This fluid is thick and slippery (like egg whites) and is contained in a bag called the joint capsule. When a load takes place at the joint, the synovial fluid lubricates the joint. The lubricating synovial fluid allows the joint to move smoothly and easily over the cushioning rubber-like cartilage. Often as we age, less synovial fluid is produced; that is one reason older people may have pain when moving.

In the beginning (approximately 6,000 years ago), Adam and Eve were made perfect and without joint pain. After they sinned by eating the forbidden fruit, the curse of nature resulted, and all things began to decay. Hence, we may now experience joint pain as we age. Did synovial fluid develop by accident and chance over millions of years? Hardly! Synovial fluid was created by God to allow us to move pain free.

...my strength fails because of my affliction, and my bones grow weak. - Psalm 31:10 (NIV)

ANATOMY

JUNE 17

The study of genetics has revealed that our DNA is degenerating rapidly! Researchers have found that our genes are accumulating copying mistakes (mutations) at a rate of 60 - 100 mutations per person per generation. These mistakes build up over time like rust slowly destroys an automobile, until it falls apart. This rate of deterioration is so rapid that geneticists are wondering why we are not extinct already. If humans have been evolving millions of years were would have long ago gone extinct from the rapid build-up of mutational mistakes.

In reality, mankind was created about 6,000 years ago and geneticists have identified approximately 5,000 genetic mistakes linked to mutations on the human genome. Thus, in the just 6.000 years since the Fall, thousands of genetic mistakes have built up and **mankind's life-expectancy has dropped from around 900 years to less than 90 years.**

Evolutionists promote the belief that mutations are a good thing; mutations supposedly enabled the uphill increase in complexity to change microbes into mankind. The study of genetics is disproving this belief - **mutations are causing our DNA to deteriorate.** We are going downhill, and fast! The rapid decay of our genetic code is a clear indication that creation is recent, just as the Bible declares; there have been at most 250 generations since the creation of Adam and Eve.

Adam lived a total of 930 years, then he died... -Genesis 5:5 (NIV)
Our days may come to 70 years, or 80, if our strength endures... -Psalm 90:10 (NIV)

JUNE 18

Aging awaits us all with accompanying grey hair, wrinkled skin, hearing and vision loss, loss of muscle mass, diminished mobility, brittle arteries, fragile bones, and slowing brain function. Aging begins at the cellular level, because every copy of every cell has more random mistakes than the cell it came from. Scientists have worked on a number of ideas for extending our lifespan with negligible results:

- There are protective caps (called telomeres) on the ends of our chromosomes and each time our DNA is copied these telomeres get shorter. Scientists thought they had discovered the ability to reverse this by rebuilding the telomeres. But the results have not worked out. Clearly there is more to aging than short telomeres.
- What about hormones? These seem to control rapid changes in our bodies that we experience at puberty and menopause. Growth and adrenal hormones also decrease with time. But adjusting hormone levels has not been shown to extend lifespans.
- Then there is the immune system. Early in life the body makes a generous supply of T-cells in our bloodstream to fight off disease. By puberty, T-cells are well stocked, but as we age, production slows. By the time a person reaches their 60s, the immune system has an ever-shrinking number of T-cells available to respond to new invaders. Yet, infusions of T-cells do not lengthen life.

Every system of our body slowly wears down due to mutation after mutation being added to every cell. The 100 trillion cells in our bodies literally mutate to death.

Aging and death are inevitable because of Adam's rebellion and our sinful actions. God's Word reveals that aging is not an entirely bad thing because after death we can finally be reunited with our Creator and Savior.

GENETICS

Wisdom is with the aged and understanding in length of days. - Job 12:12 (NIV)

JUNE 19

Ripple marks are a common type of fossil found worldwide, especially in sandstone formations. These fossilized ripple marks are identical to today's ripple marks found near beaches as water moves over the sand. They can also be found on ocean bottoms, formed by strong currents in deep water. But how can these marks be preserved in rock?

Ripple marks made in wet sand are easily wiped away, just like a sandcastle on a beach disappearing with the next tide. To preserve ripple marks, the sand must be rapidly covered by another layer containing a cementing agent such as calcium carbonate, silica, or iron. We do not see ripple marks becoming fossils today so **something very different must have happened in the past to form ripple mark fossils around the world.** What event in history had worldwide water coverage, rocks being ground into sand combined with cementing agents, ripple marks being made, and rapid coverage by other types of sediment? This common rock structure is evidence, frozen in time, of the catastrophic Flood of Noah's day.

If the LORD had not been on our side...the flood would have engulfed us, the torrent would have swept over us, the raging waters would have swept us away. – Psalm 124:1,4 (NIV)

JUNE 20

TRUTH

For over 50 years, the search for extraterrestrial intelligence (SETI) has been looking for a coded message. And what have they found? Silence, nothing, zero, zip, not a peep. **This has cost millions in tax dollars and donations, yet we continue searching for ETs even though there has been no reply.** So why continue the search?

The belief in evolution is what drives this fruitless search. It is assumed that since life evolved by chance here on Earth, it MUST HAVE evolved countless times in our vast universe. As far back as the 1950's, Nobel prize winner Enrico Fermi promoted the belief that intelligent aliens would be curious explorers. He reasoned that in a 14-billion-year-old universe there should be advanced civilizations sending starships to colonize other planets. Once the first colony was established, it would send starships to colonize new planets. Even if it took a million years to find and colonize each new planet, within 10 million years there could be 1,000 new colonies. Each of these would

in turn send out more explorers and within 20 million years, a million planets could be colonized. After 14 billion years the number of alien civilizations would be so numerous that they would be tripping over each other.

So why aren't the airwaves filled with their communications? Because life has never 'evolved' anywhere. Life DID NOT EVOLVE here on earth, chemicals NEVER COME ALIVE by themselves, and the universe is NOT billions of years old. There is NO EVIDENCE that aliens exist. The lack of extraterrestrial life is known as the Fermi paradox. **If evolution really happened all over our universe, where is everybody?** Reality is as God told us - He created the universe and everything in it during creation week about 6,000 years ago. He created Earth to be inhabited and the vastness of the universe exists to reveal His power and glory.

Wisdom is with the aged and understanding in length of days. - Job 12:12 (NIV)

JUNE 21

Back in 1971, the Occupational, Safety, and Health Administration (OSHA) mandated that construction workers wear hard hats for safety. However, the first hard hat was created decades earlier in a Tasmanian mine!

Early in the 1900's, a South African miner left his felt hat in the mineral-saturated water of the mine. Fifty years later the hat was found, and it had turned into solid rock. Calcium carbonate (think limestone) had replaced the felt, molecule-by-molecule, and left an exact replicate of the original hat - except this hard hat was made entirely from calcium carbonate.

It does not take millions of years to create fossils - just the right conditions. The year long, globe-covering Flood of Noah's day would have provided these rapid-fossil-forming conditions. **We find trillions of organisms turned into rock (fossils) in rock layers around the Earth.** The rapidly fossilizing miner's hat shows that is doesn't take millions of years to form a fossil, but just the right conditions.

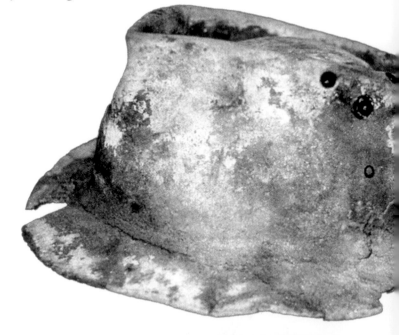

There is no wisdom, no insight, no plan that can succeed against the LORD. – Proverbs 21:30

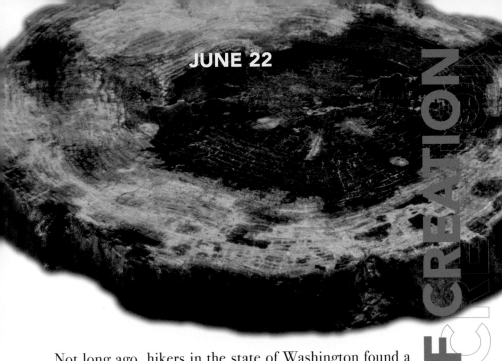

AGE OF CREATION

Not long ago, hikers in the state of Washington found a petrified fence post which had a nail imprint and marks of a strand of barbed wire. This petrified fence post was found along an old fence line dating around the late 1800s. Only part of the post remained. It was four inches long, three inches wide and two inches thick. It also showed clear markings of being a "worked' piece of wood.

It is often taught that petrified wood is millions of years old but here we see an example of wood petrifying quickly. Wood can petrify quickly if buried in hot vlcanic ash. Ash contains silica which has been melted and mixed with hot water. The buried wood soaks up the silica-rich water - rapidly replacing or surrounding each wood cell.

The farm that this piece of fence post came from is long gone but the petrified fence post remained. This fossilized human artifact shows that petrification does not take millions of years, just the right conditions!

For the earth is the Lord's, and the fulness thereof. - 1 Corinthians 10:26 (KJV)

JUNE 23

Composed of single cells large enough to see without magnification, "slime mold" (*Physarum polycephalum*) is either beautiful or disgusting, depending on your perspective. Slime mold seems to grow anywhere it is moist – in the woods, your garden, or around the yard on decaying organic matter. It feeds on microbes, molds, yeasts, mushroom spores, and bacteria. During one stage of its growth, it is protozoan-like: with no cell wall, ingesting nutrients directly, and moving like an amoeba. When propagating, it becomes more like fungi: forming fruiting bodies and sporangia which produce spores.

Slime mold does not have a central brain, but functions via thousands of connected nuclei so its information (genetic material) is spread throughout the cell. A single organism can grow as large as a foot in diameter! Each nucleus is a clone (a seemingly exact copy) of the others, yet when separated from each other they are preprogrammed to react in different ways. How do exact copies end up with different programming?

Slime molds have been phenomenally pre-programmed by the intelligent mind of their Creator. Scientists don't understand this. They throw out scientific sounding names like "emergent plasticity" or "distributed intelligence" in an attempt to explain it as occurring naturally without God. Information ALWAYS comes from an intelligent source of information. For slime mold, that information source is its creator - Jesus Christ.

Then the Lord answered Job out of the whirlwind, and said, Who is this that darkeneth counsel by words without knowledge? ...Where wast thou when I laid the foundations of the earth? declare, if thou hast understanding."
- Job 38:1-4 (KJV)

JUNE 24

For a Christian to believe the Flood of Noah was a "local event" raises many questions:

- If the Flood was local, couldn't the animals have walked to another place and Noah would not have needed to build an ark?
- If the Flood was local, couldn't the birds have flown to another area?
- We are told that **every hill**, **on Earth**, **under heaven** was covered by water (Genesis 7:19). How could God have made the extent of the Flood any clearer?
- If the Flood was a local flood, God's promise of never sending another flood has been repeatedly broken since thousands of local floods have happened around the earth.
- In Matthew 24:37-39, God likened the future coming judgment of all people to the past judgment of all people by the worldwide Flood. If humanity of Noah's day received only a partial judgment, then the future judgment of God will also be partial, which contradicts God's Word.

A worldwide Flood has enormous geological implications. It would have laid down sedimentary layers, filled with fossils, rapidly and recently. Every public school textbook states that the earth is billions of years old. Each Christian must choose, man's interpretation or God's Word (global flood). If we cannot trust what God has said about the Flood, then how can we trust what God says about the future judgment of man? God's Word is true and reliable. The worldwide Flood of Noah's day did happen exactly as described.

But as the days of [Noah] were, so shall also the coming of the Son of man be...they knew not until the flood came, and took them all away.
– Matthew 24:37,39 (NIV)

JUNE 25

The Big Bang model is filled with problems which are suppressed. A few of these major problems are:

- The belief that all matter and energy appear from nothing. If evolutionists start with "something," they have to explain where the "something" came from. Dr. Stephen Hawking starts with gravity but never explains how gravity can exist without time, space, and matter. In reality, nothing can do nothing.
- Stars cannot form via gravity pulling gas together because the Universal Gas Law shows that gas molecules always move away from high pressure. Gravity is much weaker and will never condense gas into a star and **no new star has ever been seen to form.** It is just assumed to have happened.
- Where is all the anti-matter? Big Bang mathematics requires an equal production of matter and antimatter. No one has an adequate explanation where all the anti-matter went to. This major problem is simply ignored.

The Big Bang does not work to explain the origin of the universe. Why is the Big Bang belief preferred to acknowledging that the universe was supernaturally and recently formed by an infinitely powerful Creator? Because then we come face to face with a Creator God. As Sir Arthur Keith wrote in the forward of *The Origin of Species*, the 100th anniversary edition, "*Evolution is unproved and unprovable. We believe it only because the only alternative is special creation, and that is unthinkable.*"

According to Scripture, God made the universe.

He hath made the earth by his power, he hath established the world by his wisdom, and hath stretched out the heaven by his understanding. – Jeremiah 51:15 (KJV)

JUNE 26

Our Sun, a star, is a giant ball of gases. The gases are held in place by gravitational pull. **Cosmic evolutionists say stars formed from a collapsing gas cloud or nebula and are still forming today.** This is impossible. When someone sprays perfume in the air, does it spread out or condense into a tiny spot of concentrated fragrance? Gases always spread out to fill the space they are in. The perfume molecules are not pulled together by gravity. If stars formed from natural forces, what natural forces overcame the outward-pushing gas pressure? Gases are very resistant to being compressed. Also, whenever gas is compressed, it heats up. With higher temperatures, extra pressure is created, which resists further compression. Long before a star could form, the cloud would stop compressing. Gas within stars is ONLY held in place by gravity because God supernaturally created them with the gas molecules already on Day 4. Gravity is the weakest of atomic forces and FAR too feeble to create a star.

There is also a problem with the magnetic field during compression. If any nebula collapsed, it would "concentrate" the similar charges of its magnetic field. The magnetic field would then resist being compressed further – just like similar poles of magnets cannot be forced together – like charges repel each other. **Compressing gas creates heat (driving expansion not contraction) and the magnetic field works against a gas cloud becoming a star.** Evolutionary based physics behind star formation is fraught with problems. Are new stars being formed today? NO!!! During creation week, **God spoke the stars into existence.** In Psalm 147:4 it states that God determines the number of the stars and gives to all of them a name.

ASTRONOMY

[To him] who made the great lights...the sun to govern the day, His love endures forever.
- Psalm 136:7,8 (NIV)

JUNE 27

Have you heard of decorator crabs? They love to decorate their shells. Some decorate with moss, some with algae and coral, still others with seaweed and rocks, or even small animals such as sea anemones or sea urchins. **A decorator crab grabs whatever is in its environment and that becomes its decoration.** Once done, the crab is camouflaged to blend into its surroundings. Is that a piece of coral on the move? No, it's a decorator crab with coral attached to its shell!

When a crab grows bigger it needs to molt or get rid of its now-too-small inflexible shell. As the new shell hardens, the crab takes the old decorations and places them on his new home. How do the decorations stay on the shell? Decorator crabs are specially designed with hooked bristles. Other crabs do not have this feature. These hooks on their back act like Velcro. Do we say Velcro happened by accident and chance over millions of years? No, someone took years of research to

finally make Velcro. When we see Velcro, we know there must be a Velcro maker. In the same way, when we see these hooks on the back of crabs we know there had to be a hook Maker. God even cares for a small crab's protection and provided it with hooks to help it be camouflaged.

How great are your works, LORD, how profound your thoughts! Senseless people do not know, fools do not understand. – Psalm 92:5,6

JUNE 28

Rose breeding is one of the oldest human experiments in the science of genetics. The Chinese began cultivating roses over 4,000 years ago. These beautiful flowers have been vigorously bred, yet a blue rose has remained an elusive dream...until now.

After investing more than 25 million dollars and spending 20 years on the research, geneticists have finally succeeded in producing a blue rose. This was accomplished using the "gene gun." The gene gun is a relatively new invention by Dr. John Sanford of Cornell University. It allowed scientists to remove the "blue" genes from a petunia and insert them into a rose's DNA. The rose's natural color gene was then turned off using a specific enzyme. **No amount of breeding or hybridization could have produced a blue rose, because the rose kind was not created with a gene for producing blue roses!** Evolution teaches that rose genes evolved over millions of years by accident and chance, yet it took over 20 years of expensive, purposeful work to take a petunia's already written code and insert it into the rose's DNA code. The complex instructions do not appear by accident and chance. There had to be a codemaker and that Code Maker is God.

The wilderness and the solitary place shall be glad for them; and the desert shall rejoice, and blossom as the rose... they shall see the glory of the LORD, and the excellency of our God.
– Isaiah 35:1,2 (KJV)

JUNE 29

What does it take to make a heart? That's what the researchers at Harvard University have been investigating. First, they needed to build one-chamber of the heart - the left ventricle. So, they constructed a biodegradable scaffold from fibers and then inserted stem cells from a human heart. **In just a few days, a thin wall of heart tissue grew, and the heart started to beat!** The researchers had spent 10 years in designing and making just this one chamber of the heart.

A working heart needs four chambers, not just one. Making one chamber is only a tiny step toward their goal of reproducing a functioning heart outside of the human body. This very smart team of researchers worked hard, for a very long time, and spent millions of dollars. Yet notice they used existing heart stem cells in order to achieve their success. In other words, they needed to use living tissue already designed by God. God is the original Maker of the heart. He is the One Who designed the stem cells which in turn developed into our unique heart muscle cells. These engineers just copied what had already been created. This only proves that to make a heart from scratch, one needs super-intelligence, and that describes our God.

I the LORD search the heart and examine the mind, to reward each person according to their conduct, according to what their deeds deserve.
- Jeremiah 17:10 (NIV)

JUNE 30

Heat from our constantly beating heart should kill us! Rub your two hands together and feel the heat. With each heartbeat, the muscle movement creates friction as it expands and contracts, pressing against other tissues in the chest cavity. This friction generates heat. So why aren't we dead from an overheated heart? Because our heart is located within a two-layered sack (the pericardial sac). In between the two layers is a lubricating fluid. Because the heart is essentially "floating" within this fluid, it can beat with little friction. What a phenomenal engineering design solution to a major problem!

How do evolutionists explain this? Which came first, the two-layered sac, the lubricant, or the beating heart? **To beat the heat, all three needed to be there from the beginning - the two layers and the lubricant.** And what about the properties of the lubricating fluid - it has to be just the right viscosity (thickness) and present in just the right amount. The incorrect amount of lubricating fluid in the pericardial sac is a known medical condition which can lead to death.

- Too much fluid puts pressure on our heart and affects its ability to pump blood.
- Too little fluid causes friction and makes the heart heat up and "run hot."

We have an intricately designed heart, built to pump blood throughout our body for a lifetime. All of the parts had to be present at the very beginning. It was designed by the One Who gave us life, Jesus Christ.

We praise you, God, we praise you, for your Name is near; people tell of your wonderful deeds. – Psalm 75:1 (NIV)

JULY

"GOD WILL NOT LOVE US BECAUSE WE ARE GOOD, BUT GOD WILL MAKE US GOOD BECAUSE HE LOVES US; JUST AS THE ROOF OF A GREENHOUSE DOES NOT ATTRACT THE SUN BECAUSE IT IS BRIGHT, BUT BECOMES BRIGHT BECAUSE THE SUN SHINES ON IT."

– C.S. Lewis, 1998-1963, influential Christian author and theologian, excerpt from Mere Christianity

Very rarely will anyone die for a righteous person, though for a good person someone might possibly dare to die. But God demonstrates his own love for us in this: While we were still sinners, Christ died for us.

– Romans 5:7,8 (NIV)

JULY 1

A hummingbird is one of the most energetic birds in the world! Its heart beats up to 1,200 times per minute, and even when resting, it breathes 250 times per minute. High speed video shows it flaps its wings up to 80 times **per second** while hovering. This bird burns lots of energy!

To supply that energy, it extracts nectar from 2,000 flowers each day using a long specially-designed tongue. Before 2010, it was thought that the tongue worked by "wicking up" the nectar through capillary attraction. It has since been discovered that a hummingbird tongue comes equipped with its own micro pump. As the tongue probes into the flower and touches the nectar, the tongue unzips into two long narrow tubes. The nectar is drawn in as each tube expands (creating a vacuum). The tongue is then brought into the mouth and the bird squeezes the nectar from its tongue by collapsing the tubes. The collapsed tongue is then reinserted into the flower where it touches more nectar and the process is repeated. Hummingbirds have been clocked to dip their tongues 23 times/second which means this elastic pump operates at an amazing rate of 23 times per second.

The hummingbird's pump is far more advanced than a human engineer could design! Do we say pumps happen by accident and chance? When we have a pump, we know there must be a pump maker. The hummingbird's astonishing pump Maker is God!

Lord, our Lord, how majestic is your name in all the earth! – Psalm 8:1 (NIV)

The common rose butterfly of India (*Pachliopta aristolochiae*) has large wings that are primarily black. Black is wonderful for absorbing the sun's heat; however, scientists were curious if there were other design advantages to these black wings. Upon closer examination, researchers used an electron microscope to discover that the butterfly scales had a disorderly array of tiny holes AND the sizes of these "nanoholes" varied. So, scientists used a computer to simulate how these holes affected light absorption. Surprisingly, it was shown that this randomness in both size and position was more efficient than a uniform pattern in allowing absorption over the widest spectrum of sunlight angles. In other words, this design of nanoholes trapped the sunlight from whatever angle it originated.

Next, researchers copied the butterfly wing pattern by using a thin silicon sheet with microscopic holes. With "normal" solar cells, the sun is most efficient when directly pointed at the solar cells and this requires expensive motion hardware. However, by copying the butterfly's nanoholes (with their randomized sizes and locations), the solar cells efficiently used sunlight from almost any angle. **Using God's design doubled the absorption efficiency over previous designs!** The more we study nature, the more we realize what a great Designer God is!

My mouth will speak in praise of the LORD. Let every creature praise his holy name for ever and ever. – Psalm 145:21 (NIV)

JULY 3

Is your brain like a computer? Many people think that the brain permanently stores all of the information it encounters. The fact is, we forget many things. This is actually a very good thing! One famous patient remembered so many details that he had problems distinguishing between useful and useless information. **It is not good to remember everything!** We do not remember every detail of every single event, because that much information would be too overwhelming. Our brains are selective, retaining only things which they continuously and subconsciously decide are important enough to record. The sights, noises, touches, or smells entering our brain are processed as trillions of bits of information. Our brains continuously sort information, discard useless details and latch onto anything of short-term or long-term value.

Our brains are also self-organizing. Every time you recall a memory, new connections (synapses) are made between the neurons (brain cells.) Memories go from short-term to long-term memory by reinforcement. The synapses start like the faint pathway which is left as you walk through a field of grass. Through repetition (walking the same path over and over) it soon becomes a well-worn pathway. Repetition makes the synaptic connection stronger and memory reinforced. Memories are stored in neurons or brain cells. The synapse provide access to those memories. Scientists are realizing that **there is simply too much complexity, storage ability, retrieval processes, and interdependency within our brains for evolution to explain its development by gradual modification over time.** The brain had to be a fully functional system from the beginning of its creation, and we are just beginning to understand how it works.

The Creator of Heaven and Earth, Who **remembers** everything which has ever happened and knows everything which will ever happen, chooses to **forget** our sins when we accept the blood of Jesus to cover our sins!

As far as the east is from the west, so far hath he removed our transgressions from us.
– Psalm 103:12 (KJV)

JULY 4

Memory moves from short-term to long-term when reinforced by repetition or strong emotional connections. There are two types of long-term memory: declarative memory and procedural memory.

- Declarative memory deals with facts and events; it's the "what" of a memory. What happened on a certain day, what is a platypus, what is the cube root of 64 (*the answer to that one is '4'*)?
- Procedural memory deals with "how to." How to operate your TV's remote control, how do you make someone smile, how do you make a cake?

God does not want His people to forget Him or what He has done. Interestingly, God uses declarative memory (the "what") and procedural memory (the "how to") to lock memories into our brain.

- During ceremonies such as Passover, God uses specific words repeated at these ceremonies (the "what") along with food/actions (the "how.")
- During communion (the Lord's Supper) specific words are used with food/activity to help us remember His sacrifice.
- God had the Israelites set up a memorial of stones so the miracle of the Lord would not be a faint memory testified to by only words, but would be reinforced by a physical monument at the site of the miracle.

The more senses that are involved in creating a memory, the more the brain becomes engaged and the better a memory is retained. God doesn't want us to forget all He has done for us because **that builds our assurance and faith** in Him. Our brains have been designed and are far more advanced than any computer!

ANATOMY

In the future, when your children ask you, "What do these stones mean?" Tell them that the flow of the Jordan was cut off ... These stones are to be a memorial to the people of Israel forever. - Joshua 4:6,7 (NIV)

JULY 5

When evolution is defined as: "Small changes to an organism which produce new variety with each subsequent generation," then this "type of evolution" is a fact of science. **But has this fact of science evolved into religious fantasy?** The same word, "evolution," is now assumed to have produced ever-increasing complexity as bacteria (and subsequently more complex creatures) supposedly added useful information to their DNA programming via random mutations. This is believed to have created the millions of different kinds of creatures on Earth and ultimately changed bacteria into human beings. This is absolutely impossible and has never been observed. New information is never added to DNA; duplication errors, mutation mistakes, etc., but never new information.

Biological programming turns genes "on and off" (up and down regulating), but these programmed changes are NOT moving life in the direction of increased complexity. These random mutations are destroying previously existing information and **driving all life, slowly and inexorably, toward extinction.** Every known example of mutation change is a loss, or decrease, of functioning information. Geneticists have uncovered over 5,000 mistakes on the human DNA code which result in genetic diseases, deformities, allergies, mental problems, and a multitude of health issues. None of these mutational changes have resulted in improvements to our overall survival or new "superpowers." **We inherently know which direction evolution moves.** Every mother fears, rather than welcomes, a mutation to her newborn baby.

For the wrath of God is revealed from heaven against all ungodliness and unrighteousness of men, who by their unrighteousness suppress the truth, for what may be known about God is plain to them... – Romans 1:18,19 (ESV)

JULY 6

Have you ever wondered why each day contains 24 hours? It is because of the rotation rate of the earth – it takes 24 hours to spin around one time and bring the sun back into view in the same position 24 hours later. Other planets in our solar system have much longer or shorter days. Venus takes 2/3 of a year to rotate one time. Just think of all you could get done each day! You could fit 1,300 Earths inside of Jupiter, yet it spins like a top and takes only 10 hours to rotate one time. So why don't we have shorter or longer days? Because the earth is designed perfectly to support life.

If the rotation of the earth were twice as fast, almost every mountain around the equator of the earth would be underwater as the ocean water flowed to the equator. If it was half the current speed there would be violent temperature swings as earth heated and cooled longer with each rotation. A 24 hour cycle turns out to be the perfect rotation speed! A coincidence? Hardly – God designed Earth for our benefit. The timing of our Creator is always perfect.

ASTRONOMY

Then came the woman in the dawning of the day, and fell down at the door of the man's house where her lord was, till it was light.
– Judges 19:26 (NIV)

JULY 7

Have you considered a small bird called the oxpecker and its benefit to large African mammals? The oxpecker spends its day clinging to the backs of water buffaloes, rhinos, hippos, giraffes, and antelopes. Does it just like hitching rides? No, it is busy finding ticks and other parasites infecting the animal's skin.

African animals are so comfortable having the oxpecker on board that they even allow the oxpeckers to clean inside their ears! Oxpeckers also give a loud call when danger approaches - warning the animal to run. This is a great benefit for animals such as a rhino which have extremely poor eyesight. **The oxpecker receives a meal and the African mammal not only receives pest control, but its own alert system.** It's a win-win! This is an example of symbiosis, each organism benefitting from their relationship with the other. How did this come about? Do birds normally sit on mammals? Do these mammals know that the oxpecker removes ticks and parasites? Does a mammal say, *"Ahhh, that feels good, thanks for removing that tick?"* Relationships like this do not happen by accident and chance in nature; they were designed by God.

Praise the LORD…wild animals and all cattle, small creatures and flying birds.
– Psalm 148:1,10 (NIV)

JULY 8

Why do zebras and ostriches travel together on the dry grasslands of Africa? Ostriches are the largest living bird, standing some eight feet tall, and with their keen eyesight they make for good lookouts. However, ostriches have a poor sense of hearing and smell. Zebras, on the other hand, have great hearing and smell, but have poor eyesight. **So, the ostrich looks out for the zebra's enemies and the zebra listens and smells for the ostrich's enemies.** They both help each other. In a similar manner, ostriches also interact with gazelles and antelope. This is a win-win situation that science calls mutualism.

How does the ostrich know it needs zebras (which have a good sense of smell and hearing)? How does the zebra know that an ostrich's good sense of sight will be a benefit? Does each know they are lacking senses and try to solve the problem? No. This type of mutualistic behavior is programmed into animals. When you go to a zoo, take a look and see if the zebras and ostriches are penned together. They are placed that way because God programmed them to benefit from each other's abilities.

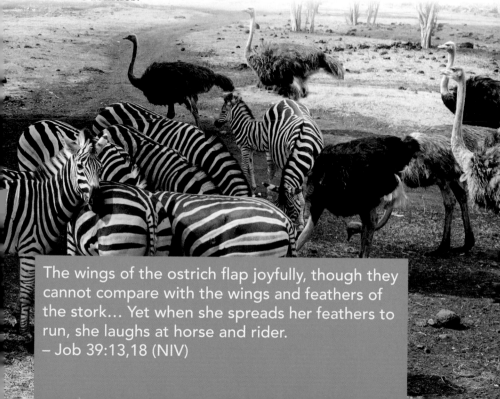

The wings of the ostrich flap joyfully, though they cannot compare with the wings and feathers of the stork... Yet when she spreads her feathers to run, she laughs at horse and rider.
– Job 39:13,18 (NIV)

BIOLOGY

JULY 9

How did animals migrate around the world so quickly after the Flood of Noah's day? There are several ways for the animals to migrate across our planet:

1.   After the Flood was the one and only Ice Age. This Ice Age caused the lowering of sea level by an estimated 300 feet. This happened as evaporated ocean water was locked up in enormous glaciers. Land bridges formed in places like the Bering Strait between Siberia and Alaska. The Indonesian Islands became a land bridge to Australia. **Kangaroos could literally have hopped to Australia!** Later, when the Ice Age ended (about 3,500 years ago) the glaciers largely melted and the sea levels rose, isolating the animals.

2.   Animals could have been on floating log mats, allowing them to be transported to locations around the earth. We witnessed such a dispersion via ocean currents in 1992 when a container ship **lost thousands of orange rubber bathtub ducks.** Within three months, these rubber duckies had floated to Indonesia, Australia, and South America; later they floated into the Arctic and Atlantic Oceans. Here is another example: after the 2011 Japanese tsunami, a debris mat 70 miles long and 2 million square feet in size was found floating out in the Pacific Ocean. During Noah's Flood, billions of trees formed large log mats – literally moving islands upon which animals released from the ark could have been transported until they found a place to disembark.

Why is Australia full of unique marsupials such as kangaroos, koala bears, and platypus? It has been found that placental animals (those with umbilical cords) out compete marsupials. Australia is absent of placental animals. Fossil marsupials have been found on every continent like the fossil marsupial lion.

When we put on our Biblical glasses, it is not difficult to understand how animals spread out, ended up in unique locations, and filled the earth after the Flood of Noah's day.

> Every beast, every creeping thing, and every fowl, and whatsoever creepeth upon the earth, after their kinds, went forth out of the ark.
> –Genesis 8:19 (KJV)

JULY 10

What would life be like without your bones? You would be like a lump of jello on the floor! Nothing would protect your brain; a good jab would probably kill you. If someone stepped on you, maybe they would step on your heart and then you would be gone. How about your lungs? Your 12 ribs form a cage to protect your heart and lungs like a shield protects Captain America. Your backbone protects your spinal cord. Your kneecap protects your knee joint. **The skull protects your brain; it's your helmet.** Interestingly, when you were born, the bones that made up your skull were not joined solidly together. Why? So, babies can pass through the birth canal. That is why babies tend to have an elongated skull. With time, the cranial bones fill in the gaps until the eight bones are fused together. Often parents remind siblings, *"Be careful of the baby's soft spot on top of the head until it fuses together."* Imagine if evolution slowly developed this system and the bones were actually fused together. Millions of moms would have died during childbirth.

Bones protect our vital areas; they act like a helmet or a shield, giving us the protection we need. Do we say that this protective gear comes about by accident and chance? That's what evolutionists believe. When we see a helmet, we know there must be a helmet maker. When we see our skull, we know there must be a skull maker. When we see ribs, we know there must be a rib maker. And Who is that great Maker of our protective "gear?" God Himself!

But you, LORD, are a shield around me, my glory, the One who lifts my head high. – Psalm 3:3 (NIV)

JULY 11

Are all viruses bad? A virus is a teeny, tiny structure that has an outside protein coat with the inside made up of nucleic acid (either DNA or RNA). One thousand viruses could fit across the width of one human hair. Viruses cannot live on their own; they need to replicate inside another living cell. Viruses are found virtually everywhere, especially in the oceans of the world where their numbers are astounding. Millions can live within a few drops of seawater!

The oceans are also teeming with bacteria because they reproduce at a phenomenal rate. The oceans could easily become overwhelmed with bacteria were it not for a virus called bacteriophages (meaning devourer of bacteria) – "phages" for short. Phages look like lunar landers with long spindly legs. The phages are 10 times smaller than the bacteria they attack. These phages "land" on a bacterium (like a lunar module landing on the moon) and inject their genetic material into the bacterium as the "lunar legs" contract. **Once the phage is inside the bacteria, it highjacks the cell's machinery** and the bacterium actually starts making more phages. In a short time, the bacterium, filled with phages, ruptures - releasing more phages which go to infect and kill other ocean bacteria.

The bacteriophages, a virus, acts to balance the total number of bacteria in ocean water, thus keeping the oceans of our world balanced and healthy. When mankind sinned, all of creation began degenerating. Some viruses have gone rogue, but originally, they were created for good - as we see with the phages being vital for the ocean's ecology by keeping the bacterial growth in check.

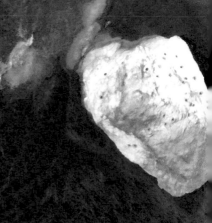

As for God, his way is perfect: The LORD's word is flawless; he shields all who take refuge in him. – Psalm 18:30 (NIV)

JULY 12

Who thinks eating oil is delicious? A newly discovered marine bacterium does! This bacterium loves to digest oil! It uses hydrocarbons as a source of energy and can utilize up to about 80% of the ingredients in an oil spill. These include xylene, toluene, and benzene. These bacteria are present throughout the world's oceans in small numbers. Once they drift into an area with oil compounds they rapidly multiply.

On April 20, 2010, an explosion on the Deepwater Horizon oil rig started the largest oil spill in recorded history. For three months, enormous amounts of oil was released into the Gulf of Mexico. It was considered the largest environmental disaster in American history! **Would the Gulf waters survive the oily muck?**

Within a month, a team of scientists discovered that bacteria were beginning to gobble up the largest oil spill in U.S. history. *"They not only out competed fellow microbes, they each ramped up their own internal metabolic machinery to digest the oil as efficiently as possible."*[1] Who would have guessed that there are several species of bacteria that eat hydrocarbons? Imagine bacteria getting fat and happy from eating oil! It was found that **the oil plume was reduced by ½ every three days**. That is amazingly rapid recovery! This is not the only scientific example of an ecosystem recovering quickly from a disaster. God has built into the earth an amazing resilience with an incredible set of checks and balances.

He lifted me out of the slimy pit, out of the mud and mire; - Psalm 40:2a (NIV)

JULY 13

God blessed us with the marvelous gift of depth perception by designing our face with two eyes. If we had a single eye or our eyes were placed very close together, we would only perceive width and height. Our brain combines a different viewing angle of the same information from each eye – giving us the ability to interpret depth, i.e. depth perception. But there are many activities which primarily use only one eye.

Did you know that every person has a dominant eye that provides a better ability when aiming, swinging, throwing, using a camera, or a variety of other eye-hand coordinated actions? Using your dominant eye-hand combination can improve your sports skills. The more precise information is given by your dominant eye because it has more neural connections to your brain than the other eye. But how can you determine which one of your eyes is dominant?

An easy way you can determine your dominant eye is to look for an upright line (edge) of an object that is at least 9 feet (3 meters) from you. Next, stretch your arm straight out, lift up your thumb and use it to cover the line. You may have to squint but keep both eyes open. Now close one eye and see if it stays lined up. If it does, then the eye you are looking with is your dominant eye. If it moves off of the line, check with the other eye. It will stay on the line with one of them; and that is your dominant eye.

We all tend to look at things through our fallen, sinful human nature. Have you considered making the Bible your dominant "eye" as you perceive truth, morality, and the world around you? God's Word and Spirit within us can help us do exactly that.

Although I want to do good, evil is right there with me...Thanks be to God, who delivers me through Jesus Christ our Lord! ...in my mind I am a slave to God's law (righteousness), but in my sinful nature a slave to the law of sin.
– Romans 7:21,25 (NIV)

JULY 14

Frozen bone-chilling Antarctica was once a lush tropical environment full of dinosaurs and tropical vegetation! Numerous dinosaur fossils have been found: ankylosaur, hadrosaur, mosasaur, pterosaurs and various sauropods (long-neck dinosaurs). **Antarctica also once had lush vegetation** as shown by the fossilized beech, gingko trees, ferns, mosses and coal beds. Scientists have even found fossils of dolphins and whales in the Vestfold hills of Antarctica's Marine Plain.

Hundred-foot-tall fossilized *Glossopteris* trees with huge flat leaves longer than your forearm have also been uncovered. The team studying these trees believe that they were covered rapidly with volcanic ash and turned to stone. *"They're actually some of the best-preserved fossil plants in the world,"* one researcher said. *"The fungi in the wood itself were probably mineralized and turned into stone within a matter of weeks, in some cases probably while the tree was still alive, ... These things happened incredibly rapidly."* It's hard to believe, but Antarctica was once a lush tropical rainforest. Now that's climate change! The Flood of Noah and the breaking apart of continents provide scientifically plausible answers for this.

FLOOD GEOLOGY

When I tried to understand all this it troubled me deeply till I entered the sanctuary of God; then I understood their final destiny.
– Psalm 73:16,17 (NIV)

ASTRONOMY

JULY 15

Did you know that the moon is moving away from us? When astronauts went to the moon, they left mirrors on the surface so that a laser light could be sent to the moon, bounce off the mirror, and return to the earth. We can measure the time this round trip takes so accurately that the exact distance to the moon can be measured within a fraction of an inch. **The moon is moving away from us at about 2 inches/year (called lunar regression).** This means the moon is getting farther away each year, and as we go back in time, the moon was closer to the earth. At this measured rate of recession, the moon would have been touching Earth less than 2 billion years ago.

It is commonly taught by evolutionists that the moon exists because material spun off of the earth as it was forming about 4.5 billion years ago. Astronomer Edouard Roche long ago calculated that from Earth's surface to 11,500 miles out, any object would be torn to pieces by Earth's gravitational forces. Therefore, **the belief that the moon came from material originating from the earth has enormous problems** because it would have been torn to pieces.

Also, if the moon were truly 4.5 billion years old, it would be much farther out in space than the distance we see today. God created the moon on Day 4 less than 10,000 year ago - which means it has only moved a mere ½ mile since creation. The simplest explanation is that the moon is not that old. The moon's distance from Earth testifies that it is young.

Let them praise the name of the LORD: for his name alone is excellent; his glory is above the earth and heaven. –Psalm 148:13 (KJV)

JULY 16

The moon is not haunted by ghosts, but does have "ghost craters." Look carefully at a full moon and you will see the lighter-colored highlands are made of rocks similar to granite and the dark-colored maria (or seas) are made of volcanic basalt-like rock. **Galileo gave maria its name four centuries ago, thinking the maria were bodies of water!**

The granite-like highlands are irregular, rugged, and saturated with craters. The darker maria are impact basins where the moon's crust was deeply fractured, creating cracks that oozed out molten lava rock from below and filled the impact basins. As the impact basins were being filled with lava, more meteors were hitting the moon, leaving small craters inside the basins. Inside these lava-filled maria basins we can see the faint outlines of these small craters (which are almost covered by lava, with only the rims being visible). **Ghost craters are craters within a crater; all that is visible is the rim of the second crater.** All lunar maria contain at least some ghost craters. Evolutionists believe it took 500 million years to fill each maria area. The evolutionary time frame cannot be true because lava couldn't remain fluid for millions of years to slowly fill the ghost craters. They would not be visible if it took millions of years to cover them.

Another observation supporting the Biblical viewpoint is where maria are located. Nearly all of the maria are on the near side of the moon (the side that faces Earth) AND in the northern hemisphere of the moon. So maria cover just one fourth of the moon. If the maria were the result of random evolutionary processes over millions of years, the maria should be equally distributed over the moon's surface. They are not. It looks like space rocks struck the northern part of the moon in just a few days before the moon had time to rotate (the moon's rotation rate is once every 30 days).

The Flood of Noah likely coincided with asteroid bombardment of the earth and moon. If this bombardment lasted only a few days, this explains why the moon was hit mostly on one side. So, when the moon is full, get out your binoculars and marvel how ghost craters are supporting Biblical truth.

...a third of the sun was struck, a third of the moon, and a third of the stars, so that a third of them turned dark. – Revelation 8:12 (NIV)

ASTRONOMY

ANATOMY

JULY 17

What is the secret ingredient which keeps you breathing? It may sound strange, but it is water! As we breathe, air passes into our lungs through a branching system called a respiratory tree. Think of the windpipe (trachea) as the **tree trunk** and bronchi as **major limbs** supplying air to the right and left lungs. Inside the lungs, the major limbs **split into branches** - smaller tubes called bronchioles. These split further into the **smallest of twig tips** - sacs called alveoli. Each person has about 300 million of these tiny sacs!

These alveoli touch each other, like a bunch of grapes. **If laid out flat, the total surface covered by an adult's alveoli would be about the size of a tennis court!** It is within the alveoli's ultra-thin walls that oxygen and carbon dioxide are exchanged. Making up these thin walls are two types of cells; one is very thin and covered with a layer of water. If this water layer was not present, the cell would almost immediately dry out and die. However, the water's surface tension could cause the alveoli to collapse. The entire system only works because there is a special chemical that reduces the water's surface tension secreted by the second type of alveolar cell. This chemical is a surfactant coating, which reduces the surface tension on the alveolus. Premature babies are **not** born with the ability to make enough surfactant and therefore have difficulty breathing. Surfactant replacement therapy helps preemies survive.

To understand surfactants, fill a small bowl with water and sprinkle ground pepper on the surface. Now add a single drop of dish soap to the water and watch the pepper scatter across the surface. The water's surface tension is broken by the soap. Soap is a surfactant. In your alveoli, there are surfactants that break the water's surface tension, thereby allowing the exchange of oxygen and carbon dioxide without collapsing the alveoli.

Does dish soap happen by accident and chance? Then why would the chemical surfactant in our lungs, which acts like dish soap, happen by accident and chance? There had to be a surfactant Maker. God knew we needed water for the alveoli cells, but also that the water had to be broken up. This is just one of a myriad of details that the great Designer of our body had to solve in order for us to have life.

Let everything that hath breath praise the Lord. Praise ye the Lord. – Psalm 150:6 (KJV)

JULY 18

The external force which supposedly guides evolution to increasing complexity is called "natural selection." However, this process can only eliminate information, NOT create new information. Here are two examples:

- In the mountain streams of Venezuela live male fishes, either brightly-colored or drab-colored. The population of either group increases or decreases depending on the predators. When there are few predators the brightly-colored male fish predominates. The female guppies then mate with the brightly-colored males and produce brightly colored guppies. When there are lots of predators, the brightly-colored males are easily seen and eaten, and the females then mate with the drab-colored males resulting in drab colored young ones. This is natural selection in action. Natural selection eliminates, it does not create new information.

- Tibetan snow lotus seeds are prized for Chinese medicine. During the last 50 years, the height of the snow lotus has decreased by 50%. Why? The people scouring the slopes believe that the taller flowering plant seeds are more potent than the shorter plants, therefore they leave the shorter plants to reproduce. The genes for tallness are slowly being removed from the Himalayas.

Evolution is not taking place; just the organism's sensors and pre-programming responding to available information. No new information is added! Natural selection can only eliminate - never create!

I will meditate on your wonderful works. They tell of the power of your awesome works-- and I will proclaim your great deeds.
- Psalm145:5,6 (NIV)

JULY 19

All over the world ancient cultures built megalithic (huge stone) structures. But why?

- Stonehenge is an ancient calendar marking the solstices. This ring of standing stones in southern England has stones 13 feet high (4.0 m) and seven feet wide (2.1 m) and **weighing about 50,000 pounds**. How were they transported and erected?

- In Baalbek, Lebanon are the ruins of a Roman temple. The temple is setting on a single foundation stone **weighing about 4 million pounds!** This was set in place by an earlier civilization. How was it transported? Even modern technology has not lifted and transported something this heavy on dry land.

- In Tiahuanaco, Peru is the "gateway of the sun." It is carved from a single block of volcanic rock **weighing 200,000 pounds.** How was it transported and erected?

- On Easter Island are carved megalithic heads. Some of these massive heads **weigh over 180,000 pounds.** Most are 12 to 15 feet high; one is 32 feet tall. How were they carved and moved?

Ancient man was obviously skillful, smart, and creative. Compare ancient man's ingenuity with NASA's movement of the 2 million pound Saturn V rocket (3.5 miles to the launch pad) in 1965. A special crawler-transporter vehicle, hundreds of people, and millions of dollars were required. Were ancient people bumbling cave men? Hardly! They were quite intelligent - just look at the megalithic structures they left behind. It is a mystery how they were able to move these stones and evolution has no answer. Man was created intelligent from the beginning.

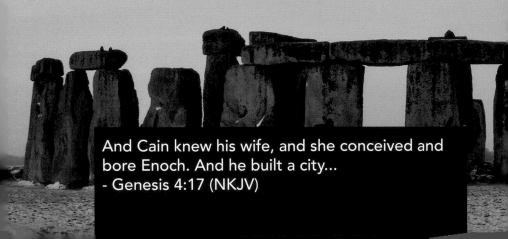

And Cain knew his wife, and she conceived and bore Enoch. And he built a city...
- Genesis 4:17 (NKJV)

JULY 20

Stonehenge in England is one of the most mysterious artifacts on earth. **This megalithic structure dates to about 4,000 years ago** with huge stones placed in concentric rings. Who built it, why, and how?

There are two types of stones at Stonehenge. The larger sarsen stones are believed to have been brought from about 20 miles away. On average, one sarsen stone weighs 50,000 pounds. Eighty-one sarsens were needed. The bluestones weighed up to 10,000 pounds, and 80 of them were used. These bluestones came from 135 miles away (as the crow flies). **Yet, they had to take a different route.** The builders brought these stones from the mountains to the coast, shipped them by boat around the coast, and finally carried them over land. Large waste piles north of the stones' excavation site indicates that the stones were shaped on site before shipment.

To fit the upright stones with the horizontal lintels, mortice holes and protruding tenons were created. In 1923, a professional mason did an experiment of shaping a single sarsen with a stone maul; he was able to remove about six cubic inches of stone per hour. Researchers estimated that it would have taken 50 masons, working 10 hours a day and 7 days a week approximately 2 years and 9 months to finish the dressing of the stones.

Then the stones had to be laid in a precise geometrical pattern. Holes were dug. Then the stones were hauled into position and stood upright. The skills required to build sophisticated megalithic structures came as a result of highly intelligent people in a stratified society. This project required designers, architects, surveyors, managers, masons, etc. A simple farming community does not generate these skills. People 4,000 years ago were not ignorant but intelligent, just as is recorded in the Bible. Man was intelligent from the beginning.

When God created man, he made him in the likeness of God. - Genesis 5:1b (ESV)

Fossils from Germany's Messel pit are fantastic! Fossilized bats have been found with bits of moths in their digestive tract and fossilized horses with leaves and grapes in their digestive tracts. But a recent "triple treat" was even more bizarre. **A fossil was found with a bug inside a lizard which was inside a snake!** All three creatures were well preserved! This is not the only time a "three in one" fossil has been found. In 2008, a fossilized shark was found which had an amphibian in its digestive tract and inside the amphibian was a spiny fish – all fossilized! A fish in an amphibian in a shark!

These fossils were "frozen in time" with undigested meals in their stomachs. Evolution, with its assumed long time periods, cannot explain this phenomenon; only a massive catastrophe could preserve these creatures fast enough. What is this recipe for making such fossils?

1. Fast coverage by sediments.
2. Lots of water so the minerals can percolate through the creatures and preserve them.
3. Deep coverage.
4. No oxygen, which would decompose the creatures/plants.

What event in history would have these conditions? The Flood of Noah's day, which took place about 4,500 years ago. It takes very special conditions to make a fossil and the Flood of Noah's day would have provided these.

Fossil perch *Paleoperca proxima* from the Messel pit, Germany

Therefore we will not fear, though the earth give way and the mountains fall into the heart of the sea, though its waters roar and foam and the mountains quake with their surging.
–Psalm 46:2,3 (NIV)

JULY 22

Was Christopher Columbus fearful of falling off the earth as he sailed westward? Was the earth really flat? Neither. Columbus read his Bible and knew Isaiah 40:22, "*It is He who sits above the _circle_ of the earth.*"

The idea that Columbus believed in a flat Earth was a bit of fiction written by an atheistic fictional writer, Washington Irving in the 1800s (Irving also wrote *Rip Van Winkle*). As far back as ~ 190 B.C., Greek mathematician Eratosthenes of Alexandria, was able to calculate the Earth's circumference within 50 miles! A century later, Hipparchus used Esarth's circumference to calculate the distance to the moon. He was only 100 miles off. **For over 3,000 years, informed people have known the earth is not flat.** Those who read the Bible also know Luke 17:34-36 which speaks of Jesus' second coming: some would be asleep at night while others would be working at daytime. This is a clear indication of a revolving sphere with day and night occurring at the same time. The idea that Columbus thought the world was flat is a myth. God's Word and science both confirm that the earth is a sphere.

I tell you, in that night there will be two in one bed. One will be taken and the other left. There will be two women grinding together. One will be taken and the other left."
- Luke 17: 34-36 (ESV)

JULY 23

Have you considered a seed? For example, an acorn weighs less than an ounce and yet it becomes a mighty oak. Within the seed is enough nutrition to get the tree started and all of the DNA information needed to direct and guide the seed (weighing a fraction of an ounce) on its transformation from a sapling to a mighty oak (weighing 200,000 pounds).

If the first acorn had to design itself by trial and error, we would still be waiting for the first oak. There are three different "faiths" attempting to explain life. The most scientifically plausible is that God programmed within each tiny acorn the information necessary to become a mighty oak. Information ONLY comes from an intelligent source and cannot arise from a purely material source. A second belief is that time, chance, and mutations (evolution) created the information necessary to create an oak tree. This is storytelling, not science. The last belief is that an active environment molded a passive non-oak tree to change it into an oak tree by a process coined "natural selection." This is also an impossibility which has never been shown to add new information.

Only the all-knowing, all-powerful God of the Bible could assemble the first oak cell complete with an estimated 26,000 genes and 1.3 billion coded parts.

All the trees of the field shall know that I am the Lord. - Ezekiel 17:24 (NIV)

JULY 24

Have you considered that some seeds plant themselves? The plant called the filaree has this ability. Its seeds have a long curve on one end and a spirally coiled shaft (style) on the other end - with the seed at its point. The seed is planted by the changes in humidity - curling when dry and straightening when wet. Because of its constantly changing shape, the **seed buries itself by slowly drilling itself into the ground!**

The wild oat (*Avena Sativa*) seed also has this ability. It has a long awn that is bent at a right angle about a quarter of the way along its length. When it gets wet, the bent awn straightens and then bends as it dries out. As the awn bends and straightens, the seed rotates. **This writhing plant also drills itself into the ground and plants itself!**

In both cases, the seed's design allows the right amount of torque and power to be applied in order to drill itself to just the right depth for proper germination. It does this without any parts twisting out of shape or breaking. Do you think this happened by random chance? Does a man-made tool, such as a drill bit in your shop, happen by accident and chance? Tools required engineering and design. The same is true of the filaree seed and the wild oat seed; they required engineering and design. **What we are witnessing are the fingerprints of God.** This is just one of the many evidences that He has left so that we will KNOW that He exists.

BIOLOGY

I will remember the deeds of the Lord; yes, I will remember your wonders of old.
- Psalm 77:11 (ESV)

One of the most beautiful and prized seashells is the cone shell of the South Pacific and Caribbean, yet it is one of the most dangerous animals in the sea! The outer beauty hides a deadly toxin which can kill humans. As the cone snail moves along the bottom of the ocean, it extends its siphon not only to take in water, and thus oxygen, but also to smell. This carnivore is like a wolf sniffing for a rabbit, only this one wants fish. Once located, the cone snail moves to its prey, extends its long proboscises (its mouth) to which is attached a harpoon with poison. Three, two, one – fire! Out shoots a poison-tipped harpoon which hits the fish and paralyzes it within seconds. So complex is this animal's venom, that no anti-venom exists. The mouth then enlarges itself and swallows the fish whole.

Evolutionists say this harpoon and poison came about by mutational accidents and chance over millions of years. Aren't weapons designed? What about the poison, did cone snails get together and say we need to tip our weapon with a poison to kill fish? NO. Snails don't think like that! What would happen if there was no harpoon to pierce the fish, how would the poison get in? Why evolve the poison without a way of stabbing it into something? What good is a harpoon without poison, it may irritate a fish to be speared, but there would be no way of killing it. Both had to be present from the beginning or no fish for supper! Weapons happening by accident and chance? Hardly! Created by God, YES!

You are the God who works wonders; you have made known your might among the peoples.
– Psalm 77:14 (ESV)

JULY 26

Have you heard of killifish (killies)? They are a very popular pet store fish because of their vibrant colors and patterns. They are not called killifish because they are aggressive, but from a Dutch word for small ditches and ponds that many of the species inhabit. The turquoise killifish live in tiny rainwater pools in Africa that exist briefly during the rainy season and then dry up. During this brief time, the adults mature within two weeks (this is the fastest maturation rate of any known vertebrate) and lay a multitude of eggs before dying. The eggs lie in the mud and develop for two to three weeks. This is very important, because these seasonal pools can dry up completely within three weeks. Once the heart and most of the body develops within the egg, the embryo goes into a dormant state (diapause). Some killies were observed to survive up to three years and hatch successfully.

Let's review: Turquoise killifish must mate and produce eggs within two weeks. They cannot give birth to live young, like guppies, because the ponds dry up too quickly. **The eggs must withstand harsh drying conditions for months, sometimes years.** There must be mechanisms within the egg to prevent false starts from small isolated rainstorms. If the fish does not mature within two weeks of hatching, they cannot spawn, and the species becomes extinct. How does evolution explain this fish's lightning-fast lifecycle? **The needed abilities and parameters for survival are too narrow to have slowly developed over time!** The annual killifish were designed to survive in these narrow conditions from the very beginning or there would be no annual killifish. Whenever we look closely at the details, we find the fingerprint of God.

Who is like you, LORD God Almighty? You, LORD, are mighty, and your faithfulness surrounds you. – Psalm 89:8 (NIV)

JULY 27

In the depths of Brazil's coconut forest, a green glow appears at night. Looking closer, **the green glow is coming from a bioluminescent mushroom.** At latest count, there were about 9,000 species of gilled mushrooms and 71 of these can glow. One of the largest is the *Neonothopanus gardneri* or flor de coco, meaning, *"coconut flower"*. This mushroom can be found attached to leaves at the base of young palm trees in coconut forests.

Since mushrooms cannot "see" light levels, botanists wondered if some other mechanism triggered their light output. First, they fooled the mushrooms by dropping the temperature. Sure enough, the mushrooms glowed an intense green. Scientists next wondered about the purpose for the green glow. They placed acrylic mushrooms on a dark forest floor emanating LED light with the same intensity and green color. Soon bugs, flies, wasps, beetles, and ants flocked to the green glow. The glowing green light and its nighttime appearance all worked to propagate the fungus spores via visiting insects.

Bioluminescence (making light by mixing together organic chemicals) is a very complex process. How do mushrooms "know" that insects see green and therefore glow with a green light? How did the mushroom know that glowing green would be needed at night and not during the day when that color would compete with all the daytime green plants? If you are ever fortunate enough to see an **eerie green glowing mushroom**, don't attribute it to some random force (like evolution). Give glory to God for His creativity.

The LORD is God, and he has made his light shine on us... You are my God, and I will praise you... - Psalm 118:27,28 (NIV)

JULY 28

Fungi are supposedly one of the least complex and earliest forms of life on earth. Yet, even the "lowly" shelf mushroom displays incredible ingenuity. **Fungi perform the important function of recycling dead plants.** Shelf mushrooms attach themselves to dead trees and slowly decompose the cellulose structure. These mushrooms can often be found attached to dead trees with their white underside releasing spores which become future mushrooms. But what happens when the tree falls down causing the white spore-releasing side of the mushroom to point sideways or upwards toward the sky?

Slowly, over a period of a month or more, the shelf mushroom moves to right itself, so once again the spores can be released downward in contact with rich forest soil. How does a sightless fungus know which direction is up and which direction is down? **This "simple life form" has the ability to sense the direction of gravity and move its entire body to line up correctly.** This requires a very complex design of sensing, programs which compare the data and select responses, and response systems. This is called Continuous Environmental Tracking (CET). CET is far more complex than Darwin's simple concept of natural selection and survival of the fittest where a changing environment supposedly molds a passive organism into something else. Humans designing a system to perform such a feat would require enormous amounts of intelligence and engineering. To believe a mushroom somehow acquired this ability by random changes over time is beyond credibility.

Whoso **walketh uprightly** shall be saved: but he that is perverse in his ways **shall fall** at once.
– Proverbs 28:18 (KJV)

Have you considered blue eyes? There is no blue pigment in the iris, so why do they look blue? Most people in the world have brown eyes; however, many of European descent have blue eyes. Our eye color comes from the amount of melanin or pigment in our irises. People with blue eyes have less pigment or melanin in their irises than brown-eyed people. Less pigment causes light hitting the iris to scatter, making the eye appear blue. In a similar way, sunlight bounces off air molecules - making the sky appear blue.

Blue eyes are a genetic mutation resulting in less melanin in the irises. Scientists discovered that two genes are involved. One gene, the HERC2 gene, inhibits the OCA2 gene resulting in less melanin or pigment being produced. **So blue-eyed people have a loss of information.** Originally, all people were brown-eyed. Is this mutation harmful? Less melanin means more light will go through the iris. Some blue-eyed people have light sensitivity, so in areas of bright sun this is actually a disadvantage. Thankfully, we have sunglasses today.

How does this fit into the Biblical perspective? Prior to the Tower of Babel, the descendants of Noah intermarried. If the mutation occurred at that time, it could have been hidden, for brown eye genes are dominant over blue eye genes. Then after the Tower of Babel, as small people groups scattered across the face of the earth in limited gene pools, blue-eye people would have married blue-eyed people, thus making blue eyes more common. We find most blue-eyed people of European descent. All blue-eyed people can be traced back to a common ancestor who originally lost the information required for brown eyes. In actuality, all people are related as we can be traced genetically and Biblically, first to Noah and his three sons and then further back to Adam and Eve.

and from thence [Babel] did the LORD scatter them abroad upon the face of all the earth.
– Genesis 11:9c (KJV)

JULY 30

You can't drink milk? **Then you're normal!** If you can enjoy a glass of milk with your chocolate chip cookies you are actually a "mutant"! When humans are infants, they produce ample quantities of lactase to digest milk. Lactase is an enzyme formed in the lining of the small intestine. This chemical is able to break down milk sugars, which are then easily digested (absorbed) by the intestines. The gene for producing lactase switches off as children are weaned. If a person has unmuted genes, that person will not be able to digest milk - resulting in gas, bloating, cramps, diarrhea and nausea. These non-mutant people are able to consume some dairy products (like cheese or yogurt), because during the process of making the cheese and yogurt, the bacteria have already fermented much of the lactose and the resulting gas was released into the atmosphere.

Originally, **Adam and Eve were made perfect** and therefore unable to drink milk into adulthood. So those who can't drink milk as adults are actually more closely comparable to the originally perfect Adam and Eve. The ability of most people to drink milk into adulthood is from a genetic mutation. This mutation is found in 95% of northern Europeans, 30 % southern Europeans and less than 10% in African and Asian people groups, yet all are relatively recent descendants of Adam and Eve. Not being able to drink milk into adulthood is actually "normal".

GENETICS

And God saw everything that he had made, and, behold, it was **very good**. And the evening and the morning were the sixth day.
– Genesis 1:31 (KJV)

JULY 31

A small river about an hour west of Dallas, Texas is famous for its dinosaur tracks in Cretaceous limestone. Since the early 1900s, thousands of tracks have been uncovered in and alongside the Paluxy River in Glen Rose, Texas. In this area are 7 layers of this sequence: clay, conglomerate, hardpan and limestone. Dinosaur tracks are found in the top limestone layer. In fact, only two specific types of dinosaur tracks are found - the Acrocanthosaurus and Sauroposeidon protelis. Only these two types of dinosaurs left prints in all 7 limestone layers. How could this happen?

Textbooks place this sediment layer at 65 to 145 million years ago – taking 60 million years to slowly form. How could the same sequence of clay/conglomerate/hardpan/limestone form in the exact same way with thousands (or millions) of years passing between each sequence? Why would the same type of dinosaur be the only animal leaving tracks, with thousands and thousands of years passing between the formation of each of the seven identical layers? From an evolutionary viewpoint it doesn't make sense, but from a Biblical viewpoint it does.

Noah's Flood would have caused the rapid formation of this Cretaceous layer as daily tides brought enormous sediment-filled waves into this area. As each tide receded, the sediment was sorted and dumped in distinct sequences of clay/conglomerate/hardpan/limestone. Animals trapped in this location would have milled around making tracks on the top limestone layer. This layer hardened enough to preserve the tracks as the next lunar cycle brought in another layer of sediment. Thus, thousands of square miles of sediment formed, all with the same dinosaur tracks made by the same herd of dinosaurs which were attempting to escape the rising flood waters of Noah's day.

This unique geological area was created in a matter of weeks, not millions of years. When we put on our Biblical glasses, there is no mystery - these dinosaur tracks were made as the flood waters rose and levels fluctuated during Noah's Flood.

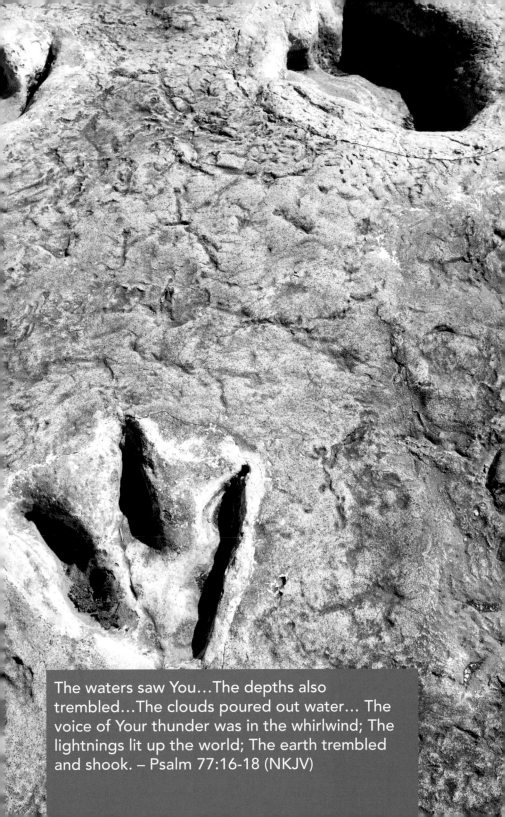

The waters saw You…The depths also trembled…The clouds poured out water… The voice of Your thunder was in the whirlwind; The lightnings lit up the world; The earth trembled and shook. — Psalm 77:16-18 (NKJV)

Aug

"WE ARE NOT RESPONSIBLE FOR THE CIRCUMSTANCES WE ARE IN, BUT WE ARE RESPONSIBLE FOR THE WAY WE ALLOW THOSE CIRCUMSTANCES TO AFFECT US; WE CAN EITHER ALLOW THEM TO GET ON TOP OF US OR WE CAN ALLOW THEM TO TRANSFORM US INTO WHAT GOD WANTS US TO BE."

- Oswald Chambers, 1874-1917, Influential Christian writer

We rejoice in our sufferings, knowing that suffering produces endurance, and endurance produces character, and character produces hope, and hope does not put us to shame, because God's love has been poured into our hearts through the Holy Spirit who has been given to us.

– Romans 5:3-5 (ESV)

Have you considered the engineering that goes into a spider web? The spider's silk is manufactured in its spinnerets, which are located at the tip of its abdomen. There are usually three pairs of spinnerets, each being a tiny cone-shaped device with a great number of spigots (sometimes over a thousand), which dispense the liquid silk. The liquid silk comes from seven glands which specialize in a certain kind of silk thread. From the gland, a tiny pumping system transports the liquid silk to the spigots. **The glands and spigots cause the silk thread to vary in thickness, stickiness, and stretchiness.**

There are 3,000 species of orb spiders, but their web designs are similar. The orb spider chooses a location and spins a Y-shaped scaffolding of radial threads. These threads are thicker, stronger, less stretchy and NOT sticky. Next the spider adds a temporary non-sticky spiral which stabilizes the web. After that, the sticky spiral is constructed, starting at the outside edges. As it spools out the thread, the spider coats it with more glue, which separates into tiny, regularly spaced beads. The spider leaves the center of the hub free of glue and skillfully moves like a tightrope walker, avoiding the sticky threads while walking on the non-sticky radial, mooring, and hub threads. Once complete, the spider sits and waits at the hub (or near the edges) for an insect to accidently fly into the web. The web vibrates as the caught prey struggles to free itself, alerting the spider that "lunch is served."

The spider needs three things to make its orb web: thread, glue, and web design. The more we examine the details, the more we realize that it had to happen all at once from the very beginning or we would have no orb spiders.

For he spoke, and it came to be; he commanded, and it stood firm.
– Psalm 33:9 (NIV)

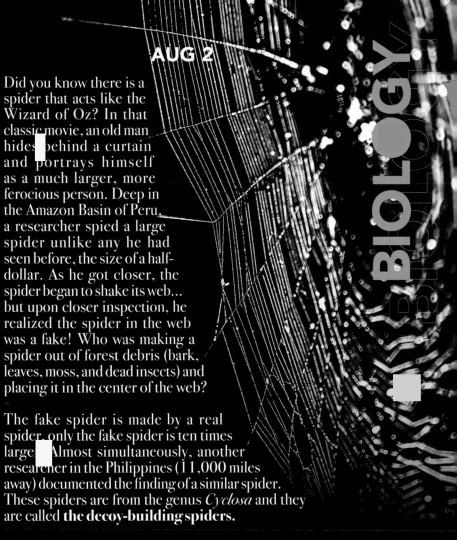

Did you know there is a spider that acts like the Wizard of Oz? In that classic movie, an old man hides behind a curtain and portrays himself as a much larger, more ferocious person. Deep in the Amazon Basin of Peru, a researcher spied a large spider unlike any he had seen before, the size of a half-dollar. As he got closer, the spider began to shake its web... but upon closer inspection, he realized the spider in the web was a fake! Who was making a spider out of forest debris (bark, leaves, moss, and dead insects) and placing it in the center of the web?

The fake spider is made by a real spider, only the fake spider is ten times large. Almost simultaneously, another researcher in the Philippines (11,000 miles away) documented the finding of a similar spider. These spiders are from the genus *Cyclosa* and they are called **the decoy-building spiders.**

How do evolutionists explain the decoy-building spider's ability to design such replicas? How does it happen in two places with an ocean separating them? How does the spider know to shake the web? The decoy-building spiders do things by instinct and instincts are programmed into an organism. That Programmer is the Almighty God.

"Holy, holy, holy is the Lord God Almighty, who was, and is, and is to come."...living creatures give glory, honor and thanks to him who sits on the throne and who lives forever and ever.
– Revelation 4:8-9 (NIV)

GEOLOGY

How does the log mat on Spirit Lake at Mount St. Helens help explain the origin of coal? On May 18, 1980, Mt. St. Helens erupted, sending a sideways explosion that downed thousands of acres of mature trees. At the same time, a huge landslide slid into Spirit Lake – creating an 800-foot tidal wave that slammed onto the surrounding hillsides. As the water came back into the lake, **it dragged more than one million downed trees into the lake**. Forty years later, many are still floating, but the trees have no bark. As the trees moved back and forth across the lake, the bark rubbed off in sheets; the waterlogged bark then dropped to the bottom of the lake. There is more than three feet of bark, branches, and waterlogged trees piled up on the bottom of the lake.

Interestingly, ten months prior to Mt. St. Helens erupting, Dr. Steven Austin was defending his dissertation of the formation of the Kentucky coal fields by floating log mats. When Mt. St. Helens blew its top, it created a real-life model of his theory. Kentucky coal beds contain abundant sheets of tree bark. **The accumulation of bark on the bottom of Spirit Lake would be the first step of coal bed formation.** If Mt. St. Helens had another eruption with an avalanche of dirt being deposited and covering the pile of tree bark, coal could then form. To make coal, pressure from overlying sediment needs to squeeze water out of the buried plant materials and heat needs to be added. Because widespread worldwide volcanism occurred during Noah's Flood, this real-life event at Mt. St. Helens, with its floating log mat, provided a small-scale model for the rapid and recent formation of coal around the globe.

...one day is with the Lord as a thousand years, and a thousand years as one day. The Lord is not slack concerning his promise... but is longsuffering...not willing that any should perish, but that all should come to repentance.
– 2 Peter 3:8,9 (KJV)

AUG 4

Throughout the course of human history, malaria has killed hundreds of millions of people. The first anti-malarial drug remained obscure to the Europeans until the 1500s A.D., at which point the conquistadors learned that the natives of South America had a malaria cure brewed from a special bark. The tree was later named after the Countess Cinchona, who returned from Peru in 1640, bringing the malaria remedy to Europe. The demand for the new drug was so great that there was soon not enough cinchona trees or "fever bark" coming from South America - so cinchona tree plantations were started in Indonesia. The active ingredient in the cinchona brew is quinine. By the 1920's, the German pharmaceutical industry had perfected quinine extraction. But once WWII started, major sources of quinine were denied to the Allies, so synthetic quinine, called chloroquine, was developed. **Chloroquine soon became the world's principal antimalarial drug.** Quinine faded into history.

Then during the 1960's, the U.S. Marines experienced a virulent strain of malaria which was chloroquine resistant. Out of desperation, doctors returned to the natural quinine - and it worked! We still use chloroquine as an antimalarial drug, but where did we get the idea to make this synthetic drug? The inspiration came from the natural product - a tree bark brew containing quinine. Chemists on their own would have probably never discovered quinine or its synthetic form, chloroquine. **God gave us the cinchona tree to help us survive in this fallen world.** Interestingly, quinine has no known function for the cinchona tree. God has provided many gifts purely for us to discover.

speak to the earth, and it shall teach thee...
- Job 12:8 (KJV)

AUG 5

Is sleep good for the brain? It has been confirmed that sleeping rejuvenates the brain. So, when your mother said, "*Get a good night's sleep*" - she was right!

Our brain uses about 20 % of our energy even though it makes up only 2% of our body weight. All of those burned calories also create waste products. **So how is the waste cleaned out of your head?** The rest of our body uses the lymphatic system to remove waste, but our brain does not use this method. Our brain and spinal column are filled with spinal fluid. When we sleep, the cerebrospinal fluid flows through the brain removing the waste - even the plaques associated with Alzheimer's disease! While we sleep, the brain's cells shrink up to 60%, allowing the spinal fluid to flow around the cells collecting the waste which is then transferred to the blood for processing. Very little spinal fluid moves while we are awake, but when asleep, spinal fluid literally sloshes through these passageways taking the toxins away and washing our brain clean. **What** a beautiful design God has created to clear our thoughts!

"... when you lie down, your sleep will be sweet." - Proverbs 3:24b (ESV)

AUG 6

What happens within our brain when we are sleeping? Brains are very busy during sleep. **They are organizing and storing information from the day's activities.** While you sleep, your brain is storing new memories and consolidating old ones. Sleep helps cement new information for better recall. Sleep also cleans our brain, clearing out the toxins. While you sleep, glial cells are feeding the brain and removing the waste. Synaptic connections that went unused during the day get marked by a protein. When microglia cells detect that mark, they prune the synapse. **In other words, your brain is being cleaned, removing thoughts that are not being accessed.** It is like the brain is cleaning the junk off your computer's hard drive so it can operate faster and better!

During sleep, the brain cells shrink by up to 60% to make room for the glial cells to clean and remove the waste. Fluid washes over the brain cells and cleans out the pruned proteins and unused memories. **Have you ever awakened thinking sharper than the night before or knowing the solution to a perplexing problem?** During your sleep, glial cells were cleaning out the trash and leaving behind information which was needed. Those are your "aha" moments. Your brain is not sleeping when you are sleeping. So, why not let God's Word permeate and restructure your mind. Just before bed, spend some time reading Scripture. Now while you sleep, the synaptic connections will be reinforced by Scripture and the other "thoughts" will be pruned. As you read, store, and recall Scripture, more synapses are made and, in a way, you are restructuring your mind.

ANATOMY

"Finally, brothers, whatever is true, whatever is honorable, whatever is just, whatever is pure, whatever is lovely, whatever is commendable, if there is any excellence, if there is anything worthy of praise, ***think about these things***."
- Philippians 4:8 (NIV)

BIOLOGY

In India and Sri Lanka there is an interesting symbiotic (win-win) relationship between an ant and a woodpecker. The Rufous woodpecker loves to eat black tree ants and the black tree ants love to eat woodpecker eggs. So what would we expect to happen if the woodpecker laid its eggs in the middle of the black tree ant colony?

In the spring of each year, when the Rufous woodpecker gets ready to lay its eggs, a nest has to be built. First, the woodpeckers look for a black tree ants' football-sized nest hanging from a tree. Once found, the woodpecker carves out a center chamber in the ant's nest, six inches in diameter. During this time, the woodpeckers do not eat the ants (their favorite food). Surprisingly, the ants do not viciously attack and sting the woodpecker (which they normally would do). Once the eggs are laid, it becomes even more bizarre. The ants do not eat the eggs. When the eggs hatch and when the baby birds appear, they are not stung by the ants scurrying around them AND the nestlings do not eat the ants.

During this entire time, the woodpeckers do not allow any other woodpeckers to eat the ants - acting as the ants' personal safety patrol. When the parents feed the nestlings, some of the leftover food is dropped and the ants are fed. How does evolution explain this relationship? How did this truce get started during nesting time? Who was the first woodpecker to lay its eggs in enemy territory? How do the nestlings know not to eat their favorite food? Here we see an ant-eating woodpecker laying eggs in an egg-eating ant nest with both living together but keeping their distance. This had to be designed from the beginning or it would not have worked. These animals do this from instinct. When we see an instinct, we know there must be an instinct Maker and He is God.

For the LORD gives wisdom; from his mouth come knowledge and understanding.
– Proverbs 2:6 (NIV)

AUG 8

Scientists in Australia decided to test the concept of slow gradual formation of fossils. Crocodiles were chosen because they are a common fossil found worldwide and often are articulated (bones aligned together) and complete.

Here is what they did:

1. Two dead carcasses were immediately buried in 8 inches (20 cm) of sand, simulating rapid burial.
2. Three carcasses were allowed to "bloat and float." Only after they sank, were they covered with 8 inches of sand, simulating delayed burial.
3. Three carcasses were not buried at all.

Here were the results:

All six of the crocodiles which were not initially buried, bloated and floated within 3-5 days and stayed afloat for 32 days. Their bones were scattered. One of the two buried crocodiles still floated to the top of the water and needed to be reburied.

Here are the obvious conclusions:

For a crocodile carcass to be preserved with the bones articulated, the crocodile had to be **buried rapidly and deeply**. Today's sediments accumulate slowly. But there was one event in history that would have had enough sediment to cover trillions of organisms rapidly and deeply. That catastrophic event would have been Noah's Flood recorded in the Bible.

When pride comes then comes disgrace, but with humility comes wisdom."
- Proverbs 11:2 (NIV)

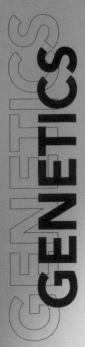

In many ways a living cell is like a complex machine made from many specifically designed parts. The most common chemical in any living cell is a protein. Each protein in a cell is made by lining up 20 smaller molecules, called amino acids. These are lined up in a specific order so that the protein will assume an exact 3-dimensional shape – not unlike the parts of any machine. The average protein is 400 amino acids long. **To randomly form the correct sequence to make even one correct protein (machine part) is essentially zero.** A typical cell has many thousands of different and specifically designed proteins (parts).

The probability of one of these 400 amino acid's long proteins randomly lining up in the correct order is once every 10^{250} tries (once in every 10 with 250 zeros times). It is estimated that there are only 10^{80} electrons in the entire universe. If the universe were 15 billion years old (10^{18} seconds), and every particle in the universe interacts with another a billion times per second (10^{12}), there still would only have been 10^{100} interactions (or chances) to make even one of the correct proteins needed for life!! Making even one of the one thousand proteins needed for even a single bacterium to form by natural evolutionary processes is the very definition of impossible. Statistical science confirms that the specific proteins needed for life would never happen via evolutionary processes. It had to be created by an all-knowing, intelligent mind. The One true God.

His wisdom is profound, his power is vast. Who has resisted him and come out unscathed?
- Job 9:4 (NIV)

AUG 10

The chemicals needed for life are very specific and only occur inside living cells. No scientist has ever found biologically useful proteins, enzymes, lipids, carbohydrates, polypeptides, or DNA fragments forming outside of a living cell. Chemicals which do form naturally are toxic to life, and therefore, not useful for forming life.

Whenever formation of life experiments are done in laboratories, the scientists start with purified chemicals which were formed by life. Thus, they are "cheating" by starting their experimentation from an invalid starting point; a starting point which would not have been present in a world without life. In spite of this "advantage," every experiment ever done by every researcher in every laboratory, after hundreds of years, thousands of attempts, and costing millions of dollars, has ALWAYS had the same result: **chemicals never come alive by themselves.** Science and experimentation clearly reveal the truth – life (and the chemicals required) had to have been created by an incredibly intelligent Designer.

"Be still, and know that I am God. I will be exalted among the nations, I will be exalted in the earth!" – Psalm 46:10 (ESV)

AUG 11

Did you realize that gorgeous green emeralds are reminders of the Flood of Noah's day? Emerald is the green variety of a mineral called beryl which comes from beryllium ore. Its mesmerizing green color is caused by two trace elements - chromium and vanadium. Forming this gem is quite a challenge, because the relatively rare ingredients are found in different types of rocks. Beryl is found in granites and black shale, while chromium and vanadium are found in volcanic basalts.

How do the beryllium, chromium, and vanadium meet? Hot water is the answer. Emeralds have been shown to form in the presence of water at temperatures between 400-650°F. Minerals were grounded up and dissolved in hot Flood waters and the three ingredients needed to make emeralds were transported, mixed, and ultimately compressed. WE DO NOT SEE THIS HAPPENING TODAY! **The Flood of Noah's day would have provided the perfect scenario for the formation of emeralds.** There would have been major earth movements throughout the Flood and LOTS of hot water. Concentrated beryllium would be near hot water, then brought into contact with chromium and vanadium from volcanic eruptions and 'voila,' an emerald is made. All as a result of the Flood.

Emerald deposits occur in very few places in the world. The Flood helps explain the rare combination of events that produced emeralds. That such beauty could come from such tragedy is a sign of God's grace. As you look at a beautiful emerald ring, know it is a souvenir from the Flood of Noah's day.

The mountains were covered as the waters surged above them more than 20 feet.
– Genesis 7:20 (CSB)

AUG 12

You may have seen intricately carved jade in the shape of Chinese dragons or beautiful pendents, but have you ever thought about how jade was formed? **When you look at jade you are seeing a souvenir from Noah's Flood.** Hard jade (jadeite) is valued as a beautiful gemstone because of its vibrant green color. Jadeite colors actually range from the most famous emerald green to white, mauves and blue. It is known by laboratory experiments that hard jade requires three conditions to form: heat between 480-1110°F, extreme pressure of 87,000-507,500 psi, and watery fluids. Forming jade requires unique conditions unlike anything on earth today. Jade deposit locations are actually adjacent to the earth's tectonic plate boundaries.

What event in history would provide these three conditions--heat, extreme stress, and watery fluids? The Flood of Noah's day! During the Flood, there were tectonic plate movements as entire continents slid to new positions. The sinking plates dragged down slivers of the continental sedimentary rocks. At great depths, heat and pressure changed the rock and released hot, salty fluids. These rising fluids crystalized into jadeite. **The Biblical Flood cataclysm provided just the right kind of rare, stressful conditions necessary to produce the beautiful jade gemstone.** When you see a beautiful sculpture from jade, know the gem was formed under unique conditions--the Flood of Noah's day.

...Where can I flee from your presence?...if I make my bed in the depths, you are there.
– Psalm 139:7,8 (NIV)

AUG 13

Scientists have long wondered why the bird-of-paradise flower has such an intense orange color. Even more intriguing are the orange seeds which maintain their brilliant color for decades. Plant pigments generally decay rapidly after cell death. After more than a year of study, researchers where stunned as they identified the source of the orange coloring. It came from bilirubin. Why the surprise? Because bilirubin is an animal pigment.

Bilirubin is a result of the breakdown of blood; plants do not have blood. **So, what's an "animal-only" pigment doing in plants?** Evolution cannot explain this. Evolution is not based on scientific observation of how new abilities developing from nothing; rather, it is a story trying to explain the existence of useful features without God. Did a plant evolve into an animal or did an animal evolve into a plant? Neither. No plant decides what chemicals to produce any more than a human being can decide to be short or tall. God designed the bird-of-paradise plant to have bilirubin, an animal pigment, so that it can have a vibrant orange color that can last for decades! No other answer adequately explains the source of its color.

Consider the lilies how they grow: they toil not, they spin not; and yet I say unto you, that Solomon in all his glory was not arrayed like one of these. - Luke 12:27

AUG 14

Have you ever wondered how your heart keeps beating? You have your own pacemaker, a cluster of specialized cells located on the upper right side of the heart. This cluster of cells, called the *sinoatrial node*, generates electrical impulses that stimulate the muscles in the upper chambers of the heart to contract, essentially saying *"beat."* The signal continues moving down to another cluster of cells above the lower chamber, which then fire, essentially saying *"beat."* The brain monitors the heart, directly controlling the heart rate and blood pressure. During a rigorous workout, your muscles need more oxygen, so the brain sends signals to increase the heart's beating rate. Simultaneously, the heart stimulates the adrenal glands to release adrenaline. Adrenaline keeps the heart rate up without further assistance from the brain. After the workout, the brain signals the adrenal glands to stop making adrenaline and the heart rate returns to normal.

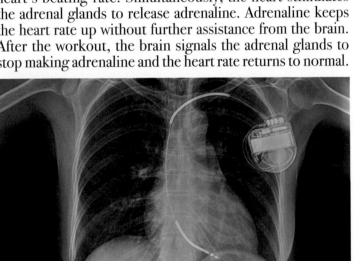

Scientists have created an artificial pacemaker. This implanted medical device helps the heart have a regular beat. Do we say that artificial pacemakers happen by accident and chance? No, years of development by engineers created the artificial pacemakers. It would be an insult to tell those engineers that their artificial pacemaker happened by accident and chance. Then why do we say our *natural* pacemaker happened by accident and chance mutations? The great engineer Himself, God, created our natural pacemaker so our heart could have a regular beat.

...the LORD that formed me from the womb *to be* his servant... my God shall be my strength.
– Isaiah 49:5 (KJV)

ANATOMY

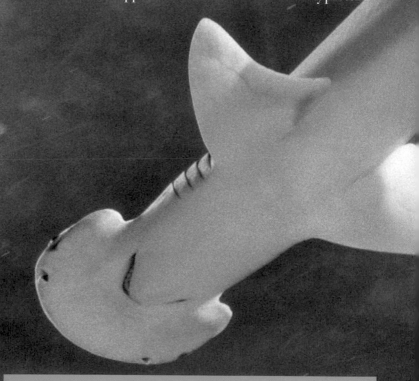

AUG 15

Shark! Beware! People tend to believe that all sharks are meat eaters. It was thought that the bonnethead shark, *Sphyrna tiburo*, was carnivorous too, until they analyzed its stomach. **Scientists found that bonnethead sharks primarily ate seagrass.** It made up over 60% of their total gut contents. Scientists thought there was no nutritional benefit for the shark from eating seagrass because the intestines were too short and there wasn't enough time to digest the fibrous plant material. For three weeks they fed the sharks 90% seagrass and 10% squid. **All the sharks gained weight**, and more than half the seagrass was being successfully digested. The scientists wrote an article entitled, "*Meet the world's first salad-eating shark*." Actually, the first salad eating shark was created about 6,000 years ago on Day 5 of Creation week. In fact, in the beginning all animals were vegetarians because the original perfect creation had no death. Since the Fall and the Flood, many animals started to supplement their diet with some meaty protein.

... to everything that creeps on the earth, in which *there is* life, *I have given* every <u>green herb</u> for food; and it was so. – Genesis 1:30 (NKJV)

AUG 16

Scientists have found a shark that glows! This 19-inch shark lives so deep in the ocean that little sunlight penetrates from above. This could be a problem, because deep in the dark ocean, a glowing shark could be seen by its prey long before it gets close enough to eat them. But this shark's lights act as an "invisibility cloak" because the velvet belly lantern shark has light emitting photophores only on its belly. **This glowing belly shark appears "invisible" to deeper fish that are looking up!**

This bioluminescent shark has a belly that glows so perfectly that it matches the light from above which hides its outline. In scientific words, the shark uses counter illumination – in simple terms, casts no shadow. The velvet belly lantern shark has ultra-sensitive eyes that measure the color and the intensity of the sunlight, allowing its belly to mimic the sunlight with similar flashes and sparkles. When its prey looks up, they see only unbroken sunlight. The shark's belly actually changes from moment to moment, matching the faint sunlight. **With this ability, the shark can either hide from its enemies or sneak up on lunch.** Do you think this glow in the dark shark happened by accident and chance? Not a chance. The imagination of God is endless!

Praise him for his mighty acts: praise him according to his excellent greatness.
– Psalm 150:2 (KJV)

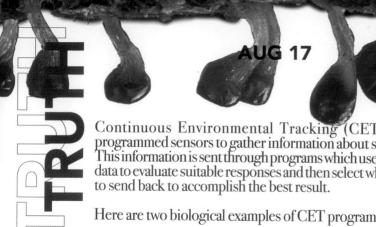

Continuous Environmental Tracking (CET) uses pre-programmed sensors to gather information about surroundings. This information is sent through programs which use the incoming data to evaluate suitable responses and then select which response to send back to accomplish the best result.

Here are two biological examples of CET programming:

1. Slime mold is a single-celled organism with no brain or nerve cells, yet it is in constant motion (up to 1.5 inches per hour.) While moving, it continually adapts to environmental changes. As a result, in the laboratory and real life, it is able to find the most nutritious foods, learn and remember undesirable foods or harmful chemicals (which can be ignored in the future), escape from traps, and move through mazes remembering the shortest routes! Slime mold has problem-solving programming equivalent to the computers running our railroads and communication networks!
2. Our individual immune cells are also programmed to react in similar ways. They store information about bacteria and viruses they have fought off in the past so they can eliminate them faster when encountering the same invaders in the future.

Some of what is "learned" is stored for future use and can even be passed on to future generations by changing their DNA programming! Slime molds can also pass information by "fusing" with one another. During fusing they lose their cell membranes while keeping their thousands of individual nuclei (where information and programming is stored) and can increase in size to over a cubic yard. Learned information is completely passed to all parts within about 3 hours of fusing.

All of this is in stark contrast to Darwin's theory of external forces molding passive organisms, which he called "survival of the fittest." When we see pre-programming, we know that an intelligent source (a creator) is required. Information (programming) can only arise from an intelligent mind.

Through thy precepts I get understanding: therefore I hate every false way.
- Psalm 119:104 (KJV)

AUG 18

Scotts Bluff National Monument in Scottsbluff, Nebraska testifies to the truth of the Bible. In 1923, the National Geological Survey sank a 6" diameter brass post into solid rock at the peak of this bluff. This post was level with the top of the rock surface in 1933, and in 2020 (87 years later), the top of the bluff had lost 14" of rock due to wind, rain, erosion, and weathering. Why is this significant? Because it proves that all of the Park's interpretive signs and their evolutionary interpretation of the area's geology could not possibly be true.

Interpretive signs in the park state that these rock formations have existed for 22 million years. Yet, the observed erosion rate of the bluff is 1.2 feet per 87 years, OR 0.01379 feet per year. The entire formation stands 800 feet above the valley, meaning that it will completely disappear in 58,000 years (800 feet)/(0.01379 feet/year) = 58,000 years). It is impossible for this formation to be millions of years old.

The evidence for the recent formation of the rock layers of the Earth is all around us. The Bible's timeframe is correct: these rock layers exist because they formed during Noah's Flood about 4,500 years ago and have been eroding ever since. The bluffs will not survive even 100,000 years at the present erosional rate. Scotts Bluff, and its observed erosion rate, testify to Biblical history being true.

Heaven and earth shall pass away, but my words shall not pass away. –Matthew 24:35 (KJV)

As you peer into the night sky, all the stars look very similar. Even looking through a telescope, the stars just seem like points of light. Yet, written thousands of years ago, the Bible stated that stars differ from one another. Is one star really different from another? Centuries after the Bible told us that this was the truth, modern astronomy has confirmed it.

Each star varies in:

- **Size:** dwarf, giant, super-giant
- **Color:** blue, white, yellow, orange, red
- **Temperature:** $5,800°F$ to $54,000°F$
- **Brightness or magnitude:** on a scale from 0 (bright) to 6 (dimmer)
- **Elements in a star:** hydrogen and helium are the most prominent, but stars also contain carbon, nitrogen, oxygen, neon, magnesium, silicon, sulfur, and iron in smaller amounts. Light coming from each star has its own unique color spectrum based on the elements present.

Each star also differs in mass, rotation rate, solar cycle, magnetic field, radius, and density. Here is yet another list, not exhaustive, of the many categories of stars:

- **Neutron star:** a minuscule 12 miles in diameter
- **Pulsar star:** a rapidly spinning neutron star that emits energy in pulses
- **Cepheid variable star:** a star that brightens and dims periodically
- **Binary star:** one star trapped orbiting another star
- **X-ray binary star:** emitting x-rays instead of light

Stars have so many variables that the probability of two stars being identical is essentially zero. It was not until telescopes were invented that the night skies revealed that no two stars are alike. Whenever the Bible speaks on science it is true!

"...for one star differs from another star in glory." - 1 Corinthians 15:41 (KJV)

AUG 20

There is an old saying that if you let a camel's nose in your tent, you'll soon find the entire camel inside. Camel's live in the desert and every drop of water is precious when living in a desert. When we breathe out, our exhaled air contains water vapor. Our human nose is short and relatively straight, but what about a camel's nose?

The camel's nose is long and filled with twisting passages. This design allows most of the water vapor from a camel's breath to stay inside its nose. But there is more to this nose! The camel's nose also acts as a heat exchanger. Those twisting passages are called turbanites and they are full of blood vessels. When a camel breathes in, the air cools the blood. This cooled blood then flows to the brain where it passes the incoming hot blood. The blood vessels are so intertwined that a heat exchange takes place. The hotter blood going to the brain is cooled to the right temperature. The camel now has a "cool head."

Do counter-current heat exchangers happen by accident and chance? Then why would we say that a camel's counter-current heat exchanger happened by mutations and chance. There had to be a counter-current heat exchanger maker and that Maker is God.

Don't let the "nose of evolutionary thinking" into the "tent of your mind." You may find yourself with the entire false evolutionary belief system taking over your "tent!"

Then they sat down to eat a meal. And as they raised their eyes and looked, behold, a caravan of Ishmaelites was coming from Gilead, with their camels bearing aromatic gum and balm and myrrh, on their way to bring them down to Egypt. - Genesis 37:25 (KJV)

ANATOMY

Nerve endings (nociceptors) which we have throughout our body are pain sensors. These nerve endings let us know when something is wrong in some part of our body. But **pain is not something that is "felt" by the sensor, it is an electrical signal interpreted by the brain**. When someone tells you that your symptoms are "all in your head," they are actually quite accurate.

- Have you ever noticed that when you have a splinter or something that really hurts the pain "goes away" if you get involved in another activity that "takes your mind" off the pain? Your brain can literally switch off a pain signal in order to concentrate on other more pressing matters!
- Another evidence that pain is actually a mind phenomenon is "phantom pain" experienced by people who lose limbs. They feel pain in an arm or leg which does not even exist anymore. The pain is in their brain, not the limb.
- Soldiers in the midst of battle often receive life threatening injuries but are so preoccupied by the urgency of the battle, that they do not even feel the pain until after the battle is over.

What a wonderful gift God has given us in the pain sensing system of our body. It alerts us to problems anywhere in our body, but we can continue to function even when pain is present by choosing to ignore pain if needed. What an awesome God we serve.

The night racks my bones, and the pain that gnaws me takes no rest. – Job 30:17 (ESV)

BIOLOGY

Have you ever thought of pain as a blessing? To answer that, we need to examine what living without pain would be like. We can do this by observing people with leprosy.

Leprosy is not a skin disease, but a deadly condition caused by a bacterium that attacks the nervous system. Leprosy bacillus destroys nerve endings that carry pain signals - resulting in the absence of feeling and pain. As a result, lepers constantly injure themselves. **People with leprosy can stick their hand into a flame without flinching.** Pain protects us. Many leprous patients have had their fingers eaten by rats in their sleep and did not even know it. If the people with leprosy had felt the pain, they would have stopped the rat. Pain tells us something is wrong. It tells us when to slow down or when we have done too much. Nothing sends us to the doctor faster than intense pain. If we never felt pain, we would rarely know something was wrong. Dr. Brand, who worked with lepers throughout his career has declared, *"I cannot think of a greater gift that I could give my leprosy patients than pain."* God in His wisdom has given us pain so we can be protected from greater harm.

There came a man full of leprosy. And when he saw Jesus, he fell on his face and begged him, "Lord, if you will, you can make me clean." And Jesus stretched out his hand and touched him, saying, "I will; be clean." And immediately the leprosy left him. – Luke 5:12,13 (KJV)

AUG 23

Hezekiah's tunnel, constructed underneath ancient Jerusalem, is so unbelievably well engineered that evolution-blinded archeologists can't believe it! Under the threat of siege, King Hezekiah completed one of the engineering marvels of the ancient world. This 1,750-foot (533 meter) tunnel is dug through the solid rock of a mountain. It starts at the Gihon Spring on the side of a cliff overlooking the Kidron Valley and was dug to the pool of Siloam. King Hezekiah needed to protect Jerusalem's only fresh water source from the advancing Assyrian army in the 8th century B.C. The project began with two teams digging from opposite ends and meeting in the middle. But this was no straight-line project: the tunnel was constructed in an S-shaped curve. **This was built 2,700 years ago before GPS and laser levels.** How the teams met together in the middle is still a mystery. Astoundingly, the elevation change from one end of the 1/3-mile-long tunnel to the other is only 12 inches (or a grade of 0.6%). Even more amazing is that the entire project took only two years to complete.

This amazing engineering feat was considered impossible and assumed to be a myth until the tunnel was discovered in 1867. That the people of this time had these capabilities is astonishing to archeologists. Radiometric dating places the tunnel in Hezekiah's time. Man has been intelligent from the beginning of time. One of the highlights for visitors to Jerusalem today is trekking through Hezekiah's Tunnel in ankle-deep water and marveling at ancient man's engineering skills.

"And when Hezekiah saw that Sennacherib had come and intended to fight against Jerusalem, he planned with his officers and his mighty men to stop the water of the springs that were outside the city; and they helped him. A great many people were gathered, and they stopped all the springs and the brook that flowed through the land, saying, "Why should the kings of Assyria come and find much water?"
- 2 Chronicles 32: 2-4 (ESV)

AUG 24

The Coconino sandstone at the Grand Canyon is famous. Sandstone is made when sand grains cement together. Evolutionary geologists say the Coconino sandstone was formed in a dry environment, the sand dune, while creation geologists say the Coconino sandstone was laid down by water during the Flood of Noah. Which explanation is correct? A team of scientists gathered four hundred samples throughout this famous rock layer and examined the sand grains under a microscope. They also visited modern desert sand dunes and collected samples of unconsolidated sand. The primary mineral in both was quartz. About 90% of the Coconino sand grains were quartz but **they also found another mineral, muscovite, which is never found in desert sand.** Muscovite is a type of mica and is extremely soft (2.5 on a scale of 10). That mica in the sand tells us something really grand.

Experiments were done. In the first one, mica rich sand (muscovite) was placed in a large jar with a propeller; causing the sand to move slowly - replicating a small migrating sand dune. Mica flakes are so fragile that after only four days they had completely disappeared! In a second experiment, water was added to a jar. After more than one year of slow agitation, the mica flakes were still visible. The two experiments confirmed that fragile mica grains are chewed up quickly in deserts, while in a watery environment, the water cushioned the collisions. **The presence of mica in the Grand Canyon's Coconino Sandstone tells us it was formed under the water.** That under-water event would have been Noah's Flood! When you visit the Grand Canyon and look at the Coconino Sandstone, be sure to say, *"Mica, mica in the sand, tell us something really grand!"* By studying and understanding the earth, we can know how the Grand Canyon was formed.

...have dominion...upon the earth.
– Genesis 1:28b (KJV)
[The Hebrew understanding of the word translated "dominion" was to study, understand, and control. We are to study, understand, and control the earth – this is science.]

AUG 25

Deserts cover one fifth of the earth's land surfaces, but only the Americas have cacti. The southwestern U.S. has more than 2,000 varieties of cactus. What design would you put into a desert plant for it to hold onto its water? Cacti open their tiny pores (stomata) to take in carbon dioxide during the night! This is opposite of most plants; they open their pores (stomata) during the daylight hours because this is when photosynthesis takes place and the carbon dioxide is needed at that time. If the cacti were to open their pores during the day, precious water would evaporate. Losing water is not good in the desert! **Cacti are designed so that during the night, stomata open up and carbon dioxide is collected and stored.** During the day, the stomata close and the previously stored carbon dioxide is used for photosynthesis. Cacti are an extremely unique plant that open their pores only at night.

The cacti have many other ingenious designs to help them survive in the desert:

- The main body of the cacti acts as a reservoir, storing water. The cacti can actually expand their diameter. Question: Can trees swell their trunks as they gather water, and then shrink their girth as they use the water? A mature saguaro can absorb 200 gallons from one rainstorm. Cacti are like sponges, so when it does rain, they collect as much water as possible!
- The outer part of the cactus is waxy. This helps retain the moisture.
- Pointy spines or "cactus needles" stop thirsty animals from getting a free drink.

Evolution teaches that cacti evolved these features over eons of time. **Yet thousands of specific programming changes would be needed to allow some sort of "pre-cactus" to survive in the desert.** What if stomata were open during the day, like other plants? *The cacti would most likely wither away and die.* What if it did not have the unusual feature of its stem expanding to hold water? *An extended dry spell would kill all the cacti.* What if there were no spines? *Animals would eat the cacti for their water.* These are just a few of the design issues that God had to think about so that cacti could survive and thrive in a harsh desert environment. Cacti show the handiwork of the Great Creator!

Can papyrus grow tall where there is no marsh? Can reeds thrive without water? - Job 8:11 (NIV)

AUG 26

The year was 1942, and six P-38 planes and two B-17 bombers left a secret U.S. Army Base in Greenland and headed for Britain to fight against Hitler. They flew directly into a blizzard; their only hope was to crash-land in southern Greenland. They landed successfully, but had to abandon their airplanes. In 1980, an airplane dealer told his friend about the lost squadron, *"All we'd have to do is shovel the snow off the wings, fill them with gas, crank them up and fly them off into the sunset. Nothing to it."*

When they arrived in Greenland, they could not find the airplanes. After diligently searching for a year, they found them 3 miles away from the original crash-landing spot because of glacial flow. **And they were 250 feet below the ice!** That is an amazing amount of ice covering the planes in less than 50 years! Most of Greenland receives less than 12 inches of snow per/year, however, southern Greenland receives much, much more. Why? Because the warm Gulf Stream flows nearby. The warm ocean waters evaporate and are blown onto the cold land, precipitating as snow, and lots of it!

Now imagine during the Flood, the fountains of the deep bursting open which brought great quantities of hot water and lava into the oceans. These warm oceans would have caused lots of evaporation and the moisture would have precipitated out onto cold land as snow in the upper latitudes and high mountains. Snow, miles deep, would have packed down over the subsequent centuries. The Lost Squadron in Greenland gives us just a glimpse of the fast build-up of snow and ice across the world during the Ice Age. The Ice Age would have been an unstoppable consequence immediately following the Flood of Noah.

Have you entered the storehouses of snow?
- Job 38:22 (NIV)

AUG 27

On July 14, 2015, after traveling for 9 ½ years, the NASA spacecraft New Horizons flew past Pluto. **The images stunned researchers: Pluto looked young!** Pluto had large mountains made of ice. One ice mountain range is 2.1 miles high; another range of ice is 1 mile high. With Pluto's frigid temperatures (-390°F), the ice is as hard as a rock, and for them to be thrust upward would require lots of energy. Yet according to the evolutionary time scale, Pluto should have been dead when this geological activity (mountains forming) took place.

NASA scientists have counted over 1,000 impact craters. Counting impact craters is one method to assign age, i.e., the more craters, the older the planet. Yet a huge heart-shaped area of Pluto, *Sputnick Planum*, **has NO impact craters AND is very smooth** - which indicates its very recent formation, i.e. recent geological activity.

Pluto's atmosphere is thin, but still extends 1,000 miles above the planet. It is 98% composed of nitrogen with small amounts of methane and carbon monoxide. When *New Horizons* passed Pluto and looked back to take a photo, the sun's light passed through the atmosphere, showing it to be *blue*. Because Pluto is small, its gravitational pull is low. This, coupled with the sun's ultraviolet light, allows its atmospheric nitrogen to escape at a rate of hundreds of tons each hour! There certainly should be *no blue skies unless this heavenly body was recently created.*

Pluto's high mountains, lack of impact craters, and blue atmosphere all proclaim it to be young.

You alone are the Lord; You have made heaven,
The heaven of heavens, with all their host.
- Nehemiah 9:6 (NKJV)

AUG 28

Pluto is not a planet anymore; it has now been downgraded to simply an object that orbits the sun beyond Neptune. This area of the solar system has much debris and Pluto is now a "Trans Neptunian Object" (TNO). The nebular hypothesis proposes that our solar system, and everything in it, was created by a rotating cloud of gas from the sun about 4.5 billion years ago. But **the characteristics of Pluto reveal that the nebular hypothesis cannot be true:**

- Pluto does not orbit on the same ecliptic or plane as the other planets but at an angle of $17°$.
- Pluto's spin is tilted so it points almost directly at the sun; it should be perpendicular to the plane.
- Pluto's orbit is highly elliptical. In fact at times, comes closer to the sun than Neptune. It should not do this if the nebular hypothesis is true.
- Pluto's moon Charon is covered with active volcanoes spewing out ammonia-rich water. If it were billions of years old, it should be cold and geologically dead.

Pluto teaches us that the nebular hypothesis is not true AND its moon shows it is young. Which leaves us with what the Bible has taught from the very beginning. God created the sun, moon, stars and planets fully formed on Day 4 of the creation week, a little over 6,000 years ago..

ASTRONOMY

"Heaven is my throne and the earth is my footstool…Has not my hand made all these things so they came into being?" declares the LORD. - Isaiah 66:1,2 (NIV)

AUG 29

If God intended no death prior to the Fall how do we explain the stingers on bees and wasps? **When a honeybee stings, the bee dies.** This happens because the stinger is plunged into the victim's flesh and as the bee flies away, the barb on the stinger causes the stinger to hold fast. Thus, the guts are literally ripped out of a bee! Did this happen before the Fall?

Due to genetic mapping, it is now acknowledged that female wasp stingers, and female honeybees' stingers, are actually modified ovipositors. An ovipositor is an insect organ used by females to deposit eggs on, or in, something. Between the male and female wasps, only female wasps sting, the same can be said for honeybees, only females have stingers. Today, the stingers of the cuckoo wasps (Chrysididae) still function as an ovipositor. What has happened since the Fall? There are two possibilities. In the beginning, stingers may have been made for a certain purpose, like an ovipositor, and then deteriorated after the Fall and are now being used as stingers. Or, God knew the Fall would happen with all its sin and death consequences. Therefore He "front-loaded" certain animals with "weapons" in a post-Fall world. In any case, God knew his creation would have to deal with sin's consequence and organisms would need weapons for protection.

For my thoughts *are* not your thoughts, neither *are* your ways my ways, saith the LORD.
– Isaiah 55:8 (KJV)

AUG 30

The explosion of knowledge in our lifetime is astounding. Consider American life in 1907:

- The average life expectancy was 47 years, many dieing from childhood deseases
- Only 14% of homes had bathtubs
- Only 8% of homes had telephones
- Most women washed their hair once a month with borax and egg yolks
- The top causes of death were influenzia, tuberculosis, and diarrhea
- The population of Las Vegas, NV was 45
- 6% of people graduated from high school

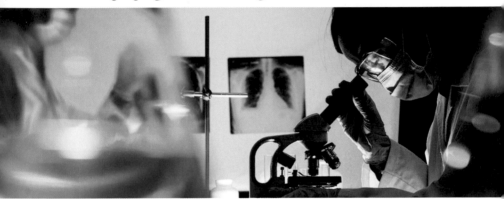

Modern science has truly revolutionized our world. But true science is doing exactly what God told us to do – taking "dominion" over creation. That means to study, understand, and control what God has made. Evolutionary science (molecules-to-man) is speculative and unproved with a goal to replace God as the creator. Evolution has actually impeded scientific progress, i.e. vestigial organs, junk DNA. As evolutionary biologist Jerry Coyne has stated, *"If truth be told, evolution hasn't yielded many practical or commercial benefits."* Let us do true science and reap the benefits.

And God said, Let us make man in our image, after our likeness: and let them have dominion over the fish of the sea, and over the fowl of the air, and over the cattle, and over all the earth, and over every creeping thing that creepeth upon the earth. – Genesis 1:26 (KJV)

AUG 31

Phew! What's that smell? It's a skunk! These nocturnal mammals of the western hemisphere are active at night. They are well designed for this:

- They have specially designed eyesight; You may notice that their eyes glow at night. In nocturnal animals, a mirror-like layer of tissue called the tapetum bounces the light back through the retina. In our eyes we do not have a tapetum and the light is just absorbed into the retina.
- Skunks have more rod cells than cone cells. Rod cells absorb very low-level light which help them see in the dark.
- Skunks are equipped with whiskers which touch and detect what and where they are walking.
- Their powerful nose is able to smell turtle eggs even if they are several inches below the surface.

But when you think "skunk," it is that awful smell that is remembered. This is their best protection. Skunks are not fast or big – making them an easy target. Owls have no trouble catching and eating them – because owls can't smell. The substance that protects skunks is sulfur containing n-buty mercaptian. But even this stinky stuff has found useful purposes.

- In the past, miners would use skunk oil to warn other miners. Skunk oil was poured into the air system during emergencies. One whiff of skunk oil and out came the miners.
- Skunk oil has a great clinging quality, so believe it or not, it was used as a perfume base, once the stinky stuff was removed. Personally, I wouldn't advertise my perfume as having a skunk base!

Skunks give a warning before firing the fog-like spray from a two-barrel gland in its rear. It first raises its tail, does a little dance while doing a handstand on its forefeet, and spreads its back legs. Then it fires. Note: You should not be watching this happen! A skunk can shoot 20 feet away and do it five to six times! If hit, old wives tales said bathe in tomato juice. It doesn't work, it just covers the smell. You want to neutralize the smell. Baking soda and hydrogen peroxide changes the composition of the skunk oil, thus removing the smell.

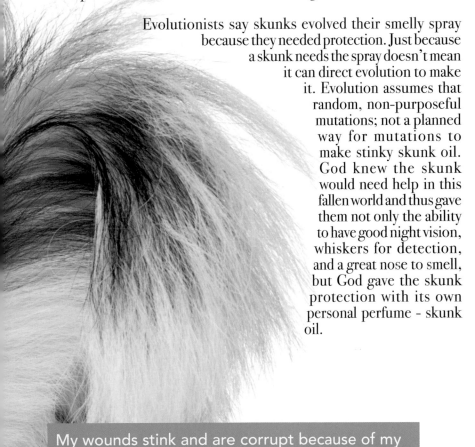

Evolutionists say skunks evolved their smelly spray because they needed protection. Just because a skunk needs the spray doesn't mean it can direct evolution to make it. Evolution assumes that random, non-purposeful mutations; not a planned way for mutations to make stinky skunk oil. God knew the skunk would need help in this fallen world and thus gave them not only the ability to have good night vision, whiskers for detection, and a great nose to smell, but God gave the skunk protection with its own personal perfume - skunk oil.

My wounds stink and are corrupt because of my foolishness. – Psalm 38:5 (KJV)

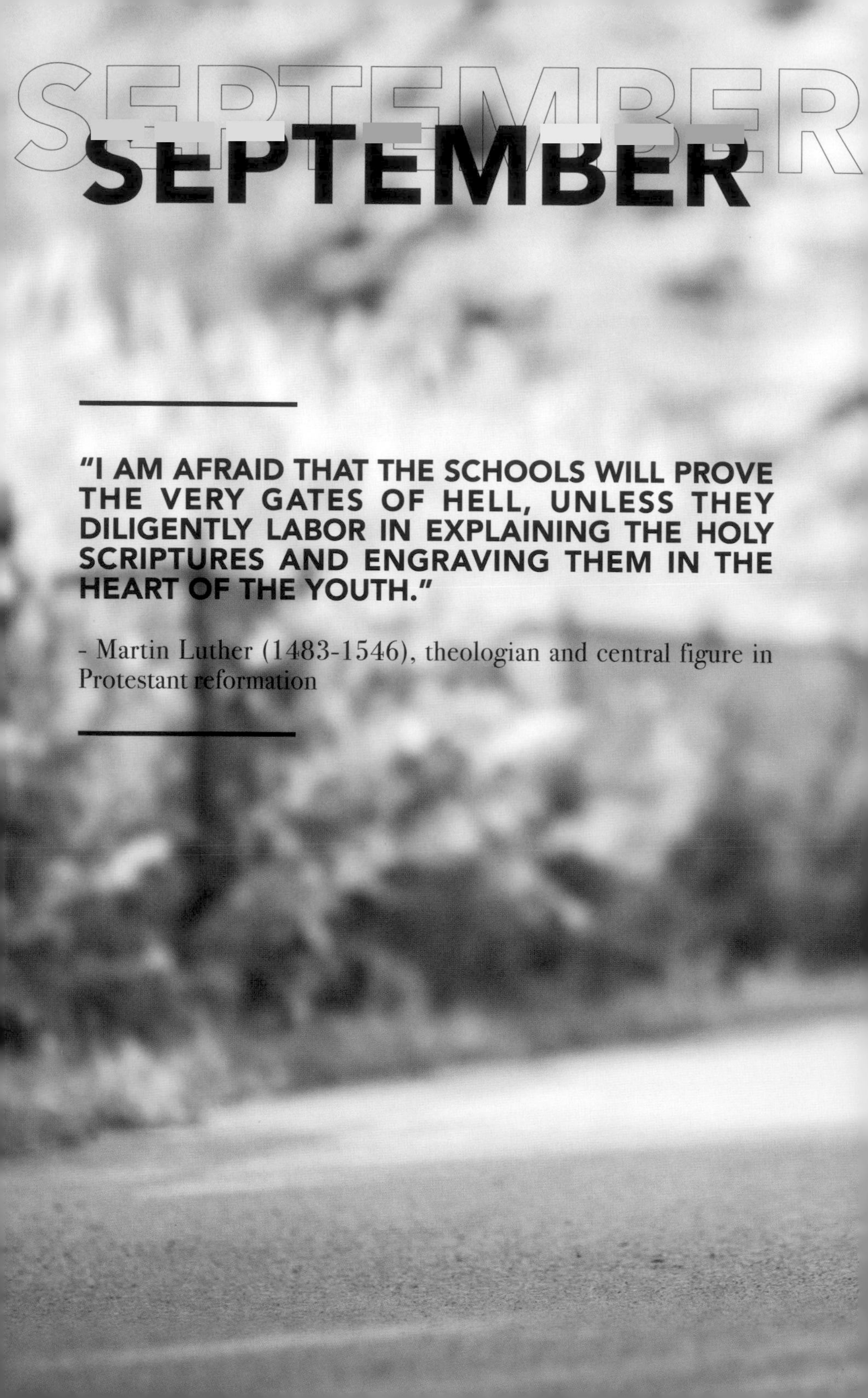

SEPTEMBER

SEPTEMBER

"I AM AFRAID THAT THE SCHOOLS WILL PROVE THE VERY GATES OF HELL, UNLESS THEY DILIGENTLY LABOR IN EXPLAINING THE HOLY SCRIPTURES AND ENGRAVING THEM IN THE HEART OF THE YOUTH."

- Martin Luther (1483-1546), theologian and central figure in Protestant reformation

---

The fear of the LORD is the beginning of knowledge: but fools despise wisdom and instruction.

– Proverbs 1:7 (KJV)

SEPTEMBER 1

Can you name the superhero that displays these powers:

- The ability to live for weeks in outer space with no oxygen.
- The ability to survive radiation 1,000 times greater than at the Earth's surface with no ill effect.
- He can't be crushed even when exposed to pressure six times greater than the Earth's deepest ocean.
- He can be boiled (+212°F) or frozen to near absolute zero (-460°F) without dying.
- The ability to be buried in a dry tomb for 100 years and when water is added come back to life!

It is not a Marvel™ superhero, but a tiny aquatic creature called the tardigrade. This tiny eight-legged, microscopic animal lives on moss around your house and eats algae. It looks like a little armored military tank, but its secret to" immortality" is the ability to totally shut down its metabolism while maintaining its cellular structure – indefinitely. So it can be boiled, frozen, crushed, dried, irradiated, and asphyxiated...yet come back to life centuries later!

The tardigrade had to have these abilities BEFORE it was exposed to these conditions. **If it did not have the ability to survive such extreme adversity <u>before</u> it was exposed to the conditions, it would not have survived.** Evolution cannot explain this animal's existence. God creates such marvels so we will KNOW He exists.

You do not even know what will happen tomorrow. What is your life? You are a mist that appears for a little while and then vanishes.
– James 4:14 (NIV)

SEPTEMBER 2

After spending twelve hours in shark infested waters, the five scuba divers scrambled onto a remote Indonesian island. Ocean currents had carried them 20 miles from their dive site - swimming to this remote island was their last chance of survival before being swept out into the open ocean. Exhausted, they crawled on shore, where **they faced another danger - the Komodo dragon.** This reptile can be 10 feet long and weigh 360 pounds. Komodo dragons have sharp, serrated teeth and investigate every new smell. They have been known to even kill and eat humans. Fortunately for the stranded and exhausted divers, throwing rocks and their weight belts at the dragon scared it away.

The castaways were rescued the next day.

This was a rare encounter, but it does give us a glimpse of life with dragons. There are many dragon legends of the past where people have fought them off or have been killed by them. Dragon is an ancient word for the extinct animal we know today only by its fossilized bones - the dinosaur. It was not until 1841 that the word, "dinosaur," was coined (meaning terrible lizard). **No one had heard the word, dinosaur, prior to that time.** Instead, people used the word, "dragon." Imagine a dinosaur in your region. People would likely have tried to avoid it, trap it, or kill it. People, whether in self-defense or for the thrill of hunting, would have killed off the dinosaurs. Who would want a life-threatening dragon/dinosaur living in their backyard?

Thou didst divide the sea by thy strength: thou brakest the heads of the dragons in the waters.
–Psalm 74:13 (KJV)

SEPTEMBER 3

Evolution by means of slow change over time contains a testable prediction: abundant transitional fossils should have resulted as organisms slowly morphed into a different type of animal. For example, a transitional fossil would be a part fish-like animal now able to walk on land. The geological column should have "simple" fossils at the bottom and more complex ones near the top with a slow transition from one to the next throughout the rock layers. The search for transitional fossils has been going on for about 170 years - ever since Darwin proposed his theory. The time has arrived. The test is finished. What have paleontologists found?

World famous evolutionary paleontologist, Stephen J. Gould stated, "*The absence of fossil evidence for intermediary stages between major transitions ... has been a persistent and nagging problem for gradualistic accounts of evolution.*" We have exposed millions of fossils, but the situation hasn't changed. Gould further stated, "*The extreme rarity of transitional forms in the fossil record persists as the trade secret of paleontology. The evolutionary trees that adorn our textbooks have data only at the tips and nodes of their branches...*"

Darwin wagered a prediction that abundant transitional fossils would eventually be found, thus proving evolution. He has lost his bet! **The fossil record clearly conflicts with the theory of gradual evolution**; there is a systematic absence of transitional fossils. What are often proposed as transitional fossils are just variations within a kind; the information was already present on the "parent's DNA." The fossil record reveals abrupt and major distinctions between very different body structures. So what's an evolutionist going to do to hang onto the belief in evolution? Gould and others have claimed that "punctuated evolution" has happened. In other words, animals changed so fast that we can't find any transitions in the fossil record. So now we have two opposing theories: one gradual and one rapid. This is not science but storytelling. The testable prediction of evolution, slow gradual change over time, has been proven wrong!

Woe to the multitude of many people, which make a noise like the noise of the seas; and to the rushing of nations, that make a rushing like the rushing of mighty waters!
- Isaiah 17:12 (KJV)

SEPTEMBER 4

The year was 1938, and a young museum curator was at a fish market on the east coast of South Africa. Surprise! What was that fish? She had never seen the likes of such! **She convinced the taxi driver to take the 127-pound blue fish into the back seat of his taxi.** At the museum, she couldn't find the fish in any of her reference books. She contacted others in the academic world, but no one could identify it. In desperation, she tried to get the county hospital morgue to refrigerate the fish, but they declined. She eventually had to have the fish preserved by taxidermy before it rotted.

A few months later, a museum curator arrived who was an expert on fish. He was stunned. **The entire academic world had been taught that the fish he was looking at had gone extinct 70 million years ago.** This was akin to finding a living dinosaur! The coelacanth was considered by evolutionists to be the bridge between fish and land animals. For generations, the textbooks listed the coelacanth as the creature which had evolved its fins into legs and crawled out of the ocean onto land. How could it still be alive? Now the search was on for where the fisherman had caught this fish. Coelacanths are deep-sea fish, usually living at depths of 500 to 800 feet. When scientists finally located a probable location, they went scuba diving. Surprise! The coelacanth wasn't walking on the ocean floor but using it fins to swim!

Evolutionists had misinterpreted EVERYTHING about the coelacanth based on a misinterpretation of the fossil record! The coelacanth was just a fish and there was not a hint of evolution. In fact, today we call coelacanths "living fossils"- creatures found in the fossil record that are still living today. As it says in the Bible, God created fish, fully formed, on Day 5 of creation week; He created mammals, fully formed, on Day 6 of creation week. Fish evolving into land animals? There is no evidence.

And when they heard that, they lifted up their voice to God with one accord, and said, Lord, thou art God, which hast made heaven, and earth, and the sea, and all that in them is.
– Acts 4:24 (KJV)

SEPTEMBER 5

Is there life on planets outside our solar system? Recently, about 4,000 extrasolar planets were examined to see if they were in the habitable zone or Goldilocks zone. Planets in the habitable zone need the distance to be "just right" from its star to have liquid water; if too close it would boil away, and if too far it would freeze. Also, the amount of UV light had to be "just right' to believe in life spontaneously appearing. If there was too much UV light the molecules would be sterilized.

After examining the 4,000 known exoplanets, only 49 were assessed to be in the habitable zone. Closer analysis revealed only 8 were possible, but 7 of the 8 were "gas giants" that would not support life. The only remaining planet was Kepler-452b discovered in 2015. This planet also has several problems – an unknown atmosphere, composition, and density. Scientists are now debating whether it might be a gas planet. One of the astrobiologists working on this research, Marcos Jusino-Maldonado wrote, "*It's getting harder to find origins of life. It seems very unlikely.*"

When we examine Earth, we find it is "just right" for life. It is a rocky planet with an atmosphere consisting of mostly nitrogen and oxygen. Pure oxygen would be very volatile. Our Sun is very stable, it is not a variable star. Earth is the perfect distance from the sun with a minor elliptical orbit. If it was wildly elliptical, we would have periods of freezing temperatures and boiling heat. Earth is a unique planet, with many more attributes which make it made "just right" for life; it's the Goldilocks principle. And who put this habitable zone together? Our Creator God!

> ... he who created the heavens, he is God; he who fashioned and made the earth, he founded it; he did not create it to be empty, but formed it to be inhabited-- he says: "I am the LORD, and there is no other." – Isaiah 45:18 (NIV)

SEPTEMBER 6

The tombs of ancient Egypt don't just contain dead bodies wrapped in ribbons of cloth; they have another mystery - human DNA. By sequencing this ancient Egyptian DNA, we can trace where the ancient Egyptians came from. So what do the mummies divulge about the origin of this early human civilization?

Recently sequenced DNA shows that Egyptians did NOT come out of Africa. Research found that mummies are genetically linked with people of the Fertile Crescent (Syria, Lebanon, Israel, Jordan, and Iraq) and the eastern population. This is consistent with the Bible, which states that early Egyptians were descended from Noah's grandson, Mizraim, who migrated in this direction from Mt. Ararat in Turkey, not Africa. DNA evidence discredits evolution.

It is an evolutionary dogma that all humans came from apelike creatures in Africa, so the DNA of the earliest advanced civilization, Egypt, should be closely related to other Africans. Yet the sequencing of ancient Egyptian DNA shows that they came from the northeast, which is a complete mystery to evolutionary thinking. Yet this is exactly what the Bible tells us. We can trust God's Word from the beginning. Science is finally catching up with God's truth!

Can you fathom the mystery of God? Can you probe the limits of the Almighty?
- Job 11:7 (NIV)

BIOLOGY

Your blood carries everything you need to stay alive. As an adult, your heart pumps five quarts of blood each minute throughout your circulatory system. The average human has about 60,000 miles of blood vessels - some as thick as a garden hose and others as thin as a thread. This tubing is like a superhighway connected to hundreds of thousands of smaller roads, all working together to help virtually every cell in your body. The blood travels from the heart through the blood vessels, which ultimately branch off into capillaries so small that blood cells have to travel single file. Here nutrients and oxygen are delivered, passing through the capillary walls. Meanwhile, carbon dioxide and waste leave the cell and are passed into the capillaries and return to the heart via veins. Your kidneys remove waste while the lungs expel the carbon dioxide.

Every cell depends upon this circulatory system for survival. Evolution believes that random mutations created all of this. Really? We would be long dead while waiting for this highway system for the blood to develop. When we see a human highway system, we know it had to have a plan and a builder. When we see a blood highway system, we know there must be a blood highway system maker, and that Maker is God."

For the life of every creature is its blood: its blood is its life. - Leviticus 17:1 (NIV)

SEPTEMBER 8

BIOLOGY

Can we grow new arteries, veins, and capillaries? Your circulatory system has three parts:

- Arteries bring nutrients and oxygen to our cells. They are bright red when oxygen rich.
- Veins return blood to the heart after dumping their load of waste to the kidneys and carbon dioxide to the lungs. Veins are closer to the skin and look blue because blood cells are dark red in veins when depleted of oxygen and appear to have a bluish tinge when viewed through the skin.
- Capillaries are the transition between the outgoing oxygen-rich blood and returning waste-filled blood. These very tiny blood vessels are as thin as a thread and red blood cells need to travel single file to pass through. It is in the capillaries that oxygen and nutrients leave the blood while carbon dioxide and cellular waste enters.

Generally, our body does not add new veins or arteries. However, **our body routinely grows more capillaries.** When you exercise, the muscles need more oxygen and food. So more capillaries are grown, allowing more oxygen and nutrients to be delivered to your muscles. That makes your body healthier.

This can be compared to a city building more roads. If all the traffic is not forced to travel on only a few roads but can travel different routes, the result is less congestion. When your body adds capillaries, you are "growing" more roads, resulting in less pressure and lowering your blood pressure. Capillaries are God-designed to be built as needed.

Son of man, mark out two roads for the sword of the king of Babylon to take… Make a signpost where the road branches off to the city.
– Ezekiel 21:19 (NIV)

SEPTEMBER 9

Have you ever thought what should be written on your tombstone? What would a man who has died twice put on his? In John chapter 11 we find the account of Lazarus who had died and had been in a tomb for four days. Jesus told the mourning crowd to move the stone away from the entrance to Lazarus' tomb.

" *'But LORD,' said Martha, the sister of the dead man, 'by this time there is a bad odor, for he has been there four days.'* "(v. 39).
The stone was rolled away, and Jesus called, "*Lazarus, Come out!*" (v. 43).

The dead man came out.

Lazarus, four days dead, was alive!

Following his resurrection, Lazarus fled to Cyprus to avoid the death threats by the religious leaders because so many Jews were coming to believe in Jesus (John 12:10). According to historical documents, Lazarus lived another 30 years on the island of Cyprus (dying at the age of 60.) On his tombstone in the church of St. Lazarus, is written "*Lazarus, Four Days Dead, Friend of Christ.*"

Death is powerful, and none escape its grip. But Jesus showed that He possessed the power to raise someone from the dead. God has that power to raise us from the dead. He has promised a bodily resurrection. Our bodies are a temple of the Holy Spirit (1 Corinthians 6:19) and will someday be transformed to a glorious body (Philippians 3:21). Our personalities, who we are, will be forever in eternity. We do not cease to exist at death. God wants you to be with Him in His glorious kingdom where there is no crying, pain, or sadness. All you need to do is "*believe in the Lord Jesus Christ and you will be saved.*" - Acts 16:31 (ESV)

Now when Jesus came, he found that Lazarus had already been in the tomb four days.
- John 11:17 (ESV)

SEPTEMBER 10

BOTANY

The mimosa, or sensitivity plant, is very unusual! **When touched, the leaflets close within seconds** and will reopen after about 30 minutes. Also, when night comes, the leaflets close and droop. In the morning, they reopen. If the leaflets are pinched hard, they fold more quickly, and even surrounding leaflets start to close. If the potted plant is dropped, the entire plant folds and droops, collapsing to a grey stick. The undersides of the leaflets are grey, while the top side is bright green. The mimosa is one of the few plants that folds upon touch. But why?

The mimosa is a low creeping shrub and very attractive to grazing animals. If any animal touches the plant and tries to eat it, it appears like a grey stick. Evolutionists believe that the plant evolved this ability so grazing animals would look for another plant to eat. If evolution were true, **why didn't other plants that are heavily eaten by grazers evolve the same ability?** Because the plant did not evolve this ability; it was created to do this from the beginning. The majesty of God is shown in His ingenuity in how to protect this plant from being devoured.

For the Lord Most High is awesome; He is a great King over all the earth. - Psalm 47:2 (NKJV)

SEPTEMBER 11

DESIGN

God could have made visible light as a single wavelength so that all light was white, instead of a blend of the seven colors of a rainbow (red, orange, yellow, green, blue, indigo and violet.) If He had done this, the entire universe would only be seen in shades of gray. The most common colors on Earth are blue and green.

Blue is common because of the expansive sky above us; it absorbs and reflects wavelengths in such a way that only the blue light is seen when looking skyward. Water also reflects the sky and often appears blue. If light was a single wavelength, the sky would be a dismal black. This is what photographs taken from the surface of the moon show. **But God chose the beauty of blue.**

Green exists primarily within plants, and plants are everywhere. Leaves are green because of the chlorophyll in the chloroplasts. Chloroplasts are incredible little factories that use sunlight to convert carbon dioxide and water to make every speck of food that ends up in every living creature, including us. Chlorophyll acts like a catalyst in this factory. **God placed beautiful green everywhere** we look! And **just for variety**, God threw in multicolored sunsets, flowers, animals, gemstones, and minerals for our enjoyment.

God could have made a drab gray universe, but He chose color. Why? Because creation reflects God's character and God is the ultimate in beauty.

He has made everything beautiful in its time. He has also set eternity in the human heart; yet no one can fathom what God has done from beginning to end.   - Ecclesiastes 3:11 (NIV)

SEPTEMBER 12

After a storm you may see a rainbow. When sunlight enters a raindrop, it is bent or refracted; this causes the raindrop to act like a prism. Longer wavelengths of light (red) are bent the least, while shorter wavelengths (violet) are bent the most. The bent light is reflected off the inside surface of the raindrop. To see a rainbow, the sun must be behind you and water droplets must be floating in the air.

The rainbow is mentioned in the Bible after the Flood of Noah's time; it is part of the covenantal promise made between God and all generations to **not destroy the earth a second time with a worldwide flood.** We also find the rainbow mentioned in Revelation as God is sitting on His throne, "and there was a rainbow around the throne, in appearance like an emerald" - Revelation 4:3b.

Every time we see a rainbow we should be reminded of God's righteous judgment of sin and God's undeserved grace and mercy: God's judgment when the Flood cleansed the earth of mankind's wickedness; God's mercy in saving eight people on the Ark. God has made a covenantal promise, as shown by the rainbow, that He will never destroy the world a second time with a worldwide flood.

"I set My rainbow in the cloud, and it shall be for the sign of the covenant between Me and the earth….; the waters shall never again become a flood to destroy all flesh"
- Genesis 9:13,15 (ESV)

SEPTEMBER 13

Siberian chipmunks live in northern Asia and eat everything from fruits to small birds. Predators of this chipmunk range from foxes to its deadly enemy - the snake. But this chipmunk has a unique way of protecting itself from snakes. It rubs its fur with the smell of snakes!

First, a Siberian chipmunk finds a dead snake carcass. Next, it cautiously approaches the dead snake, nibbling the head or tail region first. Once it is sure the snake is dead, the chipmunk applies the nibbled bits on its body fur. To do this, the chipmunk chews and then licks its fur repeatedly. The chipmunk is employing what scientists now call, "*snake scent application behavior.*" **They have even been known to apply a snake's half-solid urine to their fur.** When scientists set out dead frogs, birds, and lizard carcasses, they discovered that the chipmunks would only use the scent of dead snakes. Perhaps snake urine perfume would be a best-seller for humans afraid of snakes!

How does evolution explain this? Does a chipmunk know that if he smells like a snake, other snakes won't bother him? What chipmunk would approach a snake, its deadly enemy, to see if it were dead? Wow! God shows His creativity in how a chipmunk protects itself.

Satan disguises himself as an angel of light. Therefore it is not surprising if his servants also disguise themselves as servants of righteousness. – 2 Corinthians 11:14,15 (NKJV)

SEPTEMBER 14

How long does it take for volcanic ash to turn to stone? On January 12, 2020 the Philippine volcano, Taal, spread ash up to 60 miles away. After the eruption, it rained onto the freshly fallen ash. The ash absorbed the water to become a muddy mess and subsequently hardened into something resembling cement.

The type of rock typically made from volcanic ash is called tuff. Tuff has been used for building projects for thousands of years. Romans used it extensively and the people of Easter Island used tuff to make their Moai statues (large human faces). Geologists are typically taught that it takes thousands (to millions) of years for rock layers to form. In reality, it only takes the right conditions. After the Flood of Noah's day, rock layers could and did form quickly around the earth.

FLOOD GEOLOGY

Who is like the LORD our God, the One who sits enthroned on high, who stoops down to look on the heavens and the earth? - Psalm 113:5,6 (NIV)

TRUTH

SEPTEMBER 15

When a whale died off the coast of South Australia in 2001, its floating carcass became a tourist attraction. Authorities became worried when tourists started standing on the dead whale while sharks tore at the whale's flesh. The police bomb squad was called in to sink the whale. **They placed three explosives inside the dead whale's belly and blew a hole in the side of the whale.** The whale still refused to sink!

Observations like this show that whales and fish bloat and float when they die. Their bodies do not sink to the bottom and slowly turn into fossils. Instead, their bodies, bones and all, disappear as scavengers tear them apart. Even if parts of the fish sink to the bottom, crabs and bacteria devour the remainder. We do not see the bottoms of our lakes and oceans covered with dead animals on their way to becoming fossils. It takes special conditions to make a fossil, and the Flood of Noah's day would have provided them.

Noah's Flood would have covered billions of organisms very quickly and deeply. Then water would have percolated through the sedimentary layers picking up minerals and depositing them in the bones. That's how bones become fossils. Every continent has an abundance of fossils trapped within its sedimentary rock layers. Could the floating dead whale tourist attraction become a fossil? No, it takes special conditions, which the Flood of Noah's day provided.

You covered [the earth] with the deep as with a garment; The waters stood above the mountains.
– Psalm 104:6 (NKJV)

SEPTEMBER 16

The Philippine snout weevil is a small beetle that has rainbow-colored circles on its wing casings and thorax. These circular patches start with a blue center changing to yellow and then to red with all the colors of a rainbow represented. **The colors stay the same regardless of the angle from which the Philippine snout weevil is viewed.** This is because the colors are not produced by pigments, but by structure.

The circular patches are made from microscopic protein chitin "scales" and it is the three-dimensional size, structure, and volume of these scales which determine the color displayed. Smaller scales (with smaller crystals) reflect blue light, while the larger scales (with large crystals) reflect red light. The crystalline structure splits the sunlight like a prism, creating the rainbow of colors. If human engineers could copy this, they could apply it to paint and cosmetics. If this were possible, the hew of colors on a wall or cosmetics would remain the same regardless of the viewing angle and lighting. Human engineers have not even come close to achieving such true color fidelity. Nature's engineering has outdone human engineers. And Who is nature's Engineer? God Himself!

Our help is in the name of the LORD, who made heaven and earth. – Psalm 124:8 (KJV)

HISTORY

SEPTEMBER 17

I am often asked; How did kangaroos end up in Australia? They hopped! Remember, Noah took two of each kind of animal on the Ark. He would have taken two kangaroos. The Ark landed in the mountains of Ararat in present day Turkey and its inhabitants spread out. Until recently, evidence of kangaroos living in places other than Australia was not commonly known. However, ancient rock art (petroglyphs) of kangaroos have been found in India. Jinu Koshy, an archeologist from the University of Madras, found one of the biggest rock art complexes in India. These red ochre drawings included stick people and crude drawings of cow, deer, boar and what Koshy himself said looked like some kind of kangaroo. The rock art shows a kangaroo, including front limbs held aloft, a snout like a kangaroo, and a pouch.

There are narrow waters between Australia and Papua New Guinea (PNG) and during the peak of the Ice Age the sea levels would have dropped by hundreds of feet. The kangaroos would have crossed into Australia and PNG on land bridges. At the end of the Ice Age, the ice melted, poured into the ocean, and the sea level rose. When we put on our Biblical glasses, finding ancient rock art of kangaroos in India is not surprising!

Does this petroglyph from Ratnagiri depict a Kangaroo?

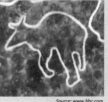 

Source: www.bbc.com   Source: www.wallpapermaiden.com

No one says, 'Where is God my Maker, who gives songs in the night, who teaches us more than he teaches the beasts of the earth and makes us wiser than the birds in the sky?'
- Job 35:10,11 (NIV)

SEPTEMBER 18

If we had a moon like Saturn's, nights with a full moon would be almost ten times brighter! Our moon has a reflectivity (or albedo) of just 12%. **Only a tiny amount of the sun's light hitting the moon is reflected to Earth at night.** Earth reflects 37% and Venus reflects 65%, while Saturn's moon Enceladus has an albedo of 99% (that's because it is covered in very reflective snow and ice).

The far side of Earth's moon's far side actually has more albedo (or reflectivity.) The far side is heavily cratered, with more than 200,000 craters, and with only 2% lunar plains. Of the moon's two sides, near and far, the near side is much less reflective. If the moon had a larger albedo, the nighttime glare would be very harsh. As it is, the moon's near side reflectivity is just right for us on earth; **the light is soft with the perfect amount of light for our needs.** It's the perfect night light; designed by God. So, take a moonlight walk and enjoy the soft light.

ASTRONOMY

Yours is the day, yours also the night; you have established the heavenly lights and the sun.
- Psalm 74:16 (ESV)

SEPTEMBER 19

On the small island nation of Palau is a lake where tourists go swimming with jellyfish! **But wait, you say,** *"Jellyfish live in ocean salt water."* There are actually about 200 known landlocked bodies of seawater, but only a few contain jellyfish. Jellyfish Lake on this South Pacific Island is the most famous.

This marine lake has indirect fissures connected to the ocean. There are millions of Golden jellyfish that thrive in this saltwater lake. This is the only place on earth to find Golden jellyfish. **But wait, you say,** *"Won't I get stung when swimming with these jellyfish?"* These particular jellyfish have stinging cells that are too small to be felt by humans. **But wait, you say,** *"Without effective stingers, how do these jellies get fed?"*

These jellies get their nutrition from the algae that live in them. In turn, the algae need sunlight for photosynthesis to take place so, every day millions of Golden jellyfish migrate across the lake following the sunlight. Golden jellyfish live in a symbiotic relationship with the algae. It is a win-win situation. The Golden jellyfish need the algae and the algae need the sunlight which the jellyfish seek out. Evolution has no adequate explaination for this relationship. The algae, living in the jellyfish would not exist if the jellyfish did not continually keep them in the sunlight. God created this relationship from the beginning. So, if you ever get a chance to swim among Golden jellyfish, marvel at not being stung as well as its symbiotic relationship with algae.

...he commanded our ancestors to teach their children...Then they would put their trust in God and would not forget his deeds but would keep his commands. – Psalm 78:5,7 (NIV)

SEPTEMBER 20

The box jellyfish, *Tripedalia cystophora*, of the Caribbean and Indo-Pacific Ocean, is known as a vicious predator! **This animal is made up of mostly water with no brain, yet it has 24 eyes!** Eight of these eyes are very much like a human eye with a lens, retina, iris, and cornea. But these eyes are only a tenth of a millimeter (1/250th of an inch) across.

Researchers were curious why a box jellyfish would need to see because most jellyfish just float along. They discovered that the box jellyfish used their eyes to keep focused on the mangrove tree canopy. By doing this, they could maintain their position near the mangrove tree root system and not be washed out to sea. They do this because their main food source is crustaceans and crustaceans are found in mangrove swamps. The jellyfish were able to see the mangrove canopy from 24 feet away. Evolutionists were **very surprised**, *"to find such a navigational system in an animal as basal as a jellyfish."* By *"basal,"* they mean a creature supposedly appearing early in the supposed evolutionary tree of life. Evolutionists continued with, *"**It is a surprise** that a jellyfish – an animal normally considered to be lacking both brain and advanced behavior - is able to perform visually guided navigation, which is not a trivial behavioral task."* **And surprised they should be** because evolution, with its belief in time and mutations, cannot explain how these complex eyes evolved in box jellyfish. Their 24 eyes to help navigate did not happen by accident and chance. The box jellyfish needed these eyes from the beginning in order to find their food. I hope you can "see" that eyes require an eye-maker. And the Maker of the 24-eye box jellyfish is our awesome God.

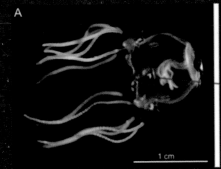

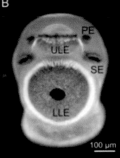

The lamp of the body is the eye. Therefore, when your eye is good, your whole body also is full of light. But when your eye is bad, your body also is full of darkness. – Luke 11:34 (NKJV)

SEPTEMBER 21

A botanist was visiting South Africa and noticed the Rat's Tail plant (*Babiana ringens*). Its long tubular red flowers were close to the ground. The scientist recalled that red tubular flowers are quite often pollinated by birds. This perked his curiosity, because birds dislike moving around near the ground where there is lots of foliage for predators to hide. So with binoculars in hand, he patiently observed the flowers. Sure enough, the "Malachite Sunbird" (*Nectarina femosa*) came for the nectar and picked up the flower's pollen; a bird was the flower's pollinator.

But what was the sunbird grasping? It was holding a spike growing close to the flower that looked like a rat's tail (hence the name of the plant.) Instead of walking around at ground level, where it could neither see predators nor fly away quickly, the sunbird perched on the Rat's Tail's spike. **The sunbird was able to reach the flower's nectar from above while perched on this rigid spike.** From this position, the Malachite sunbird could dip its long, down-curving beak directly into the flower and pollen was brushed all over its chest. When the botanist removed the spikes, the male sunbirds were far less likely to visit and pollinate those plants - resulting in half as many seeds being produced.

Evolutionists assume that the plant developed this special growth, the Rat's Tail, by some chance mutational mistake and it turned out to be useful as birds then came to visit and pollinate. This is simply storytelling. Very specific DNA instructions are needed to grow a perfectly formed and positioned spike. The Rat's Tail shows God's creativity for flower pollination. God gave the Rat's Tail a spike so a bird can perch, drink its nectar, and pollinate the flower.

The grass withers, the flower fades, But the word of our God stands forever. – Isaiah 40:8 (NKJV)

SEPTEMBER 22

Are dinosaurs still alive today? For more than 100 years, reports have been coming out of the Congo area in central Africa of a creature the natives call, *"Mokele Mbembe."* In November of 1980, **Science-80 Magazine** reported that *"in the swamp jungles of western Africa reports persist of an elephant-sized creature with smooth, brownish-gray skin, a long, flexible neck, a very long tail...and three clawed feet the size of frying pans...the animals feed on nutlike fruit of a riverbank plant and keep to the deep pools and subsurface caves of waters of this largely unexplored region...this creature, called 'Mokele Mbembe' by the natives, may actually be a dinosaur..."*

- The Likouala swamp region of the Congo is about the size of Arkansas. In 1981, Herman Regusters led explorers into Lake Tele and returned with footprint casts, droppings, and a sound recording unlike any known animal. On May 1, 1983, African biologist Marcellin Agnagna wrote a detailed report of seeing Mokele Mbembe in the shallow water of the remote Lake Tele.
- Pygmies tell explorers to look where there are not hippos or crocodiles. They report that the Mokele Mbembe fights with the hippos over the fruit of the molombo plants. According to these eyewitness reports, it kills with the blow of its tail, not the bite of its mouth. It is interesting that a tail would be a weapon. When we read Revelation 12: 4, we find the dragon [Satan] using his tail as a weapon.

A few explorers have since braved this swampy Congo jungle to search for proof of this creature's existence. So far, no additional proof has been found. If a dinosaur-like creature does exist, I do hope they find one before the last of them perishes. **God still has many discoveries waiting for us to find!**

... a dragon's tail...swept a third of the stars out of the sky and flung them to the earth.
– Rev. 12:3,4 (NIV)

SEPTEMBER 23

The word "dinosaur" is a fairly new word, coined by British scientist Sir Richard Owen in 1841. Prior to that time, these 'terrible lizards' were called by the ancient word, 'dragons.' **Stories abound across the world in ancient literature of dragon-like creatures:**

- Alexander the Great (356-323 BC) reported seeing dragons.
- Marco Polo (1254-1324 AD), during his travels in China, recorded seeing huge serpents that had short legs, claws, and large jaws with sharp teeth.
- The ancient historians Josephus (37-100 A.D.) and Herodotus (400s B.C.) wrote of winged serpents (pterosaurs).

Not only are there written accounts of dragons/dinosaurs, but **artifacts depicting dinosaurs have been found:**

- The ancient Mesopotamian Uruk civilization's cylinder seal reveals sauropods (long necked dinosaurs) in fighting position.
- The Egyptian artifact, the Narmer Palette, shows two men subduing two sauropods (long necked dinosaurs).
- The Ta Prohm temple in Cambodia (1100s A.D.) has a bas relief showing a stegosaurus. This was carved 800 years before scientists discovered fossils of stegosaurus.
- These are but a few examples of ancient artifacts showing dinosaurs/dragons.

Did man and dinosaurs live together? Ancient literature and artifacts have been found from around the world saying, "Yes!" Man saw dinosaurs in the past! They were created on Day 6 of creation week.

Now war arose in heaven, Michael and his angels fighting against the dragon. And the dragon and his angels fought back, - Revelation 12:7 (ESV)

SEPTEMBER 24

If God took a rib out of Adam to make Eve, is Adam missing a rib? As it turns out, rib bones are amazingly unique - they can grow back! If I cut my finger off, it will not grow back. In fact, there are no other bones in your body that can grow back – except your ribs.

Bones can repair themselves by adding more bone tissue around a break, but only a rib bone can regenerate an entirely new bone. There is a covering on the outside of rib bones called the periosteum. If surgeons need bone tissue to reconstruct part of our missing skeleton, they remove part of a rib for use in a bone graft but leave the periosteum. It is like taking a banana out of its peel while leaving the peel intact. As long as this membrane, the periosteum, remains, the osteoblasts inside can rebuild an entire new rib bone. Is Adam missing a rib bone? No. **God used the only bone in Adam's body capable of regenerating itself to form the body of Eve.** God knew exactly what He was doing, and science is just now confirming this amazing fact.

And the rib, which the LORD God had taken from man, made he a woman, and brought her unto the man. – Genesis 2:22 (KJV)

very lowBOTANY

SEPTEMBER 25

Is it a bee or an orchid? It's a bee orchid! This amazing flower looks like a female bee, smells like a female bee, and blooms several weeks before female bees appear each spring. Male bees emerge first and are lured to the orchid because of its scent and appearance. **So what is a male bee to do?** He tries to mate with the bee orchid!

In the process, he is dusted with pollen which the male bee deposits as it flies to another bee orchid. Evolution says the bee orchid design happened by accident and chance; that it gradually transformed itself into a flower that looks like a bee. **How does a plant which has no eyes know what a bee looks like?** How does a plant which has no nose know what a female bee smells like? Even if the plant could see and smell, how could it restructure itself to fool a male bee into

pollinating it? The bee orchid was designed to look like a female bee from the beginning or there would "bee" no bee orchids.

Consider the lilies of the field, how they grow; they toil not, neither do they spin: And yet I say unto you, That even Solomon in all his glory was not arrayed like one of these.
– Matthew 6:28b,29 (KJV)

SEPTEMBER 26

Greenhood Orchids are found in Australian forests. **This orchid emits the exotic smell of a female fungus gnat.** So of course, male fungus gnats swarm to the flower to find the good smelling girls. The male gnats land on the flower's lip. As soon as this happens, the hinged lip snaps shut, imprisoning the gnat within the flower. But all is not lost; there is a light shining...is that the exit? As the gnat crawls toward the light, he has to squeeze through a narrow tunnel lined with hairs. The first part of the tunnel has sticky liquid and some of it gets glued to his body. The second part of the tunnel has pollen which sticks to the glue. Now the gnat exits with pollen glued to its body. The orchid does not reset its lip for about an hour. This ensures that the gnat will not revisit the same flower and self-pollinate the flower. Cross-pollination makes the strongest seeds. Now the male gnat flies off...smells what he thinks is another exotic female gnat...lands on another flower's lip...another hinged lip suddenly snaps shut...the imprisoned gnat sees another exit light... crawls through another narrow tunnel...and this time, voila!!!!...the pollen on his back is removed, thus pollinating the second orchid.

What a complex system. How could all these components just "happen" by random changes and chance occurrences over time? How does an orchid, with no brain, evolve the perfect smell of a female insect? How would the orchid evolve a narrow tunnel with a light at the end? How did it evolve the glue to be positioned first and then the pollen? How did the orchid know how to reset itself, thereby avoiding self-pollination? Accident and chance? Not a chance! Perfectly designed, YES! If there is a design, there must be a Designer, and He is Jesus.

The LORD is exalted, for he dwells on high...He will be the sure foundation for your times, a rich store of salvation and wisdom and knowledge... - Isaiah 33:5,6 (NIV)

SEPTEMBER 27

Whenever astronomers find a planet circling a star where water may exist, or NASA finds water on one of the planets or moons in our solar system... it is stated as a fact that, *"life could form"* in that location. These types of statements are religious beliefs, not science. They are actually refuted by scientific observation. For instance, life has never been seen to form in any body of water all by itself - whether in oceans, lakes, ponds, swamps, laboratories, or kitchen sinks. Yet this idea of life popping into existence all over the universe is implied by textbooks, widely promoted by museums, and is the basis for the myriad of alien movies that are watched by billions of people.

Teaching students that life can appear any time water is present is analogous to telling students that because iron ore is found in a rock layer, given enough time, an automobile could appear all by itself. **We all have water in our kitchen sinks, but new forms of life are not in the process of forming there.** Brilliant scientists, spending billions of dollars over decades of effort in well-equipped laboratories around the globe, have never succeeded in bringing chemicals to life. It just NEVER happens! We all know the truth – life only exists because God made it. So don't look in your kitchen sink for the source of life. Look up to God.

You created all of them by your Spirit, and you give new life to the earth. – Psalm 104:30 (CEV)

SEPTEMBER 28

Radiometric dating is used for igneous and metamorphic rocks. As the radioactive parent element in these rocks decay into a daughter element (via a process called radioactive decay), the amount of each is assumed to reveal the age of the rock. Radiometric dating has three basic assumptions:

1. The rock starts with known quantities or ratios of the parent to daughter.
2. The decay rate is known and has not changed.
3. It is in a closed system; no leaching or contamination takes place.

Several common methods include unstable isotopes of potassium decaying to argon; rubidium decaying to strontium; and uranium decaying to lead. It is assumed to be accurate for rocks formed deep within the earth, but the assumptions cannot be proven and it often gives widely varying dates for the same rock. Researchers literally "shop" for the results they are looking for - rejecting any which disagree with their assumptions as "discordant" dates.

Methods used to date the earth at billions of years have serious problems. However, the Bible provides a fool-proof way of determining the age of the earth – an eye witness account. God's Word testifies to the earth having been supernaturally created thousands, not million or billions, of years ago.

Listen to me, you who pursue righteousness, you who seek the LORD: look to the rock from which you were hewn, and to the quarry from which you were dug. - Isaiah 51:1 (ESV)

It is commonly taught that fossils are evidence of slow processes over millions of years. Many interesting fossils have been found which refute this idea:

- Fish have been found in the midst of eating another fish. The fossil fish is halfway through swallowing another fish and did not have time to finish swallowing before it was **frozen in time**.
- Two froghopper insects in the process of mating. This act was also **frozen in time**.
- An exquisitely preserved fossil of an extinct marine reptile called an ichthyosaur. The mother ichthyosaur has almost completed giving birth to a live infant. Only the young infant's beak is still inside the mother's birth canal. The mother did not have time to finish giving birth before they were covered rapidly and **frozen in time**. It would be hard to believe that the mother would lay at the bottom of the ocean giving birth over thousands of years as she was slowly covered with sediments.

These fossils give scientific evidence that sediments quickly covered them. Finding fossils where animals are **frozen in time** is exactly what we would expect to find as a result of the worldwide Genesis Flood which happened approximately 4,500 years ago.

The earth trembled and quaked, and the foundations of the mountains shook; they trembled because he was angry.
– Psalm 18:7 (NIV)

SEPTEMBER 30

Have you considered that unicorns are mentioned in the Bible? Today's depictions of unicorns involve fantasy stories filled with flying, white, one-horned horses. Is that the unicorn that is mentioned in the King James Version of the Bible? Interestingly, the King James Bible, translated in 1611, used the word "unicorn" nine times, but it was likely referring to the rhinoceros, not some mystical white flying horse. Here is some evidence:

1. In Webster's 1828 dictionary, the first edition, there is no mention of an imaginary animal or horse-like animal in its definition of unicorn. At this time, the word unicorn was defined as: "*An animal with one horn; the monoceros. The name is often applied to the rhinoceros.*"
2. An ancient obelisk found in Nineveh shows a large single-horned creature. It looks like the giant (and now extinct) one-horned rhinoceros called the *elasmotherium*.
3. Marco Polo's description of unicorns in Sumatra sound like a rhinoceros:
   "*They have wild elephants and plenty of unicorns, which are scarcely smaller than elephants. They have the hair of a buffalo and feet like an elephant. They have a single large black horn in the middle of the forehead... They are very ugly brutes to look at.*"
4. Even today the one-horned Indian Rhino is classified as Rhinoceros *unicornis*.

Newer Bible translations use the term "wild ox" instead of rhinoceros. But rhinoceros would be a better fit and here's why. Rhinos have great strength (Numbers 23:22, 24:8). They are not suitable to use for plowing a field (Job 39:9-10). The young rhinos can skip about (Psalm 29:6). They can have either one horn (Psalm 92:10) or two horns (Deut. 33:17). Can Christians believe in unicorns? Yes, they were likely an ancient name for the one-horned rhinoceros.

God brought them out of Egypt; he hath as it were the strength of an unicorn.
– Numbers 23:22 (KJV)

OCTOBER

"A BIBLE WHICH IS FALLING APART IS USUALLY OWNED BY SOMEONE WHO ISN'T."

- Charles Spurgeon (1834-1892), Influential Christian Leader known as 'The Prince of Preachers'

All Scripture is God-breathed and is useful for teaching, rebuking, correcting and training in righteousness.

– 2 Timothy 14:16 (NIV)

OCTOBER 1

As summer comes to an end, deciduous trees start preparing for winter. The trigger which starts this process is the decrease in the amount of sunlight each day. A secondary factor is increasingly cooler temperatures. As the sunlight decreases, an abscission layer starts forming between the stem and the

branch. The flow of water to the leaf and the flow of sugar out of the slows down. Due to this decrease in water availability, chlorophyll (which causes the leaves to be green) fades away. This allows the hidden colors to show - orange or yellow. Red leaves are formed by sugar that the leaf makes but cannot get out due to the abscission layer cutting off the flow of fluids out of the leaves.

God could have made all deciduous trees turn from green leaves to brown leaves; there is no purpose for the reds, yellows or oranges, other than beauty. Why did He not make the tree leaves just wither away into drabness? Our Creator is a God who loves beauty. **Maybe God made autumn leaves beautiful just for our sheer enjoyment.** As you look at this autumn's cacophony of colors – the reds, yellows, and oranges - enjoy the beauty that God has created.

...perfect in beauty, God shines forth.
– Psalm 50:2 (NIV)

How do trees survive a bone-chilling winter? Trees are half water, and in the winter water freezes and expands. What keeps trees from bursting like frozen water pipes? Scientists have discovered two important ways in which tree cells are protected.

First, as the autumn cooling process sets in, the living cells of a tree become more pliable which allows most of the water in the cells to move into the spaces between the cells.

Second, this removal of water from within the cell concentrates the cell's sugars. This sweetened water inside each cell acts like antifreeze, lowering the freezing point to keep the cell

BOTANY

from freezing, expanding, and exploding. The water outside the cell is not sweetened and does freeze; however, these ice crystals do not puncture the pliable cell membranes.

Evolution does not explain how this came about! If it did not work the first time, we would have dead trees all over the forest with "frozen water pipes." **God designed the trees to survive and thrive in bone-chilling winters.** Don't we have a cool God!

You are my strength...my refuge... my protector.
–Psalm 31:3,4 (ABE)

OCTOBER 3

How did the English Channel form? After the Flood of Noah's day, there was the one and only Ice Age. During this time, France and England were connected by a chalk ridge over 20 miles long and 330 feet high between Dover, England and Calais, France. This ridge held back the melted water of a huge Ice Age lake which stretched across the present-day North Sea basin. The lake was dammed to the north by ice and the south by the chalk ridge. At some point during the Ice Age, water overflowed the chalk dam causing it to be breached. **As enormous amounts of flood waters poured out of this Ice Age lake, the English Channel** was rapidly eroded - leaving the famous White Cliffs of Dover. Researchers have found evidence of seven plunge holes underwater in the English Channel, all made by waterfalls. These enormous holes are over a mile wide and 300 feet deep in a straight line between Britain and France. The channel also contains 36 tear-drop shaped islands – a shape that only forms during energetic water flow.

Evolutionary geologists are rethinking their uniformitarian idea that all geological formations resulted from slow and gradual processes. More and more **evidence is being "uncovered" of regional mega-floods which followed the worldwide Flood of Noah** and continued to form the earth's

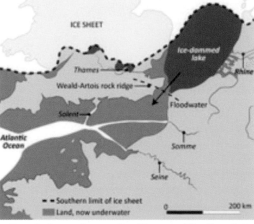

NEED FULL RES OF THIS IMAGE

topography. Other mega-floods have been the Bonneville flood in Utah, the Missoula flood in the Channeled Scablands in Eastern Washington, the mega-flood of Lake Agassiz in North America and many more oversized canyons located around the world. These interesting land forms resulted from mega-floods just after the Ice Age.

if you transgress the covenant of the LORD your God... you shall perish quickly...
- Joshua 23:16 (ESV)

OCTOBER 4

"Nobody needs their appendix," said the doctor, *"it serves no purpose."* Once labeled as a useless left-over from our purported evolutionary past, new information is emerging showing the importance of the appendix. Inside our large intestine are trillions of "good" bacteria that help us function. The large intestine is coated with "good bacteria" which prevents "bad bacteria" from penetrating the intestinal walls and the body tissues. Diarrhea clears this protective barrier from the intestinal lining. When that happens, the appendix, which stores extra "good bacteria" in a safe place, restores them into the large intestines.

Prolonged use of antibiotics is another way our "good bacteria" is removed, allowing bad bacteria to take over. *Clostridium difficile* (*C. diff*) is a common type of harmful bacteria. When the appendix is not available to restore the good bacteria, *C. diff* can cause a nasty sickness – even resulting in death. One study indicated that people whose appendix had been removed were four times more likely to suffer a recurrence of *C. diff*. Researchers have also found an increase of various gastro-intestinal cancers among those who do not have an appendix.

The appendix is an integral part of our immune system, and the idea that it is a left-over from an imaginary evolutionary past, should be discarded. Ideas have consequences, and this evolutionary idea has been very harmful to patients who had their appendix needlessly removed.

Large Intestine

Small Intestine

APPENDIX

ANATOMY

There is a way that seems right to a man, but its end is the way to death. – Proverbs 14:12 (ESV)

OCTOBER 5

BIOLOGY

What do reindeer really see in the twilight Arctic landscape? During long Arctic winters, the ground is covered with snow and the sun is very low on the horizon. What little light there is scatters, resulting in the majority of light being in the blue or ultraviolet (UV light) wavelength. Also, snow can reflect up to 90% of the UV light that falls on it. This reflected UV light is what causes a temporary but painful condition of snow blindness in humans. But for reindeer, seeing in the UV range is lifesaving. Researchers tested reindeer and found they could see beyond humans into the UV light wavelength. Curious to see what a reindeer saw, researchers used cameras that picked up UV light. Lichen, fur, and urine all absorb UV light. Lichen, a reindeer's major source of food in winter, appeared black, contrasting strongly with the white snow. Fur of animals, such as the predator wolf, was black and very easy to see. Urine was easy to see, allowing the reindeer to know if a predator or competitor was near. Thus, reindeer could easily see the things most important for their survival.

Evolution cannot adequately explain how a mammal can see in the UV range. How many reindeer would have been killed by not seeing a wolf? And what about the reindeer's source of food; they would have missed lots of lichen without UV vision. And then there is the snow blindness. Would they have been able to see at all? From the beginning, reindeer needed this super-vision to survive and thrive in one of the least hospitable climates in the world.

Take notice, you senseless ones among the peoples; you fools, when will you become wise?...Does not he who formed the eye see?
- Psalm 94:8-9 (NIV)

OCTOBER 6

Dr. Glen Jeffery became increasingly curious about the bags of reindeer eyeballs that were being sent to him. Some of the eyes were golden, while others were a deep blue color. He realized that reindeer killed in the summer had a golden reflection coming from the back of the eyeball, while those killed in the winter had a deep blue reflection. Arctic reindeer live in an extreme environment; winters are dark with the sun never rising on the shortest day of the year, while summers have almost 24 hours of sunlight. It took Dr. Jeffery and other researchers 12 years to discover how and why reindeer change their eye color from golden to deep blue as the seasons change.

In the back of the eye is a tapetum lucidum; which reflects light back into the eye for a second time. We see this in animals such as cats or deer; their eyes "glow" at night when a light is shined in their direction. Reindeer eyes have this tapetum lucidum, but theirs actually change the eye color. How does a reindeer change its eye color from gold to blue? In the dark Arctic winters, a reindeer's eyes need to be fully dilated to allow in as much light as possible. This puts pressure on the eye, which affects the spacing between the collagen fibers in the tapetum lucidum, causing the fibers to push together. The result, eye color changes from gold to deep blue. This shift to blue increases the scattering of reflected light, which activates more photoreceptors in the eye, giving the reindeer the ability to see in dim light. Then in the Arctic summer, with up to 24 hours of sunlight daily, the eye color changes back to a golden color. The ingenuity of God is amazing!

For who has known the mind of the LORD
- Romans 11:34 (NIV)

OCTOBER 7

A freshman at Eagle Rock Junior High School won first prize at the Greater Idaho Falls Science Fair. His project was to discover how many people would ban a "dangerous" chemical if only given partial (but accurate) information about its characteristics. They were asked to sign a petition demanding strict control of dihydrogen monoxide. Here are the student's reasons for eliminating this harmful chemical from our world:

- It kills thousands each year by accidental inhalation.
- It can cause severe burns in the gaseous state.
- It is so caustic that it accelerates the rusting of metals.
- It contributes to erosion.
- It has been found in the tumors of terminal cancer patients.
- If a person is dependent on this chemical, complete withdrawal results in death.

Forty-three out of fifty people signed the petition to eliminate this chemical, six were undecided and one knew the chemical in question. Dihydrogen monoxide is water or H_2O. The title of his science fair project was, *"How Gullible Are We?"* The vast majority of people, from everyday people to scientists, accept evolution because they are given only partial information and hear the word, "evolution," over and over again. The mechanisms of evolution (random mutations and natural selection) have never created life, transformed one creature into a completely different creature, or produced the information content of DNA. Evolution has been proven unscientific. As one evolutionary paleologist stated, *"Can you tell me one thing you know about evolution that is true, any one thing, any one thing that is true?"*[1]

Evolution directly contradicts the statements of the Bible and flies in the face of science and reality. How gullible are we?

See to it that no one takes you captive by philosophy and empty deceit, according to human tradition, according to the elemental spirits of the world, and not according to Christ.
- Colossians 2:8 (NIV)

OCTOBER 8

Micha L Rieser

Woolly bear caterpillars begin with the Isabella tiger moth laying eggs on plant leaves. The eggs hatch and the woolly caterpillar devours the plant's leaves. In warm climates, the woolly bear will feed for a couple of weeks before hiding in cracks, crevices, or under loose objects. **In cold climates, the woolly bear will winter over and nearly freeze solid.** The woolly bear produces a chemical (cryoprotectant) that acts like an anti-freeze and protects the organs and body tissues from being damaged from freezing. Once spring arrives, the woolly bear thaws out and soon spins a cocoon and pupates - emerging as an adult Isabella Tiger Moth. Woolly bears found in the Artic can live up to 14 years before being ready to make a cocoon. While in the cocoon, the wolly bear transforms itself. Virtually everything is reworked.

- How does a caterpillar make a cocoon and dissolve itself into a jelly and come out as a moth?
- How can a caterpillar with brown and red hair change into a moth with tan wings?
- If evolution were true, how would a caterpillar mutate both the ability and the desire to go from crawling with legs to flying with wings?
- Could genetic mistakes rework virtually everything in order to go from an egg to caterpillar to caterpillar soup inside the cocoon to a moth?

Remember, it is the moth that makes the babies, not the caterpillar. Woolly bear caterpillars and their metamorphism cry out design. **The woolly bear caterpillar life cycle had to work all at once** or it would not have happened at all. God has chosen a unique way for moths to develop and declare His glory.

Andy Reago & Chrissy McClarren

Be thou exalted, O God, above the heavens: and thy glory above all the earth; - Psalm 108:5 (KJV)

OCTOBER 9

One of the leading researchers in the area of unfossilized dinosaur tissue is microscopist Mark Armitage. Mark set up and ran the microscopy laboratory at the California State University Northridge (Los Ángeles, CA) from 2010 - 2013 with stellar performance reviews. Yet he was fired within a week of sharing with students the implications of his published paper on soft tissue inside of a fossilized triceratops horn. A lawsuit forced the university to settle on this blatant religious discrimination, allowing Mark to continue his work on unfossilized dinosaur tissue outside of the university. He has subsequently made the following discoveries:

- Upon fracturing a Triceratops horn bone, soft sheets of FIBRILLAR BONE were found (i.e. the "collagen carpet" with bone cells within it). This collagen carpet had yet to be impregnated with bone material so it was caught in a state of arrested development. Theses sheets of protein tissue were so fresh that they could be stretched and would snap back into shape.

- Multiple dinosaur fossils have been found which contain totally undecayed osteocytes (bone making cells). These fragile cells have been preserved with intricate fingerlike protrusions used to connect and construct the porous calcium structure of the bones. They look exactly like living osteocytes.

- Mark has also published the first discovery of undecayed nerve bundles (extremely tiny "wires" that carry nerve signals to and from the brain) within dinosaur bones. Again these bundles are indistinguishable from modern nerve bundles and are undecayed.

Even one of these finds is astounding evidence for the relatively recent burial of dinosaurs during the globe covering Flood of Noah only about 4,500 years ago. **Presenting all these lines of evidence to any jury looking for the truth would result in a verdict that Noah's Flood was a real event.** That means that dinosaurs were created at the same time as mankind - at the beginning of creation! They lived thousands of years ago and were buried during Noah's Flood...not millions of years ago. It also means the sedimentary rocks which these bones are buried within (covering 75% of the land surfaces of the earth) were also laid down during this worldwide flood. Thus, these rock layers could not possibly be millions of years old and the Biblical timescale of history is correct.

But from the beginning of the creation God made them (humans) male and female."
- Mark 10:6 (NIV)

OCTOBER 10

Undecayed dinosaur tissue "shouts recent creation" like nothing else, capturing people's attention, and the implications is understandable by everyone from young children to college professors. **This type of information is systematically excluded from secular education and relatively unknown.** Which is why showing this evidence to college students got Mark Armitage fired. After being unjustly fired from California State University, Mark started the non-profit **D**inosaur **S**oft **T**issue **R**esearch **I**nstitute and has continued to make astounding discoveries:

- Every dinosaur fossil Mark has examined has distinct blood vessels within the bone structure filled with clotted blood. This is a classic indication of rapid drowning, not allowing the blood to drain from vessels. How could so many dinosaurs, of different varieties and found in different locations, have all died from drowning?

- There is no sign of blood from the vessels escaping to contact any tissue outside of the vessels. This is important because it has been promoted to students that iron from the blood has preserved dinosaur tissue for 60 – 200 million years.

This idea is based on extremely limited evidence with many problems which are not reported to students. The fact that the blood clotted and remained within the vessels is definitive evidence that iron from the blood could never have reached the undecayed tissue.

These discoveries are documented in both published technical reports and his short children's books which can be downloaded from his web site (**www.DSTRI.org**). Share this stunning information with others!

All in whose nostrils was the breath of life, of all thta was in dry land, died. - Genesis 7:22 (KJV)

OCTOBER 11

The famous T.rex, nicknamed Sue, was purchased for $8.3 million dollars and has become the icon representing Chicago's natural history Field Museum. Yet this dinosaur actually testifies to Noah's Flood, not millions of years of Earth history.

The 90% complete dinosaur fossil was found alongside fossils of freshwater fish and marine shark teeth. How did ocean fossils become buried with freshwater fossils? Also, Sue is said to have lived near a "meandering river channel." If this were true, how would she have been so well-preserved? Wouldn't nearby scavengers like fish and crocodiles have eaten the remains? **Even during massive river floods, dead animal bodies are not preserved.** In this same Hell Creek formation, another T. rex has been found with soft tissue. How could soft tissue be preserved for 65 million years (the assumed age of this rock layer)? Let's look at the facts:

1. Marine and freshwater fossils washed together.
2. Well preserved T. rex and other fossils.
3. Soft tissue found in dinosaur bones.

These fossils were not preserved by a local flood; they were captured by a worldwide catastrophic disaster. These plant and animal fossils give evidence of being buried together, not living together. Raging flood waters picked up shark's teeth from the ocean and redeposited them on land - covering the T. rex. under millions of pounds of sediments before it had a chance to be scavenged and dismembered. Sue, and the entire Hell Creek formation, testifies to a worldwide flood which the Bible tells us happened about 4,500 years ago.

Go onto the ark, you and your whole family...and after seven days the floodwaters came on the earth. – Genesis 7:1,10 (NIV)

OCTOBER 12

What was that on the lavender bush - a moving flower? Farmers in South Africa can be astonished by such "*moving flowers*." But they are not flowers, they are insects called the spiny flower mantis (*Pseudocreobotr wahlbergii.*)

The spiny flower mantis is gorgeous. This insect has white wings with a green swirl, while the remainder of the body is adorned with tiny, purple flower-like structures. Looking like a flower allows the insect to ambush bees that visit the flowers. **Can a regular praying mantis reprogram its DNA to look like a frilly flower?** During this transformation of appearance, the insect would likely look less camouflaged - making it less capable to survive. Stories that try to explain evolution by step-at-a-time changes simply do not work. Evolutionists assume such beauty is the result of accident and chance. Beauty never arises from accident and chance. Beauty is designed by our Creator, Jesus Christ, as a reflection of His very nature.

When is a flower not a flower? When it is a spiny flower mantis created by God.

Come and see what God has done: he is awesome in his deeds toward the children of man. - Psalm 66:5 (ESV)

BIOLOGY

OCTOBER 13

"In 1977, the worst winter of the century struck the USA. Arctic cold gripped the Midwest for weeks on end. Great blizzards paralyzed cities of the Northeast. One desperate night in Buffalo, 8 people froze to death in their own cars... The brutal Buffalo winter may be common all through the United States. The climate experts believe that the next Ice Age is on its way. According to recent evidence, it could come sooner than anyone expected. And weather stations from the far North report that temperatures have been dropping for thirty years." That was the 1978 introduction by Leonard Nimoy of Star Trek fame. The documentary included world-leading climate scientists and was sponsored by the U.S. Army and the National Science Foundation. During the 1970s, the scientific consensus was that a new Ice Age was coming!

Today we hear the same fear-based cries, but this time, it is about the scientific consensus being certain that climate change is caused by human activity. Carbon dioxide is blamed as the cause and trillions are being spent to reduce CO_2 levels. **CO_2 is plant food; they need it for growth.** CO_2 levels in the atmosphere vary because the natural flow of CO_2 in and out of the ocean. Climate is not constant. Just like the weather, it is a complex system affected by the turbulent flow of heat through both the atmosphere and the ocean, evaporation, cloud cover, precipitation, ice sheets, vegetation growth and energy transfers. There are so many variables to keep track of! **One reason the computer was invented was to predict weather; allowing multiple complex simultaneous calculations.** Even so, look how difficult it is to predict weather even one week into the future. How much more difficult to accurately predict weather a year, 30 years, or a century into the future!

We are to be good stewards of the earth, but if we look at God's Word, man will NOT destroy the earth; God will, and it will be by fire, not climate change.

> But the day of the Lord will come as a thief in the night, in which the heavens will pass away with a great noise, and the elements will melt with fervent heat; both the earth and the works that are in it will be burned up. - 2 Peter 3:10 (NKJV)

OCTOBER 14

It is widely promoted that climate change is a man-made problem. Let's take a look at a broader view of history. In Genesis, three big famines caused by droughts took place. As Abram traveled to Canaan, Genesis 12:10 states, "*Now there was a famine in the land. So Abram went down to Egypt to sojourn there, for the famine was severe in the land.*" Abram went to Egypt because the Nile River was a reliable source for water when rainfall failed. Scripture records the next major famine in the land was during Isaac's time, "*Now there was a famine in the land, besides the former famine that was in the days of Abraham.*" (Genesis 26:1). The third great famine took place when Joseph was a top leader in Egypt. He had to help the people survive for **seven years without rain - that would be climate change!** (Genesis 41:30). Almost four thousand years ago there were three droughts over a 200 year period, illustrating extreme weather changes - without industrial pollution.

These famines fit into an Ice Age climate which followed Noah's Flood. Prior to the Ice Age, Noah's Flood warmed the oceans via massive land movement and volcanic activity. Increased evaporation and ash-filled skies drove the Ice Age that lasted for centuries following the Flood. Once the oceans cooled and the ash dissipated, the world's weather patterns changed again. As the Ice Age wound down, the Middle East changed from lush to arid. Only 3,500 years ago, the ancient Middle East area was called a "*land flowing with milk and honey*" (Exodus 33:3-5). It is now a dry desert. Is climate change caused by mankind's activities? Take a closer look at history!

They...cut down a branch with one cluster of grapes; they carried it between two of them on a pole. ...They told (Moses): "We went to the land where you sent us. It truly flows with milk and honey..." - Numbers 13:23, 27 (ESV)

OCTOBER 15

Have you considered the bittersweet nightshade (Solanum dulcamara)? When this plant's leaves are being eaten by insects, **it sends out an attractive distress aroma to attract nearby ants.** The ants immediately come and kill the devouring insects; receiving a sweet treat of nectar as a reward for their assistance. This nectar comes from the wounded leaves - it's unique and not the plant's sap. Remember, nectar usually comes from a flower and this is what bees collect. This type of unique nectar comes from the leaves.

How did the bittersweet nightshade know to make nectar instead of sap when its leaves were wounded by insects? How did the plant know that this nectar would attract ants? How did the plant know that ants would kill off the devouring insects? Plants don't think, and neither does this nightshade plant! God designed this protective system from the beginning. Many plants have flowers which provide nectar to ants, but the bittersweet nightshade is the only known plant to provide sweet nectar from wounded leaves.

Behold, you are beautiful, my love, behold, you are beautiful!... Your lips drip nectar, my bride; - Song of Solomon 4:1,11 (ESV)

OCTOBER 16

Is a Neanderthal coming to your next family reunion? **Europeans and Asians have been found to carry about 2% Neanderthal DNA!** Classic Neanderthal features (sloping foreheads and enlarged brow ridges) can actually be found to varying degrees in humans today. For example, Nicolai Valuev is a former world-champion boxer and has the classic Neanderthal features of a sloping forehead and a heavy brow ridge. Mr. Valuev likely has some Neanderthal DNA, but he is no primitive half-human. He is a highly intelligent former member of the Russian parliament.

The entire scientific community now unanimously agrees that Neanderthal man was completely human. Since sequencing the Neanderthal genome, it has been found that Neanderthals and modern man could and did interbreed. Neanderthal DNA is 99.7% identical to present-day human DNA. God created man on Day 6 of creation week, fully formed. Neanderthals are just a variation within a kind - the humankind. So is a Neanderthal coming to your next family reunion? Probably so!

[God] hath made of one blood all nations of man for to dwell on all the face of the earth.
- Acts 17:26a (KJV)

FLOOD GEOLOGY

During the Ice Age, only 30% of the land was covered with ice. But what about the rest of the world? During the Ice Age, the equatorial regions of the world, from 30° south to 30° north, received much more rainfall than they do today. Today these areas contain many hot, dry deserts. It is now widely acknowledged that during the Ice Age:

- Lake Bonneville, near Salt Lake City, Utah, would have been the size of Lake Michigan. One can see the ancient shorelines of this gigantic lake in the mountains around Salt Lake City.
- Death Valley is now one of the driest places on Earth but was once filled with 590 ft. (180 m) of water!
- In the Middle East, the Dead Sea reveals shorelines of an ancient lake which geologists call Lake Lisan. It was 870 feet higher than today's Dead Sea.
- In Australia, dry shorelines reveal an ancient Lake Eyre 80-100 feet deeper than the playa lake of that name today. It would have covered 13,513 square miles and contained 125 cubic miles of water.
- Satellite imaging has revealed a buried river landscape in Central Australia's Simpson Desert, making this desert a lush green area in the past.
- The Sahara Desert was also a well-watered, highly populated region during the Ice Age.

These once well-watered deserts are difficult to explain from an evolutionary viewpoint... but not from a Biblical viewpoint. Noah's Flood was accompanied by widespread volcanic activity and massive land movements. These processes heated the ocean's water, leaving them much warmer than today's ocean waters. Warmer oceans mean more evaporation. In the higher latitudes, the clouds would have blown onto cold land and precipitated out as snow. In the lower latitudes, it would have precipitated out as rain - and lots of it! This would have continued until the oceans cooled enough to slow the excessive evaporation. This wetter earth environment may have continued for as long as a thousand years after the Flood ended. The Biblical model clearly explains why deserts used to be well-watered.

He turns rivers into a desert, springs of water into thirsty ground, - Psalm 107:33 (NIV)

OCTOBER 18

Under Saudi Arabia's sand dunes, archeologists are finding evidence that it was once a well-watered place! Fossils of extinct jaguar, oryx, giant elephants with seven-foot-long tusks, and other forest-dwelling fossils have been found. **How surprising to find Saudi Arabia, the land of sand dunes, was once a rich green landscape!** How does this fit into the Biblical timeline?

After the Flood of Noah's time, many of the world's deserts were lush and green. The warm post-flood oceans (as a result of the fountains of the deep breaking open and the volcanic activity) would have had a high evaporation rate and produced abundant amounts of rainfall near the equator. In the higher latitudes, this moisture would have fallen as snow. This type of climate probably existed for the first thousand years following the Flood, until the oceans cooled to current conditions. Once that happened, deserts like the Sahara Desert and those in the Southwestern U.S.A. began to form. Lush green forests simply disappeared. Now that is climate change!

FLOOD GEOLOGY

All the kings of Arabia and all the kings of the mixed tribes who dwell in the desert;
- Jeremiah 25:24 (NIV)

BIOLOGY

Have you heard of a bird that deliberately eats its own feathers? This bird is a North American water bird called the grebe. **But it doesn't just snack on a few feathers - it devours hundreds of them!** It even feeds its soft contour feathers to its baby chicks! It's not that feathers are nutritional; it would be the equivalent of eating our fingernails. Yet up to fifty percent of the stomach contents of a grebe is feathers! So why would this bird eat its own feathers?

Grebes are water birds which eat lots and lots of fish, insects, and shrimp - which means they ingest lots of indigestible bones and exterior shells. The feathers protect the stomach by padding the sharp fish bones and hold them back until the bones are ready to pass through their digestive tract. A study done by Joseph Jehl and published in *Wilson Journal of Ornithology* found that the Eared Grebe actually regurgitated the feathers up to six times each night in the form of pellets. When the pellets were pulled apart, they were found to contain the hard parts of shrimp and insect skeletons.

How did a grebe know that it needed help in digestion and then solved it by eating feathers? Do we try to solve our digestive problems by eating our fingernails? This had to be programmed into the grebe from the beginning. Programming is information and information is made only by an intelligent mind. If there is a program, there must be a programmer and that Programmer is God.

The birds of the sky nest by the waters; they sing among the branches. – Psalm 104:12 (NIV)

OCTOBER 20

It was recently discovered that Jupiter has 12 more moons than previously known, giving Jupiter 79 orbiting moons - the most of any planet in our solar system. Most moons orbit the same direction as their host planet; however, Jupiter has a band of moons that orbit backwards or retrograde. This is confounding to cosmic evolutionists who believe in the Nebular Hypothesis. They believe the solar system began with a swirling cloud of dust and gas which condensed to form our planets and moons. **If this were true, then all the planets and moons should rotate and orbit in the same direction.** Think of an ice skater twirling – her arms, legs, and body must all spin in the same direction. Yet many of Jupiter's moons orbit in the opposite direction of the spinning planet.

To make matters worse, there is one moon within the retrograde band of moons, Valetudo, that orbits the "correct" way. In other words, this renegade moon is hurtling around Jupiter in the opposite direction of its immediate neighbors - risking a head-on collision with every trip. This is like going down the freeway in the wrong direction. If these moons were millions or billions of years old, Valetudo should have long ago been destroyed by a head-on collision.

Moons orbiting the wrong way are an indication that our solar system did not form over billions of years as gas and dust condensed to form planets and their moons. And the fact that Valetudo has not been destroyed by a collision is consistent with God creating the solar system quite recently. We have a planned, orderly, and young solar system, just as God has said in the first Book of the Bible.

ASTRONOMY

For as the heavens are higher than the earth, so are my ways higher than your ways, and my thoughts than your thoughts. – Isaiah 55:9 (KJV)

HISTORY

One of the great men of science was a Swedish scientist named Carl Linnaeus (1707–1778). He brought into general use the system of classifying all living organisms by genus and species - two Latin words. He was able to name thousands of plants and animals and became the *"Father of Taxonomy."* We still use this system today. Linnaeus believed that all living thing were recently created, and they reproduced after their kind. These created kinds could then be categorized with his classification system. Linnaeus recognized that there is lots of variation within major groups of animals but rejected the belief that one organism could slowly turn into a completely different critter. In actuality, a belief in evolution would have hindered the development of a classification system because **evolution implies a blurred continuum of life rather than distinctly different groups.**

Our entire taxonomy system is based on Linnaeus' belief that, *"God could be approached through the study of Nature."* He felt it was his Christian obligation to learn about God by studying *"the wonders of the created universe."* Linnaeus also said, *"The Earth's creation is the glory of God, as seen from the works of Nature by Man alone. The study of nature would reveal the Divine Order of God's creation, and it was the naturalist's task to construct a 'natural classification' that would reveal this Order in the universe."* **God is a God of order and that is revealed in the universe He created.** The more we study nature, the more we see this truth revealed.

> Blessed is the man who walks not in the counsel of the wicked, nor stands in the way of sinners, nor sits in the seat of scoffers; but his delight is in the law of the LORD, and on his law he meditates day and night. – Psalm 1:1,2 (ESV)

OCTOBER 22

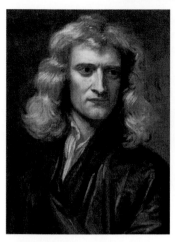

Epidemics are nothing new in history. Isaac Newton had just finished studying theology and mathematics at Cambridge University and graduated without any particular honors in 1665. Before he had time to find a job, the bubonic plague (or Black Death) spread throughout Europe. Cambridge University was closed and Isaac returned home for 18 months. During this time on the farm, he had time to think of what he had been taught and ponder problems his teachers had mentioned, such as why did the moon circles the earth.

One day as he pondered this question under an apple tree, an apple fell, and as he picked it up, he saw the moon in the sky behind it. He realized that the moon did not fly in a straight line and head out into space, because it was held in place and forced to circle the earth by gravity - the same force that caused an apple to drop toward the earth. Within a few months, Isaac Newton made breakthroughs in astronomy, light, color, physics, and mathematics. When the university opened again, his mathematics teacher realized Newton's genius and gave him a teaching position at the university. Later, Newton wrote his book, *Principia*, considered by many to be the most important science book ever published.

It was during an epidemic that Newton had time to think things through and grasp new understanding of God's creative genius. May we similarly use our time wisely.

So teach us to number our days that we may get a heart of wisdom. - Psalm 90:12 (ESV)

OCTOBER 23

What kind of mammal is as small as a cat but covered with scales? It's a pangolin, often called a 'scaly anteater.' This strange animal lives in Africa and Asia and is the only mammal in the world covered in scales - all other mammals are covered in hair. Pangolin scales are made of the same stuff as your fingernails (or reptile scales) – a tough protein called keratin.

Pangolins feed on ants and termites. Their long, sharp claws rip open insect nests and they use their long sticky tongues to reach the ants. The tongue is able to get into every crevice of a nest. They eat thousands of ants each day. **This 16 inch (40 cm) long tongue (longer than their body) doesn't even fit inside its mouth!** There is a special pocket inside the pangolin's chest to store the extremely long tongue when not in use. But that's just the start of its special design features:

- They have no teeth, so they swallow small pebbles to help grind their food like birds.
- When a pangolin starts to dig up an ant nest the ants try to attack, but the tightly fit scales provide excellent protection.
- If ants and termites start to crawl into its ears or nostrils, it closes them with specially designed muscles.
- When frightened, the pangolin tucks its head into its stomach and rolls into a ball for protection.

Evolutionists believe reptiles came before mammals and reptile scales evolved into mammal hair. Yet with the pangolin, they believe the hair turned back to scales. Is there any evidence of this? Not a shred! The oldest pangolin fossils are just like the pangolins of today - scales and all! God simply decided to make a mammal with scales like a reptile.

Have you not known? Have you not heard? The LORD is the everlasting God, the Creator of the ends of the earth. He does not faint or grow weary; his understanding is unsearchable.
– Isaiah 40:28 (ESV)

OCTOBER 24

Science finally catches up with the Bible! In Luke 10:30-35, Jesus tells the parable about the good Samaritan who came upon a wounded traveler. The good Samaritan poured wine and olive oil upon the injured man's wound and then bandaged him up. Today we know that wine contains ethyl alcohol and traces of methyl alcohol, **which are good disinfectants**. Wine cleansed the wound. Olive oil also disinfects, but also **has anti-inflammatory properties** and soothes the area.

From the Middle Ages, right up to the early 20th century, people forgot how to care for open wounds and millions died prematurely of infections. Science finally caught up with the Bible in the 1900's by using alcohol to kill germs and ointments to sooth wounds. The Bible is not a science textbook, but when it speaks on the topic, it is always true.

BOTANY

So he went to him and bandaged his wounds, pouring on oil and wine; and he set him on his own animal, brought him to an inn, and took care of him. - Luke 10:34 (NKJV)

OCTOBER 25

Why isn't your nose made of bone? Your nose is made of cartilage, a connective tissue that is strong and flexible, just like your ears. Go ahead - touch your nose, wiggle it, move it. Now gently push in on it. If your nose were made of bone and you were hit hard enough with a basketball, fist, or ran into a wall, the bone would push into your brain and **you would die!**

Our noses act like a collapsible bumper on a car. What a great design. Collapsible bumpers on our cars did not happen by accident and chance, so why would our collapsible nose? Collapsible car bumpers were designed by car engineers. Collapsible noses were designed by THE Engineer, God Almighty! So, go ahead and play football and basketball knowing that when your nose gets jarred, your collapsible nose Maker designed it so you would not die.

All things were made by him... - John 1:3a (KJV)

OCTOBER 26

"What was that on the bacterial culture?" wondered Alexander Fleming. This famous twentieth century scientist, who discovered penicillin, did not realize that he had accidentally dropped some mucus (snot) from his nose onto a bacterial culture. The place where his snot dropped had dead bacteria around it. He named this bacterial killing substance lysozyme. Scientists have now discovered that this same special enzyme is not only found in snot, but in our tears, saliva, sweat and other bodily fluids. **Your nose produces about a quart of mucus every day!**

When you are sick, bacteria killed by lysozymes turn your mucus yellow or green. This is evidence that a battle has been taking place; the lysozymes are fighting to destroy the bacterial enemy. Our body has a first line of defense against bacterial infections - lysozymes. Would anyone believe that a country's military, trained to protect us from an enemy invasion, came about by accident and chance? Then why would we say that lysozymes came about by accident and chance! Our Heavenly Father knew what our bodies would be up against and created this line of defense to protect us.

... and without him was not any thing made that was made. – John 1:3b (KJV)

OCTOBER 27

Have you ever wondered what a bird has to do to hatch a chick? To hatch a chick, the parent needs to control the temperature of the egg. Many bird eggs need a steady temperature of 99 degrees F. A bird's entire body is covered with feathers in order to keep heat in, so **how does a bird radiate enough heat to heat up eggs on a nest?** Enter in the brood patch!

During the breeding season, there is a hormonal change in which the down feathers on the bird's tummy suddenly become loose. Depending on the bird, some feathers will just fall out, and others will have to be plucked out. Ducks, for example, pull them out and use them in building their nests. Gulls and other shorebirds have three brooding patches, while songbirds and hummingbirds have one. As the feathers fall out, the tissue swells, and the blood vessels expand. The entire area can swell to five times its normal size as the internal blood vessels swell up to seven times larger. This area becomes as hot as the inside of a bird. The bird needs to find someplace to cool this hot area, *"Oh there is a cool egg. Ahhh, that cool egg pressed against the hot brood patch feels SOOOO good!"*

As that area of the egg warms up, the bird turns the egg to a cooler area to seek relief, thus heating the egg evenly! The goal is to uniformly heat the egg to its center. Also, the egg must be turned so the developing chick does not get stuck to the inside of the egg. No brood patch, no chick! Evolutionists believe this brood patch evolved over eons of time. How would the developing embryo get enough heat to incubate? Half incubated eggs do not make chicks. Eggs, from the beginning, needed a properly designed brood patch to provide the controlled heat needed to develop the next generation of birds. When we see such a design, we know there must be a designer. The Designer of a bird's brood patch is God.

For in six days the LORD made heaven and earth, the sea, and all that is in them, and rested on the seventh day. – Exodus 20:11 (ESV)

OCTOBER 28

There are four surprising things about coal that point to its Genesis Flood origin:

1. Coal is found in seams which are flat on the top and bottom.
2. Coal often contains identifiable plants.
3. The rock layers between coal seams have marine fossils.
4. Coal can be formed quickly in the lab.

Imagine a worldwide flood ripping up huge plants and trees. As they floated and bumped the bark , the waterlogged plants would drop to the bottom. The bark would pile up on the flat bottom creating a flat layer of organic-rich material. Any subsequent mud flow covering the plant debris could easily and quickly create a coal seam. This flowing mud could also carry dead marine creatures and these would become fossilized if buried deeply enough.

While Dr. Kurt Wise was studying rocks, part of his undergraduate work was to make rocks. He and his fellow students would grind up rocks and then put them in a special capsule. The capsule was then heated under high pressure. **New rocks took only minutes to form.** But, when they placed plant material in the capsule, no rock-like coal formed. What was needed? They examined coal more closely and realized that when coal is burned, it leaves "clinkers" in a stove. This unburnable part of coal is clay. So into the capsule with the plants went some clay. **Within 3-4 weeks coal had formed!** The clay acted as a catalyst. Clay comes from volcanic ash.

During the Worldwide Flood of Noah's time, thousands of volcanos were erupting ash which landed on the plants. Then they were covered by other sediments resulting in high temperatures and pressures. **By the time Noah got off the Ark, the coal had already been made and was ready for use.** It does not take millions of years to form coal, just the right conditions.

Surely God is my helper! The Lord is the provider for my life. – Psalm 54:4 (JB)

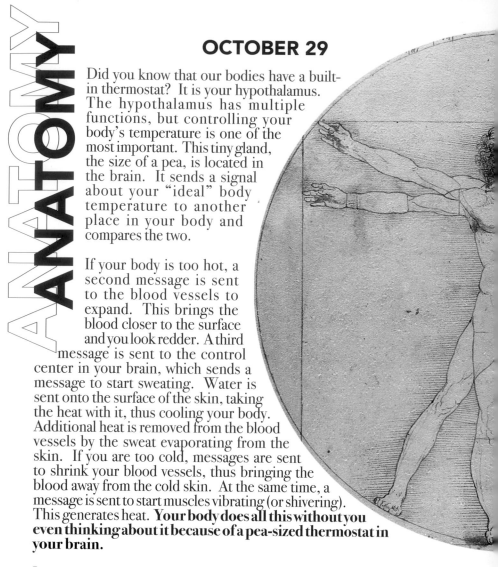

OCTOBER 29

Did you know that our bodies have a built-in thermostat? It is your hypothalamus. The hypothalamus has multiple functions, but controlling your body's temperature is one of the most important. This tiny gland, the size of a pea, is located in the brain. It sends a signal about your "ideal" body temperature to another place in your body and compares the two.

If your body is too hot, a second message is sent to the blood vessels to expand. This brings the blood closer to the surface and you look redder. A third message is sent to the control center in your brain, which sends a message to start sweating. Water is sent onto the surface of the skin, taking the heat with it, thus cooling your body. Additional heat is removed from the blood vessels by the sweat evaporating from the skin. If you are too cold, messages are sent to shrink your blood vessels, thus bringing the blood away from the cold skin. At the same time, a message is sent to start muscles vibrating (or shivering). This generates heat. **Your body does all this without you even thinking about it because of a pea-sized thermostat in your brain.**

Imagine trying to design such a temperature control system for a building. It would need sensors, feedback loops, ductwork, valves, and a control system. Everyone would acknowledge that someone engineered it. Yet, evolutionists say that our body's automatic temperature control system happened by mutational accidents and chance. Isn't our body's temperature control system much more complex and efficient than a building's temperature control system? We are fearfully and wonderfully made by the great Engineer Himself, God.

Who has put wisdom in the inward parts?
- Job 38:36 (KJV)

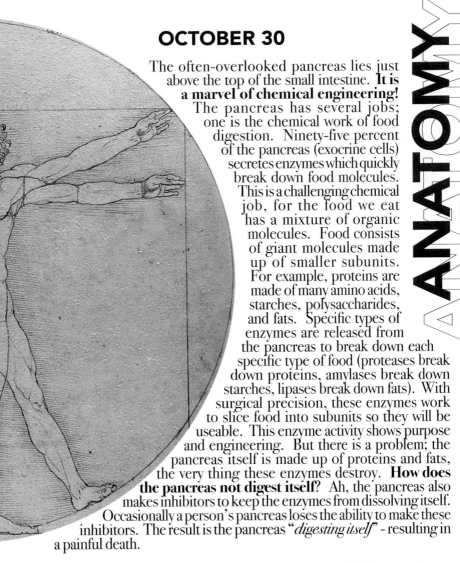

OCTOBER 30

The often-overlooked pancreas lies just above the top of the small intestine. **It is a marvel of chemical engineering!** The pancreas has several jobs; one is the chemical work of food digestion. Ninety-five percent of the pancreas (exocrine cells) secretes enzymes which quickly break down food molecules. This is a challenging chemical job, for the food we eat has a mixture of organic molecules. Food consists of giant molecules made up of smaller subunits. For example, proteins are made of many amino acids, starches, polysaccharides, and fats. Specific types of enzymes are released from the pancreas to break down each specific type of food (proteases break down proteins, amylases break down starches, lipases break down fats). With surgical precision, these enzymes work to slice food into subunits so they will be useable. This enzyme activity shows purpose and engineering. But there is a problem; the pancreas itself is made up of proteins and fats, the very thing these enzymes destroy. **How does the pancreas not digest itself?** Ah, the pancreas also makes inhibitors to keep the enzymes from dissolving itself. Occasionally a person's pancreas loses the ability to make these inhibitors. The result is the pancreas *"digesting itself"* - resulting in a painful death.

How does evolution explain a pancreas evolving? The container, corrosive chemicals, and inhibitors had to be present from the beginning. Furthermore, they all had to be present in the right amounts and with mechanisms to continuously monitor the process and repair any problems. What a glorious design. What a glorious God.

Thus says the Lord, your Redeemer, who formed you from the womb: "I am the Lord, who made all things, who alone stretched out the heavens, who spread out the earth by myself..."
- Isaiah 44:24 (ESV)

OCTOBER 31

Winter is approaching and a bear is looking for a den in order to hibernate. Some consider bears super hibernators; they can go for over three months without eating, drinking, urinating, defecating, or exercising. Bears do not experience extreme body temperature decreases like chipmunks and ground squirrels. A hibernating bear's body temperature drops less than 12°F. Respiration decreases from an average of 8 breaths/minute to less than 1 breath/minute and the heartbeat drops by 70%.

Bears live off the fat they accumulated from summer and fall. This fat tissue is processed to supply water and up to 4,000 calories a day. As the fat releases water, urea is created (a chief component of urine). **In non-hibernating animals, when urea builds up, it becomes fatal**, but in a hibernating bear, even the urea is used. It is broken down to make protein for the bear. Even though a hibernating bear drinks no water, it does not become dehydrated. Researchers discovered that bears were in "*almost perfect water balance*" after 100 days of hibernation - during which time they had not swallowed a single drop of water. Humans would be dead within 3-5 days of hving no water to drink!

When the bears are hibernating and metabolizing their body fat, their cholesterol levels become twice as high as in the summer. Yet, hibernating bears do not suffer cholesterol gallstones or hardening of the arteries, because the bear's liver secretes a substance that dissolves these gallstones. **It has been confirmed that this same chemical, a form of bile acid, can be used to dissolve gallstones in people and thus eliminates the need for surgery!** Even though the bears are curled up in a doghouse-sized space, with males losing an average of 22% of their weight, and females losing 40%, they have no degenerative bone loss. If only this diet worked that well for humans!
To survive during hibernation, vast internal changes must take place. One hundred days of no eating, no drinking, no urinating, no defecating and no exercising. This could not have happened by accident or chance. However, there is One Who created the bear with the ability to hibernate. And Who is that hibernator Maker? God Himself!

Then the beasts go into dens and remain in their places. - Job 37:8 (KJV)

NOVEMBER

"THERE ARE ONLY TWO POSSIBLE EXPLANATIONS AS TO HOW LIFE AROSE: SPONTANEOUS GENERATION ARISING TO EVOLUTION OR A SUPERNATURAL CREATIVE ACT OF GOD...THERE IS NO OTHER POSSIBILITY. SPONTANEOUS GENERATION WAS SCIENTIFICALLY DISPROVED 120 YEARS AGO BY LOUIS PASTEUR AND OTHERS, BUT THAT LEAVES US WITH ONLY ONE OTHER POSSIBILITY... THAT LIFE CAME AS A SUPERNATURAL ACT OF CREATION OF GOD, BUT I CAN'T ACCEPT THAT PHILOSOPHY BECAUSE I DO NOT WANT TO BELIEVE IN GOD. THEREFORE, I CHOOSE TO BELIEVE IN THAT WHICH IS SCIENTIFICALLY IMPOSSIBLE, SPONTANEOUS GENERATION LEADING TO EVOLUTION."

- George Wald (1906-1997), Nobel winning scientist, "The Origin of Life," Scientific America, Vol 190, pp 46-50.

If anyone causes one of these little ones--those who believe in me--to stumble, it would be better for them if a large millstone were hung around their neck and they were thrown into the sea.

– Mark 9:42 (NIV)

NOVEMBER 1

Neptune, a gas giant, is the furthest planet from the sun and has the strongest winds of any planet of our solar system. High-altitude winds have been recorded at 1,300 m.p.h. **Compared to this, a category 5 earth hurricane (sustained winds of 157 mph) is a gentle spring breeze!** Coupled with these high winds are ferocious storms. These storms are dark in color and are known to rage for years before disappearing. Jupiter's Great Red Spot is a similar, atmospheric storm lasting centuries. One of Neptune's ferocious storms was recorded to be the diameter of the earth!

Why does the planet the farthest from the sun have the most extreme winds? Neptune must have heat, and lots of it, to create such fierce windstorms. Neptune emits two-and-a-half times the heat it receives from the sun. As the heat leaves the core and radiates outward, it creates these violent storms. With no mountains or continents to slow the circulation of atmospheric gases, these winds whip around the planet at supersonic speeds. If Neptune were millions of years old, it should have gone cold long ago and have no heat to generate strong winds.

Neptune's core heat and ferocious winds both testify to Neptune's recent creation. God clearly tells us that by His power He created the heavens in six literal, normal days. Observation from science gives us the confidence that placing our faith in God's Word is justified.

Worthy are you, our Lord and God, to receive glory and honor and power…
- Revelation 4:11a (ESV)

NOVEMBER 2

Neptune has 14 moons, and the largest of Neptune's moons, Triton, orbits backwards. Evolutionists believe that the solar system was formed in an enormous cloud of gas and dust rotating in the same direction around our sun. Then, over millions of years, the dust clumped together into rocks, the rocks clumped together into bigger rocks, and enormous rocks clumped together and became planets. [In reality, actual modeling shows that these clumps would have *bounced off of each other and planets could never have formed in this way.]*

Furthermore, they propose that our solar system's gas giants (Saturn, Jupiter, Uranus, and Neptune) formed in the outer parts of our solar system because it was cold enough for ice and other gases to condense onto the planet's surface. With this evolutionary model, all planets and moons should be orbiting in the same direction.

Triton, Neptune's moon, does not fit the evolutionary model because it orbits backwards. Because Triton orbits in the opposite direction, evolutionary astronomers believe that Triton originated in the Kuiper Belt and was captured by Neptune's gravity. But this causes another problem; if Triton was captured, it should have an elliptical orbit. It does not - it has a circular orbit. In fact, it has the most circular orbit of any moon in our entire solar system!

The final nail in the cosmic evolutionary coffin is that Triton is geologically active. When Voyager 2 passed Triton, its cameras revealed geysers erupting nitrogen gas and dust particles some 5 miles (8 km) high. NASA called these eruptions ice volcanoes. If Triton is millions of years old, why are geysers still erupting? Triton is a mystery to evolutionists because it **orbits backwards** in a perfectly **circular orbit** and has **geysers that erupt**. This is not an accident; God created this moon which witnesses to the fact that our solar system is not millions of years old.

… you created all things, and by your will they existed and were created.
– Revelation 4:11b (ESV)

NOVEMBER 3

The method used by the male sandgrouse to bring water to its newly hatched chicks is so extraordinary; it was once thought to be a myth. The sandgrouse lives in some of the most parched regions of the earth, so the male often flies 20 miles away to retrieve water. But he doesn't bring it home in a bucket - he has a better method!

Once he reaches a water hole, he wades in up to his belly and starts "rocking" from side to side and shaking his belly feathers. Feathers normally repel water, but after about 15 minutes, his specially designed feathers, with coiled hair-like extensions, trap and hold some of the water. **He then flies back over the scorched desert to his nest with about two tablespoons of precious water.** In the nest, the chicks will crowd under him and use their bills like squeegees to remove water from the belly feathers. One scientist reported that, "*chicks of sandgrouse that he reared would die from thirst even if drinking water was available to them, but that they would take water from wet cotton.*"

How would evolution explain this? What if the belly feathers did not have the special design so water could be transported? This type of feather had to be there from the very beginning, or no sandgrouse chicks would have survived. When we see a design, we know there must be a designer, and the sandgrouse's feather was designed by God.

The eyes of all look to You, and You give them their food in due time. You open Your hand and satisfy the desire of every living thing.
– Psalm 145:15,16 (NIV)

NOVEMBER 4

Hidden in the mountains of Jordan is the ancient city of Petra. The red rock cliffs have been carved with palaces, a temple, tombs, and a theater. It even had an innovative water system. All of this was carved by a desert tribe more than 2,000 years ago. Petra was once a thriving trade center with an estimated population of 20,000 people. This lost and desolate city lay hidden for years until 1812, when it was rediscovered by a European explorer.

Today Petra is considered one of the Seven New Wonders of the World. Evolutionists find it hard to believe that ancient people could carve such exquisite buildings; that's because they view ancient man closer to apish hominoids. Yet, here we see gorgeous buildings that would be difficult for us to carve today. When we see Petra, we see the work of **intelligent people** and that is what God created from the beginning - intelligent people. As you gaze at this beautifully carved city, it's not a mystery that a desert tribe could do this, for God created us intelligent from the very beginning of time.

For You have made him a little lower than the angels, And You have crowned him with glory and honor.
- Psalm 8:5 (NIV)

NOVEMBER 5

How did millions of woolly mammoths get trapped in the permanently frozen muck of Northern Siberia? After the flood of Noah's day, the Arctic Ocean region would have been warm (think hot tub warm!) due to the fountains of the deep bursting forth and the multitude of volcanic eruptions. This warmth brought abundant rains and vegetation to the Arctic and resulted in a mammoth population explosion. Woolly mammoths were once widespread in the northern latitudes, especially Alaska and Siberia.

In the later stages of the Ice Age, the climate changed drastically. As the ocean surface froze, the climate became dry and arid. The temperature differences between the land and ocean created strong winds that carried enormous amounts of silt across the land surfaces. This change in climate resulted in the burial of millions of woolly mammoths within "yedomas" or "loess" – hills containing large amounts of windblown silt and ice. **These woolly mammoth bones are a witness to God's judgment on man's sin.** The worldwide catastrophic Flood created conditions causing both the Ice Age and the extinction of the woolly mammoths.

By the breath of God ice is given, and the broad waters are frozen fast. - Job 37:10 (ESV)

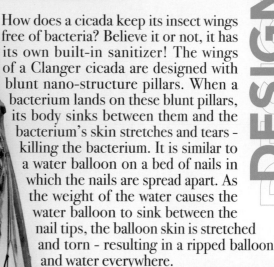

NOVEMBER 6

How does a cicada keep its insect wings free of bacteria? Believe it or not, it has its own built-in sanitizer! The wings of a Clanger cicada are designed with blunt nano-structure pillars. When a bacterium lands on these blunt pillars, its body sinks between them and the bacterium's skin stretches and tears - killing the bacterium. It is similar to a water balloon on a bed of nails in which the nails are spread apart. As the weight of the water causes the water balloon to sink between the nail tips, the balloon skin is stretched and torn - resulting in a ripped balloon and water everywhere.

The cicada's wing design is the **first known physical structure that has been shown to kill a bacterium.** No chemicals were needed. Scientists recognize a good design when they see it and are excited to see how they can use this design to make antibacterial surfaces in hospitals and public places frequented by large crowds - such as subways. Maybe the next time you grab a doorknob it will be covered with antibacterial nano-pillars copied from the wing of a cicada. Cicada wing doorknobs! Cicada wing handrails! When you see a design there must be a designer, and the Designer of antibacterial cicada wings is God.

God is exalted in his power. Who is a teacher like him? - Job 36:22 (NIV)

NOVEMBER 7

Do you realize our body has multiple systems for protecting us from invading germs?

- **Our skin** is a great first barrier, stopping billions of bacteria from entering our body.
- The skin is not only a barrier, but it has **oil glands** which produce sebum - which is an antibacterial agent able to destroy bacteria.
- **Our tears** also have an antibacterial substance killing off harmful bacteria in the eye.
- With each breath we take through our nose, invaders enter. The germs are caught in the mucus and cilia move them to the back of our **nose** and down our **throat**. They end up in the **stomach** where hydrochloric acid kills the invaders.
- **Our intestines** also work to protect us from the enemy. Good bacteria live there - not allowing the bad bacteria to take up residence.

Our body has multiple levels of protection to stop invading germs. Evolution does not explain how this came about. How did we survive before the systems purportedly evolved? Why didn't we go extinct? God created overlapping systems of protection for our body from the very beginning so we could survive and thrive.

The LORD protects you; the LORD is a shelter right by your side. – Psalm 121:5 (CSB)

NOVEMBER 8

What happens to the harmful bacteria and viruses (pathogens) that get inside your body? If left unchecked, you would die within days. What does your body do? **It sends out an army of defenders on a search and destroy mission;** this is your immune system.

Our body has a complex defense network. Neutrophils are the body's first defense, attacking the enemy. Next macrophages, larger than the neutrophils, devour the many pathogens that have escaped the neutrophils. Think of a marshmallow (macrophage) encompassing a jellybean (pathogen) and eating it. The macrophage analyzes how the pathogen is made and sends the information to the helper T-cells. The helper T-cells emit a chemical which signals the B-cells to make antibodies. Antibodies, which are Y-shaped, bind themselves to the pathogens causing them to malfunction. At the same time, killer-cells circulate throughout the body, ridding the body of damaged cells, like the cleanup crew on a battlefield. Sometimes it takes a few days for the "soldiers" to reach full strength; this is the time when you feel sick. When all the pathogens have been destroyed, suppressor T-cells tell the helper T-cells to call off the attack. **Our immune system is an amazing defense system, constantly fighting to protect us from death.**

Do we say an army happens by accident and chance? How did this army know which weapons to use to be successful? If it took millions of years for our immune system to evolve, we would not be here. Our immune system "soldiers" needed to have the right weapons to kill the enemy pathogens from the very beginning. When we see such an immune system, we know there must be an immune system Maker, and that He is God.

Proclaim this among the nations: Prepare for war! Rouse the warriors! Let all the fighting men draw near and attack. - Joel 3:9 (NIV)

NOVEMBER 9

Did you know that many flowers have "*blue halos*," which humans are unable to see but bees can? Flowers that have these *blue halos* tend to produce greater quantities of nectar, and bees, with their ability to see ultra-violet light, are drawn to these flowers. The *blue halos* act like a McDonalds's sign advertising, "Plenty of McNectar here."

These *blue halos* are created by nanoscales on the petals. When sunlight hits these tiny structures, the light is scattered, resulting in blue or ultraviolet light appearing as a halo around the nectar producing area.

Confounding any evolutionary explanation is the discovery that these *blue halos* are found in a wide variety of flower species having different petal anatomies and nanostructure spacing.

How could a flower without a brain know to create these *blue halos*? Could flowers know that bees see in the UV spectrum and then think, "We need to modify our DNA to produce structures which produce UV light?" Could flowers learn a trick of physics and create tiny ridges on their petals which altered the way light bounced back, affecting the color that is seen? Flowers could never do this by random mutations. God is the Master Creator.

I will be as the dew to Israel; he will blossom like the lily; - Hosea 14:5 (NIV)

NOVEMBER 10

The Bible explains where the one and only Ice Age fits into world history. The flood of Noah's day was followed by a 700 year-long ice age. Have you ever wondered what the world looked like at the height of the Ice Age? During the Ice Age, enormous amounts of ocean water were locked up in ice sheets, lowering ocean water levels. A NASA video reveals what Earth's surface would have looked like when the water level in the oceans dropped almost 400 feet. **When that happened, land bridges appeared.** This would have allowed humans and animals to migrate across the world.

As the ocean level dropped during the Ice Age the first land bridge appeared between Australia, New Guinea, and Tasmania. Then England was connected to Europe; there was no English Channel. Another land bridge to appear was between Russia and Alaska; the Bering Strait disappeared. These land bridges likely allowed the migration of both animals and people around the world from where the ark landed. At the end of the Ice Age, the ice melted and ran into the oceans causing the sea level to rise, isolating animals and people in their new locations. All of this happened approximately 4,500 – 3,500 years ago - resulting in the world we see today.

FLOOD GEOLOGY

He gives snow like wool; he scatters frost like ashes. - Psalm 147:16 (NIV)

Do you have eyes in the back of your head? An owl butterfly does, but they are just spots on the wings. In the middle of each brown wing is a conspicuous spot of yellow with black in the middle that resembles a light-colored iris and a large black pupil - reminiscent of a predator owl's large eyes.

This huge butterfly, with an 8-inch wingspan, lives in the tropical rainforests of Central and South America and feeds on bananas and other fruit. The owl butterfly would make a tasty morsel for a bird, but peering back at the bird are large owl eyes. Since owls will eat birds, many birds fly away from this perceived danger, not realizing they missed a delicious meal.

Evolution teaches that these eyespots happened by accident and chance over millions of years by one little mutation at a time until a perfect pattern appeared. Mutations are random events. Does throwing paint against a wall create an eye pattern? Do distinct patterns happen by accident and chance? If there is a pattern there has to be a patternmaker. Also, the pattern is not a swirl or zigzag but an eye design. How does a butterfly know it needed an eyespot to scare away a bird? It doesn't. A patternmaker is needed for the distinctive eyespots on the owl butterfly. And Who is this pattern Maker? God!

All the kings of the earth shall praise thee... they shall sing in the ways of the LORD: for great is the glory of the LORD.
– Psalm 138:4,5 (KJV)

NOVEMBER 12

Is it a dead leaf or a butterfly? Both – it's a dead leaf butterfly! These butterflies are found in tropical areas of Asia from India to Japan. When the butterfly's wings are open, they are beautifully colored with vibrant orange, deep blue, and black. **But when closed, the wings look like a dead leaf, right down to the exact leaf shape, midrib, and leaf veins.** It even has a fungus-like or lichen-like appearance that is common on the dead leaves of the tropics! Of what value is a butterfly looking like a dead leaf?

As the vibrantly colored butterfly flutters through the tropical forest and a bird starts to chase it, the butterfly drops down into the foliage and stands still with its wings closed. The wings now look like a dead leaf. Birds pursuing this butterfly are often unable to find it. Evolution will tell you that this butterfly slowly evolved this "dead leaf" look over time. Even if a butterfly knows what a dead leaf looks like, can it cause its DNA to mutate to have the color, shape, veins, and fungus-covering of a dead leaf? And how did the butterfly know it needed this coloration only on the underside of the wing? What if it got it wrong and the mutations were on the top side? The camouflage would then be hidden when it landed and closed its wings. Now the bright colors would make it a sitting duck to predators! Butterflies rest with their wings closed.

Did all this happen by accident and chance? Hardly. The only alternative is the intelligent design of the butterfly's wings to look like a dead leaf. Also, that Designer had to know that a butterfly rests with its wings closed. Who is that someone? That Someone is God! He cares about even the protection of a lowly butterfly.

One generation shall praise Your works to another, And shall declare Your mighty acts. I will meditate on the glorious splendor of Your majesty... - Psalm 145:4,5 (NKJV)

BIOLOGY

BIOLOGY

The Corsican Blue Tit, a small bird which lives on the French island of Corsica, uses fragrant plants to kill bacteria in its nest. During field studies, scientists discovered that this little bird lined its nest in various sprigs of aromatic plants such as mint, lavender, or curry. When the eggs were laid, the female bird continued to bring fresh, fragrant herbs to the nest. If the scientists removed the herbs, the parent birds replaced them quickly. Researchers discovered that the aromatic herbs acted as a disinfectant for the nests, creating a sterile environment for the chicks. The herbs gave the chicks a health boost!

Chicks living in nests lined with aromatic plants grew faster and had a higher proportion of red blood cells than those that were not richly adorned with the aromatic plants. **In addition to making their nests beautiful, the Blue Tit was protecting its young from disease.** Evolutionists should ask themselves, how do these birds know this, and how is this knowledge passed on? Does a bird understand that its chicks are healthier when exposed to herbs? And if so, how does it know which herbs to choose? How did the Blue Tit know that mint, lavender and other aromatic herbs act like a disinfectant cleanser? When we use a disinfectant for our homes, we know there must be a cleanser maker. The Maker of the cleanser used by the Blue Tit is God. Jesus Christ is the Cleanser of our sins.

If we confess our sins, he is faithful and just to forgive us our sins and to cleanse us from all unrighteousness. -1 John 1:9 (ESV)

NOVEMBER 14

Name a plant that thrives in intense heat and can be eaten all the way to the ground and still survive - the answer is grass! In Genesis 1:11-13, plants were created, and grass is so important that it is listed as one of three broad categories of plant life.

Grass is both the most abundant and important of land vegetation. I know what you are thinking, what's the big deal about grass – it is such a pain to mow! But grass provides far more than a nice lawn...grass literally feeds the world! Essentially all grain (wheat, rice, corn, barley, alfalfa, etc....) are a grass which produces the grains needed to feed everything from chickens to cattle. In addition, grass provides other functions:

- It is eaten directly by everything from horses, sheep, cattle, pigs, goats, and deer.
- It provides food for the entire ecological food chain – starting with grasshoppers, ants, and other insects...which provide food for mice, birds, bats, snakes, and frogs... which provide food for larger mammals.
- It provides a habitat and nesting material for a host of insects, birds, mammals, and reptiles.
- It prevents erosion of land surfaces, allowing larger plants to take root.

All of this is possible because of God's design for grass – thriving in high heat/light environments, fast growing/propagating, and growing from the bottom up (rather than from the tips out) so that when eaten it is not killed. The 9,000 species of grass give glory to God and showcase His creativity.

And God said, "Let the earth put forth grass..."
– Genesis 1:11 (ASV)

NOVEMBER 15

Many people stand at the rim of the Grand Canyon in awe of its size but **there are hundreds of Grand Canyon-sized gashes in the earth under our oceans.** There are almost 10,000 underwater canyons lying perpendicular to the shoreline of continents. They are not trenches; trenches run parallel to the shoreline and are fault structures. Submarine canyons are erosional and most are not associated with current rivers coming off continents. The average submarine canyon is 30 miles long and 350 feet deep. The Bering Canyon is the longest (310 miles long), located near the Aleutian Islands of Alaska. The Monterey Canyon is the most studied submarine canyon - located near Monterey, California - it is 300 miles long (including its fan) and 7.5 miles wide, with a maximum depth of 5,600 feet. Submarine canyons are too deep and large to have been formed by river erosion; so what cut these deep canyons?

Towards the end of Noah's Flood, as the continents were rising, the floodwaters poured off the continents in enormous sheets. As the flood level dropped, the waters became channelized, eroding today's continental valleys (today's rivers conveniently follow these eroded channels). The eroded sediments were deposited on the continental shelf. As the sediments accumulated, some of them slid down the continental slope. **At first, the sliding sediment would erode a shallow canyon, but as the sediments accelerated, they caused deeper and deeper erosion - resulting in the formation of submarine canyons**. Submarine canyons are one more piece of evidence that supports the reality of the Biblical Flood.

Ocean Floor

Who shut in the sea with doors when it burst out from the womb, when I made clouds its garment and thick darkness its swaddling band, and prescribed limits for it and set bars and doors, and said, 'Thus far shall you come, and no farther, and here shall your proud waves be stayed'? - Job 38: 8-11 (ESV)

NOVEMBER 16

What's a guyot? It is an undersea volcano with a flat top. There are thousands of these guyots on the ocean bottom, especially in the western Pacific. **These flat-topped volcanoes currently sit at an average depth of 5,000 feet below sea level.** Why don't these seamounts have peaks like other volcanic cones? How did they become flat?

Almost all scientists agree that water currents near the ocean's surface shaved them smooth across the top. But how did they all get so far below sea level?

1. The volcanos formed while the ocean basins were very shallow.
2. Ocean currents near the surface removed the tops of the volcanos.
3. The ocean basins sank down carrying these flattened volcanos a mile deep into the newly deepened ocean basins.

But when did the ocean basins sink thousands of feet? This happened at the end of the Flood of Noah's day as the continents rose above the ocean's surface and the newly formed ocean basin cooled and sank down. Great tectonic forces were reshaping the earth. Guyots are not only evidence of the ocean basins sinking, but a reminder of Noah's Flood when the entire surface of the earth was rapidly changing.

1500 m

GUYOT

Volcanic submarine mountain

Truncated by waves near sea level

The mountains rose, the valleys sank down to the place that you appointed for them.
— Psalm 104:8 (ESV)

NOVEMBER 17

Our respiratory system has an extremely efficient air purification system. Every breath you take into your body is filled with dust, pollen, bacteria, and viruses. So how are all the dirt and accompanying germs removed?

The first line of defense are nose hairs which catch the "dirt." Next, as the air travels through the nose, it passes through the conchae. The conchae in your nasal passage is full of twists and turns. This disrupts the air flow, making air travel like a twisting roller coaster - going this way and that way instead of in a straight line to the lungs. As air slams against the walls at each turn, the mucus on the walls collects the dirt and germs. At the same time, the air is warmed by the many blood vessels in your nose, and water evaporates from the mucus to humidify the air. The dirt and germs now collected in the mucus are propelled toward your throat by tiny beating hairs called cilia until it reaches the throat and is swallowed - plunging into the **acid bath of death** in your stomach. Mucus also contains special chemicals which kill bacteria and viruses. When you are sick, these bacteria are killed and turn your mucus yellow or green. Eighty percent of the time, yellow or green mucus (snot) means a bacterial infection.

The air purification system continues as the air now moves to the trachea, bronchi and bronchioles - each filled with more mucus and cilia. This mucus catches the vast majority of dirt and germs not caught in your nose. Every day you operate one of the most efficient air purification systems in the world and you don't even think about it! In 24 hours, some 2,640 gallons of air are cleaned, warmed, and humidified. This purification system is also fully portable. Little maintenance is needed; it can operate for a lifetime in a variety of climates, hot or cold. How much is this machine worth? It is priceless!!! **Mankind's most advanced air purification system can't begin to match the one God built!**

Let everything that has breath praise the Lord. Praise the Lord! ~Psalm 150:6 (NIV)

NOVEMBER 18

Evolutionary concepts have invaded our thinking about cultures. Evolution assumes that apish creatures evolved... to "hunter-gatherer" societies...to agricultural societies...to industrial societies and so on. When anthropologists discover a hunter-gatherer society, they assume that they were primitive because they never developed into an agricultural society. Let's test that concept with the indigenous people of the Chatham Islands.

About 1,000 years ago, Polynesian farmers colonized New Zealand. Some of these travelers (the Moriori) colonized the Chatham Islands, which are about 500 miles east of New Zealand. The Moriori people reverted from an agricultural society to hunter-gatherer society. Why? Because the islands were too cold to grow tropical crops. No crops meant no storage of extra produce, which meant no extra food to feed bureaucrats, chiefs, armies, and specialists - so they became hunter-gatherers. **They were not primitive or less evolved; they were just coping with their situation.**

In some ways, hunter-gatherers can be superior to farmers, depending on the environment. For example, the Norse farmers of Greenland were replaced by the Inuit (Eskimo) hunter-gatherers. This is nothing new. The Bible teaches us that before the Flood of Noah's time, people had farms and built cities. After the Flood, the descendants of Noah built the city of Babel, God confused their language, and they dispersed to fill the earth. As they journeyed, they were hunter-gatherers until they found a new place to settle. They were not primitive; they were coping with the changing environment the best they could.

These are the clans of Noah's sons...From these the nations spread out over the earth after the flood. – Genesis 10:32 (NIV)

FLOOD GEOLOGY

NOVEMBER 19

If there was a worldwide flood, where is all the water?

The Flood mentioned in Genesis was a worldwide flood; it began with a special rain of "*40 days and nights*" and all of the "*fountains of the great deep*" opened up. The Flood continued for one year. During the first five months, the waters rose and covered all land surfaces. "*Every hill under the whole heaven was covered.*" God's judgment upon sin was to totally destroy all life on land that had the "breath of life." The floodwaters cleansed the earth.

Towards the end of the Flood, all current mountains of the earth rose up and the valleys sank low, resulting in the water rushing off the continents into the oceans. **This explains why fossils of ocean creatures that once lived on the ocean floor can be found on the highest mountain peaks.** Today this flood water fills the oceans of the world which cover about 70% of the globe. Many parts of the ocean are extremely deep. The deepest is the Marianas Trench, located in the Pacific Ocean. It is almost seven miles deep; compare this with Mt. Everest at about 5 ½ miles high. If the earth's surface were completely leveled, as smooth as a ping pong ball, the oceans would cover the entire globe to a depth of about a mile and a half. Here is a satellite picture of the Pacific Ocean. Water everywhere! Where is the Flood water? The water from the Flood is still here; it is found in the earth's oceans.

[The earth is the LORD's]...he founded it on the seas and established it on the waters.
- Psalms 24:2 (NIV)

NOVEMBER 20

Do you realize the earth has the perfect amount of water? Water has an amazing ability to hold heat (heat capacity) and **this is very important for our survival.** In fact, it has the highest heat capacity of all liquids (except liquid ammonia.) If there was less water, the earth would experience far more drastic temperature changes from day to night and season to season. Notice how deserts are extremely hot during the day and extremely cold at night. Desert temperatures swing greatly because there is little water present to absorb heat during the day and release it at night – thus moderating temperature swings.

Fortunately, Earth has a lot of water compared to its land mass. The surface of the earth is 70% water covered. Try this experiment to see the ability of water to hold heat. Hold an air-filled balloon over a candle flame. It bursts immediately as the heat melts the latex skin of the balloon. Now hold a water-filled balloon over the flame. The water will soak up the heat of the flame, even to the point of boiling, without breaking. **Water can store a lot of heat!**

The deep oceans can store enormous amounts of heat from the sun and release it slowly – preventing rapid worldwide temperature swings. This helps regulate Earth's climate and prevent constant, massive worldwide storms. God designed this planet for our benefit in every possible way – right down to the amount and characteristics of water.

The sea is his, for he made it, and his hands formed the dry land. Oh come, let us worship and bow down; let us kneel before the Lord, our Maker! - Psalm 95:5,6 (ESV)

NOVEMBER 21

Dinosaurs eating grass? Yes, a fossilized duck billed dinosaur has been found with pieces of grass, leaves, and phytoliths stuck in its teeth. Phytoliths are microscopic structures made of silica. Plants take up silica from the soil and deposit it within their leaf cells. In 2005, dinosaur dung was found with phytoliths uniquely produced by grass. So, what is the big deal, don't lots of carnivores eat vegetation? Here is the discrepancy:

- For over 50 years it has been taught as a scientific fact that grass had not evolved until 55 million years ago.
- Dinosaurs were supposed to have disappeared 60 million years ago – 5 million years before grass existed.
- How could dinosaurs be eating something which would not appear upon the earth for another 5 million years?

What did evolutionists do with this discrepancy? They simply changed the evolutionary story to say that grass evolved 11 million years earlier. So much for infallible dating methods! However, if we put on our Biblical glasses, we realize that God created grasses on Day 3 of creation week and dinosaurs on Day 6 of the same week. From a Biblical perspective, dinosaurs would have and did eat grass from the moment of their creation. That is exactly what we find in the fossil record! The tool of science, if properly used, eventually catches up with Scripture.

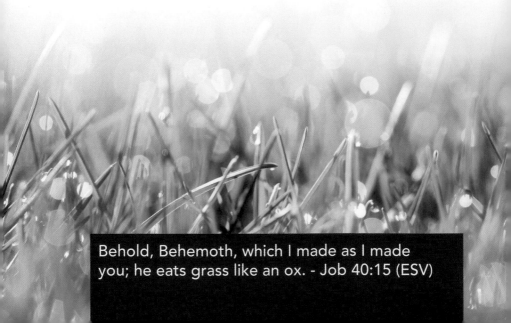

Behold, Behemoth, which I made as I made you; he eats grass like an ox. - Job 40:15 (ESV)

NOVEMBER 22

What is a fruit? A fruit is the fleshy product of a plant that contains seeds and can be eaten. A fruit is a seed container! **God in His creativity takes a flower and turns it into a fruit, so seeds can develop!** Our vegetable gardens contain many fruits including cucumbers, squash, peppers, and tomatoes. So why are all of these commonly considered as vegetables?

In 1893, the Supreme Court proclaimed that the tomato was a vegetable, even though botanically it is a fruit. The 1883 Tariff Act taxed imported vegetables but not fruit, yet tomatoes were included in the taxation. John Nix, an importer of tomatoes, sued on the grounds that tomatoes were a fruit and should not be taxed. The court ruled that tomatoes are commonly seen as vegetables because they are eaten as part of the main course instead of as a dessert. Therefore, they could continue to be taxed!!! Ignoring science and finding an excuse to continue raising tax revenue, the court also ruled that cucumbers, squash, peas, and beans were vegetables, even though botanically they are fruits.

When your Mom says, *"Children eat your vegetables!"*, you can politely respond, *"I am done with my vegetables, peas are a fruit."* Or perhaps if you are hungry between meals try asking your Mom for a "fruit snack." When she asks what kind of fruit you'd like, you can respond, *"A chocolate bar."* Chocolate can be considered the product of a fruit because it is made from cocoa beans, the seeds inside the fruit of a cocoa tree. Eating chocolate is eating a fruit, scientifically speaking. **Knowing science can be very useful!**

How sweet are your words to my taste...
- Psalm 119:103 (ESV)

BOTANY

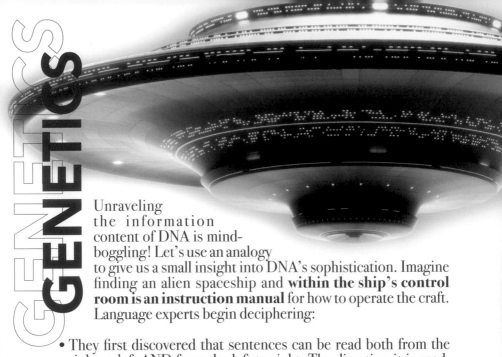

GENETICS

Unraveling the information content of DNA is mind-boggling! Let's use an analogy to give us a small insight into DNA's sophistication. Imagine finding an alien spaceship and **within the ship's control room is an instruction manual** for how to operate the craft. Language experts begin deciphering:

- They first discovered that sentences can be read both from the right to left AND from the left to right. The direction it is read, determines the meaning of the text.
- Next it is discovered that the same sentences have different meanings in different languages. Imagine reading chapter 1 in English. Then, the same words on the same pages could be read in French to get a completely different message.
- They also discovered that the manual contained an entirely different set of information by only reading every third letter. And if you started at different positions and skipped every third letter, yet more meanings were revealed.
- Needing a quiet place to work on deciphering the tablet, one of the linguists took the tablet into the ship's galley. When she opened the document, she noticed some of the letters had been "greyed out." Reading just the highlighted letters, she found one meaning but when the tablet was taken to the navigation deck, other letters were "greyed out" and a different message appeared. The information changed depending on where the book was read!

Our DNA has this same astonishing level of "data compression!" **Scientists have only scratched the surface of deciphering DNA.** An information system with this level of complexity and sophistication can only come from an incomprehensibly intelligent Being, who is God.

And these are but the outer fringe of his works; how faint the whisper we hear of him!
- Job 16:14 (NIV)

NOVEMBER 24

Sometimes when you are standing outside on a dark night, you may see a "shooting star." But, is it really a star? NO! It is a random space rock speeding through our atmosphere, burning up with tremendous frictional heat, causing light to streak across the sky. If it is a large enough chunk of rock, it will not entirely burn up, but hit the earth and make an impact crater. How many impact craters are here on Earth? It is estimated that there are about 100. How many impact craters are on the moon? There are 5,185 moon craters that are more than 12 miles across, but **if you count the craters less than one-half mile in diameter, it brings the total to about one million!** Why are there more craters on the moon than on Earth?

Earth has an atmosphere which burns up space rocks; the moon does not. Without our atmosphere, rocks could be routinely plummeting through our homes at night. Fortunately, our atmosphere is almost 50 miles thick, and as space rocks encounter it, friction is produced, and rocks are disintegrated. Did our atmosphere develop by chance over millions of years? If so, we should find billions of meteorites buried within the rock layers of the earth. We do not. Our atmosphere was set up from the beginning to protect life on Earth. It did not happen by accident and chance; our atmosphere was created by God to protect us! So as you "wish upon a falling star," thank the One who made it all possible.

ASTRONOMY

In the beginning, Lord, you laid the foundations of the earth, and the heavens are the work of your hands. – Hebrews 1:10 (NIV)

Ancestory.com is all the craze, with people tracing their ancestry to cultures all over the world. But did you know that some people, like the Queen of England, **can trace their genealogies all the way back to Adam?** How is that possible?

In Genesis 5 and 10 are a genealogical list from Adam to Noah. Noah was the tenth generation from Adam. Noah had three sons (Japheth, Shem, and Ham) - from which all people today have descended. The descendants of Japheth moved to Europe and India. In Europe, the people kept meticulous records. Queen Elizabeth II can trace her lineage back to Noah based on the six Anglo-Saxon royal houses (Anglia, Kent, Lindsey, Mercia, Northumbria, and Wessex) and then to Adam. Many other royal houses in Europe can also trace their lineage to Adam. In the book, *After the Flood*, Bill Cooper lays out these genealogical tables, all based on historical documents from the ancient world. What a family reunion these people could have with charts of ancestors going all the way to Adam!

But of course, **we are all descendants of Adam** - just as the Bible states. We have not ascended from a bacterium as evolution teaches. God made man, Adam, from the dust of the ground, breathed into him the breath of life, and man became a living soul. We are the crown of His creation.

This is the book of the generations of Adam.
- Genesis 5:1a (ESV)

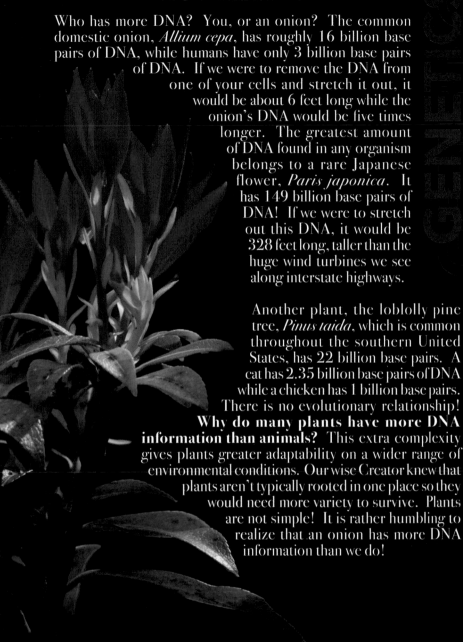

Who has more DNA? You, or an onion? The common domestic onion, *Allium cepa*, has roughly 16 billion base pairs of DNA, while humans have only 3 billion base pairs of DNA. If we were to remove the DNA from one of your cells and stretch it out, it would be about 6 feet long while the onion's DNA would be five times longer. The greatest amount of DNA found in any organism belongs to a rare Japanese flower, *Paris japonica*. It has 149 billion base pairs of DNA! If we were to stretch out this DNA, it would be 328 feet long, taller than the huge wind turbines we see along interstate highways.

Another plant, the loblolly pine tree, *Pinus taida*, which is common throughout the southern United States, has 22 billion base pairs. A cat has 2.35 billion base pairs of DNA while a chicken has 1 billion base pairs. There is no evolutionary relationship! **Why do many plants have more DNA information than animals?** This extra complexity gives plants greater adaptability on a wider range of environmental conditions. Our wise Creator knew that plants aren't typically rooted in one place so they would need more variety to survive. Plants are not simple! It is rather humbling to realize that an onion has more DNA information than we do!

God opposes the proud but gives grace to the humble. – James 4:6 (ESV)

It's a warm summer night just at dusk, and the field is full of tiny lights. What are they? Fireflies! A firefly is a beetle that glows with a light. How do fireflies glow? They glow because of a chemical reaction in their lower abdomen. Fireflies produce one of the most efficient lights in the world. Almost 100% of the energy from the chemical reaction becomes light while producing no heat. **This is particularly important for fireflies since the light source is inside of its body.** Old-fashion incandescent light bulbs produce 10% light and 90% heat!

Bioluminescence is the production and emission of light by a living organism. It occurs through a chemical reaction. How does this chemical reaction work in a firefly? Oxygen enters through tubes in its body, reacts with the chemical luciferin, the enzyme luciferase, and other chemicals - producing light. When the oxygen flow is cut off, the light goes out. A firefly **controls the oxygen flow like an on/off switch on the wall!**

Fireflies also need a special window for the light to pass through. The abdomen of the firefly has 3 layers: window (cuticle), light-producing middle (photogenic), and the reflective dorsal layer. The light producing middle layer produces light in all directions. The light can pass through the window (cuticle) directly or it can reflect off the reflective dorsal layer and then go out through the window. The window layer is also uniquely designed to transmit the optimal wavelength of light produced by the firefly. Male fireflies send a Morse code-like signal to females waiting on the ground. When the correct light signal is seen, the female beams back an answer and the two fireflies are able to find each other.

How do evolutionists explain the signaling system? **Did Morse code happen by accident and chance?** How do they explain the source of the complex chemicals needed for making light? How do they explain the on/off switch? When we see light, there has to be a light-maker and that light-Maker is God.

And God said, Let there be light: and there was light. – Genesis 1:3 (KJV)

NOVEMBER 28

Have you ever thought about how plants that grow under the canopy of a forest get the sunlight they need? Most of the sunlight entering a dense forest is captured by tall trees, with those under the tall trees receiving only filtered light. Plants under the canopy receive only 2-7% of the sunlight. A plant needs sunlight to survive. Take a closer look at shade-loving plants. They are deep green, which means they have more chlorophyll (chlorophyll makes the leaf green) than leaves in direct sunlight. This chlorophyll is part of the mechanism needed to make plant sugars (food) and more is needed to compensate for the lower levels of sunlight.

Begonia plants have dark green leaves, but they also have something even more amazing. **They have their own magnifying lens built into their leaves.** These "lenses" allow the little sunlight that is received to be concentrated and photosynthesis to take place. **Therefore, begonias grow well in shady places.** If a begonia is placed in direct sunlight the concentration of sunlight is too high and the leaves die.

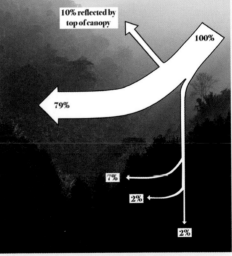

10% reflected by top of canopy

100%

79%

7%

2%

2%

How did the begonia know it needed more sunlight? How would it know to mutate its cells to become miniature magnifying lenses? How did the begonia know that magnifying lenses would concentrate sunlight? Begonias just aren't that smart. But the Designer of their microscopic magnifying lenses [God] is intelligent beyond comprehension!

Blessed is he whose help is the God of Jacob, whose hope is in the LORD his God.
– Psalm 146:5 (ESV)

NOVEMBER 29

Do you realize you are mutating to death? On an individual level, every time a cell divides, new mutations occur. Every year you live adds mutations on top of previous mutations. On average, a typical 15-year-old has 6,300 mutations while a 60-year-old has about 40,000 mutations. We are literally mutating to death with an upper limit of 70 to 120 years.

On a population level, we are also degenerating. Every generation has accumulated more mutations than the last. Every person has approximately **100 new mutation**s (akin to spelling errors) in their genome at birth. That means every human being accumulates about 100 new mutations per person per generation. Fortunately, most of these mutations have a very small effect. Yet as one population geneticist has stated, "*We are inferior to cavemen.*" Our fitness is weakening! Darwin had it wrong, we are not improving in complexity; we are deteriorating!

Viruses mutate even more quickly. The virus H1N1 caused the Spanish Flu of 1918 that killed millions of people. This particular virus has disappeared by mutating itself to death; by 2009, the Spanish Flu virus went extinct (except for those in freezers). All genomes, from humans to viruses, are degenerating. Genetic entropy is real! As humans we are only about 200 to 300 generations away from Adam and Eve. Why is this degeneration happening? SIN. Adam and Eve disobeyed God by eating a forbidden fruit and we have been deteriorating ever since. The evolutionists' idea that humans have been evolving upwards for millions of years contradicts what true scientific evidence reveals. If deep time (millions of years) were true, the human race would have long ago gone extinct. Sin and its results can be depressing, but sin can point us to the Savior. Our spirit and soul will live forever...some place - either with the Savior in Heaven or with Satan in Hell.

For God so loved the world that He gave his only begotten Son, that whosoever believeth in him should not perish, but have everlasting life. - John 3:16 (KJV)

NOVEMBER 30

Have you thought about a fly? What makes it alive? If I swatted a fly it's dead, right? Well, why doesn't it come back to life? It has all the "right stuff" present for life, yet it is still dead. All the parts are present to make the fly. All I have done is rearrange the parts, so why doesn't it come back to life? That's because life comes from life--not just because the necessary chemicals are present. Dead things do not make living creatures; this is call spontaneous generation.

In the 19th century, Louis Pasteur, disproved this theory and discovered the law of biogenesis, that **living things come from living things**. We know that only a living fly can make another fly. Life is more than just having the right chemicals present under the right conditions. Life comes from life. God told us this from the beginning in Genesis 1:24, "Then God said, 'Let the earth bring forth living creatures after their kind.'"

Behold, to the LORD your God belong heaven and the heaven of heavens, the earth with all that is in it. – Deuteronomy 10:14 (ESV)

DECEMBER

DECEMBER

"WE CAN EASILY MANAGE IF WE WILL ONLY TAKE, EACH DAY, THE BURDEN APPOINTED TO IT. BUT THE LOAD WILL BE TOO HEAVY FOR US IF WE CARRY YESTERDAY'S BURDEN OVER AGAIN TODAY, AND THEN ADD THE BURDEN OF THE MORROW BEFORE WE ARE REQUIRED TO BEAR IT."

- John Newton (1725-1807), Former slave ship captain who became a prominent Christian pastor and wrote the song, Amazing Grace.

Come to me, all you who are weary and burdened, and I will give you rest. Take my yoke upon you and learn from me, for I am gentle and humble in heart, and you will find rest for your souls. For my yoke is easy and my burden is light.

– Matthew 11:28-30

DECEMBER 1

God created everything "very good" in the beginning of creation; so why did God make mosquitoes? One possibility is that mosquitoes were just created to be another insect feeding on flowers. **Did you realize that mosquitoes still drink nectar?** In fact, nectar is the main food of a mosquito diet. How does a mosquito find this nectar? It has three primary tools: CO_2 detectors, heat-sensors, and chemicals sensors.

- Flowers emit CO_2 and mosquitoes are drawn to this CO_2 - via their carbon dioxide detectors. Mosquitoes also locate you by tracking the CO_2 in your breath.
- It has been found that flowers emit heat to attract pollinators; some plants can increase their flower's temperatures over 50°F above the surrounding air temperature. Mosquitoes are also drawn to us by our body heat.
- Mosquitoes also have the ability to detect certain specific chemicals coming from flowers. Surprisingly, human breath and skin emit 9 of the 20 chemicals that these mosquito-friendly flowers possess.

So why do mosquitoes suck our blood when they can just drink nectar? Males still drink only nectar, but females need the blood for a healthy batch of eggs. Flowers may no longer provide all the nutrients a mosquito needs, so they seek out human blood. A recent study in *Nature* concluded that blood-sucking mosquitoes may have arisen from nectar-eating mosquitoes. The original mosquitoes were created with the right tools to find the flowers they needed for survival. These flowers may have gone extinct or decreased in availability, which left mosquitoes in desperate need of an additional source of nutrition... and that is you! In the beginning, God created mosquitoes to use their three main tools to find flower nectar. **Today those tools are being used to find you.**

...and God saw that it was good.
- Genesis 1:25b (KJV)

DECEMBER 2

Do you realize that most engaged or married women in North America wear evidence that God created a **young earth**? It's their diamond ring.

Diamonds were created deep within the earth in the "diamond stability zone" during creation week. We can conclude this because diamonds have the same radioisotope markers as the earth's foundation rock layers. **During the Flood**, because massive tectonic movements were happening around the earth, these diamonds were blasted 90 miles to the surface - carried on molten blobs of kimberlite and lamproites up through "*diamond pipes*." Laboratory simulations show that the ascent had to be between 6-19 m.p.h. Any slower and the carbon would have reverted to soft graphite. Any faster and the carbon would not have had the time to restructure into the hard diamond structure. Thus, the diamonds would have arrived at the surface within 7-20 hours.

Geologists claim that diamonds are 1-3 billion years old, YET recent analysis found carbon-14 (^{14}C) within diamonds. Diamonds are made from carbon and one isotope of carbon (^{14}C) has a half-life of only 5,730 years. So, finding even a single molecule of ^{14}C in diamonds is proof that they formed less than 100,000 years ago. Diamonds are one of the hardest natural substances, so the interior ^{14}C could not have come from modern contamination. This is highly significant! Diamonds testify that both their formation, and the earth's formation, happened quite recently. Every time you look at a diamond ring, let it be a reminder that the earth was recently created.

The sin of Judah is written...with the point of a diamond: it is graven upon the table of their heart, and upon the horns of your altars;
- Jeremiah 17:1 (KJV)

DECEMBER 3

Plants need to be pollinated in order to make seeds and propagate. There are two basic methods of pollination: 90% by animals, and 10% by wind. Evolutionists claim that wind pollination is a primitive, inefficient, wasteful method. Let us consider a world with no wind pollination.

Prairies and coniferous forests generally form large monocultures (the cultivation of a single crop in a given area.) God foresaw the need to quickly pollinate vast monocultures, so He designed wind pollination. Many of the world's most important crop plants are wind pollinated. These include rice, corn, barley, oats and wheat. Many economically important trees are wind pollinated - such as pines, firs, and hardwood trees. If there was no wind pollination of our crops, the world would face massive starvation. Without wind pollination in the forests, the lumber for homes would be prohibitively expensive.

Furthermore, consider the billions of acres of grasslands with their small inconspicuous florets that need to be pollinated. Without wind pollination, an insect would need to travel to each grass floret and individually pollinate it. That would propagate the need for trillions more insects such as gnats and "*no-see-ums*." **With bees, wasps, gnats, and no-see-ums EVERYWHERE, our lives would be miserable.**

Contrary to what evolution believers' state, wind pollination is neither primitive nor inefficient. It is a well-designed system! God cares for us by providing food (grains), shelter (trees for wood structures), and comfort (less insects) through wind pollination.

The wind blows where it wishes, and you hear its sound, but you do not know where it comes from or where it goes. So it is with everyone who is born of the Spirit. – John 3:8 (ESV)

DECEMBER 4

Plants do not move, so there are a wide variety of ways their seeds are spread (wind, gravity, animals, insects). One the most fascinating methods are "exploding" seed pods. For many plants, the energy for the explosive opening of seed pods was thought to come from the drying out of the pods. This isn't the case with the Popping Cress (*Cardamine hirsuta*). Their pods explode while they are still hydrated and green.

Plants do not have muscles, so for a plant to produce rapid movements is a unique curiosity. **The popping cress seeds shoot out from the pod like fireworks**. Their explosive movement is so fast that advanced high-speed cameras were needed to capture the action. The seeds accelerate to thirty-two feet/second in about half a millisecond. After much study, scientists discovered that this explosive acceleration was linked to the pod walls' ability to store elastic energy throughout its growth process and then release the energy at the perfect stage of development. The outer seed pod's hydrated cells use the internal water pressure to contract in such a way that generates tension. As the cells are pressurized, they expand in depth while contracting in length. The cells are shaped like microscopic hinges, causing the seed pod to flatten and then explosively coil open. This unique hinged cell wall has only been found in this one plant species. This is an example of a specially created plant with active sensors, pre-programmed algorithms, and communication systems.

Because God is left out, "evolution" is given credit for this amazing dispersal method, but no one has ever explained how such a complex cell structure could develop in a step-by-step evolutionary manner. The Popping Cress gives testimony to the Master Designer's incredible cleverness. Praise belongs to God, not evolution, for such marvels.

Remember that you should exalt His work...All men have seen it... - Job 36:24,25 (NASB)

BOTANY

ANATOMY

DECEMBER 5

Have you ever wondered why the end part of the human spinal column is called the tailbone? The name stuck because evolutionists believe that this is a useless leftover part (a vestigial feature) of human evolution when "our evolutionary ancestors" had tails. This is a fairy tale. For over 150 years, the tailbone has been promoted as the poster child of "useless features." After Darwin proposed vestigial features as an evidence for evolution, over 100 human organs and features were compiled and taught as such to medical students. **Today, essentially every item on the list has been shown to serve useful functions.** Rather than give up on the ill-conceived notion, evolutionists have modified the definition of vestigial features to include anything which no longer serves its "original" function. But this is a meaningless definition, because how can anyone prove the "original function" of something clearly designed to serve a current function!

Now let's reconsider our "useless tailbone." Do you like to sit, stand, and go to the bathroom? The "tailbone," or more accurately the coccyx, is enormously important, for it is the place to which many muscles, tendons, and ligaments are attached. Twelve muscles alone are anchored to the coccyx which allow for such "useless functions" as standing erect, supporting pelvic organs, and assisting in bowel movements. There would be no dancing, jumping, running, sitting upright, or a multitude of other human activities without our coccyx. This critical bone is neither leftover nor useless. We need to be calling it our coccyx. "*Ouch, I just fell on my coccyx!*" In doing so, we are not continuing the false idea that we once had tails AND we can give glory to the God who made us "fearfully and wonderfully."

Always being prepared to make a defense to anyone who asks you for a reason for the hope that is in you; yet do it with gentleness and respect. – 1 Peter 3:15 (ESV)

DECEMBER 6

Ingenious calendar structures demonstrate the intelligence of ancient mankind. There are so many examples that the study of these structures is given a special name – archaeoastronomy. Here are a few examples:

- **Stonehenge in England** This structure has rings of megaliths (huge standing stones) which mark the summer and winter solstices.
- **Chaco Canyon's Sun Dagger in New Mexico, U.S.A.** Three large rock slabs leaning against a cliff were set up so that shafts of sunlight passed through onto a spiral petroglyph. The sun dagger's location varied throughout the year to mark significant astronomical dates.
- **The Medicine Wheel high in the Bighorn Mountains, Wyoming, U.S.A.** These stones are arranged in the shape of a wheel, 80 feet across with 28 spokes. The center has a pile of rocks, large enough to sit in. The arrangement marks the summer solstice and other astronomical alignments.
- **El Castillo at Chichen Itza in the Yucatan Peninsula, Mexico** This Mayan pyramid is known for the "Snake of Sunlight." On only 2 days each year the late afternoon sun casts a shadow in the shape of a wriggling snake, slowly descending 120 feet until it joins the serpent's head at the bottom of the stairway. This marks the first day of spring or fall (spring and fall equinox).

Summer Soltice

Winter Soltice

SUN DAGGER

These are just a few examples of the discoveries that have been made in the field of archaeoastronomy. Man, from the very the beginning of creation, has shown great intelligence and creativity!

And God said, "Let there be lights in the expanse of the heavens to separate the day from the night. And let them be for signs and for seasons, and for days and years..."
- Genesis 1:14 (ESV)

DECEMBER 7

Does your footprint on a beach become a fossil? For a dinosaur footprint (or any footprint) to be preserved requires special conditions:

1. If the ground is too dry - no footprint, if it is too wet - the sides cave in.
2. The track must be covered by the right kind of sediment.
3. It cannot be exposed to erosion (wind, rain, freeze/thaw) before it is buried.
4. It must be covered rapidly, but gently. If filled violently, the track is destroyed.
5. After burial, it cannot be destroyed by worms and burrowing animals.
6. The sediment containing the track must be rapidly turned to rock.

It is difficult to preserve a fossil track, yet the rock layers of the earth contain billions of fossilized tracks! The Flood of Noah's day provided the perfect track preservation conditions. During the Flood, **dinosaurs not on the Ark would have tried to escape the rising waters.** The Flood was not a simple event of water smoothly covering the land. Instead, during the early part of the Flood, there would have been frequent sea-level oscillations. As the Earth's crust was shifting, tsunamis would have swept across the globe and some land surfaces would have been exposed for many days and then covered rapidly. Desperate dinosaurs would have found these exposed land areas and climbed onto the freshly laid down sediments and made tracks. As the Flood continued, **the rising floodwater would have rapidly buried these tracks.** Then the rocks would have hardened. At the end of the Flood, waters rushed off the continent, exposing some of these tracks. It takes special conditions to make a fossil dinosaur track. Fossilized dinosaur tracks are a testimony to a worldwide Flood!

"O Lord, make me know my end and what is the measure of my days; let me know how fleeting I am! - Psalm 39:4 (ESV)

DECEMBER 8

The more scientists study DNA, the more they are finding "messages within messages." DNA is a language made of four letters. In comparison, English has 26 letters which are reshuffled to make thousands of words. French, German, Italian, etc. use the same letters but assign different meanings to the different arrangements. DNA's four "letters" are actually complex chemicals that are abbreviated A, T, C, and G. Scientists initially thought the letters were only the instructions to make specific proteins. Now, geneticists are finding that if the DNA is read by combining three letters, they make entirely new words (codons) which give instructions for either making proteins OR regulating these proteins.

Codons also act like a "pause" button for the assembling of the proteins so it can be folded properly. **If a protein is folded wrong, it will not work.** Proteins act like parts in a machine which require exactly the correct three-dimensional shape to function properly. Even more complex is the discovery that certain genes code for more than one protein, i.e., dual-coding genes. In this case, both genes had to have existed simultaneously for the correct protein to be produced. What scientists are realizing is that the DNA is much, much more complicated than originally believed. It is like hiding a language within a language within a language!

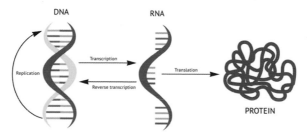

Imagine, the world's most complex language system is located within every cell of your body (except red blood cells)! **We are just on the cusp of deciphering this hidden message within a message.** And while great advances are taking place to understand this marvel of nature, the belief in evolution is suppressing the acknowledgement of the source of this wonder. The language of DNA is the language of life, and life only comes from God.

My substance was not hid from thee, when I was made in secret, and curiously wrought in the lowest parts of the earth. –Psalm 139:15 (KJV)

DECEMBER 9

Science works by forming a belief (called a hypothesis or theory) and collecting observations to determine how well they fit within this framework. The classic scientific method teaches that a theory cannot be fully verified, but can only be "falsifiable" and evidence should be sought to prove the belief wrong. Yet once a belief is established, this is seldom done. Instead, within science, and in every other area of life, once a belief is established the brain literally becomes blind to anything which contradicts the firmly established belief (often called a paradigm or pattern of thinking). Psychologists call this well-known phenomena "confirmation bias" and "change blindness." Confirmation bias is the tendency to only notice things that agree with your beliefs. Change blindness is the failure of the brain to even register things that are different than expected.

A classic 1949 experiment revealed just how powerfully a paradigm can blind people to the truth. People were briefly shown a series of playing cards that included a black four of hearts and red six of spades. (Hearts are always red, not black. While spades are always black not red.) Essentially everyone identified ALL the cards as normal. When shown the cards over and over and asked to look for something wrong, most still identified the abnormal cards as normal. Some subjects became increasingly agitated and could not even name the suit of the abnormal card. One person stated, "I don't know what color it is now or whether it is a heart or a spade. My God, I'm no longer sure what a spade looks like!" The same thing has happened in the area of evolutionary science.

Evolution and its expected timeframe form the foundational paradigm for almost every area of science. For over a hundred years science students in biology, geology, astronomy, cosmology, paleontology, and all of the earth sciences are taught that it is a fact that the earth and universe are billions of years old and everything exists as the result of evolutionary processes by slow cosmic, chemical, and biological changes. This is the paradigm, pattern, and belief which most students will then continue using as they interpret observations. With each passing generation an increasing proportion of scientific experts (and the general population and media) have literally become blind to any other possibility - even when shown observations that reveal these evolutionary assumptions and time frames could not possibly be true.

> ...they neither glorified him as God nor gave thanks to him, but their thinking became futile and their foolish hearts were darkened.
> - Romans 1:21 (NIV)

DECEMBER 10

Can the vast majority of scientists be completely wrong and continue in erroneous beliefs even when presented with proof that what they believe could not possibly be true? The history of science is replete with such examples. A particularly tragic example involves the treatment of cholera right up into the twentieth century. From the time of the Greek physician Hippocrates (460 B.C) onward, medical students were taught that health involved the complex interaction between external factors such as meteorological conditions, topography, and air quality. This formed the medical communities' paradigm for understanding what causes human disease for the next 2,400 years. Based on this belief, the cure for cholera was taught by the medical community to be the withholding of fluids and bleeding patients to remove "bad blood." The death rate from cholera before the 1900s was 50-70%.

Cholera is caused by bacteria from contaminated water and results in extreme diarrhea and vomiting. Death by dehydration can happen within days. The cure (lots of fluids, administering salty water, and removing sources of sewage contaminated water) was known to the medical community for almost 70 years - long before implemented:

- Anton van Leeuwenhoek handcrafted the first microscope and observed the first bacteria in the seventeenth century – 200 years before scientists accepted microorganisms, such Vibrio cholera (cholera), as the cause for many diseases.
- In the 1830s, physicians William Stevens and William O'Shaughnessy independently showed that administering salty water to patients dropped the cholera death rate from 50% to 4%. Yet the evidence was rejected and mocked by experts because it contradicted the Hippocratic paradigm.
- In 1854, anesthesiologist John Snow showed that removing a source of contaminated water in cholera plagued London districts dropped the infection rate from 60% to 7%. In spite of a 600-page report on his finding to the London Medical Society, his well-documented and publicized observations were summarily dismissed and ridiculed.

The medical community was not looking for truth, just whatever fit into their current beliefs. An estimated 40 million people needlessly died of cholera between 1800-1900. Today the same thing is happening with the belief in molecules-to-man evolution. No matter how strong the evidence showing that these beliefs are wrong, and the Bible is accurate and true, the evidence is simply rejected. In this century, evolution is blinding hundreds of millions to the truth of the Bible, resulting in an eternity separation from their Savior.

Professing themselves to be wise, they became fools, – Romans 1:22 (KJV)

DECEMBER 11

ASTRONOMY

Have you considered Saturn's rings? These rings appear solid, but powerful telescopes reveal each ring is composed of billions of particles of dust, rocks, and ice ranging in size from a grain of sand to a house. The rings are very thin and flat, ranging from 32 feet thick (10 meters), up to 0.6 miles (1 kilometer). Each ring orbits at its own rate. One of the rings even looks braided! The rings and gaps are so distinct that they have even been given individual names. The only reason we can see these beautiful rings from Earth is because Saturn is tilted sideways.

Evolutionists believe the rings developed billions of years ago when objects like asteroids, comets or moons crashed and left the debris circling. **When the space probe Cassini flew by Saturn, it measured the gravitational pull on the rings and found it to be too faint for the rings to have survived for billions of years.** Also, Cassini revealed that the ice rings were too clean to be billions of years old. With all the dust and debris in space, they should be much dirtier. Astronomy is showing us that Saturn's rings are young. How old is the universe? When we do the math of the genealogies in the Bible, we find the universe is some 6,000 years old. Saturn's rings give evidence for a recently created solar system.

By faith we understand that the universe was created by the word of God, so that what is seen was not made out of things that are visible. – Hebrew 11:3 (ESV)

DECEMBER 12

The space probe Cassini also surprised astronomers with up-close pictures revealing that Saturn's moon system appeared to have been recently created!

Titan, Saturn's large, smog shrouded moon, does <u>not</u> have a global ocean of ethane. Instead, the equatorial region had "ice dunes." These ice dunes are made of ice crystals coated with acetylene, benzene, and other complex organic molecules. Scientists were able to simulate the creation of these complex organic molecules by exposing acetylene to cosmic rays and found they would have accumulated quickly. Titan's sand dunes **indicate that Titan is young**.

Another moon of Saturn, Enceladus, has south pole geysers. These geysers are spewing ice at supersonic speeds and in such great volumes they have significantly contributed to Saturn's magnetosphere - effecting Saturn's magnetic field. Not only that, but the leftover particles that do not land on the moon are contributing to the E-ring around Saturn. AND, radar is showing that Enceladus is also spray-painting the other moons! **Active geysers on Enceladus indicate a young moon.**

Saturn's rings, Titan's ice dunes, Enceladus's ice-spewing geysers all witness to Saturn's recent creation.

ASTRONOMY

By the word of the Lord the heavens were made, and by the breath of his mouth all their host.
- Psalm 33:6 (ESV)

DECEMBER 13

The ground is dry and parched and the drought has taken its toll. The woodcock family of a mom and four chicks are famished. Suddenly, the mama lays her body flat on the ground and begins drumming the surface of the earth with her wings. **Minutes later the family is well fed.** How did the mama woodcock feed her family? When she drummed on the ground's surface, the vibrations sound like raindrops. Earthworms which had burrowed deep to find moist soil quickly propel themselves to the surface in fear of drowning. How did the mama woodcock know that earthworms were afraid of drowning, and that drumming her wings would sound like rain causing the earthworms to come to the surface?

- Woodcocks are equipped with super-sensitive feet that can actually feel earthworms burrowing in the ground and know their exact location.
- Most birds' ears are located on either side of their head, but the woodcock's ears are located between the bill and eyes - helping them hear the earthworms.
- Its flexible bill tip works like a tweezers, opening and closing in tiny spaces – allowing it to grab earthworms quickly before they escape.
- The highly sensitive nerve endings on the bill's tip inform the woodcock that the earthworm has been gripped.

The woodcock is magnificently designed by God!

Praise be to the LORD, for he showed me the wonders of his love… – Psalm 31:21 (ESV)

DECEMBER 14

Where is the largest desert in the world? Antarctica! That's right, the central part of Antarctica, which is bitterly frigid, has the largest desert on Earth. A desert is a place that does not receive much moisture. Even today, these polar regions are the driest on Earth, with the South Pole receiving less precipitation than the Sahara Desert. Antarctica receives about an inch of water (in the form of snow) each year. **It's a desert - a polar desert.** If it is a desert, then where did the ice sheets, averaging over one mile in thickness, come from?

At the end of the Flood of Noah's day, about 4,500 years ago, the mountains rose, and the Flood waters raced off the continent into the oceans. These ocean waters would have been much warmer than they are today - from the North Pole all the way to the South Pole because of massive earth crust upheavals, plate movements, earthquakes, volcanoes, and more. Interestingly, a powerful ocean current (called a gyre) encircles Antarctica. Very warm post–Flood ocean waters would have evaporated year after year, moving moisture laden air onto the cold central Antarctica land surface, and precipitated out as snow, eventually compressing into ice sheets. When the oceans had cooled to their present equilibrium, evaporation slowed dramatically. Which brings us to today: Antarctica is a polar desert. The ice sheets on Antarctica are a remnant from the post-Flood Ice Age which started over 4,000 years ago.

He thunders with his majestic voice. He says to the snow, 'Fall on the earth,' and to the rain shower, 'Be a mighty downpour.' - Job 37:4,6 (NIV)

There are many hungry predators in the ocean; that's why many small creatures swim in large groups. But one fish doesn't! This foot-long, vertical striped animal is called the pilot fish. It prefers to hang out with a hungry predator shark. **Pilot fish swim alongside the shark and the shark acts like its**

personal bodyguard. In return, the pilot fish eats parasites on the shark's skin and is even known to enter a shark's mouth to nibble away food debris. It's a win-win relationship; the pilot fish gets protection and the shark gets to be parasite free with a no-cost dental care plan.

How did this relationship get started? Sharks eat fish. Which pilot fish was the first brave fish to enter into the shark's mouth to clean it up? Evolution says this symbiotic relationship happened by accident and chance. **If so, how many pilot fish were eaten before the sharks realized they would be beneficial?** This type of relationship with a hungry-fish-eating-predator shark and a pilot fish had to be designed from the beginning. If designed, there must be a Designer, and He is God.

Whatever the LORD pleases He does, In heaven and in earth, In the seas and in all deep places. – Psalm 135:6 (NKJV)

DECEMBER 16

The largest crocodiles in Africa live along the Nile River and are capable of killing animals as large as a water buffalo or wildebeest. So why would such a ferocious creature lay still in the water with its mouth open while a bird flies in and out? This bird, the Egyptian Plover, cleans the croc's teeth by removing any decaying meat.

At the end of the dental cleaning, why isn't the crocodile thinking, *"clean teeth, free meal?"* Snap. But no, when the cleaning is finished, the plover flies away. **I want to know which Egyptian Plover tried this first!** What was it thinking? How did the crocodile know that the plover would clean its teeth? How does evolution explain this mutualistic relationship? The crocodile and plover work with instincts. Both had to have the instinct at the same time for this mutually beneficial relationship to work. Instincts are pre-programmed operational information. They are programmed codes and systems which we don't fully understand. The source of coded information is always intelligence, not the random mutational processes of microevolution.

Bear one another's burdens, and so fulfill the law of Christ. – Galatians 6:2 (NKJV)

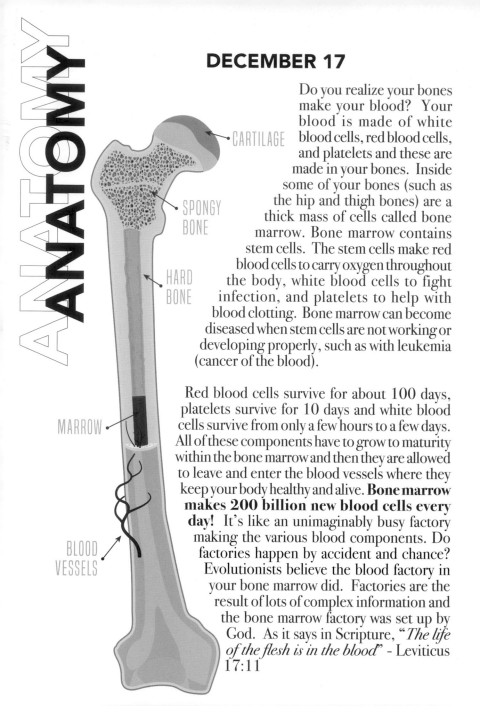

ANATOMY

DECEMBER 17

CARTILAGE

SPONGY BONE

HARD BONE

MARROW

BLOOD VESSELS

Do you realize your bones make your blood? Your blood is made of white blood cells, red blood cells, and platelets and these are made in your bones. Inside some of your bones (such as the hip and thigh bones) are a thick mass of cells called bone marrow. Bone marrow contains stem cells. The stem cells make red blood cells to carry oxygen throughout the body, white blood cells to fight infection, and platelets to help with blood clotting. Bone marrow can become diseased when stem cells are not working or developing properly, such as with leukemia (cancer of the blood).

Red blood cells survive for about 100 days, platelets survive for 10 days and white blood cells survive from only a few hours to a few days. All of these components have to grow to maturity within the bone marrow and then they are allowed to leave and enter the blood vessels where they keep your body healthy and alive. **Bone marrow makes 200 billion new blood cells every day!** It's like an unimaginably busy factory making the various blood components. Do factories happen by accident and chance? Evolutionists believe the blood factory in your bone marrow did. Factories are the result of lots of complex information and the bone marrow factory was set up by God. As it says in Scripture, *"The life of the flesh is in the blood"* - Leviticus 17:11

A cheerful heart is good medicine, but a crushed spirit dries up the bones.
- Proverbs 17:22 (NIV)

DECEMBER 18

The universe is filled with galaxies of three types – elliptical, spiral, and irregular. Some of the most beautiful galaxies have a spiral shape. One-third of all known galaxies are spiral. **Yet NONE should exist if they are billions of years old!** A spiral galaxy has a flat disc shape with a central bulge and looks like a rotating wheel with the spokes of stars spiraling out away from the massive central hub. Our Milky Way galaxy is a spiral galaxy and our solar system is located in one of the arms. We are located about 2/3 of the way from the center, allowing us to see the stars of our galaxy stretching across the night sky like a splash of spilt milk on a tabletop.

The evolutionary idea that a Big Bang happened about 14 billion years ago and stars within spiral galaxies formed relatively shortly thereafter has a problem. Spiral galaxy arms rotate slowly but, the hub rotates faster; this would result in a twisted mess. IF the spiral galaxies are billions of years old, we should not see spiral galaxies. We see lots of spiral galaxies; therefore, spiral galaxies testify to a young universe.

ASTRONOMY

Lift up your eyes and look to the heavens: Who created all these? He who brings out the starry host one by one and calls forth each of them by name. Because of his great power and mighty strength, not one of them is missing.
– Isaiah 40:26 (NIV)

DECEMBER 19

The knowledge of the one true God has been preserved in the Polynesian culture. The Maori people of New Zealand left the Middle East sometime after Abraham, Isaac, Jacob, and Joseph lived - about 3,800 years ago - and journeyed west through Indo-Malayan regions, ending up in Hawaii. When the Hawaiian culture was overrun by enemies from Tahiti, many fled to New Zealand. These Maori people brought with them the knowledge of God, creation, and other Biblical events.

The Maori have stories about God making the first people from the dirt and stories about Eve and a snake. Their stories also tell of a great ancestor known as Lua-Nu'u who left his country and traveled south. He was commanded by God to introduce circumcision for all his descendants. He had two sons, one by a slave girl and the other by a "chieftainess." He went up a mountain to sacrifice to his God. Lua-Nu'u is Abraham of the Bible. Their stories also include references to Jacob and Joseph. **All of this prior to any missionary contact!**

The Maori priests had knowledge of a Supreme Being named Io (pronounced Ee-or). These are a few of His attributes/names: Supreme, Everlasting, The Parent (The parent of heavens, worlds, clouds, animals, including man), Source of Knowledge, and The Giver of All. Genesis events such as the global Flood and Tower of Babel are also known within the Maori culture. The Maori people of New Zealand, and other Polynesian cultures, have preserved the knowledge of the one true God and the real history of humanity for thousands of years. The truth of the Bible is not limited to just the Jews and Christians; **God has left a witness of true history among the nations.**

For the grace of God that brings salvation has appeared to all men - Titus 2:11 (NKJV)

DECEMBER 20

Who would have thought that a small tribe of ancient Native Americans, known as the Delaware Indians, would have a document containing information similar to the first chapters of Genesis? Symbols written on birch bark recounted their history and were passed down to each generation. Here is just a sample of this document which contains information from the beginning of time: *"At the beginning, the sea everywhere....the Great Spirit moved, everlasting, invisible, omnipresent... Bringing forth sky, earth, heavens, day, night, stars, birds, beasts, immortals, all were delighted, carefree, happy, ...But then, very secretly, an evil snake, came to the earth, wickedness...death. All of this was long ago in the land beyond the great Flood,... Flooding.., Filling.., Smashing..., Drowning..... Nenabush (Noah), grandfather of humanity... the Great Flood ended... Living in cave shelters, their home was icy... they followed great game herds North where it was less cold..."*

This document, called the Wallam Ollum (The Red Record), parallels Genesis with the Creation of the world, the Fall, and the Flood. Several hundred years after the Flood, the Delaware Indians would have been one of the many groups leaving the tower of Babel with their own distinct language. This group traveled north to Siberia. At the beginning and middle of the Ice Age, Siberia contained vast, warm grasslands just right for mammoths and other game. How can we reach the Native Americans with the Gospel of Christ? Show them that Christianity is not just a Western religion but that their ancient fathers knew and believed in the same one true Great Spirit of the Bible.

The God who made the world and everything in it is the Lord of heaven and earth and does not live in temples built by human hands.
– Acts 17:24 (NIV)

DECEMBER 21

An important clue for the Ice Age is finding large boulders whose mineral composition does not match the surrounding area. These are called erratics. Whenever you are traveling and see a huge, out of place boulder, ask yourself, "*Boulder, boulder on the ground, tell us something very profound.*" Most likely, it rode to its present location on a glacier. Where did all these glaciers come from? The one and only time in history when ocean temperatures and other conditions were right to create an Ice Age occurred after the Flood of Noah's day. Here are some famous erratic locations:

- At Yosemite National Park visit Olmsted Point where strange boulders have been left behind by a melting glacier. A glacier plucked these large boulders and moved them here.
- At Mendenhall Glacier Visitor Center in Juneau, Alaska, you will meet Eric the Erratic. Eric rode a glacier and arrived 7 miles from its origin.
- At Glacier National Park (Montana), erratics are throughout the park. Either the glacier picked up the large boulders or the boulders fell on top of the glacier from a nearby mountain. They rode the glacier many miles before the ice melted, leaving behind the erratics.
- At Pipestone National Monument (MN) are erratics called the "Three Maidens." It is estimated that it was originally one huge boulder about 50 feet in diameter and because of freezing and thawing action, it has split into six pieces.

Erratics testify to a recent Ice Age which is a direct consequence of the real Worldwide Flood of Noah's day.

And all flesh died that moved on the earth, birds, livestock, beasts, all swarming creatures that swarm on the earth, and all mankind.
– Genesis 7:21 (ESV)

Pollen can be a problem for those with allergies, but it is also a problem for evolutionists. Pollen comes from flowering plants and trees. On an evolutionary scale, flowering plants evolved long after the dinosaurs. Yet since the 1960s, pollen has been discovered in the rock layers where it should not be found. The Precambrian layer in the Grand Canyon (a layer believed to have been laid down long before seed plants are thought by evolutionists to have evolved) revealed specific pollen grains from pine trees, oak trees, and flowers.

Not only has pollen been found in the Grand Canyon Precambrian layer, but in the Roraima formation in South America. The scientists studying this Precambrian formation found the flower pollen in metamorphic rock. How could there be pollen from flowering plants before flowering plants evolved? As one researcher stated, "we offer no solution to the paradox" and this is "*a highly intriguing geological problem.*" **These out of place fossils have huge implications.**

Fossil pollen is causing the geologic column, with its long ages, to collapse. Fossil pollen in Precambrian rocks is a mystery to evolutionists; but not for a creationist, the simplest explanation is that the fossil record does not show the evolution of life over billions of years. The fossil record is a record of what got caught in the year-long Flood of Noah's time. Fossil pollen grains give evidence that the Bible is true and that is nothing to sneeze at!

And God said, "Let the earth sprout vegetation, plants yielding seed, and fruit trees bearing fruit in which is their seed, each according to its kind, on the earth." - Genesis 1:11(ESV)

DECEMBER 23

What looks like a stick but is not a stick? A stick insect. These insects are found virtually worldwide. They are the masters of disguise, with most looking like sticks. But just for variety, God made others to look like leaves, bark, moss, or lichen. Each stick insect blends perfectly into their surroundings. **Amazingly, stick insects do not just look like sticks; they act like sticks by swaying in the wind.**

Even more astonishing, the stick insect's eggs are camouflaged to look like seeds! The stick insects found in New Mexico glue their eggs onto grass. But not just any grass; only the grass which the parents feed on. Their eggs exactly resemble the seeds of this grass, right down to the shape and position where they are glued onto the grass.

Evolution teaches that stick insects evolved slowly from other kinds of insects over time. Wouldn't an insect that looked only half like a stick, "stick out" even more? If insects that did not look like sticks were surviving just fine, then why evolve to look like a stick? When we see such a disguise, we know there must be a disguise maker who created this information. Disguises do not happen by accident and chance. God knew that stick insects would experience the ramifications of man's sin, with its curse of death - so He gave these insects imaginative disguises to help them survive.

"I am the Alpha and the Omega," says the Lord God, "who is, and who was, and who is to come, the Almighty." - Revelation 1:8 (NIV)

DECEMBER 24

What has **9 brains**, 3 hearts, and blue blood? The octopus. This brainy animal has one main brain but was also created with a "mini-brain" in each arm. He has **blue blood** because its blood is copper-based instead of iron-based.

He is also the **master of camouflage!** He can instantly change his skin to perfectly match his background (e.g., a coral reef). An octopus' skin has three layers. The top layer contains tens of thousands of tiny packets of different colors that contract or expand in seconds. The middle layer has reflective cells that create iridescence. The bottom layer bounces back incoming light. Also, the body does shape-shifting. The muscles are tightly packed fibers arranged in three directions: transverse, longitudinal, and oblique - **allowing the octopus to mimic** seaweed, coral and other shapes. In addition, researchers curious about the octopus' **super-sucking suction cups** copied the design...and sure enough... we now have super-sucking suction cups. How did the octopus evolve all these traits? He didn't. God created this blue-blooded, brainy, camouflaging, mimicking, super-suction cup covered creature to showcase His creativity!

For by Him all things were created that are in heaven and that are on earth, visible and invisible, whether thrones or dominions or principalities or powers. All things were created through Him and for Him.
– Colossians 1:16 (NKJV)

DECEMBER 25

The birth of Jesus is so significant that two Gospels (Matthew and Luke) give us numerous details surrounding the event. But it is the Gospel of John (John 1:1-14) which provides the greatest implication of Jesus birth.

- *¹ In the beginning was the Word, and the Word was with God, and the Word was God. ² He was in the beginning with God. ³ All things were made through Him, and without Him nothing was made that was made. ⁴ In Him was life, and the life was the light of men. ⁵ And the light shines in the darkness, and the darkness did not comprehend it...*

- *¹⁰ He was in the world, and the world was made through Him, and the world did not know Him. ¹¹ He came to His own, and His own did not receive Him. ¹² But as many as received Him, to them He gave the right to become children of God, to those who believe in His name: ¹³ who were born, not of blood, nor of the will of the flesh, nor of the will of man, but of God.*

- *¹⁴ And the Word became flesh and dwelt among us, and we beheld His glory, the glory as of the only begotten of the Father, full of grace and truth.*

Notice that in 4 ways (the underlined passages) God's Word makes it emp[...]ly clear that Jesus created all things. He created the universe (time, space, matter, energy), the world (and all life on earth), and every person. Why is this so important? Because once it is denied that all these things were supernaturally created by Jesus (God), the only thing left is to pretend that everything made itself (evolution). Yet it is an impossibility to explain life by evolution. The DNA of life contains enormous amounts of complex information. Matter contains no inherent information. Evolution and random mutations have never been shown to produce complex information; only intelligence produces information. Once Jesus is removed as literal Creator, it is a simple matter to make him a symbolic, irrelevant figure rather than a literal Savior who died for our sins. Thus, people live in increasing darkness as they progressively deny what God has revealed to us about both creation and salvation.

Verses 12-13 (**bolded**) are the most noteworthy of all. What is the solution to the darkness of mankind? For those willing to know the Truth, God is the one who opens their eyes to the light. We cannot open our own eyes, just as a convict cannot choose to free himself. Verse 13 points out that we are not spiritually born into salvation by being of a certain bloodline ("not of blood"), or by following our heart ("the will of flesh"), or by following religious rules ("the will of man") – but only by believing what Jesus did for us (Romans 5:8).

For this reason, the most significant event in the history of the universe happened and is commemorated on December 25 of each year - Jesus was born ("*the Word became flesh*").

But God demonstrates His own love toward us, in that while we were still sinners, Christ died for us. – Romans 5:8 (NIV)

DECEMBER 26

Did you know that a beaver has its own comb? We recently had a conversation with a Northwoods trapper who showed us the foot of a beaver. On each of its hind legs was one large toenail that was double. *"Without double toenails it would be impossible for the beaver to scrape mud and other debris off its body."* The trapper continued, *"These double toenails are also necessary for the beaver to stimulate the oil glands that emit a substance to waterproof the fur."*

This unusually double toenail allows the beaver to apply and reapply the special waterproofing oil. Without this coating of oil on their fur, beavers would become water soaked, not withstand the cold winter water temperatures, and die. Beavers have been created with their own built-in comb, one on each hind leg, to remove mud and distribute oil throughout their fur. Clasping the foot of the beaver, the trapper firmly stated, *"Now let some evolutionist try to convince you that this double toenail came about by accident! This double toenail had to be there from the beginning or the beaver would have died."*

The heavens are yours, and also the earth; you founded the world and all that is in it.
– Psalm 89:11 (NIV)

DECEMBER 27

Radiohalos are minute spheres of discoloration often found in translucent minerals (biotite and muscovite) within granite. These polonium halos formed when radioactive polonium decayed, creating a discolored sphere within the biotite's crystalline structure. Here are the implications:

A. The polonium had to have entered the granite crystal while the rock was molten. There is no known way for it to have entered the biotite crystalline structure after it had formed and hardened.
B. If the granite were molten when the decay occurred, no spherical discoloration would be captured in its as yet unformed crystal structure. In other words, if the crystal structure of the biotite has not hardened within days of the polonium decay discoloration occurring, the radiohalos disappear.
C. Naturally occurring polonium has isotopes with half-lives from a fraction of a second to 138 days. Thus, any trapped polonium within a cooling granite would have decayed within 138 days of the granite forming.
D. The existence of these radiohalos is proof that enormous granite formations cooled rapidly, not over thousands of years. **This had to be a supernatural creation event.**

Granite is the most common "basement rock" forming the very structure of the earth's foundational rock layers. Polonium halos have been found by the trillions in granite all over the world. How can granite, which from an evolutionary presumption took millions of years to solidify and cool, preserve these polonium radiohalos? **It is an impossibility.** But from a Biblical viewpoint, these halos were "frozen in an instant of time" and preserved. The existence of polonium halos in granite means that the granite formed, solidified, and cooled rapidly – instantaneously or over a matter of days. Polonium halos provide rock solid evidence that the very foundation of the earth was created rapidly and not over billions of years.

Come, let us sing for joy to the LORD; let us shout aloud to the Rock of our salvation.
– Psalm 95:1 (NIV)

DECEMBER 28

We would like to wrap-up this book on the overwhelming evidence for the Biblical view of origins by discussing why so many intelligent and highly educated people seem to be blind to the evidence for creation. By understanding the intellectual blindness of the world around us, we are more likely to become aware of our own areas of blindness.

There are multiple reasons why the majority of scientists and educators believe and promote only an evolutionary perspective. One of the most powerful is the bias which occurs when only one viewpoint is taught. Psychologists call this "confirmation bias."

For generations, students have been taught to view things from a naturalistic perspective which leaves God out of their thinking. These students go on to become future educators who reinforce this viewpoint even more strongly with each passing generation. By defining science as allowing only the examination of natural causes, one of the two possibilities for our existence (creation) is not even considered. Thus, the only alternative to evolution (creation) becomes forgotten (and even ridiculed). When the truth is assumed to be wrong before even looking for an answer, believing in the wrong answer is guaranteed. The Bible makes the same observation in Proverbs 18:17.

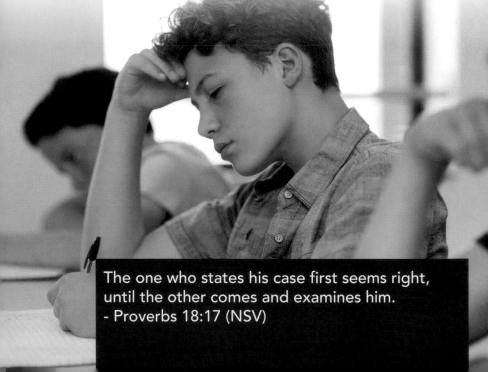

The one who states his case first seems right, until the other comes and examines him.
- Proverbs 18:17 (NSV)

DECEMBER 29

How can scientific "experts" promote and believe the obvious falsehoods that everything came from nothing (cosmic evolution) and that all forms of life are a result of random changes which turned bacteria into people (biological evolution)? This belief change did not happen overnight, but has been the result of a slow hundred year-long transformation within the scientific community. However, there is a vocal and active minority of scientists who look at the same rocks, biology, genetics, and laws of science and come to a completely different conclusion about our origin, but their voice is ridiculed, suppressed, and largely excluded from educational input.

All of our beliefs are the result of something we have been told in the past. Once this is established as a fact, our minds will automatically filter observations through this fixed mental framework. The mind subconsciously rejects that which does not "fit" what we have been taught and accepted as truth. Psychologists call this "change blindness."

The world around us has been repeatedly told false information concerning our origin while the truth is censored or ridiculed. When generations of public educated children are given only evolutionary explanations for life, they form a framework of "truth" which comes to accept that belief as reality. This is called a "paradigm" and they may not even realize that they need to look for another option. As a result, some relevant scientific data or even the truth may be overlooked. They literally become blind to any other possibility. Once a framework of what is the truth forms in the human mind, it becomes very difficult to view things in any other way. Even when shown that a belief could not be true, it is still accepted as true. As the father of modern psychology, Dr. William James noted, *"There is nothing so absurd that it cannot be believed, if repeated often enough."* The Bible calls this, "hardening of the heart."

The heart is deceitful above all things, and desperately wicked: who can know it?
– Jeremiah 17:9 (KJV)

DECEMBER 30

The second force blinding people to the reality of Biblical creation is the powerful effect of peer pressure. **There is enormous pressure to conform.** All people have a tendency to be influenced by the opinions of others. No one is immune to this. This is why companies spend billions advertising products and polls are widely publicized showing what is most popular.

Scientists and professors are also influenced by consensus thinking. An enormous amount of money is spent to promote evolution. Tiny amounts are spent to promote creation. The only research that gets serious funding is for evolution. Furthermore, any researcher who promotes a creation viewpoint, or even openly questions evolution, will find it extremely difficult to get their papers published and risk their academic career, teaching position, and future earning ability.

Also, any teacher or professor who dares to teach students an alternative puts their livelihood in jeopardy. Thus, even if they have doubts about what they are required to teach, they often remain silent about these doubts.

Ultimately what is at stake is the trustworthiness of God's Word. Will we choose to believe the truth or believe a lie. As a lie becomes overwhelmingly accepted, those in the minority will increasingly come under persecution. Eventually, any attempt to expose "the lie" will be ignored, suppressed, and ridiculed. We are increasingly seeing this happening in all areas of life – politics, education, morality, and science.

For although they knew God, they neither glorified him as God nor gave thanks to him, but their thinking became futile and their foolish hearts were darkened. Although they claimed to be wise, they became fools... Therefore God gave them over in the sinful desires...They exchanged the truth about God for a lie, and worshipped and served created things rather than the Creator.
- Romans 1:22,24,25 (NIV)

DECEMBER 31

My friend's father recently died at a ripe old age and he asked the doctor what killed his father.

"*Nothing*," answered the doctor.
Surprised, my friend responded, "*But he's certainly dead, something must have killed him!*"
"*Well*," responded the physician, "*Everything.*"

The doctor was explaining that as we age, essentially every organ, system, and cell in our body weakens, deteriorates, wears out, and fails. Nothing specific causes our natural death but eventually everything in our body kills us. Throughout our life, with every division of every cell, tiny mistakes (mutations) start to build up until the body's ability to repair and ignore these mistakes fail. It is pure fantasy to believe modern medicine will ever extend lives indefinitely because every one of our 100 trillion cells begin to degrade as soon as we are born. Only one person out of 6,000 (0.017%) will live to be 100 years old. Only 1 out of 20 (0.47%) will live to 90. The death rate for humans is 100%. Why? **Because we have rebelled against our Creator (Romans 23:3), are desperately wicked (Isaiah 64:6), and the penalty for our sinful lives is physical death and without our Savior - eternal separation from God (Romans 6:23).**

Why are we ending our creation devotional with such a downer of a subject? Because it is the reality of our pending death which should focus our attention on the true source of our hope for the future. King Solomon noted in Ecclesiastes 7:2 that, "*It's better to go to a funeral than to attend a feast; funerals remind us that we all must die.*" Christians have far more than some vague hope for the future, we have an **absolute assurance** that there is life after our death, and we are just passing through this life on our way to a much better existence. It is our prayer that you will see that plants, animals, people, etc., did not originate by accident and chance but had a Creator. This Creator is also your Savior who died in your place. He is trying to get our attention by what He has made so you will seek and find Him. He tells us in the Bible that He wants to spend eternity with us. By accepting the payment He made for our sins, the fear of death, and any fear about what comes after death, is exchanged for joyful expectation. We hope those who have read this book will ponder the evidence and seek out our Savior, Jesus Christ.

I write these things to you who believe in the name of the Son of God that you may KNOW that you have eternal life. – 1 John 5:13 (ESV)

TOPIC INDEX

BOTANY
6-Jan
22-Jan
25-Jan
12-Feb
16-Feb
24-Feb
31-Mar
4-May
22-May
23-Jul
24-Jul
13-Aug
25-Aug
10-Sep
15-Oct
24-Oct
9-Nov
26-Jan
23-Feb
20-Mar
15-Apr
20-Apr
21-Apr
22-Apr
3-May
27-Jul
28-Jul
21-Sep
25-Sep
26-Sep
1-Oct
2-Oct
15-Oct
14-Nov
22-Nov
28-Nov
3-Dec
4-Dec
22-Dec
31-Dec

DESIGN
8-Jan
15-Jan
27-Jan

13-Feb
12-Mar
12-Apr
12-Apr
16-Apr
23-Apr
24-Apr
5-May
5-May
18-May
5-Jun
2-Jul
11-Sep
12-Sep
27-Oct
3-Nov
6-Nov
20-Nov
13-Dec

FLOOD GEOLOGY
2-Jan
11-Jan
12-Jan
17-Jan
24-Jan
29-Jan
31-Jan
3-Feb
21-Feb
22-Feb
3-Mar
11-Mar
29-Mar
30-Mar
13-Apr
14-Apr
19-Apr
7-May
8-May
13-May
25-May
3-Jun
4-Jun
19-Jun
24-Jun

9-Jul
14-Jul
21-Jul
3-Aug
8-Aug
11-Aug
12-Aug
24-Aug
3-Sep
4-Sep
14-Sep
15-Sep
23-Sep
29-Sep
3-Oct
11-Oct
17-Oct
18-Oct
5-Nov
10-Nov
15-Nov
16-Nov
19-Nov
2-Dec
7-Dec
14-Dec
21-Dec

GENETICS
14-Jan
20-Feb
14-Mar
3-Apr
9-Apr
10-Apr
6-May
17-Jun
17-Jun
18-Jun
28-Jun
29-Jul
30-Jul
9-Aug
10-Aug
6-Sep
9-Oct
23-Nov

26-Nov
29-Nov
8-Dec

HISTORY
5-Jan
21-Jan
30-Jan
2-Feb
5-Feb
6-Feb
11-Feb
23-Mar
24-Mar
25-Mar
4-Apr
7-Apr
8-Apr
9-May
17-May
21-May
31-May
19-Jul
20-Jul
22-Jul
23-Aug
26-Aug
9-Sep
17-Sep
30-Sep
21-Oct
22-Oct
4-Nov
18-Nov
25-Nov
6-Dec
19-Dec
19-Dec
20-Dec

TRUTH
7-Jan
7-Feb
14-Feb
25-Feb
27-Feb
4-Mar

18-Mar
26-Mar
5-Apr
27-Apr
10-May
30-May
6-Jun
8-Jun
14-Jun
20-Jun
5-Jul
18-Jul
4-Aug
17-Aug
29-Aug
22-Sep
27-Sep
7-Oct
13-Oct
14-Oct
28-Oct
21-Nov
27-Nov
30-Nov
9-Dec
25-Dec
28-Dec
29-Dec
30-Dec

SUBJECT INDEX

VERSE INDEX

Reference	Date	Reference	Date	Reference	Date
Pro. 3:5,6	12-Apr	Psa. 77:12	1-Jun	Psa. 145:21	2-Jul
Pro. 8:29	19-Apr	Psa. 77:14	25-Jul	Psa. 145:5b,6	18-Jul
Pro. 9:10	7-Jan	Psa. 77:16-18	31-Jul	Psa. 145:8,9	9-Feb
Pro. 12:17	6-Feb	Psa. 78:2,4	12-May	Psa. 146:5	28-Nov
Pro. 12:22	5-Feb	Psa. 78:5,7	19-Sep	Psa. 146:6	16-Apr
Pro. 14:12	4-Oct	Psa. 86:10	13-Mar	Psa. 147:4	26-Feb
Pro. 17:22	17-Dec	Psa. 89:8	26-Jul	Psa. 147:7	29-Jan
Pro. 18:17	28-Dec	Psa. 89:11	26-Dec	Psa. 147:8	24-Feb
Pro. 20:12	15-Jun	Psa. 90:2	7-May	Psa. 147:10,11	3-Apr
Pro. 21:30	21-Jun	Psa. 90:10	17-Jun	Psa. 147:16	10-Nov
Pro. 25:2	22-Jun	Psa. 90:12	22-Oct	Psa. 148:1,10	7-Jul
Pro. 28:18	28-Jul	Psa. 92:6,7	27-Jun	Psa. 148:13	15-Jul
Pro. 30:28	1-Mar	Psa. 93:3	3-Mar	Psa. 148:3	8-Feb
Psa. 1:1,2	21-Oct	Psa. 94:8-9	5-Oct	Psa. 148:7	2-Feb
Psa. 3:3	10-Jul	Psa. 95:1	27-Dec	Psa. 150:2	16-Aug
Psa. 8:1	1-Jul	Psa. 95:3,5	20-Jan	Psa. 150:6	17-Jul
Psa. 8:3,4	9-Mar	Psa. 95:5-6	20-Nov		17-Nov
Psa. 8:5	4-Nov	Psa. 96:2,3	5-Jun	Rev. 1:8	23-Dec
Psa. 8:9	25-Apr	Psa. 96:6	19-May	Rev. 4:11a	1-Nov
Psa. 9:1	31-Dec	Psa. 96:12a,13	3-May	Rev. 4:11b	2-Nov
Psa. 11:2	24-Mar	Psa. 97:1	11-May	Rev. 4:8,9	2-Aug
Psa. 11:3	23-Mar	Psa. 97:6	16-May	Rev. 8:12	16-Jul
Psa. 17:7a	31-Mar	Psa. 98:1a	2-Apr	Rev. 12:3,4	22-Sep
Psa. 18:15	8-May	Psa. 98:4a,7	20-May	Rev. 12:7	23-Sep
Psa. 18:30	11-Jul	Psa. 100:3	20-Apr	Rev. 15:3	22-Jan
Psa. 18:7	29-Sep	Psa. 103:12	3-Jul	Rev. 21:4	21-Aug
Psa. 19:1	20-Jun	Psa. 104:6	15-Sep	Rom. 1:18,19	5-Jul
Psa. 24:1	1-Jan	Psa. 104:8	16-Nov	Rom. 1:20	27-Jan
Psa. 24:2	19-Nov	Psa. 104:12	19-Oct	Rom. 1:22,24,25	30-Dec
Psa. 29:10,11	24-Jan	Psa. 104:24	27-Apr	Rom. 1:25	14-Jan
Psa. 29:3,4	17-Jan	Psa. 104:25,26	28-Apr	Rom. 11:34	6-Oct
Psa. 31:3,4	2-Oct	Psa. 104:27	26-Apr	Rom. 12:1b	23-Jan
Psa. 31:10	16-Jun	Psa. 104:29	15-Mar	Rom. 12:2	8-Jun
Psa. 31:21	13-Dec	Psa. 104:30	27-Sep	Rom. 12:2	9-Dec
Psa. 33:6	11-Dec	Psa. 105:2	10-Feb	Rom. 12:3	12-Apr
Psa. 33:9	1-Aug	Psa. 105:5	23-Apr	Rom. 12:4	15-Oct
Psa. 33:13,14	2-Feb	Psa. 107:33	17-Oct	Rom. 12:5	19-Dec
Psa. 34:8	19-Jan	Psa. 108:5	8-Oct	Rom. 21,23	30-May
Psa. 37:14,15	9-May	Psa. 113:2,3	23-Feb	Sos. 4:1,11	15-Oct
Psa. 38:5	31-Aug	Psa. 113:5,6	14-Sep	Titus 2:11	19-Dec
Psa. 39:4	7-Dec	Psa. 114:6,7	14-Apr		
Psa. 40:2	12-Jul	Psa. 117:2	27-May		
Psa. 42:11b	8-Aug	Psa. 118:27,28	27-Jul		
Psa. 46:1	26-Jan	Psa. 119:64	19-Feb		
Psa. 46:10	10-Aug	Psa. 119:73	9-Jan		
Psa. 46:2,3	21-Jul	Psa. 119:89	3-Jan		
Psa. 47:2a	10-Sep	Psa. 119:103	22-Nov		
Psa. 48:1a	22-May	Psa. 119:104	17-Aug		
Psa. 50:10	1-Apr	Psa. 119:135,136	18-Apr		
Psa. 50:2	1-Oct	Psa. 121:1,2	13-Apr		
Psa. 54:4	28-Oct	Psa. 121:5	7-Nov		
Psa. 55:9	20-Oct	Psa. 121:7	13-Jan		
Psa. 56:8	17-Apr	Psa. 124:1,4	19-Jun		
Psa. 57:5	4-May	Psa. 124:8	16-Sep		
Psa. 58:4	15-Feb	Psa. 135:6	15-Dec		
Psa. 63:1	28-Feb	Psa. 136:25,26	29-May		
Psa. 66:5	12-Oct	Psa. 136:3,4	16-Feb		
Psa. 67:2	4-Apr	Psa. 136:7,8	26-Jun		
Psa. 69:34	5-Mar	Psa. 136:9	24-Apr		
Psa. 72:18	27-Mar	Psa. 138: 4,5	16-Nov		
Psa. 72:19	1-May	Psa. 139:13	4-Mar		
Psa. 73:16,17	14-Jul	Psa. 139:14	4-Jan		
Psa. 74:13	2-Sep	Psa. 139:15	8-Dec		
Psa. 74:15	21-Mar	Psa. 139:16	2-Jun		
Psa. 74:16	18-Sep	Psa. 139:7,8	12-Aug		
Psa. 75:1	30-Jun	Psa. 145:4,5a	12-Nov		
Psa. 77:11	24-Jul	Psa. 145:15,16	3-Nov		

REFERENCES

3-Jan Guide to the Human Body, ICR, Harvest House publisher, Eugene, OR, 2015, p.14-15

4-Jan Faulkner,Danny, Ph.D., Comets and the age of the solar system   https://creation.
com/comets-and-the-age-of the-solar-system, retrieved 8/12/20   Stillman, W.E.,
The Lifetime and renewal of comets, Proceedings of the Second International Conf.
on Creationism, Vol. 2, pp. 267-278

5-Jan Bergman, Jerry, "Ota Benga: The Sory of the pygmy on Display in a Zoo," CRSQ, vol.
30, De,. 1993, p. 140-147

6-Jan https://ww.fs.fed.us/wildflowers/ethnobotany/resins.shtml, retrieved 5/15/20

7-Jan https://answersingenesis.org/human-body/brain/bigger-brain-better/, retrieved
7/1/20

8-Jan https://answersingeneis.org/birds/peregrine-falcon-natures-top-gun/, retrieved
4/22/2020

10-Jan https://www.npr.org/sections/health-shots/2017/07/27/5394736773/slug-slime-
inspires-scientists-to-invent-sticky-surgical-glue, retrieved 7/1/20

11-Jan "Dinosaur Fossil in Mame Enviroment", Creation 40(2)2018, p.7
https://creation.com/dead-whales-telling tales, Retrieved 4/9/2020.   https://creation.
com/focus-253

12-Jan Morris, John D. and Frank J. Sherwin, The Fossil Record Unearthing Nature's History
of Life. ICR, 2010, p.41 https://davidson.weizmann.ac.il/en/online/askexpert/life_sci/
have-any-fossilized-whole-skulls-dinosaurs-ever-been-found#:~:text=Currently%20
it%20is%20estimated%20that,of%20completing%20the%20full%20picture

13-Jan Cook, David, "Daddy, don't swallow me!", Creation Magazine, back cover vol. 31 no.
1, December 2008-February 2009

15-Jan https://phys.org/news/2016-02-penguin-feathers-ice-proof.html, retrieved 4/24/2020
"Cool Features Keep Penguins Warm", Creation 39(2)2017 p. 11

16-Jan Catchpoole, David, "Aboriginal Knowledge Amazes Evolutionist Astronomer",
Creation 37(4) 2015, 25-27

17-Jan Nelson, Vance, Untold Secrets of Planet Earth: Flood Fossils, Untold Secrets of Planet
Earth Publishing Co., Red Deer, Alberta, Canada, 2014, p.98

18-Jan https://answersingenesis.org/human-body/nerve-distribution-sensitive-topic/
https://www.scienceworld.ca/resource/tactile-sensitivity/, retrieved 5/5/2020

19-Jan http://bioweb.uwlax.edu/bio203/s2008/niemi_riss/interactions.htm, retrieved
5/19/2020

20-Jan https://www.newsweek.com/upside-down-jellyfish-stinging-water-prey-mucus-
grenades-1487163, retrieved 5/19/2020

21-Jan https://creation.com/a-tale-of-ancient-toothpaste, retrieved 7/20/20

22-Jan https://answersingenesis.org/evidence-for-creation/god-created-plant-pollinator-
partners/, retrieved 7/21/2020

23-Jan Heather Brinson Bruce, "Speedsters of the Serengeti", https://answersingenesis.org/
mammals/speedsters-serengeti/, retrieved 5/4/2020

24-Jan Oard, Michael J. Dinosaur Challenges and Mysteries. Creation Book Publishers,
Atlanta, Georgia, USA. 2011, 99-108.

25-Jan https://www.piquenewsmagazine.com/whistler-news/naturespeak-skunk-cabbage-is-
a-bears-bff-2498039, retrieved 6/29/2020

26-Jan https://theconversation.com/skunk-cabbage-blooms-are-a-stinky-herald-of-
spring-39217, retrieved 6/29/2020

28-Jan The Catastrophic Geology of Mount St. Helens by Dr. Tim Clarey, ICR, https://
www.youtube.com/watch?v=5IJ6SLbNsWk&feature=youtu.be&utm_
source=phplist8603&utm_medium=email&utm_content=HTML&utm_
Available+%2B+ICR+News%3A+Mars%2C+Dinosaurs%2C+and+more%21,
retrieved 5/25/2020

29-Jan https://answersingenesis.org/amphibians/super-sticky-spit-how-a-frog-gets-a-meal/,
retrieved 4/18/2020

30-Jan "Smart Neandertals used aspirin and Penicillin?" Creation 39 (3) 2017 p. 7
https://www.discovermagazine.com/planet-earth/ailing-neanderthals-used-penicillin-
and-aspirin

31-Jan https://link.springer.com/referenceworkentry/10.1007%2F978-1-4419-0465-2_1891
https://www.bible.ca/tracks/taylor-trail.htm, Picture: Encyclopedia of Global
Archaeology, 2014 Edition, "Prehistoric Human Footprint Sites"   https://www.icr.
org/article/laetoli-footprints-out-step-with-evolution

1-Feb https://www.geneva.edu/blog/faith/can-christians-teach-science, retreived 9/19/2020

2-Feb https://answersingenesis.org/aquatic-animals/unicorn-sea/, retrieved 4/18/2020

3-Feb Clarey, Dr. Tim, "Flood Model Solves Antarctica Rainforest Mystery". Acts and Facts
49(6) 9

5-Feb Bergman, Jerry, "The Piltdown Hoax's Influence on Evolution's Acceptance",
Creation Research Society Quarterly, volume 36, December 1999 p. 145-154

6-Feb https://creation.com/fresh-look-at-nebraska-man, retrieved 5/26/2020
7-Feb Cosner, Lita and Carter, Robert, "The Majestic Gorilla", Creation 42(2)2020 p. 28-31

8-Feb https://creation.com/heliopause
9-Feb https://creation.com/practical-pouches, retrieved 3/25/2020
10-Feb https://creation.com/australias-amazing-kangaroos-and-the-birth-of-their-young, https://www.echidnawalkabout.com.au/kangaroo-joey-facts/, retrieved 6/10/2020

11-Feb Trumbull, H. Clay, "Jonah in Nineveh", Journal of Biblical Literature, Vol. 2, No.1, 1892, p. 56
12-Feb https://creation.com/patriarchs-of-the-forest, retrieved 7/21/2020   https://usda.gov/media/blog/2011/04/21/methuselah-bristlecone-pine-thought-be-oldest-living-organism-earth#:~:text=The%20Inyo%20National%20Forest%20is,up%20to%20nearly%205%2C000%20years, retrieved 7/21/2020
13-Feb https://creation.com/incredible-human-hand
15-Feb https://www.sciencenewsforstudents.org/article/dangerous-meal, retrieved 5/18/2020   https://www.sciencemag.org/news/2007/11/shrewd-snake-savors-deadly-meal, retrieved 5/16/20
16-Feb https://pza.sanbi.org/welwitschia-mirabilis, retrieved 4/7/2020   https://answersingenesis.org/biology/plants/mystery-plant-of-the-desert/, retrieved 4/7/2020
19-Feb Snelling, Andrew, (2018, May-June), "Mudrocks in Minutes", Answers Magazine, p. 38-39
22-Feb "Amazingly Preserved Leaves", Answers Magazine, October-December 2016, p.37

23-Feb https://nature.berkeley.edu/news/2016/08/sunflowers-move-clock, retrieved 5/6/2020   https://www.npr.org/sections/thetwo-way/2016/08/05/488891151/the-mystery-of-why-sunflowers-turn-to-follow-the-sun-solved, retrieved 5/16/20
24-Feb Catchpoole, David, "Hear Bee, Make Nectar" Creation, 41:4, 2019, back cover

26-Feb https://www.amnh.org/explore/news-blogs/news-posts/to-hunt-the-platypus-uses-its-electric-sixth-sense, retrieved 4/21/2020   https://creation.com/the-platypus-1986 https://answersingenesis.org/mammals/the-platypus/
27-Feb   https://en.wikipedia.org/wiki/Gravity, retreived 10/15/20
28-Feb   https://www.sciencemag.org/news/2019/11/could-desert-beetle-help-humans-harvest-water-thin-air   https://www.bbc.com/news/science-environment-35650518
29-Feb   Rupe, John and Sandford, John, Ph. D., Contested Bones, FMS publication, 2017 www.contestedbones.org
1-Mar Retrieved 5/1/2020 https://answersingenesis.org/creepy-crawlies/bolas-spiders-eight-legged-gauchos/
2-Mar https://answersingenesis.org/evidence-for-creation/design-in-nature/amazing-design-scuba-spiders/, retrieved 4/18/2020   https://www.sciencemag.org/news/2011/06/underwater-spider-spins-itself-aqualung#, retrieved 4/18/2020
3-Mar Sarfati, Jonathan, "Could the Flood have been Tranquil?" Creation 39(3)2017, p. 38-39
4-Mar Giglio, Louie, Indescribable 100 Devotions about God and Science, Passion publishing, Tommy Nelson, p.170-171
5-Mar https://www.mbari.org/barreleye-fish-with-tubular-eyes-and-transparent-head/, retrieved 5/16/2020   The Mystery of the Barreleye Fish, https://www.youtube.com/watch?v=rIwHd7u9Q0U, retrieved 5/16/2020
6-Mar https://answersingenesis.org/aquatic-animals/fish/fishy-source-sunscreen/, retrieved 4/21/2020
7-Mar https://youtu.be/j043X_S_tGA
8-Mar https://www.icr.org/article/opossums-in-neighborhood-relevant-to-human-health/, retrieved 4/8/2020
9-Mar https://creation.com/mercury-more-marks-of-youth, retrieved 8/7/2020
10-Mar https://creation.com/planets-uranus-and-neptune, retrieved 3/5/2020
11-Mar https://creation.com/early-arguments-for-deep-time-3, retrieved 10/12/20
12-Mar https://answersingenesis.org/human-body/whole-new-you/, retrieved 7/4/202

13-Mar https://answersingenesis.org/aquatic-animals/fish/antarctic-icefish-cozy-below-freezing/, retrieved 4/22/2020
14-Mar Guliuzza, Randy, Ph.D., Acts and Facts, 49:11, ICR.org, November 2020
16-Mar https://answersingenesis.org/human-body/the-breath-of-life/, retrieved 6/9/2020

17-Mar   https://www.care2.com/causes/celebrity-rabbit-suffers-from-cancer-causing-cottontail-papilloma-virus.html, retrieved 12/4/18   Catchpoole, David, "Bunnies cute and cursed" , Creation, 41(1) 2019, p. 30.
19-Mar   https://answersingenesis.org/human-body/time-everything-your-body-internal-clock/, retrieved 7/21/2020
20-Mar   The Corpse Flower: Behind the Stink, National Geographic, https://www.youtube.com/watch?v=l-uK5ulLBr8, retrieved 6/29/2020   https://www.livescience.com/51947-corpse-flower-facts-about-the-smelly-plant.html#:~:text=One%20of%20

the%20world's%20largest,for%20the%20plant's%20strong%20odor, retrieved 6/29/2020

21-Mar   Morris, J. 2009, "A Classic Polystrate Fossil". Acts & Facts, 38 (10): 15

22-Mar   Juby, Ian A. "The Fossil Cliffs of Joggins, Nova Scotia, Creation Research Society Quarterly, Volume 43, June 2006. p. 48-53   https://creation.com/joggins-polystrate-fossils, retrieved 7/6/2020

23-Mar   Jonathan Park: The Hunt for Beowulf volume IV, Study Guide, The Vision Forum, Inc, 97-107.

24-Mar   Rupe, John and Sandford, John, Ph. D., Contested Bones, FMS publication, 2017, pp.53-76   Jonathan Park: The Hunt for Beowulf, volume IV, Study Guide, The Vision Forum, Inc, 97-107, 2017   Bergman, Jerry, Ph.D., Useless Organs, pp.91-121, 2019

25-Mar   Denton, Michael, Ph.D., Inherently Wind, DVD presentation on Scopes Monkey Trial, www.Answersingenesis.org

26-Mar   https://creation.com/pascals-wager, retrieved 10/15/20

27-Mar   "Tuxedo-Tailed Deception", Answers Magazine, vol. 12 no.6, November-December 2017, p.23

28-Mar   https://rcannon992.com/2018/07/03/eu-migrants-influx-of-silver-y-moths/ and https://www.sciencedirect.com/science/article/pii/S0960982208005022, retrieved 5/29/2020

29-Mar   DeYoung, Donald, B., Dinosaurs and Creation, Baker Books, Grand Rapid, MI, 2000. 50-55

30-Mar   https://creation.com/sensational-australian-tree-like-finding-a-live-dinosaur https://creation.com/living-fossils-enigma, retrieved 4/10/2020

1-Apr   https://carnegiemnh.org/identical-quadruplets-every-time/

2-Apr   https://www.livescience.com/amp/20763-procreation-station-species-craziest-pregnancy.html

3-Apr   Catchpoole, David, "Polka Dotted Zebra", Creation 42(2)2020, p.39

4-Apr   https://www.smithsonianmag.com/history/the-worlds-most-famous-nurse-florence-nightingale-180974155/, retrieved 4/20/2020

5-Apr   https://www.livescience.com/474-controversy-evolution-works.html https://creation.com/whale-evolution-fraud, retrived 9/7/20

7-Apr   Martin, Charles, Flood Legends Global Clues of a Common Event. Master Books, Green Forest, AR. 2009, p. 41-43,128-129

8-Apr   Truax, E. A. 1991, Genesis According to the Miao People, Acts & Facts, 20 (4), To read the complete song check out www.icr.org/article/341/

11-Apr   https://creation.com/nickel-concentration-indicates-youthful-oceans, retrieved 3/26/2020

12-Apr   http://people.eku.edu/ritchisong/birdbrain2.html, retrieved 4/30/2020 Stott, John, Birds our Teachers, Baker Books, Grand Rapids, Michigan, 1999, p.21

13-Apr   https://www.bbc.com/news/world-43789527, retrieved 4/9/20   https://www.icr.org/article/volcanic-ash-turns-to-stone-in-months/, retrieved 4/9/20

14-Apr   Lung, Stacy, (2016). Wisconsin' Flood Journey, Self-published

15-Apr   "Beggar Tick Seeds Sprout After 350 Years in Salt Water", Creation Research Society Quarterly, volume 24, December 1987, p. 144

16-Apr   https://creation.com/oyster-twist, retrieved 10/26/2020

18-Apr   https://www.reviewofophthalmology.com/article/the-eye-and-the-nosewhats-the-connection

19-Apr   Oard, Michael, "Continental Margins there rapid formation during flood runoff", Creation, 39(4)2017, pp. 41-44

20-Apr   https://answersingenesis.org/human-body/brain/your-pituitary-a-miniscule-master/, retrieved 7/3/2020

22-Apr   Mollen, Cora and Larry Weber, Fascinating Fungi of the North Woods, Kollath and Stensaas Publishing, Duluth, MN 55802, p.100-101

23-Apr   Thomas, Brian Ph.D., "Why Don't Raindrops Bomb Butterfly Wings?", ICR, Acts and Facts 49 (8), Aug 2020, P.20

24-Apr   www.creationastronomy.com is a great source for astronomy information from a Biblical perspective

25-Apr   Cserhati, Matthew, "Owls Masters of the Night Sky", Creation 42(3), 2020, p.29

26-Apr   Character Sketches, Institute in Basic Youth Conflicts, Inc. Rand McNally and Co., 1976, vol. 1, p.30

27-Apr   https://www.livescience.com/60227-babylonian-clay-tablet-trigonometry.html, retrieved 8/28/2017

28-Apr   Martin, Charles, Flood Legends Global Clues of a Common Event, Master Books, Green Forest. AR., 2009, p. 10-12   Wieland, Carl and Wiskur, David, Dragons of the Deep, Master Books, Green Forest, AR, 2005, p.30-32

30-Apr   Psarris, Spike, "Our Goldilocks Cosmos," Conference: In the Beginning: The Origin of the Universe, Society of Creation, 6/6/2020

1-May Chapman, Geoff, More Weird and Wonderful, Creation Resources Trust, 2000, p.10

2-May Cosner, Lita, "What's Your Address?", Creation, 40(3)2018 p.55.   https://creation.

com/incredible-kinesin, retrieved 6/24/2020

3-May https://creation.com/caring-for-creation, retrieved 5/6/2020

4-May https://theconversation.com/how-dung-beetles-are-duped-into-rolling-and-burying-seeds-66692, retrieved 10/28/2020

7-May https://answersingenesis.org/geology/grand-canyon-facts/when-and-how-did-the-grand-canyon-form/, retrieved 7/7/2020

8-May https://answersingenesis.org/geology/grand-canyon-facts/when-and-how-did-the-grand-canyon-form/, retrieved 7/7/2020

9-May Coulter, Ann, Godless: The Church of Liberalism, Crown Publishing Group, a division of Random House, Inc., New York, 2006. p.268-275

10-May https://www.icr.org/article/what-would-need-change-for-dinosaur-evolve-into-bi, retrieved 4/30/2020 https://www.c-r-t.co.uk/uploads/downloads/127/file/ow-129-web.pdf, retrieved 4/30/2020

11-May https://www.discoverwildlife.com/animal-facts/birds/facts-about-southern-cassowary/, retrieved 7/9/2020 https://animals.sandiegozoo.org/animals/cassowary https://www.rainforesttrust.org/seven-things-probably-dont-know-cassowary/, retrieved 7/9/2020

12-May https://www.allaboutbirds.org/news/soul-mates-nutcrackers-whitebark-pine-and-a-bond-that-holds-an-ecosystem-together/, retrieved 7/22/2020 Dr. Carl Werner, Evolution: The Grand Experiment, 2007. New Leaf Publishing

13-May https://answersingenesis.org/biology/plants/how-did-we-get-all-this-coal/, retrieved 2-25-2019 Group in conjunction with Audio Visual Consultants, Inc. p.224

14-May https://answersingenesis.org/mammals/the-bloodhound-natural-born-smeller/

15-May https://answersingenesis.org/astronomy/age-of-the-universe/an-evaluation-of-astronomical-young-age-determination-methods-i-solar-system/, retrieved 5/9/2020 https://sci.esa.int/documents/33321/35974/1567259603006-ESLAB40-Proc_307063-Osinski.pdf#:~:text=On%20Earth%2C%20however%2C%20erosion%2C,being%20recognized%20each%20year%20(Fig., retrieved 5/9/2020 retrieved 5/9/2020 https://www.liebertpub.com/doi/10.1089/ast.2019.2085, retrieved 5/9/2020

16-May O'Brien, Jonathan, "Ceres Surprises", Creation, 41(3)2019. p. 145

17-May Wise, David A., "Modern Medicine is not so Modern", Creation Research Society Quarterly, Volume 30, June 1993, p.18-19

18-May DeYoung, Donald, Weather and the Bible, 1992. p. 67-68

19-May https://www.livescience.com/54121-birds-use-alligators-as-bodyguards.html, retrieved April 15, 2020

20-May https://www.latimes.com/science/la-xpm-2012-nov-08-la-sci-sn-crocodile-jaws-more-sensitive-than-human-fingertips-20121108-story.html, retrieved 5/6/2020

21-May Chittick, Donald E., The Puzzle of Ancient Man. Creation Compass, Newberg, Oregon. 1998. p.101-107 Swift, Dennis, Secrets of the Ica Stones and Nazca Lines, p. 91

23-May Retrieved 4/9/2020 https://answersingenesis.org/dinosaurs/when-did-dinosaurs-live/solid-answers-soft-tissue/

24-May "Bird's oil gland preserved for '48 million years', Creation 40(2)2018, p.7

28-May https://answersingenesis.org/human-body/vestigial-organs/vestigial-organs-evidence-for-evolution/, retrieved 7/3/2020

29-May https://www.nhpr.org/post/something-wild-salamander-plant-or-animal-yes#stream/0, retrieved 4/15/2020 https://www.fllt.org/the-symbiotic-relationship-of-algae-and-spotted-salamanders/, retrieved 4/15/2020

31-May The Truth Project, Lesson 10: The American Experiment, Focus on the Family Publications, DVD curriculum, 2011

1-Jun https://betterknowafish.com/2013/05/07/amazon-leaffish-monocirrhus-polyacanthus/, retrieved 8/31/ 2020

2-Jun https://www.shorelinevision.com/cornea/, retrieved 5/77/2020

3-Jun https://creation.com/oroville-dam-spillway-crisis-california, retrieved 6/30/2020

4-Jun http://hugefloods.com/Bonneville.html https://www.icr.org/article/red-rock-pass-spillway-bonneville-flood, retrieved 5/30/2020

5-Jun http://bugoftheweek.com/blog/2013/2/3/passionate-about-passion-fruit-zebra-longwing-butterflies-iheliconius-charitoniusi https://heliconius2015.wordpress.com/2015/04/19/heliconius-butterflies/, retrieved 7/22/2020 https://www.nytimes.com/2000/08/01/science/in-death-defying-act-butterfly-thrives-on-poison-vine.html, retrieved 7/22/2020

6-Jun Cosner, Lita, "Ethiopia's 'Little Edens' The Dominion Mandate in Action", Creation, 41(3)2019. P. 16-17

8-Jun Coleman, William L. Singing Penguins and Puffed-Up Toads. Bethany House Publisher, Mpls, MN, 55438. 1981. p.56-57.

9-Jun Bergman, Dr. Jerry, "Werner von Braun: The Father of Space Flight", Acts and Facts, 1/2015 p. 20-21 https://www.newworldencyclopedia.org/entry/Wernher_von_Braun, retrieved 4/20/2020 Excerpts from an original interview in "Applied Christianity", Bible-Science Newsletter, May 1974, p.8

10-Jun "The Farther We Probe into Space, the Greater my Faith": C.M.Ward's account of His

Interview with Dr. Warner von Braun (1966) Springfield, MO: Assemblies of God, 17 pp. Mini-pamphlet   https://en.wikipedia.org/wiki/James_Irwin, extracted 9/19/2020
11-Jun https://en.wikipedia.org/wiki/Buzz_Aldrin, extracted 9/19/2020
12-Jun https://en.wikipedia.org/wiki/Apollo_13, extracted 9/19/2020
15-Jun https://creation.com/the-fish-with-four-eyes-anableps
17-Jun https://creation.com/created-or-evolved, retrieved 6/24/2020
18-Jun https://answersingenesis.org/suffering/why-do-we-age/, retrieve 7/4/2020
19-Jun https://www.creationsciencetoday.com/18-Fragile_Surface_Features html   https://www.icr.org/article/surface-features-require-rapid-deposition/
20-Jun Bates, Gary "The Fermi Paradox", Creation, 38(4)2016, p.53-55 retrieved 3/5/2020 https://creation.com/fermi-paradox
21-Jun https://www.evolutionisamyth.com/dating-methods/rapid-fossilization-miners-hat-found-petrified-after-being-left-in-a-mine-for-50-years/, extracted 11/20/20
22-Jun Snelling, Andrew, Ph.D., What is Radiocarbon Dating?, https://www.youtube.com/watch?v=Pyxq3mEiMYA
23-Jun https://www.livescience.com/ancient-squid-attack-fossilized.html, retrieved 6/5/2020

25-Jun Coles, Peter and Lucchin, Francesco, Cosmology: The Origin and Evolution of Cosmic Structure, Second edition (2002), page 152
26-Jun Lisle, Jason, Taking Back Astronomy, Master Books, Green Forest, AR 726, 2007, p.85

27-Jun https://oceana.org/marine-life/cephalopods-crustaceans-other-shellfish/decorator-crab, retrieved 4/25/2020
28-Jun Gordon, Howard, "The Blue Rose", Creation Magazine, 41(2), p. 46-47
29-Jun "Engineers Copy (Some) of God's Heart Design," Creation 42(1), 2020, p.11
30-Jun Pocket guide to Human Body, Answers in Genesis, Petersburg, Kentucky, USA, p.43.

1-Jul https://creation.com/hummingbird-superhero, retrieved on November 28, 2018
2-Jul https://www.theengineer.co.uk/butterfly-wings-inspire-efficient-light-absorbing-surface-solar-cells/ https://creation.com/butterfly-solar-cell, retrieved 5/30/2020
3-Jul https://answersingenesis.org/human-body/brain/what-memories-are-made-of/, retrieved 7/3/2020
6-Jul https://www.popsci.com/earth-spin-faster/
7-Jul https://wildearth.tv/2018/01/oxpeckers-role-animal-kingdom/
8-Jul https://www.sunnysports.com/blog/symbiotic-relationships-bird-world/, retrieved on April 4/15/2020
9-Jul Statham, Dominic, 2013, Migration After the Flood, DVD, Creation Ministries International

11-Jul Sherwin, Frank. "An Ocean of Viruses". Acts and Facts 49(6) 14
12-Jul Brown, D. The Washington Post, Aug 25, 2010).   The Rapid BioTruthal Recovery of Mount St. Helens by Frank Sherwin, ICR   https://www.youtube.com/watch?v=gqemfpOzdBM&feature=youtu.be&utm_source=phplist8603&utm_medium=email&utm_content=HTML&utm_w+Available+%2B+ICR+News%3A+Mars%2C+Dinosaurs%2C+and+more%21, retrieved 5/26/2020
14-Jul https://www.bbc.com/news/science-environment-12378934   https://www.antarctica.gov.au/about-antarctica/environment/geology/antarctic-prehistory, retrieved 4/10/2020 https://www.atlasobscura.com/articles/did-antarctica-ever-have-trees http://www.glencoe.com/sec/science/webquest/content/fossils2, retrieved 2/26/20
15-Jul https://creation.com/the-moons-recession-and-age, retrieved 2/26/2020
18-Jul Catchpoole, David, "Isn't it Obvious? Natural selection can eliminate but never create!", Creation 39(1), 2017, p. 38-41
20-Jul Tyler, David J, "Megaliths and Neolithic Man," Creation Research Society Quarterly, volume 16, June 1979, p.47-58
21-Jul Greshko, Michael, "Amazing Nesting Doll" Fossil Reveals Bug in Lizard in Snake, National Geographic, September 7, 2016   http://news.nationalgeographic.com/2016/09/snake-fossil-palaeopython-trophic-levels-food/, retrieved 6-26- 2017
22-Jul https://creationmoments.com/sermons/who-said-the-earth-was-flat/, retrieved 7/29/2020

24-Jul Wilson, Fred, Brochure: Filaree, Institute for Creation Research, 1996
26-Jul https://answersingenesis.org/aquatic-animals/fish/rapidly-reproducing-killifish-defy-evolution/, retrieved 4/21/2020
27-Jul https://answersingenesis.org/evidence-for-creation/design-in-nature/gods-design-for-bioluminescence/, retrieved 5/12/2020
29-Jul Catchpoole, David and Carter, Robert, "Blue Eyes Mutation," Creation, 40(3)2018, p.26-27

30-Jul https://creation.com/lactose-intolerance, retrieved 5/29/2020
1-Aug https://answersingenesis.org/creepy-crawlies/ultimate-web-designer/, retrieved 4/27/2020

2-Aug https://creation.com/spider-decoys https://www.wired.com/2014/01/more-decoy-spiders-philippines/, retrieved 4/24/2020
3-Aug How does the log mat at Mount St. Helens help explain the origin of Coal? - Dr. Steve Austin https://www.youtube.com/watch?v=W4a6oWZQ2ok
4-Aug Lumsden, Richard D., "Sources and Applications of Botanical Alkaloids Offer Evidence of

Creative Purpose and Design", Creation Research Society Quarterly, volume 30, December 1993, p.132-139

5-Aug "Sleep Rejuvenates the brain" Creation Magazine 37(4)2015: 9, retrieved 7/1/2020 https://answersingenesis.org/human-body/brain/gods-gift-sleep/, retrieved 7?1?20

6-Aug https://www.brainscape.com/blog/2012/03/facts-about-your-gray-matter/ https://conquerseries.com/how-to-delete-porn-from-your-brain/ https://www.nih.gov/news-events/nih-research-matters/how-sleep-clears-brain, retrieved 6/10/2020

7-Aug https://www.profraguram.com/musings--reflections/the-woodpecker-the-ants, retrieved 4/15/2020   https://www.lookandlearn.com/blog/22138/the-ant-and-the-woodpecker/, retrieved 4/15/2020

8-Aug Neller, Ron, "Dead Crocodiles Down Under", Creation 39(3)2017, p. 14-15

9-Aug Grigg, Russell, M.S., Creation 13(1):30–34, "Could monkeys type the 23rd Psalm?" https://creation.com/could-monkeys-type-the-23rd-psalm, retrieved 6/10/2020

11-Aug   https://answersingenesis.org/geology/rocks-and-minerals/emeralds-treasures-from-catastrophe/, retrieved 6/12/2020

12-Aug https://answersingenesis.org/geology/rocks-and-minerals/jade-beauty-under-pressure/, retrieved 6/12/2020

13-Aug   http://www.creationmagazine.com/creation/2017_volume_39_issue_2?pg=32#pg32

14-Aug   Brinson Bruce, Heather, "Heart-Constantly Beating Death", A Pocket Guide to the Human Body, Answers In Genesis, Petersburg, Kentucky, 2011, p.44-45

15-Aug   David Catchpoole, "Salad Eating Sharks", Creation 40(4)2018, backcover.

16-Aug   https://answersingenesis.org/aquatic-animals/fish/sharks-in-a-new-light/, retrieved 4/22/2020

17-Aug   https://www.icr.org/article/What-Came-First-Chicken-or-Egg/, retrieved 7/31/2020

20-Aug   https://spatialexperiments.wordpress.com/2016/09/16/countercurrent-heat-exchange-in-desert-animals/,retrieved 8/11/ 2020   https://blogionik.org/blog/2016/05/05/camel-living-air-conditioner/, retrieved 8/11/20

22-Aug   Gillen, Alan L., Body by Design, Master Books, Green Forest, AR, 2001, p.94

23-Aug   The Story of Hezekiah's Tunnel https://www.youtube.com/watch?v=2QAW5k_bCB0, retrieved 5/27/2020   Bartz, Paul. A., Letting God Create Your Day Volume 6, Creation Moments, Foley, MN, p. 52

24-Aug   https://answersingenesis.org/geology/mica-mica-sand-tell-us-something-really-grand/, retrieved 7/7/2020

26-Aug   Were WWII planes really found under the ice in Greenland? - Dr. Larry Vardiman https://www.youtube.com/watch?v=CNyIAerXTEU/, retrieved 5/27/20

27-Aug   https://creation.com/media-center/youtube/pluto-another-young-planet-creation-magazine-live-7-1, retrieved 7/20/20   https://creation.com/pluto, retrieved 7/20/20

28-Aug   https://creation.com/a-lesson-from-pluto/, retrieved 6/12/20

29-Aug   Cosner, Lita, 2016, "Wasps Nature's pest control", Creation Magazine, 38 (4) 16-19 http://creation.com/no-death-before-fall/ retrieved 8/11/20

31-Aug   https://creation.com/lasting-impressions, retrieved 7/8/2020

1-Sep Reference: Copley, J., Indestructible, New Scientist, posted on new-scientist.com on October 1999, accessed April 2, 1999

2-Sep https://answersingenesis.org/reptiles/danger-of-komodo-dragons/, retrieved 5/2/2020

3-Sep Hedtke, Randall. "How Gradual Evolution is Disproved in the Textbooks", Creation Research Society Quarterly, Volume 36, December 1999. p. 136-144

4-Sep https://www.smithsonianmag.com/smart-news/1930s-curator-discovered-living-fossil-well-sort-180967616/, retrieved 5/19/2020

6-Sep "Mummy DNA Supports Biblical History", Creation 40(1)2018, p.8

9-Sep https://www.youtube.com/watch?v=_IefyFvLuAw

10-Sep   Geering, Esme, "Tom and Jenny at the Botanical Gardens", Creation, 20(3) June-Aug 1998, p.37   https://www.sciencefocus.com/nature/why-do-mimosa-plants-close-when-touched/, retreived 5/23/20

13-Sep   Kobayashi,Tomoninchi, Snake Scent Application Behavior in the Siberian Chipmunk, 1981   https://www.jstage.jst.go.jp/article/pjab1977/57/5/57_5_141/_pdf https://creationmoments.com/sermons/those-clever-siberian-chipmunks-3/, retrieved 5/23/2020

14-Sep   https://www.icr.org/article/volcanic-ash-turns-to-stone-in-months/, retrieved 4/9/20 https://en.wikipedia.org/wiki/Taal_Volcano, https://en.wikipedia.org/wiki/Tuff, retrieved 4/9/2020

15-Sep   https://creation.com/whale-explodes-fossil-theory, retrieved 6/1/2020

16-Sep   Borg, Julie. "A Beautiful Design Humans Can't replicate", World magazine   https://world.wng.org/content/a_beautiful_design_humans_can_t_replicate, posted 10/04/18

17-Sep   https://www.icr.org/article/indian-kangaroo-pictographs-challenge-evolution/, retrieved 6/26/2020

18-Sep   https://earthsky.org/tonight/moons-dark-side-faces-earth

19-Sep   https://coralreefpalau.org/research/marine-lakes/jellyfish-lake/, retrieved 5/20/2020

21-Sep   Plant has evolved a specialist bird perch by Jennifer Carpenter https://www.bbc.com/news/science-environment-14788701, retrieved 5/29/2020

22-Sep   https://creation.com/sea-monsters-more-than-a-legend   https://www.

genesispark.com/exhibits/evidence/cryptozooTruthal/apatosaurs/mokele-mbembe/, Retrieved 7/8/2020   https://creation.com/mating-fossilized-insects, retrieved 6/2/2020
23-Sep   "Dragon Encounters at the ICR Center", Acts and Facts, 49 (4), April 2020, p.16

24-Sep   https://answersingenesis.org/human-body/the-amazing-regenerating-rib/, retrieved 4/10/2020
26-Sep   https://creation.com/the-love-trap, retrieved 7/20/2020
29-Sep   https://creation.com/frozen-feeding, retrieved 6/2/2020   https://creation.com/
buried-birth, retrieved 6/2/2020
30-Sep   http://midwestapologetics.org/blog/?p=351
2-Oct   https://northernwoodlands.org/outside_story/article/trees-survive-winter-cold, retrieved 2/6/2019
4-Oct   Statham, Dominic, "Appendix Functional, but still evidence for evolution?", Creation,40(2), 2018, p. 17-19
5-Oct   https://www.sciencedaily.com/releases/2011/05/110526064627.htm, retrieved 5/2/2020

6-Oct   Catchpoole, David. (2017, July-September). "Reindeer Eyes". Creation 39(2). back cover.

7-Oct   Comfort, Eat, Scientific Facts in the Bible, Bridge Logos Publishers, Gainesville, Florida, 2001, p.74   https://www.washingtonpost.com/archive/opinions/1997/10/21/
dihydrogen-monoxide-unrecognized-killer/ee85631a-c426-42c4-bda7-ed63db993106/
Retrieved 11/10/2020
8-Oct   http://bioweb.uwlax.edu/bio210/s2013/clinton_kevi/facts.htm, retrieved 7/18/2020

9-Oct   https://dstri.org/, retrieved 10/15/21   Armitage, Mark, and Beltran,
Debra, Old Stretchy The Dinosaur Bone Cell, Dinosaur Soft Tissue Research Institiue, ISBN 978-0-578-14682-9, 2017
10-Oct   https://dstri.org/, retrieved 10/15/21   Armitage, Mark, and Beltran,
Debra, Old Stretchy The Dinosaur Bone Cell Discovers Nanotyrannus, Dinosaur Soft Tissue Research Institiue, ISBN 978-1-64999-662-6, 2020
11-Oct   Cos, Gavin. "How Hell Creek supports the Bible," Creation, 41(3), 2019, p.42-43

12-Oct   https://www.thedodo.com/in-the-wild/woman-finds-incredible-bug-flower-mantis, retrieved 3/31/2020
14-Oct   Thomas, Brian, "Does Scripture Say Anything about Climate?", Acts and Facts, 49(6) 20
15-Oct   "Will Bleed for Protection", Answersmagazine, vol. 11 (4), 2016, p.30
16-Oct   https://allrus.me/tallest-and-heaviest-russian-boxer-nikolai-valuev/
Christopher Rupe, Christopher and Sanford, John, Contested Bones, FMS Publications, 2017, p. 29-51
17-Oct   Oard, Michael, Well-Watered Deserts", Creation, 42(2)2020, p. 46-49
18-Oct   Creation Magazine, 36(4) 2014. p.7   https://www.atlasobscura.com/articles/
reindeer-may-not-be-able-to-fly-but-they-do-have-ultraviolet-vision
19-Oct   Character Sketches, Institute in Basic Youth Conflicts, Inc. Rand McNally and Co., 1976, vol. 1, p. 97   http://web.colby.edu/mainebirds/2017/12/, retrieved 4/7/202
20-Oct   "Jupiter's oddball moon must be young", Creation, 41(3)2019, p.7
21-Oct   https://answersingenesis.org/evidence-for-creation/god-created-plant-pollinator-partners/
22-Oct   Tiner, John Hudson, Exploring Planet Earth, Master Books, 2001, p. 54-55
23-Oct   Chapman, Geoff, More Weird and Wonderful, Creation Resources Trust, 2000, p.28

24-Oct   http://www.eternal-productions.org/101science.html # 81, retrieved 7/31/2020
https://faseb.onlinelibrary.wiley.com/doi/abs/10.1096/fasebj.30.1_supplement.1036.5, retrieved 7/31/2020
25-Oct   https://study.com/academy/lesson/lysozyme-definition-function-structure.html, retrieved July 18, 2018
27-Oct   https://journeynorth.org/tm/robin/BroodPatch.html, retrieved 8/1/2020
28-Oct   https://isgenesishistory.com/surprising-things-coal-flood/, retrieved 5/1/2020
30-Oct   http://www.discovercreation.org/documents/Spring2003.pdf, retrieved 7/23/2020

1-Nov https://creation.com/planets-uranus-and-neptune, https://creation.com/neptune-monument-to-creation, retrieved 3/5/2020
2-Nov https://creation.com/age-of-the-earth
3-Nov https://www.audubon.org/news/why-would-bird-carry-water-its-feathers, retrieved 4/28/2020   https://sora.unm.edu/sites/default/files/journals/condor/v069n04/
p0323-p0343.pdf, retrieved 4/28/2020
5-Nov DeYoung, Donald, Weather and the Bible, 1992, pp.118-119   https://icr.org/article/
woolly-mammoth-mystry-finally-solved/, extracted 3/20/21.
6-Nov https://youtu.be/zUYGIxQNcWU
7-Nov Alexandria, Virginia, Time Life, Understanding science and nature: Human Body, 1992, p.128-129
8-Nov Fulbright, Jeannie, and Ryan, Brooke, Exploring Creation with Human Anatomy and Physiology, Apologia Educational Ministries, Inc. Anderson, IN, 2010 p.221
9-Nov http://www.sciencemag.org/news/2017/10/flower-petals-have-blue-halos-attract-bees

Flower petals have "blue halos" to attract bees by Virginia Morell, Oct. 18, 2017

10-Nov "NASA Animation Exposed Ice Age Land Bridges" Creation 42 (3) 2020. https://sealevel.nasa.gov/resources/100/video-watch-glaciers-rise-fall-in-thousands-of-years-per-second/, retrieved 7/17/20

11-Nov Retrieved 7/18/2020 "Butterfly Rainforest Moment: Owl Butterfly" https://www.youtube.com/watch?v=TiYmassj4TA

12-Nov https://www.arkinspace.com/2018/07/the-dead-leaf-butterfly-camouflage-king.html, retrieved 7/17/20 https://www.butterflyidentification.com/orange-oakleaf.htm, retrieved 7/17/20

13-Nov Blue tits embrace 'aromatherapy' by Matt Walker http://news.bbc.co.uk/earth/hi/earth_news/newsid_8199000/8199726.stm, retrieved 5/21/2020

15-Nov Oard, Mike, Flood by Design, Master Books, Green Forest, AR, 2008, p. 88-92

16-Nov Oard, Mike, Flood by Design, Master Books, Green Forest, AR, 2008, p. 46-48 https://creation.com/how-did-the-waters-of-noahs-flood-drain, retrieved 7/6/2020

18-Nov https://creation.com/moriori-hunter-gatherers, retrieved 7/25/2020

21-Nov "'Early Cretaceous' Dinos Sand their Teeth into…Grass", Creation, 42 (3), 2020, p.7

24-Nov Statham, Dominic, "The Mysterious Alien Tablet", Creation, 41(3)2019, p. 39-41

25-Nov Cooper, Bill, After the Flood, New Wine Press, United Kingdom, 1995 https://answersingenesis.org/bible-timeline/genealogy/how-many-human-generations-are-there-from-adam-until-today/, retrieved 9/12/2020

26-Nov http://www.sciencemag.org/news/2010/10/scienceshot-biggest-genome-ever, retrieved April 7, 2020

27-Nov https://creation.com/firefly-lanterns-led-lenses, retrieved April 7, 2020

29-Nov Sanford, John, Ph.D., "The TRuth about Genetics", Origins Truth Conference, 10/3/2020

1-Dec https://www.icr.org/article/why-mosquitoes-attack-mystery-solved, retrieved 10/26/2020

2-Dec https://answersingenesis.org/geology/rocks-and-minerals/dazzling-diamonds-special-delivery/, retrieved 2-25-2019

3-Dec Austin, Stephen B., "God Created Wind Pollination", Alpha Omega Institute, Think and Believe Newsletter http://www.discovercreation.org/documents/Spring2003.pdf, retrieved 5/30/2020

4-Dec https://phys.org/news/2016-06-mathematical-cress-catapults-seeds-air.html, retrieved 5/30/2020

5-Dec http://www.wnd.com/2013/02/human-tailbone-evidence-of-evolution/

6-Dec http://mexicolesstraveled.com/itzacosmology.html, retrieved March 30, 2020 https://www.atlasobscura.com/places/bighorn-medicine-wheel https://en.wikipedia.org/wiki/Fajada_Butte, retrieved March 30, 2020

7-Dec Oard, Michael J., Dinosaur Challenges and Mysteries, Creation Book Publishers, Atlanta, Georgia, 2011, 85-96

8-Dec Parker, Gary and Mary, The Fossil Book, Master Books, Green Forest, AR. 2006, p.13-14

9-Dec Shah, Sonia, Pandemic, MacMillan Publishing, 2016, pp. 141-158

10-Dec Shah, Sonia, Pandemic, MacMillan Publishing, 2016, pp. 141-158

11-Dec https://answersingenesis.org/astronomy/solar-system/saturn-jewel-creators-showcase/

12-Dec Coppedge, David, 'Latest Cassini Findings Confirm: Saturnian System is Young!", Creation, 42(2)2020, p. 25-27

13-Dec https://answersingenesis.org/animal-behavior/a-wonderfully-bizarre-bird, retrieved 4/4/202

14-Dec https://www.universetoday.com/27064/what-is-the-largest-desert-on-earth/, retrieved 4/4/2020 https://answersingenesis.org/environmental-science/ice-age/do-ice-cores-show-many-tens-of-thousands-of-years/, retrieved 4/4/2020

15-Dec https://www.thedodo.com/how-one-genius-little-fish-con-672797576.html

16-Dec https://www.factmonster.com/math-science/biology/plants-animals/animal-partnerships

18-Dec https://www.icr.org/article/evidence-for-young-world/, retrieved 3/27/2020

19-Dec https://creation.com/maori-memories-of-the-creator https://creation.com/maori-creator-io

20-Dec www.searchforthetruth.net, For an in depth look at the Red Record see The Rocks Cry Out, lesson 2

21-Dec https://answersingenesis.org/creation-vacations/yosemite-national-park/ vacations/glacier-national-park-montana/ https://answersingenesis.org/creation-vacations/mendenhall-glacier-visitor-center/

22-Dec https://creationmoments.com/sermons/tiny-time-bombs/ https://creation.com/fossil-pollen-in-grand-canyon-overturns-plant-evolution https://creation.com/pollen-paradox, retrieved 7/25/2020

23-Dec https://simple.wikipedia.org/wiki/Stick_insec http://animals.sandiegozoo.org/animals/stick-insect

24-Dec https://creation.com/the-octopus, retrieved 11/13/20202

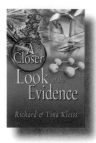
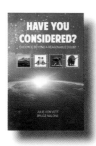

OTHER CREATION BOOKS
BY SEARCH FOR THE TRUTH MINISTRIES

Brilliant

A full-color book containing history from all over the world that points to and supports a biblical timeline.

(8 x11, 128 pages)

Censored Science

A stunning, full-color book containing fifty of the best evidences for biblical creation. Examine the information all too often censored, suppressed, or ignored in our schools. Every page is a visual masterpiece. Perfect for students.

(8 x11, 112 pages)

Search for the Truth

This book is the result of a 15-year effort to bring the scientific evidence for creation into public view. Search for the Truth is a compilation of 100 individual articles originally published as newspaper columns, summarizing every aspect of the creation model for our origin.

(8 x 11, 144 pages)

SEE ALL OF OUR RESOURCES AT **WWW.SEARCHFORTHETRUTH.NET**

God's ONLY plan for our SALVATION

The Lord Jesus Christ explained salvation as being born again. Nicodemus, a religious man, came to Jesus one night wanting to *"see the kingdome of God."* Jesus gave him an answer saying to him: *"You must be born again"* (John 3:7).

Nicodemus did not really understand this answer, and he asked how it was possible for a man to experience another physical birth. Jesus explained what He meant by saying that for a man to go to heaven, he must be born again spiritually. Jesus Christ explained, *"That which is born of the flesh is flesh, and that which is born of the Spirit is spirit"* (John 3:6).

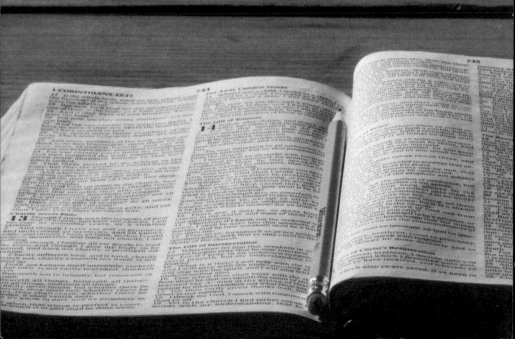

Jesus was making it clear that the first birth is a flesh birth, but the second birth is a spiritual birth. God is a Spirit (John 4:24), and being born again means that the second birth is to be born of God in a spiritual birth.

To be born again (or to be saved, as the book of Romans describes salvation) is to believe that Jesus Christ paid the penalty for your sins and literally rose from the dead. You must trust completely. The Bible tells us that the penalty, or punishment of sin is death. God told Adam if he disobeyed and ate of the forbidden tree, the penalty for that sin would be death. The Bible tells us that all have sinned and come short of the glory of God. (Romans 3:23).

Jesus Christ never sinned. As God in the flesh, He lived a perfect and sinless life. Jesus Christ could have stood before God the Father and rightfully claimed that He had never sinned and therefore did not deserve to die. Why then did Christ die on the cross?

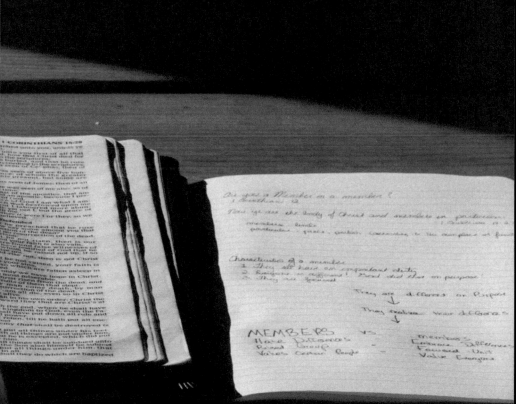

When Jesus Christ died on the cross, He was paying the penalty for the sin of all mankind. Our sin and the judgment of our sin were laid on Him, and by dying on the cross, He paid the penalty that really was ours to pay. He did not deserve to die but He died for us. *But God commendeth his love toward us, in that while we were yet sinners, Christ died for us.* (Romans 5:8) *For the wages of sin is death, but the gift of God is eternal life through Jesus Christ our Lord.* (Romans 6:23)

To be saved, you must put your faith (belief) in Jesus Christ as being the One who paid the penalty for your sin, you must trust completely in what He has done for you to provide salvation. *But as many as received Him, to them gave He power to become the sons of God, even to them that believe His name.* (John 1:12). *For whosoever shall call upon the name of the Lord shall be saved.* (Romans 10:13). If you understand and believe these things, turn to Jesus Christ to be your Savior; accept His gift of salvation that He offers to you.

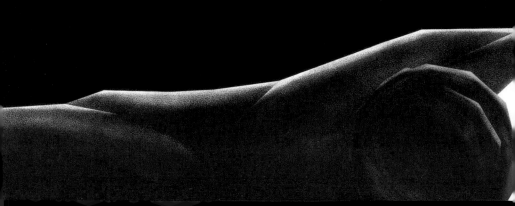

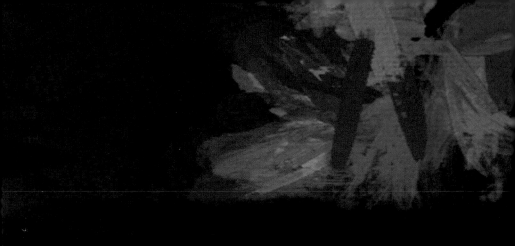

In Luke 18:13, the sinner prayed, *"God be merciful to me a sinner."* If you believe these things, you can turn to Jesus Christ and accept His gift of salvation. No amount of good works or other prayers at church will save you. It is God that saves you. Just take God at His word and receive His salvation by faith. You may want to pray something like this:

> God, I know that I am a sinner. I believe Jesus Christ paid the penalty for my sin by His death on the cross. I believe He rose from the dead and at this very moment wants to be my Savior. I turn to Him now and receive the gift of salvation and everlasting life. Save me.

If you have made this decision to believe in Jesus Christ to be your Savior, we'd like to know about it and help you further in your new life in Christ.

For help, contact us on our website:
searchforthetruth.net

CREATION CURRICULUM:

THE ROCKS CRY OUT CURRICULUM

Bring the most visual, interactive, and relevant series on the evidence to creation to your church, fellowship, or youth group! Filmed at locations across America with video illustrations and animations, these lessons are not a boring technical lecture.

These 45 minute classes enable the non-scientist to bring the evidence for biblical creation to their home or church. This curriculum uses short, personal narrative-style teachings to connect God's Word with science and history, i.e *"the real world"*. Leaders guide included with each set.

Perfect for small group, home school, or Sunday school groups of all ages, *The Rocks Cry Out* show how EVERY area of science confirms Biblical Truth in a visual masterpiece that rivals a National Geographic special. Volume I contains lessons 1-6, Volume II contains lessons 7-12, Volume 3 contains lessons 13-18

See all of our resources at www.searchforthetruth.net

SEARCH FOR THE TRUTH
MAIL-IN ORDER FORM
See more at www.searchforthetruth.net

Call us, or send this completed order form
(other side of page) with check or money order to:

Search for the Truth Ministries
3255 Monroe Rd.
Midland, MI 48642
989.837.5546 or truth@searchforthetruth.net

PRICES

	Item Price	2-9 Copies	10 Copies	Case Price
DEVOTIONAL SPECIAL (4 books)	$45.00	-	Mix or Match	-
Have You Considered (Hardback)	$13.95	$8.96/ea.	$8.00/ea.	call
Inspired Evidence (Softcover book)	$11.95	$8.96/ea.	$6.00/ea.	call
A Closer Look at the Evidence (Hardback)	$13.95	$8.96/ea.	$8.00/ea.	call
Without Excuse (Hardback)	$13.95	$8.96/ea.	$8.00/ea.	call
Censored Science (Hardback)	$16.95	$11.95/ea.	$8.00/ea.	call
Brilliant (Hardback)	$16.95	$11.95/ea.	$8.00/ea.	call
Search for the Truth (book)	$11.95	$8.96/ea.	$6.00/ea.	call
6 DVD Creation Curriculum (Specify Vol.) with Leader Guide	$25	-	-	call

MAIL-IN ORDER FORM

RESOURCE	Quantity	Cost each	Total
DEVOTIONAL SPECIAL (4 books)			
Inspired Evidence (Softcover Book)			
A Closer Look at the Evidence(Hardback)			
Have You Considered (Hardback)			
Without Excuse (Hardback)			
Censored Science (Hardback)			
Brilliant (Hardback)			
Search for the Truth (book)			
Rocks Cry Out (specify which volume)			
Tax deductible Donation to ministry			

	Subtotal
Normal delivery time is 1-2 weeks	MI residents add 6% sales tax
	Shipping add 15% of subtotal
For express delivery	TOTAL ENCLOSED
increase shipping to 20%	

SHIP TO:

Name: ——————————————————————

Address: ——————————————————————

City: ——————————————————————

State: ——————————————— Zip: ———————————

Phone: ——————————————————————

E-mail: ——————————————————————